SEVENTH ED...

THE LEGAL ENVIRONMENT OF
BUSINESS

RYAN H. PACE

Kendall Hunt
publishing company

Cover image © Shutterstock.com

Kendall Hunt
publishing company

www.kendallhunt.com
Send all inquiries to:
4050 Westmark Drive
Dubuque, IA 52004-1840

Contents

About the Author

Ryan H. Pace, M.Tax, J.D., LL.M., is a professor of taxation at Weber State University. He teaches graduate and undergraduate courses in taxation and business law. Mr. Pace also serves as the Director of the Master of Accounting program, the Master of Taxation program, and the Center for Tax Education & Research at Weber State. Prior to his teaching career, Mr. Pace was a full-time attorney in Arizona and Utah. Mr. Pace graduated from New York University with a Master of Laws degree in taxation after receiving his Juris Doctor with honors from Washburn University School of Law. He also received a Master of Taxation degree from Arizona State University and his Bachelor of Science degree from the University of Utah. Mr. Pace has written several articles in the area of taxation and participated in many continuing education programs and academic conferences. He has written four other textbooks published by Kendall Hunt Publishing. Those titles are *Business Entity Taxation, Individual Taxation, Corporate Taxation, and Partnership Taxation.*

Part I

Introductory Concepts

Chapter 1

The United States Constitution and Its Purposes

The law impacts decisions we make each day. For example, should you exceed the speed limit to make it to class on time, or should you be late to class? Are you free to voice your opinion about government and its leaders? The law also significantly impacts decisions business leaders must make. Suppose an employee refuses to work on Saturdays because of sincerely held religious beliefs, but the employer needs the employee to work on Saturdays. Can the employer fire the employee? What if the employee refuses to conform to the employer's dress code? To what extent must an employer accommodate an employee's disability?

Effective business leaders must know the legal environment in which they operate. As a current or future business leader, you will be at a competitive advantage the more you know about the law. Additionally, you will benefit in your personal life by knowing the fundamental principles of law.

Laws are rules established by government and enforced by government. Violation of law could result in punishment by the government (*e.g.*, prison, fines) or an obligation to pay another party that may have been harmed by the wrongdoing (*e.g.*, breach of contract). The rule of law provides predictability and stability for individual and business activity within a community, state, and nation. The people of the United States have established the **Constitution** to provide a system of government to benefit society and to make and enforce laws.

The Constitution was adopted in 1787 and ratified by the states soon thereafter. The Constitution has 27 amendments.

James Steidl/Shutterstock.com

The drafters of the Constitution considered it necessary to provide a short statement regarding the purposes of the Constitution. This statement is called the **Preamble** to the Constitution.

What Do You Think?

Should the Constitution be construed and interpreted in a liberal manner to reflect contemporary societal norms and behaviors, or should it be construed strictly in a more traditional manner consistent with the original intent of the drafters?

As you proceed through this text and study the various laws and regulations, ask yourself whether those laws further the purposes of the Constitution. Those purposes are worth repeating:

- To form a more perfect union
- To establish justice
- To insure domestic tranquility
- To provide for the common defense
- To promote the general welfare
- To secure the blessings of liberty to ourselves and our posterity

Of course, there is much debate on how the Constitution should be interpreted. Should the Constitution be interpreted strictly according to the drafters' original intent? Should it be interpreted taking into account factors of contemporary society that did not exist over 200 years ago (*e.g.*, high-powered weapons, surveillance equipment, instant communications, high-speed vehicles, progressive social norms, etc.)? Lawyers, judges, lawmakers, scholars, and others have differing views on how the Constitution should be interpreted. You may recall reading about or watching confirmation hearings of nominees to the United States Supreme Court. Often, senators will question the nominee regarding how the nominee plans to interpret the Constitution and other laws.

The Constitution establishes three different branches of government: the executive branch, legislative branch, and judicial branch. Each branch has distinct authority and power to impact law. None of the branches of government, however, can unilaterally amend the Constitution. The Constitution is the supreme law of the land, subject to the will of *the people* to change it. The president cannot unilaterally change it. Congress cannot unilaterally change it. The courts can interpret it, but cannot change its wording. Indeed, the Constitution itself provides the manner in which it can be amended.

Thus, both the House of Representatives and the Senate must pass the proposed amendment by a two-thirds margin and three-fourths of the state legislatures must ratify it.

All laws must fall within the scope of the Constitution. Otherwise, the courts will strike down the law as being "unconstitutional" if the law is subsequently challenged. The particular law would then be ineffective and unenforceable.

QUESTIONS FOR REVIEW

1. According to the Preamble, what are the Constitution's purposes?

2. In what year was the U.S. Constitution adopted?

3. What are the three branches of government?

4. How is the Constitution amended?

5. How many amendments does the Constitution have?

6. In your opinion, how successfully have the people of the United States governed themselves?

7. Refer to the U.S. Constitution in the Appendix. What Article discusses the powers and duties of the executive branch of government?

8. Refer to the U.S. Constitution in the Appendix. What Article discusses the powers and duties of the legislative branch of government?

9. Refer to the U.S. Constitution in the Appendix. What Article discusses the powers and duties of the judicial branch of government?

INTERNET ACTIVITIES

1. One of the purposes of the Constitution as set forth in the Preamble is to "insure domestic tranquility." Discuss how this phrase has been interpreted.

2. One of the purposes of the Constitution as set forth in the Preamble is to "promote the general welfare." Discuss how this phrase has been interpreted.

Chapter 2

The Organization of Government

The United States Constitution provides for three branches of government—legislative, executive, and judicial. You likely are at least generally familiar with the organization of the United States government, but it is critical that we review this information so that you can better appreciate and understand the laws and regulations that we will discuss in future chapters.

The Legislative Branch of the Federal Government

Constitutional Provision Establishing the Legislative Branch

> **UNITED STATES CONSTITUTION**
>
> **Article 1, Section 1.** All legislative Powers herein granted shall be vested in a Congress of the United States, which shall consist of a Senate and House of Representatives.

Notice that the term "Congress" refers to *both* the Senate and House of Representatives. Since these two legislative bodies are of significant importance in the law-making process, we will review the characteristics of both the Senate and the House.

The Senate

> **UNITED STATES CONSTITUTION**
>
> **Article 1, Section 3.** The Senate of the United States shall be composed of two Senators from each State, [elected for a term of] six Years; and each Senator shall have one Vote. . . .
>
> No Person shall be a Senator who shall not have attained to the Age of thirty Years, and been nine Years a Citizen of the United States, and who shall not, when elected, be an Inhabitant of that State for which he shall be chosen. . . .
>
> The Vice President of the United States shall be President of the Senate, but shall have no Vote, unless they be equally divided.

The **Senate** currently has 100 members. Approximately one-third of the Senate seats are up for election every two years. The leader of the Senate is referred to as the "Majority Leader." He or she is a member of the majority party (either Democrat or Republican, as the case may be) and typically oversees the conducting of Senate business.

The Senate is composed of many committees called "standing committees." Each senator typically serves on at least one of these committees. These committees include, among others:

- Appropriations
- Armed Services

- Budget
- Finance
- Foreign Relations
- Homeland Security and Governmental Affairs
- Veterans' Affairs

These committees are further broken down into subcommittees. These committees and subcommittees play an important role in the legislative process, as we will discuss later in the chapter.

Members of the Senate engage in debate on the Senate floor. Interestingly, senators typically do not have time limits when they speak on the Senate floor. Consequently, sometimes senators will threaten a **filibuster**, which means that they will delay a vote on the bill by making very long speeches. Other senators can end a filibuster by invoking **cloture**, which means that three-fifths (60) of the senators would have to vote in favor of ending the debate. In most votes on bills under consideration, however, a simple majority is all that is needed to pass the bill.

What Do You Think?

Should a senator be able to delay or impede a vote on a bill merely by talking endlessly on the Senate floor?

The House of Representatives

UNITED STATES CONSTITUTION

Article 1, Section 2. The House of Representatives shall be composed of Members chosen every second Year by the People of the several States. . . .

No Person shall be a Representative who shall not have attained to the age of twenty five Years, and been seven Years a Citizen of the United States, and who shall not, when elected, be an Inhabitant of that State in which he shall be chosen.

The **House of Representatives** has 435 voting members representing the states according to population. A member of the House is elected for a two-year term. Like the Senate, the House of Representatives has many committees on which members serve. Examples of these House committees are:

- Appropriations
- Armed Services
- Budget
- Education and Labor
- Foreign Affairs
- Homeland Security
- Transportation and Infrastructure
- Ways and Means

The committees also have subcommittees that consider proposed bills. Members of the House debate proposed bills on the floor of the House, but unlike senators, members of the House have time limits, sometimes as short as a minute or two. Typically, all that is needed to pass a bill in the House is a majority vote.

Overview of the Legislative Process

To become law, a bill must make its way through the legislative process. This section briefly summarizes that process.

First, a bill is introduced by a member of Congress (Senate or House). The member of Congress that introduces the bill is often referred to as the bill's "sponsor." Sometimes, more than one member of Congress introduces a bill and is considered a co-sponsor.

Second, the bill is referred to a committee or subcommittee. These committees often hold hearings and consider other evidence about the merits of the bill. If approved by a subcommittee, the bill will go to the appropriate full committee. Upon approval by the full committee, the bill makes its way to the floor of the House of Representatives or Senate, as the case may be.

Third, the bill is debated in the House or the Senate. If a bill originates in the House, and the

House passes the bill, the bill must go to the Senate for approval also. Likewise, if the Senate passes a bill, the bill must go to the House for approval. Often, however, the legislative process slows down because one chamber of Congress changes the wording of the bill from what was passed by the other chamber. This necessitates a reconciliation of the two different bills. This is often done in a "conference committee" where representatives of each chamber will negotiate and perhaps compromise on a commonly worded bill. If they cannot agree, the bill dies. If they do agree on a revised bill, the bill goes back to the House and Senate for debate and a vote.

Finally, once the House and Senate both approve the same bill, the bill then goes to the president for signature. At this point, Article 1, Section 7 of the Constitution (quoted below) explains the process that follows.

As the Constitution points out, Congress can override a presidential veto with a two-thirds vote. This is a perfect example of the **checks-and-balances** system that we have in the United States, where one branch of government can stop another branch of government from exercising too much power.

Once a bill becomes law, that particular law usually then becomes part of the **United States Code.** The United States Code contains current federal statutory law. The Code consists of 54 "Titles." Each title contains law on a different subject. For example, Title 11 is Bankruptcy, Title 17 is Copyrights, Title 26 is the Internal Revenue Code, Title 35 is Patents, and Title 50 is War and National Defense. As you might imagine, each title is quite large and typically consists of several volumes of law.

What Do You Think?

Is the legislative process currently too cumbersome? If so, how could it be improved?

Understanding the legislative process and the characteristics of the Senate and House of Representatives is critical in the successful study of law.

The Executive Branch of the Federal Government

The executive branch of government administers and enforces the law. The president, cabinet, and federal agencies are all part of the executive branch.

UNITED STATES CONSTITUTION

Article 1, Section 7

. . .

Every Bill which shall have passed the House of Representatives and the Senate, shall, before it becomes a Law, be presented to the President of the United States; If he approves he shall sign it, but if not he shall return it, with his Objections to that House in which it shall have originated, who shall enter the Objections at large on their Journal, and proceed to reconsider it. If after such Reconsideration two thirds of that House shall agree to pass the Bill, it shall be sent, together with the Objections, to the other House, by which it shall likewise be reconsidered, and if approved by two thirds of that House, it shall become a Law. . . .

Constitutional Provision Establishing the Executive Branch

The Constitution did not originally limit the number of terms a person could serve as president. After Franklin D. Roosevelt was elected as president four times, however, the Constitution was amended (Twenty-second Amendment) to restrict a person from being elected president for more than two terms.

The president obviously has a multitude of responsibilities. The Constitution does not list them all, but it is worth mentioning a few responsibilities and powers of the president that the Constitution does specifically enumerate (Article II, Section 2).

Notice the checks-and-balances built in to some of these provisions, particularly where the Senate must consent to treaties and appointments to the Supreme Court.

jiawangkun/Shutterstock.com

The president, of course, has numerous advisors and assistants to help carry out the daily tasks of administering government. The executive branch consists of several departments. The department leaders are appointed by the president and constitute the **cabinet**.

The Cabinet

The cabinet is composed of 15 executive departments. The executive that leads each department is referred to as the "secretary" of the particular department (except for the Department of Justice, whose executive is called the Attorney General). The departments are as follows:

- Agriculture
- Commerce

- Defense
- Education
- Energy
- Health and Human Services
- Homeland Security
- Housing and Urban Development
- Interior
- Justice
- Labor
- State
- Transportation
- Treasury
- Veterans Affairs

These departments and the many agencies within the respective departments play a critical role in enforcing and administering the law.

Federal Agencies

Agencies within each department are specialized in particular areas of law. For example, the Department of Transportation includes the following agencies, among others:

- Federal Aviation Administration (FAA)
- Federal Highway Administration (FHWA)
- Federal Motor Carrier Safety Administration (FMCSA)
- Federal Railroad Administration (FRA)
- Federal Transit Administration (FTA)
- Maritime Administration (MARAD)
- National Highway Traffic Safety Administration (NHTSA)

Other departments have several agencies under their umbrella as well. As another example, the Department of Labor includes the following agencies, among others:

- Employee Benefits Security Administration (EBSA)
- Employment & Training Administration (ETA)
- Mine Safety & Health Administration (MSHA)

- Occupational Safety & Health Administration (OSHA)
- Pension Benefit Guaranty Corporation (PBGC)

The importance of agencies and their influence on business law cannot be overstated. Indeed, businesses often face a difficult task in understanding and complying with the voluminous administrative regulations, rulings, and procedures promulgated by governmental agencies.

What Do You Think?

Do government agencies regulate business too much or too little?

The Judicial Branch of the Federal Government

The judicial system exists to resolve conflict and interpret and apply the law to a particular set of facts. This chapter will discuss generally the organization of the judicial branch and the United States court system.

Constitutional Provision Establishing the Judicial Branch

CONSTITUTION OF THE UNITED STATES

Article III, Section 1. The judicial Power of the United States shall be vested in one supreme Court, and in such inferior Courts as the Congress may from time to time ordain and establish. The Judges, both of the supreme and inferior Courts, shall hold their Offices during good Behaviour, and shall, at stated Times, receive for their Services, a Compensation, which shall not be diminished during their Continuance in Office.

Congress has, in fact, established courts inferior to the Supreme Court. These courts include district courts and courts of appeal.

United States District Courts

United States District Courts are the trial courts in the federal court system and are the initial courts to hear cases. Every state has at least one United States District Court.

In order for a federal court to have **jurisdiction** to hear a case, the controversy must (1) involve a federal question (*i.e.*, federal law), or (2) involve a situation where every defendant is a citizen of a different state than every plaintiff (*i.e.*, "diversity of citizenship"), and the amount in controversy is over $75,000. If either of these requirements is met, then the federal courts have what is referred to as **subject matter jurisdiction**. If neither of these requirements is met, then the litigants must take their case to state court. The term "jurisdiction" means that a court has authority to hear the case based upon the issues and parties involved.

In addition to subject matter jurisdiction, a court must also have **personal jurisdiction** over the defendant in the case. This applies in both federal and state cases. For example, suppose Marino, a resident of California, sues Anthony, a resident of Florida, for breach of contract. The amount in controversy is $100,000. Can Marino sue Anthony in an *Illinois* federal court? An Illinois court can only hear the case if the court has personal jurisdiction over Anthony. A court has personal jurisdiction over a defendant if the defendant has some level of minimum contacts with the particular state in which the court sits and the defendant has purposefully transacted business in the state, committed a wrongful act in the state, or owns property in the state. In short, requiring a defendant to go to another state to defend a lawsuit must meet the constitutional requirement of fairness. So, unless Anthony has minimum contacts with Illinois, Marino must sue him in Florida or some other state that may have

personal jurisdiction over Anthony. If more than one court has jurisdiction over a case, then the issue becomes a question of **venue**. Sometimes litigants will disagree about where the case should be heard when multiple courts have jurisdiction. Ultimately, however, a judge will decide where proper venue is if the litigants can not agree.

Circuit Courts of Appeal

The losing party at the district court level has the right to appeal the district court decision to one of the U.S. Circuit Courts of Appeal. The particular court to which the person appeals the decision depends upon the circuit court that has jurisdiction. Figure 1 on the next page illustrates the jurisdiction of the respective courts of appeal.

A person appealing a case out of a district court in Texas, for example, would appeal to the Fifth Circuit Court of Appeals.

When a case is heard on appeal, the process is different than at the trial court level. On appeal, there is no trial, witnesses, jury, etc. Rather, the lawyers for both sides submit **appellate briefs** to the judges. The briefs review the facts, apply the law to the facts, and try to persuade the appellate judges to arrive at a particular conclusion. Of course, the party who lost at the district court level will explain why he or she believes the district court judge made an error that should be reversed (*e.g.*, admitted evidence that should have been excluded, gave incorrect jury instructions, etc.). The judges will typically also hear oral arguments from the lawyers involved in the case before the judges decide to affirm or reverse the district court's decision.

United States Supreme Court

The party that loses the case at the circuit court level has one last possible appeal—to the United States Supreme Court. The United States Supreme Court is not required to hear the case, however. In fact, the Court reviews relatively few cases each year as a percentage of cases seeking

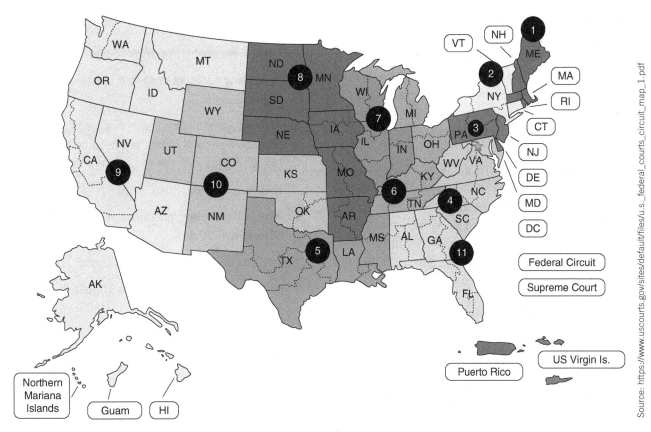

FIGURE 1. Map illustrating the jurisdiction of respective courts of appeal.

review. If the Supreme Court decides to review a case, it will issue a **writ of certiorari**. The Court typically grants a writ of certiorari for those cases that have significant constitutional implications or in cases where two or more circuit courts are split regarding the issue and the issue needs to be resolved.

A member of the United States Supreme Court is nominated by the president and confirmed by the Senate. The Court is composed of nine justices, with one serving as the Chief Justice.

Common Law Legal Systems and Civil Law Legal Systems

Laws passed by legislative bodies (*e.g.*, Congress and state legislatures) are called **statutes**. At the local level, however, laws passed by city councils and county commissions are typically called **ordinances** instead of statutes. These statutes and ordinances often do not cover every conceivable transaction or activity in our complex society. Consequently, courts analyze situations based upon an interpretation of the Constitution, statutes, ordinances, and upon legal principles that have evolved over long periods of time primarily through other court decisions. The evolution of law through court decisions has become known as the **common law**. In countries where common-law principles are adopted, such as the United States and England, courts typically rely on prior court decisions to assist in deciding the case at hand. The earlier court decisions are said to have established **precedent**. The concept of precedent is sometimes called *stare decisis*, which in Latin basically means "to let it stand." Courts typically rule consistently with precedent, but they are not absolutely required to do so if the facts warrant an overruling of the precedent. Keep in mind, however, that lower-level courts are bound by higher court rulings that are directly on point.

Some countries do not place as much emphasis on prior court decisions and do not adopt the common law legal system. The countries that give little or no weight to prior judicial decisions are said to have adopted **civil law** legal systems. Many European countries have a civil law legal system. Important note: the term "civil law" in referring to a legal system distinct from the common law legal system is different from the use of the term "civil law" (*e.g.*, contract law, property law, corporate law, etc.) when distinguishing it from "criminal law" (*e.g.*, murder, robbery, embezzlement, etc.).

State and Local Governments

Most state governments are organized in a manner similar to the federal government. State constitutions establish executive, legislative, and judicial branches for that state. Governors sign bills passed by the state legislatures in order to create statutory law. State court systems are also similar to the federal system. This can be somewhat confusing because many states identify their courts by the same names, *i.e.*, district courts, appellate courts, and a supreme court. Local governments also typically have some form of the three branches of government (*e.g.*, mayors, city councils, and municipal courts).

QUESTIONS FOR REVIEW

1. What is meant by the term "Congress"?

2. How many senators are there in the United States Senate?

3. At what age does a person become eligible to serve as a senator? Must a person be born in the United States in order to be a senator?

4. How long is a senator's term?

5. Who is the current president of the United States Senate?

6. What is a filibuster? What is cloture?

7. Name four committees in the United States Senate.

8. How many voting members are in the United States House of Representatives?

9. At what age does a person become eligible to serve as a member of the United States House of Representatives? Must a person be born in the United States in order to be a member of the House of Representatives?

10. How long is a U.S. House of Representatives member's term?

11. Name four committees in the United States House of Representatives.

12. Explain the legislative process.

13. What is necessary for Congress to override a presidential veto?

14. What is the United States Code?

15. Name the two senators that represent your state.

16. Which member of the United States House of Representatives represents the district in which you live?

17. At what age does a person become eligible to serve as president of the United States?

18. What are some of the president's specific responsibilities outlined in the Constitution?

19. Name five of the 15 departments of the federal government.

20. Explain generally the structure of the federal court system.

21. What is subject matter jurisdiction? Personal jurisdiction?

22. Explain the requirement(s) that must be met in order for a case to be heard in federal court.

23. What is a "writ of certiorari"?

24. What is meant by the term "common law"? Precedent?

INTERNET ACTIVITIES

1. Visit the U.S. House of Representatives website at www.house.gov. Which House committees does your representative serve on?

2. Visit the United States Senate website at www.senate.gov. Which Senate committees do the two senators from your state serve on?

3. Find a table of contents of the United States Code. What area of law is found in Title 35? Title 49?

4. Visit www.whitehouse.gov. Who is the president's current Chief of Staff? Deputy Chiefs of Staff? Senior Advisors?

5. Visit www.whitehouse.gov. Explain the order of succession if the president is unable to serve (*e.g.*, vice-president is first).

6. Visit the websites of two departments other than the Department of Transportation and Department of Labor. Who is the Secretary of each of the two departments? List the agencies within each of the two departments.

7. Visit the website of the United States Supreme Court at www.supremecourt.gov.

   a. Who are the nine justices of the United States Supreme Court?

   b. What is the case name of the most recent decision issued by the Court? When was the case decided?

8. Answer the following questions regarding your state and local governments.

   a. Who is the governor of your state?

   b. When was your state's constitution adopted?

   c. What is the official name of the agency that issues vehicle license plates in your state?

   d. What is the official name of the tax collection agency in your state?

   e. Name the lawmaker that represents your district in the state legislature.

   f. Who is the chief justice of the highest court in your state?

   g. How many justices are on the highest court in your state?

   h. Who is the mayor of the city in which you live? Identify the city. If you live in an area that does not have a mayor, identify the closest city and the name of its mayor.

Chapter 3

Law and Ethics

Is every law ethical? Is every ethical decision legal? These questions are sometimes difficult to answer, and to some extent, the answers vary depending upon a person's own moral philosophy and ethical belief system. While understanding fundamental legal principles is important for every businessperson, ethical principles should not be ignored. Many laws encompass generally accepted ethical and moral views of society (*e.g.*, it is wrong to take someone else's life, steal someone else's property, etc.). Violating these laws exacts punishment from the government on behalf of society. Many decisions business leaders have to make, however, are not as clear-cut. Throughout this text, we will cover various areas of law so you can be at least generally familiar with the legal environment in which a business operates. Nevertheless, you should always remember any ethical issues that may arise as well. This chapter sets forth some ethical issues to consider as you progress throughout this course and when you make business decisions in the future.

Fundamental Approaches to Ethical Decision-Making

In an ideal world, people would make decisions that are both legal and ethical. Unfortunately, this is not always the case. Some decisions may be legal but not ethical, while other decisions may be ethical but not legal. For example, lying is sometimes legal (*e.g.*, lying to your friend that you recently caught a fish that was 18 inches long when, in fact, you measured it to be only 10 inches long) and sometimes illegal (*e.g.*, lying when on the witness stand while under oath to tell the truth). Whether lying or some other act is *ethical*, however, is a different question.

Broadly speaking, there are two basic approaches to ethical decision-making—formalism and consequentialism.

Formalism

The **formalism** approach to solving ethical dilemmas basically mandates that a person should act in a manner that he or she believes that everyone should act. If you believe it would be unacceptable for everyone to act in the same way, then you should not act that way. For example, if you believe that lying is inherently wrong and immoral, then it is your duty not to lie and no one else should lie either regardless of the consequences. In other words, society as a whole benefits by everyone's being honest all the time.

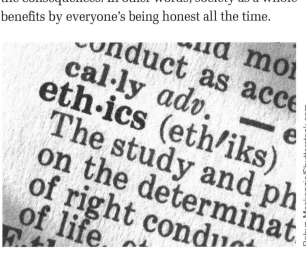

Robyn Mackenzie/Shutterstock.com

Consequentialism

In contrast to formalism, **consequentialism** focuses on the consequences of the action rather than the action itself. If the action benefits most of the people most of the time, then the action is moral. For example, suppose Dan has a girlfriend, Jessica. Jessica just purchased a new outfit and asks Dan his opinion regarding whether it looks good on her. Suppose Dan really thinks the outfit looks terrible, but he nevertheless tells Jessica that the outfit looks fabulous. Dan reasons to himself that if he tells the truth, it may hurt Jessica's feelings or cause her to be upset with him. Dan clearly focused on the consequences of his action rather than the action itself.

What Do You Think?

Assume you have a job interview next Tuesday. You have been informed that the interview process will take almost all day. You realize that you will not be able to make it to work next Tuesday at your current job. How do you proceed with your current employer?

1. Should you tell the truth? If so, would your current job be in jeopardy? Would your employer think you are disloyal and, as a result, not consider you in the future for a raise or promotion?

2. Should you lie? For example, you could tell your current employer that you need the day off because you have to go to the doctor.

3. Should you just wait until Tuesday morning and "call in sick"?

Which of these alternatives are legal? Which are ethical? Are you influenced most by the formalist approach or consequentialist approach to ethical decision-making?

Profits vs. Ethics

Suppose you are the president of a manufacturing business that manufactures fireworks, including firecrackers. Your company has a strong safety record, and you stand by the safety of your products. An employee brings to your attention that the company has recently received several telephone calls and emails from customers whose hands have been burned due to certain fireworks malfunctioning. In fact, one recent complaint was that a young boy lost a finger because of a malfunctioning fuse on a firecracker. As a result, you anticipate that the boy's parents might file a lawsuit against your company in the near future. You subsequently assign some employees to perform additional tests on the fireworks to determine safety. They report to you that, on average, one out of 10,000 firecrackers may prematurely explode because of a faulty fuse. What do you do next? Do you recall all the firecrackers currently on the market? (Ignore the fact that the government may eventually mandate a recall.) Do you need additional information before you make the decision? Does it matter how much it will cost to recall the firecrackers? Does it matter how much it will cost to redesign the product to prevent future injuries? Does it matter how much a judge or jury may award your customer in a lawsuit against your company?

One of the most famous court cases that relates to the interaction of law and ethics involved Ford Motor Company. The case involved a flaw in gas tank design in the Ford Pinto model. The case was tried in California. (See Illustrative Court Case 3.1.)

Evidence in the case showed that Ford had estimated the number of future fatalities and injuries due to the defective gas tank. Then, Ford calculated the average dollar value of a life and the dollar value for the estimated deaths and injuries. Ford then multiplied the number of estimated deaths and injuries by the respective average dollar values. The result was compared to the cost of fixing the faulty gas tanks. Ford made the decision not to fix the gas tanks.

Grimshaw v. Ford Motor Company

Court of Appeal of the State of California

119 Cal.App. 3d 757 (1981)

[**Note:** For convenience of the reader, the following language is from the official California Reports Summary.]

An automobile manufactured by [Ford] unexpectedly stalled on a freeway and erupted into flames when it was rear-ended by a car proceeding in the same direction. The driver of the stalled car suffered fatal burns and a passenger suffered severe and permanently disfiguring burns on his face and entire body. The passenger and the heirs of the driver sued [Ford] on the theory of strict liability for a design defect in the car's gas tank, and, following a six-month jury trial, verdicts were returned in favor of [the passenger and heirs of the driver]. The passenger was awarded over $2 million compensatory damages and $125 million punitive damages, while the heirs were awarded over $550,000 in compensatory damages. . . . [Ultimately, the court drastically reduced the punitive damages awarded to the passenger by the jury.]

The Court of Appeal affirmed. . . . The court rejected [Ford's] contention that the term "malice" as used in [a California statute] authorizing punitive damages, required an evil motive, an intention to injure the person harmed, and that the term was conceptually incompatible with [the manufacturing] and marketing of a defectively designed product. The court held the term "malice" as used in the statute included not only a malicious intention to injure the specific person harmed, but conduct evincing a conscious disregard of the probability that the actor's conduct will result in injury to others. . . . The court held there was ample evidence to support a finding of malice and corporate responsibility therefore, noting that through the result of crash tests [Ford] knew that the car's fuel tank and rear structure would expose consumers to serious injury or death in a low speed collision, and that [Ford] could have corrected the design defects at minimal cost but deferred corrections by engaging in a cost-benefit analysis balancing human lives and limbs against corporate profits.

What Do You Think?

1. Assume that Ford met all *legal requirements* for safety standards for vehicles at that time. Was it inherently unethical for Ford to employ a cost/benefit analysis relating to the value of lives?

2. Which of the two basic approaches to ethical decision-making did Ford use?

3. If you were a judge or on a jury, how would you go about determining how much money a life is worth?

The Enron scandal is another noted situation where the pursuit of profits compromised ethical decision-making. Thousands of people lost their livelihoods, jobs, retirement savings, etc. Because of the Enron scandal and other companies' "bad" behavior, Congress acted swiftly in enacting laws providing much more strict oversight of corporate executives and public accounting firms regarding financial matters.

Businesses sometimes get themselves into trouble by using questionable sales tactics or providing misleading information to customers in an attempt to get the customer to purchase products or services. Consider the following press release from the Federal Trade Commission (Illustrative Press Release 3.1).

Federal Trade Commission

March 27, 2019

FOR RELEASE

Office Depot, Inc. and a California-based tech support software provider have agreed to pay a total of $35 million to settle Federal Trade Commission allegations that the companies tricked customers into buying millions of dollars' worth of computer repair and technical services by deceptively claiming their software had found malware symptoms on the customers' computers.

Office Depot has agreed to pay $25 million while its software supplier, Support.com, Inc., has agreed to pay $10 million as part of their settlements with the FTC. The FTC intends to use these funds to provide refunds to consumers.

"Consumers have a hard enough time protecting their computers from malware, viruses, and other treats," said FTC Chairman Joe Simons. "This case should send a strong message to companies that they will face stiff consequences if they use deception to trick consumers into buying costly services they may not need."

In its complaint, the FTC alleges that Support.com worked with Office Depot for nearly a decade to sell technical support services at its stores. Office Depot and Support.com used PC Health Check, a software program, as a sales tool to convince consumers to purchase tech repair services from Office Depot and OfficeMax, Inc., which merged in 2013.

The Office Depot companies marketed the program as a free "PC check-up" or tune-up service to help improve a computer's performance and scan for viruses and other security threats. Support.com, which received tens of millions of dollars in revenue from Office Depot, remotely performed the tech repair services once consumers made the purchase.

The FTC alleges that while Office Depot claimed the program detected malware symptoms on consumers' computers, the actual results presented to consumers were based entirely on whether consumers answered "yes" to four questions they were asked at the beginning of the PC Health Check program. These included questions about whether the computer ran slow, received virus warnings, crashed often, or displayed pop-up ads or other problems that prevented the user from browsing the Internet.

The complaint alleges that Office Depot and Support.com configured the PC Health Check Program to report that the scan found malware symptoms or infections whenever consumers answered yes to at least one of these four questions, despite the fact that the scan had no connection to the "malware symptoms" results. After displaying the results of the scan, the program also displayed a "view recommendation" button with a detailed description of the tech services consumers were encouraged to purchase—services that could cost hundreds of dollars—to fix the problems.

The FTC alleges that both Office Depot and Support.com have been aware of concerns and complaints about the PC Health Check program since at least 2012. For example, one OfficeMax employee complained to corporate management in 2012, saying "I cannot justify lying to a customer or being TRICKED into lying to them for our store to make a few extra dollars." Despite this and other internal warnings, Office Depot continued until late 2016 to advertise and use the PC Health Check program and pushed its store managers and employees to generate sales from the program, according to the complaint.

(Continued)

The Commission alleges that both companies violated the FTC Act's prohibition against deceptive practices.

In addition to the monetary payment, the proposed settlement also prohibits Office Depot from making misrepresentations about the security or performance of a consumer's electronic device and requires the company to ensure its existing and future software providers do not engage in such conduct. As part of its proposed settlement, Support.com cannot make, or provide others with the means to make, misrepresentations about the performance or detection of security issues on consumer electronic devices.

The Commission vote authorizing the staff to file the complaint and stipulated final orders was 5-0. The FTC filed the complaint and stipulated final orders in the U.S. District Court for the Southern District of Florida. NOTE: The Commission files a complaint when it has "reason to believe" that the law has been or is being violated and it appears to the Commission that a proceeding is in the public interest. Stipulated final orders have the force of law when approved and signed by a District Court judge.

Codes of Conduct

Most professions have adopted codes of conduct that members of the profession should follow. These codes do not replace applicable law that may regulate a professional's conduct, but do provide guidelines for ethical behavior.

Individual companies may also adopt codes of conduct or codes of ethics. These codes typically address issues relating to confidentiality, accounting controls, conflicts of interest, discrimination, harassment, fraud, etc. Of course, at a minimum, business managers should inform employees about expected ethical standards of behavior within the company.

In summary, while learning the fundamental legal principles contained in this text, always keep in mind ethical issues as well. See if you can identify courses of action along the way that may be legal, but still unethical.

QUESTIONS FOR REVIEW

1. Explain the formalism approach to ethical decision-making.

2. Explain the consequentialism approach to ethical decision-making.

3. Can you think of a scenario where a decision would be ethical, but illegal? Discuss.

4. Suppose you have a business law exam that the instructor has placed in a testing center, and you have a three-day window to take the exam at your convenience. This is your second exam in the course. You decide to take the exam on Day 1. On Day 2, suppose a friend of yours who is also in the class asks you the following questions:

   a. Have you taken the business law exam yet?

   b. Was the exam difficult?

   c. Do the multiple-choice questions have four possible answers or five?

   d. How do you feel you did on the exam?

   e. I plan on taking the exam tomorrow. How do you suggest I study for the exam tonight so I am prepared to take it tomorrow?

   f. Was this exam more difficult than the first exam?

   g. How long were you in the testing center taking the exam?

   h. Did the instructor include any questions about the *Ford* case?

Which of the above questions do you believe are unethical for your friend to ask you? Which of the above questions do you believe it is unethical for you to answer?

5. Summarize the Federal Trade Commission's press release contained in the chapter.

INTERNET ACTIVITIES

1. Find a summary of the Enron scandal. In your opinion, what specific unethical decisions did Enron executives make?

2. Search for any particular company's code of conduct or code of ethics.

   a. What is the name of the company?

   b. Name at least four specific topics directly addressed by the code of conduct or code of ethics.

   c. Does the policy provide a person or department for employees to consult if they need guidance, have complaints, or have a question regarding the code of conduct?

   d. In your opinion is there any reason a company may not want to formally adopt a code of conduct or code of ethics?

Part II

The Constitution and the Business Environment

Chapter 4

The Supremacy Clause, Commerce Clause, and Full Faith and Credit Clause

What happens when a federal law and a state law are conflicting? How much authority does a state government have in regulating business within its own borders? Are state judges in one state required to recognize the decisions of judges in other states?

The answers to all of these questions are important to understand the fundamental legal environment of business. A discussion of the applicable constitutional provisions is presented here.

Supremacy Clause

The United States has a system of government referred to as **federalism**. This basically means that we have more than one government that can make and enforce laws. Most of us are subject to at least three levels of government—federal, state, and local. Because of this multilayer system of government, laws at one level may conflict with laws at another level. Article VI of the Constitution addresses the situation where a state law may conflict with a federal law.

Article VI establishes that federal law is supreme to state law when there is a conflict. The United States Supreme Court case that follows (Illustrative Court Case 4.1) explains this principle.

> **UNITED STATES CONSTITUTION**
> ## Article VI
>
> . . .
>
> This Constitution, and the Laws of the United States which shall be made in Pursuance thereof; and all Treaties made, or which shall be made, under the Authority of the United States, shall be the supreme Law of the Land; and the Judges in every State shall be bound thereby, any Thing in the Constitution or Laws of any State to the Contrary notwithstanding.
>
> . . .

Commerce Clause

States have considerable interest in commercial activity occurring within the state's borders. For example, what if a state legislature passed a law that prohibited any vehicle weighing more than 10 tons from driving on its roads because such vehicles may cause more road damage than lighter vehicles? Would such a law be enforceable? What if every state had such a law? Even if just one state had this law, how would this law affect interstate commerce?

Watters v. Wachovia Bank

Supreme Court of the United States

550 U.S. 1 (2007)

[**Note**: For convenience of the reader, the following language is from the Syllabus of the case as provided by the U.S. Supreme Court Reporter of Decisions.]

National banks' business activities are controlled by the National Bank Act (NBA) . . . and regulations promulgated thereunder by the Office of the Comptroller of the Currency (OCC). OCC is charged with supervision of the NBA and, thus, oversees the banks' operations and interactions with customers. . . . The NBA grants OCC, as part of its supervisory authority, visitorial powers to audit the banks' books and records, largely to the exclusion of other state or federal entities. . . . The NBA specifically authorizes federally chartered banks to engage in real estate lending . . . and "[t]o exercise . . . such incidental powers as shall be necessary to carry on the business of banking." [Citation omitted]. Among incidental powers, national banks may conduct certain activities through "operating subsidiaries," discrete entities authorized to engage solely in activities the bank itself could undertake, and subject to the same terms and conditions as the bank. [Citation omitted.]

Respondent Wachovia Bank is an OCC-chartered national banking association that conducts its real estate lending business through respondent Wachovia Mortgage Corporation, a wholly owned, North Carolina-chartered entity licensed as an operating subsidiary by OCC, and doing business in Michigan and elsewhere. Michigan law exempts banks, both national and state, from state mortgage lending regulation, but requires their subsidiaries to register with the State's Office of Insurance and Financial Services (OIFS) and submit to state supervision. Although Wachovia Mortgage initially complied with Michigan's requirements, it surrendered its Michigan registration once it became a wholly owned operating subsidiary of Wachovia Bank. Subsequently, petitioner Watters, the OIFS Commissioner, advised Wachovia Mortgage it would no longer be authorized to engage in mortgage lending in Michigan. Respondents sued . . . contending that the NBA and OCC's regulations preempt application of the relevant Michigan mortgage lending laws to a national bank's operating subsidiary. Watters responded that, because Wachovia Mortgage was not itself a national bank, the challenged Michigan laws were applicable and were not preempted.

Held:

1. Wachovia's mortgage business, whether conducted by the bank itself or through the bank's operating subsidiary, is subject to OCC's superintendence, and not to the licensing, reporting, and visitorial regimes of the several States in which the subsidiary operates.

. . .

To prevent inconsistent or intrusive state regulation, the NBA provides that "[n]o national bank shall be subject to any visitorial powers except as authorized by Federal law . . . ." [Citation omitted.] Federally chartered banks are subject to state laws of general application in their daily business to the extent such laws do not conflict with the letter or purposes of the NBA. But when state prescriptions significantly impair the exercise of authority, enumerated or incidental under the NBA, the State's regulations must give way.

. . .

A national bank may engage in real estate lending through an operating subsidiary, subject to the same terms and conditions that govern the bank itself; that power cannot be significantly impaired

(*Continued*)

or impeded by state law. Though state law governs incorporation-related issues, state regulators cannot interfere with the "business of banking" by subjecting national banks or their OCC-licensed operating subsidiaries to multiple audits and surveillance under rival oversight regimes.

. . .

[A]ffirmed.

The drafters of the Constitution believed that interstate commerce was very important to the United States economy and that businesses engaged in interstate commerce should not be subject to undue burdens created by individual states. Consequently, they addressed the issue in the Constitution.

Only Congress—and not the states—has the power to pass laws and regulations governing *inter*state commerce. A United States Supreme Court case (Illustrative Court Case 4.2) discusses the application of this concept.

Consider another Supreme Court case addressing the issue whether a state can require a seller to collect and remit a sales tax to the state even if the seller does not have a physical presence in the state (Illustrative Court Case 4.3).

UNITED STATES CONSTITUTION

Article I, Section 8. The Congress shall have the Power to . . . regulate Commerce with foreign Nations, and among the several States, and with the Indian Tribes; . . .

ILLUSTRATIVE COURT CASE 4.2

Hunt v. Washington State Apple Advertising Commission

Supreme Court of the United States

432 U.S. 333 (1977)

[**Note:** For convenience of the reader, the following language is from the Syllabus of the case as provided by the U.S. Supreme Court Reporter of Decisions.]

[Washington State Apple Advertising Commission], a statutory agency for the promotion and protection of the Washington State apple industry and composed of 13 state growers and dealers chosen from electoral districts by their fellow growers and dealers, . . . brought this suit challenging the constitutionality of a North Carolina statute requiring that all apples sold or shipped into North Carolina in closed containers be identified by no grade on the containers other than the applicable federal grade or a designation that the apples are not graded. [In short, North Carolina required that the U.S. Department of Agriculture (USDA) label be on the containers or the containers should have no label at all. Thus, this law prohibited containers from having a Washington label on them. Washington State Apple Advertising Commission filed suit challenging that the] statute unconstitutionally discriminated against commerce insofar as it affected the interstate shipment of Washington apples.

Held:

(Continued)

. . .

3. The North Carolina statute violates the Commerce Clause by burdening and discriminating against the interstate sale of Washington apples.

(a) The statute raises the costs of doing business in the North Carolina market for Washington growers and dealers while leaving unaffected their North Carolina counterparts, who were still free to market apples under the federal grade or none at all.

(b) The statute strips the Washington apple industry of the competitive and economic advantages it has earned for itself by an expensive, stringent mandatory state inspection and grading system that exceeds federal requirements. By requiring Washington apples to be sold under the inferior grades of their federal counterparts, the North Carolina statute offers the North Carolina apple industry the very sort of protection against out-of-state competition that the Commerce Clause was designed to prohibit.

(c) Even if the statute was not intended to be discriminatory and was enacted for the declared purposes of protecting consumers from deception and fraud because of the multiplicity of state grades, the statute does remarkably little to further that goal, at least with respect to Washington apples and grades, for it permits marketing of apples in closed containers under no grades at all, and does nothing to purify the flow of information at the retail level. Moreover, Washington grades could not have led to the type of deception at which the statute was assertedly aimed, since those grades equal or surpass the comparable federal standards.

(d) Nondiscriminatory alternatives to the outright ban of Washington State grades are readily available.

ILLUSTRATIVE COURT CASE 4.3

South Dakota v. Wayfair, Inc.

Supreme Court of the United States

585 U.S. _____ (2018)

[**Note:** For convenience of the reader, the following language is from the Syllabus of the case as provided by the U.S. Supreme Court Reporter of Decisions.]

South Dakota, like many States, taxes the retail sales of goods and services in the State. Sellers are required to collect and remit the tax to the State, but if they do not then in-state consumers are responsible for paying a use tax at the same rate. Under *National Bellas Hess, Inc. v. Department of Revenue of Ill.*, 386 U.S. 753, and *Quill Corp. v. North Dakota*, 504 U.S. 298, South Dakota may not require a business that has no physical presence in the State to collect its sales tax. Consumer compliance rates are notoriously low, however, and it is estimated that *Bellas Hess* and *Quill* cause South Dakota to lose between $48 and $58 million annually. Concerned about the erosion of its sales tax base and corresponding loss of critical funding for state and local services, the South Dakota Legislature enacted a law requiring out-of-state sellers to collect and remit sales tax "as if the seller had a physical presence in the State." The Act covers only sellers that on an annual basis deliver more than $100,000 of goods or services into the State or engage in 200 or more separate transactions for the delivery of goods or services into the State. Respondents, top online retailers with no employees or real estate in South Dakota, each meet the Act's minimum sales or transactions requirement, but do not collect the State's sales tax. South Dakota filed suit in state court, seeking a declaration that the Act's requirements are valid and applicable to respondents and an injunction requiring respondents to register for licenses to collect and remit the sales tax. Respondents sought summary judgment, arguing that the Act is unconstitutional. The trial court granted their motion. The State Supreme Court affirmed on the ground that *Quill* is controlling precedent.

(*Continued*)

Held:

Because the physical presence rule of *Quill* is unsound and incorrect, *Quill Corp. v. North Dakota*, 504 U.S. 298, and *National Bellas Hess, Inc. v. Department of Revenue of Ill.*, 386 U.S. 753, are overruled.

(a) An understanding of this Court's Commerce Clause principles and their application to state taxes is instructive here.

(1) Two primary principles mark the boundaries of a State's authority to regulate interstate commerce: State regulations may not discriminate against interstate commerce; and States may not impose undue burdens on interstate commerce. These principles guide the courts in adjudicating challenges to state laws under the Commerce Clause.

(2) They also animate Commerce Clause precedents addressing the validity of state taxes, which will be sustained so long as the (1) apply to an activity with a substantial nexus with the taxing State, (2) are fairly apportioned, (3) do not discriminate against interstate commerce, and (4) are fairly related to the services the State provides. See *Complete Auto Transit, Inc. v. Brady*, 430 U.S. 274, 279. Before *Complete Auto*, the Court held in *Bellas Hess* that a "seller whose only connection with customers in the state is by common carrier or . . . mail" lacked the requisite minimum contacts with the State required by the Due Process Clause and the Commerce Clause, and that unless the retailer maintained a physical presence in the State, the State lacked the power to require that retailer to collect a local tax. . . . In *Quill*, the Court overruled the due process holding, but not the Commerce Clause holding, grounding the physical presence rule in *Complete Auto's* requirement that a tax have a "substantial nexus" with the activity being taxed.

(b) The physical presence rule has long been criticized as giving out-of-state sellers an advantage. Each year, it becomes further removed from economic reality and results in significant revenue losses to the States. These critiques underscore that the rule, both as first formulated and as applied today, is an incorrect interpretation of the Commerce Clause.

. . .

(2) When the day-to-day functions of marketing and distribution in the modern economy are considered, it becomes evident that Quill's physical presence rule is artificial, not just "at its edges," but in its entirety. Modern e-commerce does not align analytically with a test that relies on the sort of physical presence defined in Quill. And the Court should not maintain a rule that ignores substantial virtual connections to the State.

(3) The physical presence rule of *Bellas Hess* and *Quill* is also an extraordinary imposition by the Judiciary on States' authority to collect taxes and perform critical public functions. . . . By giving some online retailers an arbitrary advantage over their competitors who collect state sales taxes, *Quill's* physical presence rule has limited States' ability to seek long-term prosperity and has prevented market participants from competing on an even playing field.

(c) Stare decisis can no longer support the Court's prohibition of a valid exercise of the States' sovereign power. If it becomes apparent that the Court's Commerce Clause decisions prohibit the States from exercising their lawful sovereign powers, the Court should be vigilant in correcting the error. It is inconsistent with this Court's proper role to ask Congress to address a false constitutional premise of this Court's own creation. The Internet revolution has made Quill's original error all the more egregious and harmful. The Quill Court did not have before it the present realities of the interstate marketplace, where the Internet's prevalence and power have changed the dynamics of the national economy. The expansion of e-commerce has also increased the revenue shortfall faced by States seeking to collect their sales and use taxes, leading the South Dakota Legislature to declare an emergency. The argument, moreover, that the physical presence rule is clear and easy to apply is unsound, as attempts to apply the physical presence rule to online retail sales have proved unworkable.

If states pass laws regulating interstate commerce, even if the federal government has not yet addressed the specific issue, the law is unconstitutional. This concept that the states must leave interstate commerce alone even if the federal government has not yet regulated the specific issue is called the **dormant Commerce Clause**.

It may be difficult to think of situations where a state law does not substantially affect interstate commerce. Nevertheless, a United States Supreme Court case (Illustrative Court Case 4.4) discusses a situation where a state was successful.

Notice in this case that the fee was purely on trucks carrying loads from one location in Michigan to another location in Michigan. Thus, according to the Supreme Court, this was a constitutional law regulating *intra*state commerce that did not substantially affect *inter*state commerce.

What Do You Think?

*In the **Hunt** case, do you think North Carolina's purpose for passing the law was really to protect consumers from deception and fraud, or do you think the purpose was to protect its own apple growing industry from out-of-state competitors, such as apple growers from Washington?*

Full Faith and Credit Clause

Assume that you own a construction business. You construct a building for someone, but that person does not pay you for your services. You bring a lawsuit against the person in the state in which you both live. The judge rules in

---

ILLUSTRATIVE COURT CASE 4.4

American Trucking Associations, Inc. v. Michigan Public Service Commission

Supreme Court of the United States

545 U.S. 429 (2005)

[**Note**: For convenience of the reader, the following language is from the Syllabus of the case as provided by the U.S. Supreme Court Reporter of Decisions.]

[American Trucking Associations, Inc.], a trucking company engaged in both interstate and intrastate hauling and a trucking association, asked Michigan courts to invalidate the state's flat $100 annual fee imposed on trucks engaged in intrastate commercial hauling, . . ., claiming that it discriminates against interstate carriers and imposes an unconstitutional burden on interstate trade because trucks carrying both interstate and intrastate loads engage in less intrastate business than trucks carrying only intrastate loads. . . .

Held:

Michigan's fee does not violate the dormant Commerce Clause. That Clause prevents a State from "jeopardizing the welfare of the Nation as a whole" by "plac[ing] burdens on the flow of commerce across its borders that commerce wholly within those borders would not bear." [Citation omitted.] Applying this Court's dormant Commerce Clause principles and precedents here, nothing in [the Michigan law] offends the Commerce Clause. The flat fee is imposed only on intrastate transactions. It does not facially discriminate against interstate or out-of-state activities or enterprises. It applies evenhandedly to all carriers making domestic journeys and does not reflect an effort to tax activity taking place outside of the State. Nothing in this Court's case law suggests that such a neutral, locally

(Continued)

focused fee or tax is inconsistent with the dormant Commerce Clause. That is not surprising, since States impose numerous flat fees on local business and service providers, *e.g.*, insurers and auctioneers. The Constitution neither displaces States' authority to shelter their people from health and safety menaces nor unduly curtails their power to lay taxes to support state government. The record, moreover, shows no special circumstances suggesting that Michigan's fee operates as anything other than an unobjectionable exercise of the State's police power. Neither does it show that the flat assessment unfairly discriminates against interstate truckers. . . .

your favor. A month after the court's judgment, you still have not been paid. You find out that the person who owes you money has moved to another state. What do you do? Must a court in the other state recognize the judgment you had against the person in your state? Or Must you sue the person again in the other state? The Constitution addresses whether one state must give credit to laws and judicial decisions in other states (Article IV, Section 1).

UNITED STATES CONSTITUTION

Article IV, Section 1. Full Faith and Credit shall be given in each State to the public Acts, Records, and judicial Proceedings of every other state. . . .

Thus, as a result of the Full Faith and Credit Clause of the Constitution, you should be able to request that the courts in the other state enforce the judgment of the court in your state.

QUESTIONS FOR REVIEW

1. What is federalism?

2. Explain how the Supremacy Clause impacts business activity.

3. Explain how the Commerce Clause impacts business activity.

4. What is the dormant Commerce Clause?

5. Explain how the Full Faith and Credit Clause impacts business activity.

6. Summarize the *Watters v. Wachovia Bank* case.

7. Summarize the *Hunt v. Washington State Apple Advertising Commission* case.

8. Summarize the *South Dakota v. Wayfair* case.

9. Summarize the *American Trucking Associations, Inc. v. Michigan Public Service Commission* case.

INTERNET ACTIVITIES

1. Find the landmark United States Supreme Court case of *Gibbons v. Ogden*, 22 U.S. 1 (1824).

   a. What was the issue in this case?

   b. Did the law in question violate the Constitution? If so, which clause(s) of the Constitution?

   c. Summarize the Court's analysis.

2. Find the landmark United States Supreme Court case of *NLRB v. Jones & Laughlin Steel Corp.*, 301 U.S. 1 (1937).

   a. What was the issue in this case?

   b. Did the Supreme Court hold that Jones and Laughlin Steel violated federal law? If so, in what way?

   c. Summarize the Court's analysis.

Chapter 5

Freedom of Speech, Freedom of the Press, Free Exercise Clause, and the Establishment Clause

In this chapter, we continue to review certain provisions of the Constitution that impact business and the legal environment in which businesses operate.

As mentioned in Chapter 1, the Constitution has 27 Amendments. The first ten of these amendments are collectively called the Bill of Rights. Of the ten amendments, the First Amendment is considered by many to be the most important.

FIRST AMENDMENT TO THE UNITED STATES CONSTITUTION

Congress shall make no law respecting an establishment of religion, or prohibiting the free exercise thereof; or abridging the freedom of speech, or of the press; or the right of the people peaceably to assemble, and to petition the Government for a redress of grievances.

Notice that several issues are contained in the First Amendment, including freedoms of religion, speech, and assembly. Moreover, Congress can not establish a religion nor prohibit the people from petitioning the government for a redress of grievances. Books can and have been written solely on the First Amendment. We obviously cannot study each First Amendment issue in great detail in this text. A working knowledge of some of these important issues is in order, however.

Another significant concept to keep in mind is that even though the First Amendment states that "Congress shall make no law. . . ," the Fourteenth Amendment also subjects *states* to the same restrictions.

FOURTEENTH AMENDMENT TO THE UNITED STATES CONSTITUTION

Section 1. All persons born or naturalized in the United States, and subject to the jurisdiction thereof, are citizens of the United States and of the state wherein they reside. No State shall make or enforce any law which shall abridge the privileges or immunities of citizens of the United States; nor shall any State deprive any person of life, liberty, or property, without due process of law; nor deny to any person within its jurisdiction the equal protection of the laws. . . .

In short, government at all levels must not restrict the individual rights that we have, as recognized by the Constitution.

Freedom of Speech

Perhaps the most fundamental right that we have in the Bill of Rights is the freedom of speech. The courts apply different standards, however, depending upon whether the speech in question is by an individual or a business.

Individuals

Individuals have very strong freedom of speech rights. We can express our views and opinions on most any subject, even on politics and government, without fear of being imprisoned by the government.

Samuel Acosta/Shutterstock.com

Nevertheless, this freedom of speech is not unlimited. Public safety concerns can override the freedom of speech in some situations. A typical example of this, of course, is that you cannot yell "Fire!" in a crowded theater when there is, in fact, no fire. Consider whether you agree with the Supreme Court in the following case (Illustrative Court Case 5.1) involving a restriction on free speech.

Notice that the court case illustrates a situation where the government [in this case, a school district] can often impose restrictions on speech by regulating the time, manner, and place where speech can occur if other competing government interests (*e.g.*, public safety) are involved. Nevertheless, when regulating an individual's speech, the government must show that the restriction is *necessary* to further a *compelling* government interest.

ILLUSTRATIVE COURT CASE 5.1

Morse v. Frederick

Supreme Court of the United States

551 U.S. 393 (2007)

[**Note**: For convenience of the reader, the following language is from the Syllabus of the case as provided by the U.S. Supreme Court Reporter of Decisions.]

At a school-sanctioned and school-supervised event, . . . Morse, the high school principal, saw students unfurl a banner stating "BONG HiTS 4 JESUS," which she regarded as promoting illegal drug use. Consistent with established school policy prohibiting such messages at school events, Morse directed the students to take down the banner. When one of the students who had brought the banner to the event—[the student] Frederick—refused, Morse confiscated the banner and later suspended him. The school superintendent upheld the suspension, explaining . . . that Frederick was disciplined because his banner appeared to advocate illegal drug use in violation of school policy. [The school board also upheld the suspension.] . . . Frederick filed suit . . . alleging that the school board and Morse had violated his First Amendment rights.

Held:

Because schools may take steps to safeguard those entrusted to their care from speech that can reasonably be regarded as encouraging illegal drug use, the school officials in this case did not violate the First Amendment by confiscating the pro-drug banner and suspending Frederick.

(a) Frederick's argument that this is not a school speech case is rejected. The event in question occurred during normal school hours and was sanctioned by Morse as an approved social event at which the district's student-conduct rules expressly applied. Teachers and administrators were

---

among the students and were charged with supervising them. Frederick stood among other students across the street from the school and directed his banner toward the school, making it plainly visible to most students. Under these circumstances, Frederick cannot claim he was not at school.

. . .

(c) A principal may, consistent with the First Amendment, restrict student speech at a school event, when that speech is reasonably viewed as promoting illegal drug use. . . .

What Do You Think?

What if in the Morse case the person displaying the sign was an adult and not a student of the school? Would the Court have ruled differently? What if the student displayed the sign at an event that was not school-sanctioned?

Remember, the First Amendment applies to the *government's* restriction on speech. Private employers have considerable ability to restrict the speech of employees. Can a private employer fire someone for saying or doing something in violation of the employer's policies? Generally speaking, the answer is yes. Private employers are not subject to the same restrictions as the government. Also, employers often have the ability to fire employees for no cause at all. For example, suppose you place derogatory remarks about your boss's spouse on your Facebook page. You are certainly free to express your opinion on the matter, but it will likely get you fired.

Businesses

Businesses also have rights to express their interests through advertising, marketing, packaging, etc. This type of speech is often called "commercial" speech. The United States Supreme Court has addressed the extent to which government can restrict commercial speech. See Illustrative Court Case 5.2.

ILLUSTRATIVE COURT CASE 5.2

Central Hudson Gas & Electric Corp. v. Public Service Commission

Supreme Court of the United States

447 U.S. 557 (1980)

[**Note**: For convenience of the reader, the following language is from the Syllabus of the case as provided by the U.S. Supreme Court Reporter of Decisions.]

Held:

A regulation of [the] New York Public Service Commission which completely bans an electric utility from advertising to promote the use of electricity violates the First and Fourteenth Amendments.

(a) Although the Constitution accords a lesser protection to commercial speech than to other constitutionally guaranteed expression, nevertheless the First Amendment protects commercial speech from unwarranted governmental regulation. For commercial speech to come within the First Amendment, it at least must concern lawful activity and not be misleading. Next, it must be determined whether the asserted governmental interest to be served by the restriction on commercial speech is substantial. If both inquiries yield positive answers, it must then be decided whether the regulation directly advances the governmental interest asserted, and whether it is not more extensive than is necessary to serve that interest.

(Continued)

...

(d) [The State's] regulation, which reaches all promotional advertising regardless of the impact of the touted service on overall energy use, is more extensive than necessary to further the State's interest in energy conservation which, as important as it is, cannot justify suppressing information about electric devices or services that would cause no net increase in total energy use. In addition, no showing has been made that a more limited restriction on the content of promotional advertising would not serve adequately the State's interests.

In summary, the *Central Hudson* case held that for a government restriction on lawful commercial speech to be constitutional, the restriction must meet a three-part test.

- The government must have a *substantial* interest in restricting the speech;
- The restriction on the speech must *directly* advance the government's interest; and
- The restriction cannot be more extensive than necessary to serve the government's interest.

Consider a little twist on the commercial speech issue. Suppose a cosmetic surgeon hires a marketing company to create a billboard advertisement. The marketing company recommends that the surgeon feature a current or former customer that is pleased with the surgeon's services. The surgeon obtains the consent of a patient to pose in a swimsuit to show the positive results of her recent cosmetic surgery. The marketing company then places the advertisement on a billboard along a busy freeway. Not surprisingly, many motorists complain that the advertisement is inappropriate, offensive, immoral, and should be taken down. Consequently, the city orders the advertisement to be taken down claiming that the advertisement is "offensive" and violates one of its city ordinances, which reads as follows:

> No offensive advertisements shall be placed within the city limits.

Is the city's order to remove the billboard advertisement a violation of the surgeon's First Amendment right to free speech? You probably recognize the issue here: who decides what "offensive" means? The surgeon could argue that the ordinance is not specific enough and that the term "offensive" is too broad and open to a wide variety of interpretations. In this regard, if a law restricting speech is not specific enough or is too vague, the courts could rule that the law is unconstitutional under the **overbreadth doctrine**.

Unprotected Speech

Some speech is not protected by the First Amendment. Speech that is "obscene" is not protected. This would include child pornography, for example. Threatening speech and actions that would incite riots are other examples of speech that are not protected. Additionally, if you defame someone's character, either verbally or in writing, you could be sued for defamation, which includes slander and libel (discussed in Chapter 11).

Freedom of the Press

Due to the value we place on freedom of the press, the United States does not have just one news channel that is operated by the government. In many other countries, the government strictly controls what information is relayed to its citizens. The freedom of the press enjoys significant protection, much like the freedom of speech. For example, newspapers cannot be forced by the government to print certain information. Neither can the government prevent a newspaper from printing information that the newspaper has in its possession. In other words, the government cannot impose **prior restraints** on the press. Of course, the term "press" includes media outlets beyond just newspapers.

Although the Constitution protects freedom of the press, that doesn't mean the press can publish or broadcast anything it wants without consequences. The press can be sued for defamation for publishing or broadcasting false information about people. For example, tabloids often get sued by celebrities who claim that the tabloids published intentionally false stories about them.

The government has been successful in some cases in limiting the freedom of the press. For example, the Federal Communications Commission (FCC) prohibits certain words (*i.e.*, "filthy" words) from being said on the air. The FCC imposes fines on press outlets that violate these regulations.

Free Exercise Clause and Establishment Clause

Two other critical components of the First Amendment address religion.

Free Exercise Clause

The Constitution guarantees the people the freedom of religion. We can freely exercise our sincerely held religious beliefs without government interference. This is not absolute, however. What if parents allow a sick child to die rather than administer medicine because the parents sincerely believe that God will save the child if it is God's will? Are the parents guilty of a crime? What if some people form a "religion" and use an illegal drug as a sacrament? Could the government prohibit such activity, even though the organizers claim it is a sincerely held religious belief? What if someone's sincerely held religious beliefs appear to discriminate against someone else? Consider the following United States Supreme Court case (Illustrative Court Case 5.3).

Freedom of religion certainly is an issue in the workplace as well. To what extent must an employer accommodate your sincerely held religious beliefs?

ILLUSTRATIVE COURT CASE 5.3

Masterpiece Cakeshop, Ltd., et al. v. Colorado Civil Rights Commission, et al.

Supreme Court of the United States

584 U.S. ___ (2018)

[**Note:** For convenience of the reader, the following language is from the Syllabus of the case as provided by the U.S. Supreme Court Reporter of Decisions.]

Masterpiece Cakeshop, Ltd., is a Colorado bakery owned and operated by Jack Phillips, an expert baker and devout Christian. In 2012 he told a same-sex couple that he would not create a cake for their wedding celebration because of his religious opposition to same-sex marriages—marriages that Colorado did not then recognize—but that he would sell them other baked goods, *e.g.*, birthday cakes. The couple filed a charge with the Colorado Civil Rights Commission (Commission) pursuant to the Colorado Anti-Discrimination Act (CADA), which prohibits, as relevant here, discrimination based on sexual orientation in a "place of business engaged in any sales to the public and any place offering services . . . to the public." Under CADA's administrative review system, the Colorado Civil Rights Division first found probable cause for a violation and referred the case to the Commission. The Commission then referred the case for a formal hearing before a state Administrative Law Judge (ALJ), who ruled in the couple's favor. In so doing, the ALJ rejected Phillips' First Amendment claims: that requiring him to create a cake for a same-sex wedding would violate his right to free speech by compelling him to exercise his artistic talents to express a message with which he disagreed and would violate his right to the free exercise of religion. Both the Commission and the Colorado Court of Appeals affirmed.

(Continued)

Held:

The Commission's actions in this case violated the Free Exercise Clause.

(a) The laws and the Constitution can, and in some instances must, protect gay persons and gay couples in the exercise of their civil rights, but religious and philosophical objections to gay marriage are protected views and in some instances protected forms of expression. . . . While it is unexceptional that Colorado law can protect gay persons in acquiring products and services on the same terms and conditions as are offered to other members of the public, the law must be applied in a manner that is neutral toward religion. To Phillips, his claim that using his artistic skills to make an expressive statement, a wedding endorsement in his own voice and of his own creation, has a significant First Amendment speech component and implicates his deep and sincere religious beliefs. His dilemma was understandable in 2012, which was before Colorado recognized the validity of gay marriages performed in the State and before this Court issued *United States v. Windsor*. . . . Given the State's position at the time, there is some force to Phillips' argument that he was not unreasonable in deeming his decision lawful. State law at the time also afforded storekeepers some latitude to decline to create specific messages they considered offensive. Indeed, while the instant enforcement proceedings were pending, the Sate Civil Rights Division concluded in a t least three cases that a baker acted lawfully in declining to create cakes with decorations that demeaned gay persons or gay marriages. Phillips too was entitled to a neutral and respectful consideration of his claims in all the circumstances of the case.

(b) That consideration was compromised, however, by the Commission's treatment of Phillips' case, which showed elements of a clear and impermissible hostility toward the sincere religious beliefs motivating his objection. As the record shows, some of the commissioners at the Commission's formal, public hearings endorsed the view that religious beliefs cannot legitimately be carried into the public sphere or commercial domain, disparaged Phillips' faith as despicable and characterized it as merely rhetorical, and compared his invocation of his sincerely held religious beliefs to defense of slavery and the Holocaust. No commissioners objected to the comments. Nor were they mentioned in the later state-court ruling or disavowed in the briefs filed here. The comments thus cast doubt on the fairness and impartiality of the Commission's adjudication of Phillips' case.

Another indication of hostility is the different treatment of Phillips' case and the cases of other bakers with objections to anti-gay messages who prevailed before the Commission. The Commission ruled against Phillips in part on the theory that any message on the requested wedding cake would be attributed to the customer, not the baker. Yet the Division did not address this point in any of the cases involving requests for cakes depicting anti-gay marriage symbolism. The Division also considered that each bakery was willing to sell other products to the prospective customers, but the Commission found Phillips' willingness to do the same irrelevant. The State Court of Appeals' brief discussion of this disparity of treatment does not answer Phillips' concern that the State's practice was to disfavor the religious basis of his objection.

(c) For these reasons, the Commission's treatment of Phillips' case violated the State's duty under the First Amendment not to base laws or regulations on hostility to a religion or religious viewpoint. The government, consistent with the Constitution's guarantee of free exercise, cannot impose regulations that are hostile to the religious beliefs of affected citizens and cannot act in a manner that passes judgment upon or presupposes the illegitimacy of religious beliefs and practices. [Citation omitted.] Factors relevant to the assessment of governmental neutrality include "the historical background of the decision under challenge, the specific series of events leading to the enactment or official policy in question, and the legislative or administrative history, including contemporaneous statements made by members of the decisionmaking body." [Citation omitted.] In view of these factors, the record here demonstrates that the Commission's consideration of Phillips' case was neither tolerant nor respectful of his religious beliefs. The Commission gave "every appearance," of adjudicating his religious objection based on a negative normative "evaluation of the particular justification" for his objection and the religious grounds for it, but government has no role in expressing or even suggesting whether the religious ground for Phillips' conscience-based objection is legitimate or illegitimate. The inference here is thus that Phillips' religious objection was not considered with the neutrality required by the Free Exercise Clause. The State's interest could have been weighed against Phillips' sincere religious objections in a way consistent with the requisite religious neutrality that must be strictly observed. But the official expressions of hostility to religion in some of the commissioners' comments were inconsistent with that requirement, and the Commission's disparate consideration of Phillips' case compared to the cases of the other bakers suggests the same.

[R]eversed.

We will discuss these issues in Chapter 32 as they relate to employment discrimination.

Establishment Clause

The First Amendment prohibits government from establishing a religion. This concept is frequently called the **separation of church and state**. Of course, this is quite different from some countries in the world today that have unified government and religion.

The Establishment Clause has been tested frequently in the courts. Some of these controversies include:

- Prayer in public schools
- "In God We Trust" printed on U.S. currency
- The phrase "one nation under God" in the pledge of allegiance
- A Christmas tree in front of city hall
- The Ten Commandments hanging on the wall in a courtroom
- Tax deductions for contributions to churches, private religious schools, and other religious organizations
- Teaching creationism in public schools

A major court case in the Establishment Clause area is *Lemon v. Kurtzman*, 403 U.S. 602 (1970). This United States Supreme Court case basically provided a three-part test to determine whether a government action violates the Establishment Clause. In short, for a law not to violate the Establishment Clause, the law must:

Ricardo Reitmeyer/Shutterstock.com

What Do You Think?

Which of the issues in the preceding bullet points do you think violate the Establishment Clause?

- Have a secular (rather than religious) purpose;
- Not have the primary effect of advancing or inhibiting religion; and
- Not result in an "excessive government entanglement" with religion.

QUESTIONS FOR REVIEW

1. With respect to the First Amendment, what is the significance of the Fourteenth Amendment?

2. What is the overbreadth doctrine?

3. What are some examples of unprotected speech?

4. Regarding the freedom of the press, explain the prohibition on prior restraints.

5. Assume that the United States Postal Service issues a stamp with a picture of Mother Teresa on it. Does this violate the Establishment Clause by favoring Catholicism over other religions? Why or why not?

6. Summarize the *Morse v. Frederick* case.

7. Summarize the *Central Hudson Gas & Electric Corp. v. Public Service Commission* case.

8. Summarize the *Masterpiece Cakeshop, Ltd v. Colorado Civil Rights Commission* case.

INTERNET ACTIVITIES

1. Find the United States Supreme Court case *New York Times Co. v. United States*, 403 U.S. 713 (1971).

   a. What was the issue or issues in the case?

   b. What was the holding of the Court?

   c. Summarize the Court's analysis.

2. Find the United States Supreme Court case *Wisconsin v. Yoder*, 406 U.S. 205 (1972).

   a. What was the issue or issues in the case?

   b. What was the holding of the Court?

   c. Summarize the Court's analysis.

Chapter 6

Privileges and Immunities Clause, Due Process Clause, and Equal Protection Clause

As discussed in Chapter 5, the Constitution preserves significant rights to the people. This chapter covers even more Constitutional rights that are important to understand.

Privileges and Immunities Clause

Can a state favor its own residents over out-of-state residents? The Constitution directly addresses this issue.

UNITED STATES CONSTITUTION

Article IV, Section 2. The Citizens of each State shall be entitled to all Privileges and Immunities of Citizens in the several States.

As set forth in a United States Supreme Court case [*Paul v. Virginia*, 8 Wall. 168 (1869)], the purpose of the Privileges and Immunities Clause is:

to place the citizens of each State upon the same footing with citizens of other States, so far as the advantages resulting from citizenship in those States are concerned. It relieves them from the disabilities of alienage in other States; it inhibits discriminating legislation against them by other States; it gives them the right of free ingress into

other States, and egress from them; it insures to them in other States the same freedom possessed by the citizens of those States in the acquisition and enjoyment of property and in the pursuit of happiness; and it secures to them in other States the equal protection of their laws. It has been justly said that no provision in the Constitution has tended so strongly to constitute the citizens of the United States one people as this.

The *Hicklin* case that follows (Illustrative Court Case 6.1) addresses a situation where the state of Alaska attempted to favor its own residents in obtaining employment.

Despite cases such as *Hicklin*, the courts have ruled that in some situations, treating out-of-state residents differently is constitutional. For example, public universities can charge out-of-state students higher tuition, and states can charge out-of-state residents higher fees for hunting and fishing licenses.

Due Process Clause

The Constitution guarantees the people basic fairness when interacting with the government. The Fourteenth Amendment as shown on the following page, provides this protection.

The language in the latter part of the amendment includes the right to "due process" of law and "equal protection" of the laws. We will discuss

Hicklin v. Orbeck

Supreme Court of the United States

437 U.S. 518 (1978)

[**Note**: For convenience of the reader, the following language is from the Syllabus of the case as provided by the U.S. Supreme Court Reporter of Decisions.]

[Some nonresidents] of Alaska challenged in state court the constitutionality of the "Alaska Hire" statute (which was enacted professedly for the purpose of reducing unemployment within the State) that requires that all Alaskan oil and gas leases, easements or right-of-way permits for oil and gas pipelines, and unitization agreements contain a requirement that qualified Alaska residents be hired in preference to nonresidents.

. . .

Held:

2. Alaska Hire violates the Privileges and Immunities Clause . . . .

. . .

(a) Though the Clause "does not preclude disparity of treatment in the many situations where there are perfectly valid independent reasons for it," it "does bar discrimination against citizens of other States where there is no reason for the discrimination beyond the mere fact that they are citizens of other States." [Citations omitted.]

(b) Even under the dubious assumption that a State may validly alleviate its unemployment problem by requiring private employers within the State to discriminate against nonresidents, Alaska Hire cannot be upheld, for the record indicates that Alaska's unemployment was not attributable to the influx of nonresident jobseekers, but rather to the fact that a substantial number of Alaska's jobless residents were unemployed either because of lack of education and job training or because of geographical remoteness from job opportunities.

FOURTEENTH AMENDMENT TO THE UNITED STATES CONSTITUTION

Section 1. All persons born or naturalized in the United States, and subject to the jurisdiction thereof, are citizens of the United States and of the state wherein they reside. No State shall make or enforce any law which shall abridge the privileges or immunities of citizens of the United States; nor shall any State deprive any person of life, liberty, or property, without due process of law; nor deny to any person within its jurisdiction the equal protection of the laws.

"due process" in this section and "equal protection" in the next section.

Courts have interpreted the Due Process Clause as consisting of two distinct parts—"procedural" due process and "substantive" due process.

Procedural Due Process

Procedural due process refers to the concept that the government must provide a fair process before depriving the person of life, property, or liberty. This is interpreted to mean that a person must receive notice of the proposed government action, and the person must be given an opportunity to be heard and voice his or her concerns in front of the appropriate government agency or tribunal. For example, suppose a state agency that regulates the licensing of certified public accountants (CPAs) in the state proposes to revoke the license of a particular CPA because of alleged violations of a state regulation. In such a case, the Procedural Due Process Clause would require that the state give the CPA notice of the proposed action and an opportunity to be heard prior to the state's decision to revoke the CPA's license.

Substantive Due Process

Substantive due process refers to the concept that government laws must be rationally related to a legitimate government interest. In other words, the focus is not on procedural fairness of the

---

ILLUSTRATIVE COURT CASE 6.2

County of Sacramento v. Lewis

Supreme Court of the United States

523 U.S. 833 (1998)

[**Note**: For convenience of the reader, the following language is from the Syllabus of the case as provided by the U.S. Supreme Court Reporter of Decisions.]

After petitioner James Smith, a county sheriff's deputy, responded to a call along with another officer, Murray Stapp, the latter returned to his patrol car and saw a motorcycle approaching at high speed, driven by Brian Willard, and carrying Philip Lewis, . . ., as a passenger. Stapp turned on his rotating lights, yelled for the cycle to stop, and pulled his car closer to Smith's in an attempt to pen the cycle in, but Willard maneuvered between the two cars and sped off. Smith immediately switched on his own emergency lights and siren and began high-speed pursuit. The chase ended after the cycle tipped over. Smith slammed on his brakes, but his car skidded into Lewis, causing massive injuries and death. [The personal representative of Lewis's estate] brought this action . . . alleging a deprivation of Lewis's Fourteenth amendment substantive due process right to life.

Held:

A police officer does not violate substantive due process by causing death through deliberate or reckless indifference to life in a high-speed automobile chase aimed at apprehending a suspected offender.

. . .

(b) . . . Protection against governmental arbitrariness is the core of due process, . . . including substantive due process, . . ., but only the most egregious executive action can be said to be "arbitrary" in the constitutional sense, . . .; the cognizable level of executive abuse of power is that which shocks the conscience, ... In the circumstances of a high-speed chase aimed at apprehending a suspected offender, where unforeseen circumstances demand an instant judgment on the part of an officer who feels the pulls of competing obligations, only a purpose to cause harm unrelated to the legitimate object of arrest will satisfy the shocks-the-conscience test. Such chases with no intent to harm suspects physically or to worsen their legal plight do not give rise to substantive due process liability. . . . Smith was faced with a course of lawless behavior for which the police were not to blame. They had done nothing to cause Willard's high-speed driving in the first place, nothing to excuse his flouting of the commonly understood police authority to control traffic, and nothing . . . to encourage him to race through traffic at breakneck speed. Willard's outrageous behavior was practically instantaneous, and so was Smith's instinctive response. While prudence would have repressed the reaction, Smith's instinct was to do his job, not to induce Willard's lawlessness, or to terrorize, cause harm, or kill. Prudence, that is, was subject to countervailing enforcement considerations, and while Smith exaggerated their demands, there is no reason to believe that they were tainted by an improper or malicious motive.

---

government law or action; rather, the focus is on the fairness of the law or action itself. Consider the United States Supreme Court case (Illustrative Court Case 6.2) on the previous page.

Notice that in *County of Sacramento v. Lewis* the Court refers to the "shocks-the-conscience" test. In short, the government's action must "shock the conscience" in order to violate substantive due process. Of course, the courts have to look at this issue on a case-by-case basis and in the context of each unique factual circumstance.

Also applicable to the Due Process Clause is an individual's right to privacy. Although the Constitution does not specifically address privacy rights for individuals, the United States Supreme Court has recognized privacy as a fundamental right protected by the Due Process Clause of the Fourteenth Amendment. Of course, *Roe v. Wade*, 410 U.S. 113 (1973), which provided certain privacy rights to women seeking abortions, is a famous case in this area. As technology has continued to advance, however, several additional controversial issues have arisen. For example, some people argue that detailed screening and searches at airports is a violation of a person's right to privacy. Others say that the government's ability in some instances to monitor email communications, cellular telephone calls, and internet traffic is all a violation of privacy rights. Other people, in turn, argue that some of these actions are necessary to protect the public from terrorist and other criminal activity.

What Do You Think?

How much individual privacy rights are you willing to give up to allow the government a greater ability to discover planned terrorist acts or other potential dangers?

Equal Protection Clause

Another critical component of the Fourteenth Amendment is the Equal Protection Clause. "Equal protection" in this context basically means that government should treat people equally unless there is a justifiable reason to treat them differently. Consider the following hypothetical. Suppose the U.S. Air Force establishes regulations that require fighter pilots be at least 5'4" in height, but not more than 6'5" in height. Thus, "short" and "tall" people would not qualify to be fighter pilots. Is the government (via the Air Force) discriminating against short and tall people? Is the reason for the discrimination justifiable?

What Do You Think?

Which of the following hypothetical criteria do you think would be acceptable for the Air Force to include in its qualifications for a person to be eligible for fighter pilot training? Why?

- Must be at least age 21 and under age 29 - *rational*
- Must be a college graduate - *rational*
- Must be a U.S. Citizen - *rational*
- Must be a male - *intermediate*
- Must be born in the United States - *smct*
- Must have 20/20 vision - *rational*
- Must be a Christian - *smct*
- Must have at least one year prior flying experience - *rational*
- Must have never lived in a foreign country for longer than a year (unless on a U.S. military base) - *rational*

Clearly, it is reasonable for the government to establish regulations regarding who can become a fighter pilot. People will inevitably be placed in classifications. But at what point is the reason for treating someone differently a violation of the person's rights under the Equal Protection Clause?

Andrea Izzotti/Shutterstock.com

The courts apply different levels of scrutiny to government action when the question of equal protection arises. Discrimination by the government on the basis of some classifications (*e.g.*, age, height, weight) receives lower scrutiny by the courts than discrimination based on other classifications (*e.g.*, race, religion, national origin). The following paragraphs discuss each of the three distinct standards that the courts have developed—(1) the *strict scrutiny* test; (2) the *intermediate scrutiny* test; and (3) the *rational basis* test.

Strict Scrutiny Test

The courts will use the strict scrutiny test in cases involving "suspect" classifications (*e.g.*, race, religion, national origin) or fundamental rights (*e.g.*, freedom of speech, right to vote). This basically means that the court will very closely scrutinize the reason why the government is favoring or discriminating against someone based upon a certain classification. Consider the *Adarand Constructors, Inc. v. Pena* United States Supreme Court case that follows (Illustrative Court Case 6.3).

In short, in strict scrutiny cases the government must show that the classification is *necessary* to promote a *compelling* government interest. Otherwise, the government action will be struck down as unconstitutional.

Intermediate Scrutiny Test

The courts have developed the intermediate scrutiny test in cases involving government classifications based on gender. Consider the *United States v. Virginia* United States Supreme Court case on the following page (Illustrative Court Case 6.4).

ILLUSTRATIVE COURT CASE 6.3

Adarand Constructors, Inc. v. Pena

Supreme Court of the United States

515 U.S. 200 (2005)

[**Note**: For convenience of the reader, the following language is from the Syllabus of the case as provided by the U.S. Supreme Court Reporter of Decisions.]

Most federal agency contracts must contain a subcontractor compensation clause, which gives a prime contractor a financial incentive to hire sub-contractors certified as small businesses controlled by socially and economically disadvantaged individuals, and requires the contractor to presume that such individuals include minorities or any other individuals found to be disadvantaged by the Small Business Administration (SBA). The prime contractor under a federal highway construction contract containing such a clause awarded a subcontract to a company that was certified as a small disadvantaged business. . . . Adarand Constructors, Inc., which submitted the low bid on the subcontract but was not a certified business, filed suit against . . . federal officials, claiming that the race-based presumptions used in subcontractor compensation clauses violate the equal protection component of the Fifth Amendment's Due Process Clause. . . . [T]he Court of Appeals assessed the constitutionality of the federal race-based action under a lenient standard, resembling intermediate scrutiny. . . .

(Continued)

Held:

. . .

2. All racial classifications, imposed by whatever federal, state, or local governmental actor, must be analyzed by a reviewing court under strict scrutiny.

. . .

(c) . . . [T]he Fifth and Fourteenth Amendments protect persons, not groups. It follows from that principle that all governmental action based on race—a group classification long recognized as in most circumstances irrelevant and therefore prohibited—should be subjected to detailed judicial inquiry to ensure that the personal right to equal protection has not been infringed. Thus, strict scrutiny is the proper standard for analysis of all racial classifications, whether imposed by a federal, state, or local actor. . . .

(d) The decision here makes explicit that federal racial classifications, like those of a State, must serve a compelling governmental interest, and must be narrowly tailored to further that interest. . . . Requiring strict scrutiny is the best way to ensure that courts will consistently give racial classifications a detailed examination, as to both ends and means.

[The Supreme Court ultimately sent this case back down to the lower courts to apply a strict scrutiny standard of judicial review to the issue rather than an intermediate scrutiny standard of judicial review.]

ILLUSTRATIVE COURT CASE 6.4

United States v. Virginia

Supreme Court of the United States

518 U.S. 515 (1996)

[**Note:** For convenience of the reader, the following language is from the Syllabus of the case as provided by the U.S. Supreme Court Reporter of Decisions.]

Virginia Military Institute (VMI) is the sole single-sex school among Virginia's public institutions of higher learning. VMI's distinctive mission is to produce "citizen-soldiers," men prepared for leadership in civilian life and in military service. Using an "adversative method" of training not available elsewhere in Virginia, VMI endeavors to instill physical and mental discipline in its cadets and impart to them a strong moral code. Reflecting the high value alumni place on their VMI training, VMI has the largest per-student endowment of all public undergraduate institutions in the Nation. The United States sued Virginia and VMI, alleging that VMI's exclusively male admission policy violated the Fourteenth Amendment's Equal Protection Clause. . . .

Held:

1. Parties who seek to defend gender-based government action must demonstrate an "exceedingly persuasive justification" for that action. [Citation omitted.] Neither federal nor state government acts compatibly with equal protection when a law or official policy denies to women, simply because they are women, full citizenship stature—equal opportunity to aspire, achieve, participate in and contribute to society based on their individual talents and capacities. To meet the burden of justification, a State must show "at least that the [challenged] classification serves 'important governmental objectives and that the discriminatory means employed' are 'substantially related to the achievement

of those objectives.'" [Citation omitted.] . . . The heightened review standard applicable to sex-based classifications does not make sex a proscribed classification, but it does mean that categorization by sex may not be used to create or perpetuate the legal, social, and economic inferiority of women.

2. Virginia's categorical exclusion of women from the educational opportunities VMI provides denies equal protection to women.

(a) Virginia contends that single-sex education yields important educational benefits and that provision of an option for such education fosters diversity in educational approaches. . . . However well this plan serves Virginia's sons, it makes no provision whatever for her daughters.

(b) Virginia also argues that VMI's adversative method of training provides educational benefits that cannot be made available, unmodified, to women, and that alterations to accommodate women would necessarily be so drastic as to destroy VMI's program. It is uncontested that women's admission to VMI would require accommodations, primarily in arranging housing assignments and physical training programs for female cadets. It is also undisputed, however, that neither the goal of producing citizen-soldiers . . . nor VMI's implementing methodology is inherently unsuitable to women. . . .

3. The remedy proffered by Virginia—maintain VMI as a male-only college and create VWIL as a separate program for women—does not cure the constitutional violation.

(a) . . . The constitutional violation in this case is the categorical exclusion of women, in disregard of their individual merit, from an extraordinary educational opportunity afforded men. Virginia chose to leave untouched VMI's exclusionary policy, and proposed for women only a separate program, different in kind from VMI and unequal in tangible and intangible facilities. VWIL affords women no opportunity to experience the rigorous military training for which VMI is famed. Kept away from the pressures, hazards, and psychological bonding characteristic of VMI's adversative training, VWIL students will not know the feeling of tremendous accomplishment commonly experienced by VMI's successful cadets. . . .

In intermediate scrutiny cases the government must show that the classification is *substantially* related to an *important* government interest. Virginia's male-only public education institution could not meet this standard with regard to the exclusion of women. Consequently, VMI's admission policies were ruled unconstitutional as a violation of the Equal Protection Clause.

What Do You Think?

Do you agree with the United States Supreme Court that an *intermediate scrutiny* test to government classifications based on gender should apply rather than a *strict scrutiny* test?

Rational Basis Test

The courts use the rational basis test for all classifications not contained in the strict scrutiny or intermediate scrutiny tests. This would include, for example, classifications based on height, weight, age, eyesight, business regulation, etc. Consider the *City of Cleburne v. Cleburne Living Center, Inc.* United States Supreme Court case that follows (Illustrative Court Case 6.5).

In short, in rational basis cases, the government must show that the classification is *rationally related* to a *legitimate* government interest. This burden is nearly always met by the government, but the *Cleburne* case illustrates a situation where the government did not meet that burden, and the government's action (*i.e.*, a city ordinance in this case) was declared unconstitutional.

City of Cleburne v. Cleburne Living Center, Inc.

Supreme Court of the United States

473 U.S. 432 (1985)

[**Note**: For convenience of the reader, the following language is from the Syllabus of the case as provided by the U.S. Supreme Court Reporter of Decisions.]

. . . Cleburne Living Center, Inc. (CLC), which anticipated leasing a certain building for the operation of a group home for the mentally retarded, was informed by [the city] that a special use permit would be required, the city having concluded that the proposed group home should be classified as a "hospital for the feebleminded" under the zoning ordinance covering the area in which the proposed home would be located. Accordingly, CLC applied for a special use permit, but the City Council, after a public hearing, denied the permit. CLC and others . . . then filed suit against the city and a number of its officials, alleging that the zoning ordinance, on its face and as applied, violated the equal protection rights of CLC and its potential residents. The District Court held the ordinance and its application constitutional. The Court of Appeals reversed, holding that mental retardation is a "quasi-suspect" classification; that, under the applicable "heightened-scrutiny" equal protection test, the ordinance was facially invalid because it did not substantially further an important governmental purpose; and that the ordinance was also invalid as applied.

Held:

1. The Court of Appeals erred in holding mental retardation a quasi-suspect classification calling for a more exacting standard of judicial review than is normally accorded economic and social legislation.

(a) Where individuals in a group affected by a statute have distinguishing characteristics relevant to interests a State has the authority to implement, the Equal Protection Clause requires only that the classification drawn by the statute be rationally related to a legitimate state interest. When social or economic legislation is at issue, the Equal Protection Clause allows the States wide latitude.

(b) Mentally retarded persons, who have a reduced ability to cope with and function in the everyday world, are thus different from other persons, and the States' interest in dealing with and providing for them is plainly a legitimate one. . . . The equal protection standard requiring that legislation be rationally related to a legitimate governmental purpose affords government the latitude necessary both to pursue policies designed to assist the retarded in realizing their full potential. . . .

2. Requiring a special use permit for the proposed group home here deprives [CLC] of the equal protection of the laws . . . . Although the mentally retarded, as a group, are different from those who occupy other facilities—such as boarding houses and hospitals—that are permitted in the zoning area in question without a special permit, such difference is irrelevant unless the proposed group home would threaten the city's legitimate interests in a way that the permitted uses would not. The record does not reveal any rational basis for believing that the proposed group home would pose any special threat to the city's legitimate interests. Requiring the permit in this case appears to rest on an irrational prejudice against the mentally retarded, including those who would occupy the proposed group home and who would live under the closely supervised and highly regulated conditions expressly provided for by state and federal law.

QUESTIONS FOR REVIEW

1. What protections does the Privileges and Immunities Clause provide?

2. What protections does the Due Process Clause provide?

3. What is "procedural" due process?

4. What is "substantive" due process?

5. What protections does the Equal Protection Clause provide?

6. Explain the three different standards of review that courts implement when analyzing government actions that bring into question the Equal Protection Clause (*i.e.*, strict scrutiny, intermediate scrutiny, and rational basis).

7. Summarize the *Hicklin v. Orbeck* case.

8. Summarize the *County of Sacramento v. Lewis* case.

9. Summarize the *Adarand Constructors v. Pena* case.

10. Summarize the *United States v. Virginia* case.

11. Summarize the *City of Cleburne v. Cleburne Living Center* case.

INTERNET ACTIVITIES

1. Find the United States Supreme Court case *Griswold v. Connecticut*, 381 U.S. 479 (1965).

   a. What was the issue or issues in the case?

   b. What was the holding of the Court?

   c. Summarize the Court's analysis.

2. Find the United States Supreme Court case *Gratz v. Bollinger*, 539 U.S. 244 (2003).

   a. What was the issue or issues in the case?

   b. What was the holding of the Court?

   c. Summarize the Court's analysis.

3. Find the United States Supreme Court case *Grutter v. Bollinger*, 539 U.S. 306 (2003).

   a. What was the issue or issues in the case?

   b. What was the holding of the Court?

   c. Summarize the Court's analysis.

Part III

Methods of Resolving Disputes

Chapter 7

The Litigation Process

One very important component of a civilized society is the manner in which disputes are resolved. In underdeveloped countries, people who have been wronged may take the law into their own hands or seek revenge through violent means. Although many would argue that the dispute resolution methods in the United States could be improved, our process still is one of the most stable systems in the world.

There are multiple ways to resolve disputes, including negotiation, mediation, arbitration, and litigation. This chapter focuses on the general litigation process in the United States, while Chapter 8 discusses the other of dispute resolution alternatives.

Before the Lawsuit

A person who suffers harm or believes he or she has been wronged in some way has a right to sue the wrongdoer. In many situations, however, the parties may try to resolve their differences without going to court. For example, in a contract dispute, one party may first formally demand—perhaps via a letter from an attorney— that the other party perform its obligations. If, however, the parties are unable to resolve the dispute on their own, litigation is an option. Litigation can be a lengthy process and very costly because of the fees attorneys charge to handle the case. In short, the decision to go to court should not be made without considering the risks and related costs.

If the case is a *criminal* case, the person accused of the crime must be **indicted** by a **grand jury**, or in states that do not use the grand jury system, a judge will hold a **preliminary hearing** to determine the sufficiency of the evidence against the person accused. The grand jury or preliminary hearing procedure allows the prosecution to present evidence to the grand jury or judge to show that enough evidence exists against the person to warrant a trial. (In some situations, the government will file an **information** rather than going through the grand jury process to obtain an indictment.) Guilt or innocence of the defendant is not determined at this stage; rather, the question to be decided is whether evidence is sufficient to proceed to trial. A grand jury is a group of citizens similar to the jury that is seated for a trial (*i.e.*, a **petit jury**), but a grand jury usually consists of more people. When the defendant appears before the judge to plead guilty or not guilty to the indictment or information, this process is referred to as the **arraignment**. Also in criminal cases, the defendant can enter into a **plea bargain** wherein he or she agrees to plead guilty in return for reduced charges or a reduced recommended prison sentence. The process in some states may be a bit different than the general process discussed here.

Parties to the Lawsuit

If the case is a *civil* (as opposed to a criminal) case, the party who initiates the lawsuit by claiming that some other party has caused harm (physical, emotional or monetary) is called the **plaintiff**. The

Hein v. Freedom from Religion Foundation, Inc.

Supreme Court of the United States

551 U.S. 587 (2007)

[**Note:** For convenience of the reader, the following language is from the Syllabus of the case as provided by the U.S. Supreme Court Reporter of Decisions.]

The President, by executive orders, created a White House office and several centers within federal agencies to ensure that faith-based community groups are eligible to compete for federal financial support. No congressional legislation specifically authorized these entities, which were created entirely within the Executive Branch, nor has Congress enacted any law specifically appropriating money to their activities, which are funded through general Executive Branch appropriations. [Freedom from Religion Foundation, Inc.], an organization opposed to Government endorsement of religion and three of its members, brought this suit alleging that . . . the directors of the federal offices violated the Establishment Clause by organizing conferences that were designed to promote, and had the effect of promoting, religious community groups over secular ones. The only asserted basis for standing was that the individual respondents are federal taxpayers opposed to Executive Branch use of congressional appropriations for these conferences.

Held: . . . [Freedom from Religion Foundation, Inc. and its members] lack standing.

1. Federal-court jurisdiction is limited to actual "Cases" and "Controversies." U.S. Const., Art. III. A controlling factor in the definition of such a case or controversy is standing, ..., the requisite elements of which are well established: "A plaintiff must allege personal injury fairly traceable to the defendant's allegedly unlawful conduct and likely to be redressed by the requested relief." [Citation omitted.]

2. Generally, a federal taxpayer's interest in seeing that Treasury funds are spent in accordance with the Constitution is too attenuated to give rise to the kind of redressable "personal injury" required for Article III standing.

. . .

5. . . . [Freedom from Religion Foundation, Inc. and its members] neither challenge any specific congressional action or appropriation nor ask the Court to invalidate any congressional enactment or legislatively created program as unconstitutional. That is because the expenditures at issue were not made pursuant to any Act of Congress, but under general appropriations to the Executive Branch to fund day-to-day activities. These appropriations did not expressly authorize, direct, or even mention the expenditures in question, which resulted from executive discretion, not congressional action. The Court has never found taxpayer standing under such circumstances.

. . .

party whom the plaintiff sues is called the **defendant**. If the defendant also has a claim against the plaintiff, the defendant can file a **counterclaim**. Sometimes, the defendant believes that someone else contributed to the plaintiff's alleged injury or harm and causes a **third-party defendant** to be brought into the lawsuit. In such a situation, the defendant would file a **cross-claim**. Of course, as discussed in Chapter 2, the court must have both subject-matter jurisdiction regarding the issue in the case and personal jurisdiction over the parties in the case.

Standing to Sue

In order for the plaintiff to bring a case that the court will decide, the plaintiff must have **standing** to sue. This means that the plaintiff has been harmed in some way and seeks payment or restitution from the person who committed the harm. For example, suppose your friend is in an automobile accident because someone ran a red light. Your friend suffered severe injuries. Can *you* sue the person who ran the red light? The answer is no because you do not have standing to sue. Your friend is the one who has standing to sue. If a plaintiff brings a case in which the plaintiff has no standing, the court will dismiss the case. Consider the *Hein v. Freedom from Religion Foundation, Inc.* United States Supreme Court case (Illustrative Court Case 7.1) on the previous page.

Because the plaintiffs in the *Hein* case did not have standing, the courts did not address the merits of their argument regarding whether the executive branch actions had violated the Establishment Clause.

Pleadings

A person initiates a lawsuit by filing with the court a document called a **complaint**. The complaint sets for the facts involved and states what award (or "damages") the plaintiff is seeking. The complaint and a **summons** are served upon the defendant to inform the defendant of the lawsuit and to explain how long the defendant has to file an **answer** to the plaintiff's complaint. The answer will admit or deny the assertions made by the plaintiff in the complaint. If the defendant fails to timely file an answer, the plaintiff will prevail by default. The complaint and answer are called the **pleadings**. The defendant can also file a counterclaim, if any, at the same time as the answer.

Pretrial Motions

Once the pleadings have been filed, one party may believe that legal justification exists for the case to be dismissed or for the judge to decide the case without proceeding to a trial. In these situations, the lawyer for a party will file a **motion**. A very common motion is a **motion to dismiss**, which the defendant files to try to persuade the judge that the plaintiff has stated no claim upon which the plaintiff could prevail or perhaps that the court does not have jurisdiction to hear the case. Another common motion is a **motion for summary judgment**. This motion basically asks the judge to decide the case based upon the facts presented because there are no issues of fact for a jury to decide, and the judge can decide the case as a matter of law. Other motions may be made at this point, but we will not discuss them here.

Discovery

One or more parties in a case may not have all the information necessary to prepare for trial. The other party and witnesses, for example, may have valuable information. The process of obtaining this information from other parties and from witnesses is called **discovery**. In the discovery process, the lawyers in the case often ask questions to potential witnesses and to the other parties in the

case, including the plaintiff and defendant. This process of asking questions is called a **deposition**. If the questions are presented to the other parties or witnesses in writing, these questions are called **interrogatories**. If a person refuses to answer a question in a deposition or in an interrogatory, the lawyers may contact the judge in the case to decide whether the person must answer the question.

The Trial

Jury Selection

If the parties have requested a jury trial, a jury must be selected. Typically, the court will send out a summons to a pool of potential jurors and bring them into the courtroom so the lawyers of the parties in the case can question the potential jurors. This process is called *voir dire*. The lawyers typically can remove a limited number of potential jurors without giving a reason why. The lawyers exercise a **peremptory challenge** to do so. Peremptory challenges cannot be discriminatory, however (*e.g.*, based on race or gender). Consider the following *Edmonson v. Leesville Concrete Co.* United States Supreme Court case (Illustrative Court Case 7.2).

Although the *Edmonson* case addressed discrimination based on race in a civil case, the same prohibition applies to criminal cases as well during the *voir dire* process.

Opening Statements

Once the jury is impaneled, the judge will instruct the lawyers to begin the trial with **opening**

ILLUSTRATIVE COURT CASE 7.2

Edmonson v. Leesville Concrete Co.

Supreme Court of the United States

500 U.S. 614 (1991)

[**Note:** For convenience of the reader, the following language is from the Syllabus of the case as provided by the U.S. Supreme Court Reporter of Decisions.]

Edmonson sued . . . Leesville Concrete Co. in the District Court, alleging that Leesville's negligence had caused him personal injury. During *voir dire*, Leesville used two of its three peremptory challenges authorized by statute to remove black persons from the prospective jury. . . . Edmonson, who is black, requested that the court require Leesville to articulate a race-neutral explanation for the peremptory strikes. The court refused . . . and the impaneled jury, which consisted of 11 white persons and 1 black, rendered a verdict unfavorable to Edmonson. . . .

Held: A private litigant in a civil case may not use peremptory challenges to exclude jurors on account of race.

(a) Although the conduct of private parties lies beyond the Constitution's scope in most instances, Leesville's exercise of peremptory challenges was pursuant to a course of state action and is therefore subject to constitutional requirements. . . . [T]he action in question involves the performance of a traditional governmental function . . . since the peremptory challenge is used in selecting the jury, an entity that is a quintessential governmental body having no attributes of a private actor. Furthermore, the injury allegedly caused by Leesville's use of peremptory challenges is aggravated in a unique way by the incidents of governmental authority . . . since the courtroom is a real expression of the government's constitutional authority, and racial exclusion within its confines compounds the racial insult inherent in judging a citizen by the color of his or her skin.

. . .

---

statements. The lawyer for the plaintiff will speak to the jury and explain that the facts will show why the plaintiff should win. Of course, the defendant's attorney will explain that the facts will show why the defendant should win. In short, the purpose of the opening statements is basically to give the jury an overview of the case and get jurors familiar with the disputed facts.

What Do You Think?

To what extent do you think a jury is swayed by an eloquent, likeable lawyer even though the facts of the case may not be in the lawyer's client's favor?

Presentation of Evidence and Examination of Witnesses

After the opening statements, the plaintiff will then present evidence. This is done through the examination of witnesses and submission of documents that are relevant to the case. The plaintiff has the first opportunity to call witnesses. The plaintiff's lawyer then questions the witness in what is called a **direct-examination**. Once the plaintiff's lawyer is finished questioning the witness, the defendant's lawyer then may ask questions of the witness on **cross-examination**. Sometimes, the plaintiff's lawyer will then follow up with more questions on **redirect-examination**. The defendant's lawyer then can follow up with **recross-examination**. Of course, the witnesses swear to tell the truth and face penalties of perjury if they lie under oath.

Once the plaintiff concludes presenting evidence, it is the defendant's turn to call witnesses and present evidence. Sometimes, however, the defendant will file a **motion for a directed verdict** at this point, basically asking the judge to rule in favor of the defendant because, as a matter of law, the plaintiff failed to present sufficient evidence to warrant further proceedings.

Closing Statements

Depending on the number of witnesses and the complexity of the case, the presentation of evidence and examination of witnesses can last as short as a few hours or as long as several months. But, once the presentation of the evidence concludes, the lawyers have one last chance to wrap

Tom Mc Nemar/Shutterstock.com

up their client's case by making **closing statements** to the jury. Again, the lawyer will try to persuade the jury why the plaintiff or the defendant, as the case may be, should win the case.

Jury Instructions

Once the closing statements have concluded, the judge will then instruct the jury on how to proceed. The judge typically explains the applicable law and sets forth the questions of fact that the jury must decide. The jury instructions are very important, and the lawyers in the case often disagree about how the jury instructions should be phrased. In fact, the

Arthur Andersen LLP v. United States

Supreme Court of the United States

544 U.S. 696 (2005)

[**Note**: For convenience of the reader, the following language is from the Syllabus of the case as provided by the U.S. Supreme Court Reporter of Decisions.]

As Enron Corporation's financial difficulties became public, [Arthur Andersen], Enron's auditor, instructed its employees to destroy documents pursuant to its document retention policy. [Arthur Andersen] was indicted under [federal law], which make[s] it a crime to "knowingly . . . corruptly persuad[e] another person . . . with intent to . . . cause" that person to "withhold" documents from, or "alter" documents for use in, an "official proceeding." The jury returned a guilty verdict, and the Fifth Circuit affirmed, holding that the District Court's jury instructions properly conveyed the meaning of "corruptly persuades" and "official proceeding" . . .; that the jury need not find any consciousness of wrongdoing in order to convict; and that there was no reversible error.

Held: The jury instructions failed to convey properly the elements of a "corrup[t] persuas[ion]" conviction. . . .

. . . .

(b) The jury instructions failed to convey the requisite consciousness of wrongdoing. Indeed, it is striking how little culpability the instructions required. For example, the jury was told that, even if petitioner honestly and sincerely believed its conduct was lawful, the jury could convict. The instructions also diluted the meaning of "corruptly" such that it covered innocent conduct. The District Court based its instruction on the Fifth Circuit Pattern Jury Instruction . . ., which defined "corruptly" as "knowingly and dishonestly, with the specific intent to subvert or undermine the integrity" of a proceeding. However, the court agreed with the Government's insistence on excluding "dishonestly" and adding the term "impede" to the phrase "subvert or undermine," so the jury was told to convict if it found [Arthur Andersen] intended to "subvert, undermine, or impede" governmental factfinding by suggesting to its employees that they enforce the document retention policy. These changes were significant. "[D]ishonest[y]" was no longer necessary to a finding of guilt, and it was enough for [Arthur Andersen] to have simply "impede[d] the government's factfinding ability." "Impede" has broader connotations than "subvert" or even "undermine," and many of these connotations do not incorporate any "corrupt[ness]" at all. Under the dictionary definition of "impede," anyone who innocently persuades another to withhold information from the Government "get[s] in the way of the progress of" the Government. . . . A "knowingly . . . corrup[t] persuade[r]" cannot be someone who persuades others to shred documents under a document retention policy when he does not have in contemplation any particular official proceeding in which those documents might be material.

What Do You Think?

Was it unfair to Arthur Andersen LLP to be convicted of a crime only to have the conviction overturned by the United States Supreme Court because of faulty jury instructions?

party that ultimately loses the case can appeal on the basis of faulty jury instructions. Consider the *Arthur Andersen LLP* United States Supreme Court case (Illustrative Court Case 7.3).

Verdict and Judgment

After receiving the jury instructions, the members of the jury then deliberate and reach conclusions on the factual questions presented to them by the judge. In civil cases, the jury is often asked to decide how much, if any, damages to award to the plaintiff. In criminal cases, the jury must decide if the defendant is guilty of the crime in question. The jury then informs the judge of the decision, *i.e.*, the **verdict**, and the judge enters into a judgment. Of course, if the trial was not a jury trial, there is no jury verdict and the judge decides who is the prevailing party.

Posttrial Motions

Once the jury has returned a verdict, the losing party still has a couple of options. First, the losing party can file a motion requesting a **judgment notwithstanding the verdict** (sometimes also called a "judgment as a matter of law"). As you might expect, it is quite rare for a judge to grant such a motion and enter into a judgment that directly contradicts the jury's verdict. The losing party may also make **a motion for a new trial**, but unless there was some gross error made during the trial by the judge, such motion will likely not be granted.

Other Issues in the Litigation Process

Does the plaintiff have the burden to persuade the judge or jury, or does the defendant? What happens if you win a case, but the losing party fails to comply with the court's judgment? These are a couple of other issues worthy of discussion here.

Burden of Proof

If the jury is deciding guilt or innocence in a criminal case, the government has the burden to show that the defendant is guilty **beyond a reasonable doubt**. Of course, this is a very high standard and, in some cases, it is possible for truly guilty people to be found not guilty because the government failed to meet the high standard.

If a judge or jury is deciding a civil case (as opposed to a criminal case), the applicable standard is **preponderance of the evidence**. This basically means that the evidence weighs more in favor of one party than the other. Of course, this is a much lower standard than the beyond a reasonable doubt standard used in criminal cases. In a few narrow situations, a standard of **clear and**

convincing evidence may apply, which is a higher standard than "preponderance of the evidence" but lower than "beyond a reasonable doubt."

Enforcing a Judgment

It is not uncommon for a plaintiff (the judgment creditor) to win a court case, but be unable to collect the judgment from the defendant (the judgment debtor). Perhaps the debtor has few assets with which to pay the creditor. In such cases, the creditor can request the judge to order an **execution** of the judgment. This basically consists of a sheriff's seizing the property of the debtor, selling it, and remitting the proceeds to the creditor under the judge's supervision. Another mechanism for a creditor to obtain funds from the debtor is through **garnishment**. An example of this is when the debtor's employer withholds wages from the debtor and remits the wages to the court, after which the court remits the funds to the creditor.

Appeals

The losing party at the trial court level, in most cases, has the right to appeal the judgment to a court of appeals. The appellate court does not hold a trial as did the trial court. Rather, the appellate court hears arguments from the lawyers in the case about whether mistakes were made at the trial court level, such as faulty jury instructions or the admission of prejudicial evidence that should have been excluded, etc. Courts of appeal typically consist of three or more judges who hear the **oral arguments** of the lawyers and read the **legal briefs** filed by the parties involved. The judges then issue an opinion either **affirming** or **reversing** the trial court result or, in some situations, **remanding** the case back down to the trial court for further proceedings. On appeal, the party who is appealing is called the **petitioner** or **appellant**. The party that prevailed at the lower court level is called the **respondent** or **appellee**. The party that loses at the court of appeals can then appeal to an even higher court (typically, the applicable state supreme court or the U.S. Supreme Court). These higher courts of appeal, however, in most situations have discretion whether to hear the case or let the appellate court's decision stand.

QUESTIONS FOR REVIEW

1. Explain what the following legal documents are:

   a. complaint

   b. answer

   c. counterclaim

   d. crossclaim

   e. pleadings

   f. motion to dismiss

   g. motion for summary judgment

   h. motion for a directed verdict

   i. motion for judgment notwithstanding the verdict

   j. legal brief

2. What is an indictment?

3. What is a preliminary hearing?

4. What is an arraignment?

5. What is a plea bargain?

6. What does it mean to have "standing"?

7. What is a deposition?

8. What is an interrogatory?

9. Explain the purpose of the opening statements and closing statements by the lawyers in a trial.

10. What is a garnishment?

11. What is the burden of proof standard in criminal cases?

12. What is the burden of proof standard in civil cases?

13. Explain generally the litigation process.

14. Summarize the *Hein v. Freedom from Religion Foundation, Inc.* case.

15. Summarize the *Edmonson v. Leesville Concrete Co.* case.

INTERNET ACTIVITIES

1. Find the United States Supreme Court case *Snyder v. Louisiana* , 552 U.S. 472 (2008).

   a. What was the issue or issues in the case?

   b. What was the holding of the Court?

   c. Summarize the Court's analysis.

Chapter 8

Negotiation, Mediation, and Arbitration

As mentioned in Chapter 7, the litigation process can be lengthy, costly, and frustrating. Nevertheless, litigation is sometimes necessary. Other methods of resolving disputes are available, however. We will discuss negotiation, mediation, and arbitration in this chapter. Negotiation, mediation, and arbitration are all forms of **alternative dispute resolution (ADR)**.

Negotiation

Of course, one way for parties to attempt to resolve their dispute is through **negotiation**. This method is typically very inexpensive compared to other dispute resolution methods. The parties must be willing to engage in negotiation, however, and the parties likely must be willing to compromise. Negotiation skills are important not just when there is a dispute to resolve. Negotiation takes place in everyday commercial transactions (*e.g.*, negotiating the price of an automobile, selling or buying products online, etc.). When negotiation is successful, the parties often can settle the matter and continue their business relationship.

Mediation

Mediation involves an independent third party, a **mediator**, who attempts to help the disputing

Mehmet Dilsiz/Shutterstock.com

parties come to an agreement or settlement. The mediator usually receives a fee for his or her services. Although mediators are frequently lawyers, a mediator is not required to be a lawyer. Perhaps the parties do not feel comfortable engaging in negotiations without a third party present, or perhaps negotiation has been tried but failed.

The mediator (in contrast to an arbitrator) will not make a decision in favor of one party or another; rather, the disputing parties ultimately agree to settle the matter in some manner. Increasingly, courts are ordering disputing parties to attempt mediation before fully litigating the issue. This often occurs in family law matters such as child custody and divorce.

Arbitration

Arbitration is a much more formal process than negotiation or mediation. Typically, the disputing parties will agree on an independent third party, an **arbitrator**, who is likely an expert regarding the issue or issues in dispute. The referral of a dispute to arbitration is called a **submission**. The parties present witnesses and other evidence and try to convince the arbitrator(s) that their position is correct. The arbitrator reviews the issues in dispute, each party's position on the issues, and the relevant facts. In short, the process is similar to a trial. The arbitrator(s) then announces their decision, called an **award**.

Arbitration clauses are quite common in contracts. Basically, the arbitration provision in the contract commits both parties to resolve any future dispute through arbitration rather than litigation. A large company with many customers, for example, may desire an arbitration clause in their contracts so that the company ultimately lessens the risk of incurring enormous litigation costs because of a large number of lawsuits.

Federal law is supportive of arbitration provisions in contracts. The Federal Arbitration Act illustrates this point (Illustrative Federal Statute 8.1).

ILLUSTRATIVE FEDERAL STATUTE 8.1

9 U.S.C. § 2

§ 2. Validity, irrevocability, and enforcement of agreements to arbitrate

A written provision in . . . a contract evidencing a transaction involving commerce to settle by arbitration a controversy thereafter arising out of such contract or transaction, or the refusal to perform the whole or any part thereof, or an agreement in writing to submit to arbitration an existing controversy arising out of such a contract, transaction, or refusal, shall be valid, irrevocable, and enforceable, save upon such grounds as exist at law or in equity for the revocation of any contract.

The courts rarely overturn arbitration awards, but it is possible if, for example, the arbitration proceedings were plagued with fraud, bias, procedural error, etc. But courts typically will not overturn arbitration awards because the arbitrator made a mistake. Consequently, a potential disadvantage of submitting to arbitration is the strong reluctance of the courts to change the award.

Sometimes, the question arises whether a party who signed a contract with an arbitration clause in it really must submit to arbitration. When an arbitration clause is in a contract, the courts will typically enforce the arbitration clause and not allow a party to go directly to litigation even if the argument is that the contract is illegal. Consider the following United States Supreme Court case (Illustrative Court Case 8.1).

Buckeye Check Cashing Inc. v. Cardegna

Supreme Court of the United States

546 U.S. 440 (2006)

[**Note**: For convenience of the reader, the following language is from the Syllabus of the case as provided by the U.S. Supreme Court Reporter of Decisions.]

For each deferred-payment transaction respondents entered into with Buckeye Check Cashing, they signed an Agreement containing provisions that required binding arbitration to resolve disputes arising out of the Agreement. Respondents sued in Florida state court, alleging that Buckeye charged usurious interest rates and that the Agreement violated various Florida laws, rendering it criminal on its face. The trial court denied Buckeye's motion to compel arbitration, holding that a court rather than an arbitrator should resolve a claim that a contract is illegal. . . . A state appellate court reversed, but was in turn reversed by the Florida Supreme Court, which reasoned that enforcing an arbitration agreement in a contract challenged as unlawful would violate state public policy and contract law.

Held:

Regardless of whether it is brought in federal or state court, a challenge to the validity of a contract as a whole, and not specifically to the arbitration clause within it, must go to the arbitrator, not the court. . . . First, as a matter of substantive federal arbitration law, an arbitration provision is severable from the remainder of the contract. . . . Second, unless the challenge is to the arbitration clause itself, the issue of the contract's validity is considered by the arbitrator in the first instance. . . . Third, this arbitration law applies in state as well as federal courts. . . . The crux of respondents' claim is that the Agreement as a whole (including its arbitration provision) is rendered invalid by the usurious finance charge. Because this challenges the Agreement, and not specifically its arbitration provisions, the latter are enforceable apart from the remainder of the contract, and the challenge should be considered by an arbitrator, not a court.

Sometimes, state law and federal law mandate that parties must submit to arbitration before they take their case to the courts. Consider the following Washington state statute (Illustrative State Statute 8.1).

Whether voluntary or mandatory, arbitration is certainly an alternative to litigation. Parties should seriously consider their alternative dispute resolution options before rushing into litigation.

RCW 7.06.020

. . . .

(2) If approved by majority vote of the superior court judges of a county which has authorized arbitration, all civil actions which are at issue in the superior court in which the sole relief sought is the establishment, termination or modification of maintenance or child support payments are subject to mandatory arbitration. . . .

QUESTIONS FOR REVIEW

1. What do the letters ADR stand for?

2. Explain the advantages and disadvantages of mediation.

3. Explain the advantages and disadvantages of arbitration.

4. Why might state and federal laws require some disputes to be mediated before bringing them to court?

5. Summarize the *Buckeye Check Cashing v. Cardegna* case.

INTERNET ACTIVITIES

1. Conduct a web search for *mediators* in your local area. Scrutinize their websites. Are they effective? How would you go about choosing a mediator to help you resolve a dispute?

2. Conduct a web search for *arbitrators* in your local area. Scrutinize their websites. Are they effective? How would you go about choosing an arbitrator to help you resolve a dispute?

Part IV
Criminal Law

Chapter 9

Criminal Law and the Constitution

Perhaps the area of law that receives the most headlines and news stories is criminal law. In civil societies, there must be punishment for those individuals that engage in acts that harm others and society as a whole. People who violate criminal laws risk losing their liberty by being sentenced to time in prison. Obviously, even business leaders commit crimes and are punished for those crimes. Consequently, understanding the fundamentals of criminal law and related constitutional protections is relevant when studying the legal environment of business.

The Constitution provides protections to the people from the government's overreaching when it investigates and prosecutes crimes. In this chapter, we will discuss provisions of the Constitution that provide important rights and protections to those individuals suspected of or accused of committing a crime.

Fourth Amendment

When does a police officer have the right to enter your house? Search your car? Search your person? The Fourth Amendment to the Constitution provides the fundamental principles regarding searches and seizures.

FOURTH AMENDMENT TO THE UNITED STATES CONSTITUTION

The right of the people to be secure in their persons, houses, papers, and effects, against unreasonable searches and seizures, shall not be violated, and no Warrants shall issue, but upon probable cause, supported by Oath or affirmation, and particularly describing the place to be searched, and the persons or things to be seized.

Thus, generally speaking, individuals are protected against "unreasonable searches and seizures" by the government, and the government must have "probable cause" in order to get a warrant to conduct a search. A **warrant** is issued by a judge upon law enforcement's explanation to the judge that there is probable cause for an arrest, search, or seizure. In general, **probable cause** exists if, given the facts and circumstances, a law enforcement officer has reasonable grounds to believe that a person has committed a crime or, in the case of searching or seizing property, whether such property is contraband, stolen, or useful as evidence to show that a crime has been committed.

The Supreme Court has decided numerous cases involving the Fourth Amendment, and much can be

Lisa F. Young/Shutterstock.com

written on the subject. Nevertheless, we will focus on the fundamental principles here. The Fourth Amendment's language is very broad, and the courts have interpreted the Fourth Amendment in a manner that provides some exceptions to requiring law enforcement to obtain a warrant before conducting a search. For example, a law enforcement officer, in most cases, can conduct a warrantless "pat down" of an individual in connection with a lawful arrest. Other limited exceptions to the need for a warrant include searching public school property, individuals and their luggage at airports, and vehicles at border crossings, among other exceptions. The Fourth Amendment's strongest protection against unreasonable searches and seizures by the government is in the individual's home. Consider the following Supreme Court case (Illustrative Court Case 9.1).

ILLUSTRATIVE COURT CASE 9.1

Kyllo v. United States

Supreme Court of the United States

533 U.S. 27 (2001))

[**Note:** For convenience of the reader, the following language is from the Syllabus of the case as provided by the U.S. Supreme Court Reporter of Decisions.]

Suspicious that marijuana was being grown in . . . Kyllo's home in a triplex, agents used a thermal-imaging device to scan the triplex to determine if the amount of heat emanating from it was consistent with the high-intensity lamps typically used for indoor marijuana growth. The scan showed that Kyllo's garage roof and a side wall were relatively hot compared to the rest of his home and substantially warmer than the neighboring units. Based in part on the thermal imaging, a Federal Magistrate Judge issued a warrant to search Kyllo's home, where the agents found marijuana growing. After Kyllo was indicted on a federal drug charge, he unsuccessfully moved to suppress the evidence seized from his home and then entered a conditional guilty plea. The Ninth Circuit ultimately affirmed, upholding the thermal imaging on the ground that Kyllo had shown no subjective expectation of privacy because he had made no attempt to conceal the heat escaping from his home. Even if he had, ruled the court, there was no objectively reasonable expectation of privacy because the thermal imager did not expose any intimate details of Kyllo's life, only amorphous hot spots on his home's exterior.

Held:

Where, as here, the Government uses a device that is not in general public use, to explore details of a private home that would previously have been unknowable without physical intrusion, the surveillance is a Fourth Amendment "search," and is presumptively unreasonable without a warrant.

(a) The question whether a warrantless search of a home is reasonable and hence constitutional must be answered no in most instances, but the antecedent question whether a Fourth Amendment "search" has occurred is not so simple. This Court has approved warrantless visual surveillance of a home, [citation omitted], ruling that visual observation is no "search" at all. . . . In assessing when a

(*Continued*)

search is not a search, the Court has adapted [the] principle [that] a "search" does not occur—even when its object is a house explicitly protected by the Fourth Amendment—unless the individual manifested a subjective expectation of privacy in the searched object, and society is willing to recognize that expectation as reasonable. . . .

(b) [I]n the case of the search of a home's interior—the prototypical and hence most commonly litigated area of protected privacy—there is a ready criterion, with roots deep in the common law, of the minimal expectation of privacy that *exists*, and that is acknowledged to be *reasonable*. To withdraw protection of this minimum expectation would be to permit police technology to erode the privacy guaranteed by the Fourth Amendment. Thus, obtaining by sense-enhancing technology an information regarding the home's interior that could not otherwise have been obtained without physical "intrusion into a constitutionally protected area," [citation omitted], constitutes a search—at least where (as here) the technology in question is not in general public use. This assures preservation of that degree of privacy against government that existed when the Fourth Amendment was adopted.

(c) Based on this criterion, the information obtained by the thermal imager in this case was the product of a search. The Court rejects the Government's argument that the thermal imaging must be upheld because it detected only heat radiating from the home's external surface. Such a mechanical interpretation of the Fourth Amendment was rejected in [a prior Supreme Court case]. . . . [Adopting the Government's argument] would leave the homeowner at the mercy of advancing technology—including imaging technology that could discern all human activity in the home. Also rejected is the Government's contention that the thermal imaging was constitutional because it did not detect "intimate details." Such an approach would be wrong in principle because, in the sanctity of the home, *all* details are intimate details.

(d) Since the imaging in this case was an unlawful search, it will remain for the District Court to determine whether, without the evidence it provided, the search warrant was supported by probable cause—and if not, whether there is any other basis for supporting admission of that evidence.

In the *Kyllo* case, law enforcement obtained evidence by using a thermal device that detected warmer temperatures in one part of the residence. According to the Supreme Court, using this thermal device without a warrant violated the Fourth Amendment because it was a "search" of the residence. Do you agree? What about the fact that law enforcement did, in fact, find marijuana in the residence when police later went inside? Does that matter?

An individual's reasonable expectation of privacy rights varies depending upon the facts and circumstances of every situation. For example, a person's reasonable expectation of privacy may differ depending on whether the person is in an automobile, or at the airport or sporting event, etc. The courts have recognized that a person does indeed have a lower expectation of privacy when outside his or her residence; consequently, the government's burden is less in these situations.

Fifth Amendment

The Fifth Amendment is another Constitutional provision that provides individuals with significant protections.

FIFTH AMENDMENT TO THE UNITED STATES CONSTITUTION

No person shall be held to answer for a capital, or otherwise infamous crime, unless on a presentment or indictment of a Grand Jury, except in cases arising in the land or naval forces, or in the Militia, when in actual service in time of War or public danger; nor shall any person be subject for the same offence to be twice put in jeopardy of life or limb; nor shall be compelled in any criminal case to be a witness against himself, nor be deprived of life, liberty, or property, without due process of law; nor shall private property be taken for public use, without just compensation.

As you can see, the Fifth Amendment contains numerous protections to individuals. We will focus on the right to remain silent.

Some people may argue that, in addition to the rights we have under the First Amendment, the "right to remain silent" is one of the most important

Miranda v. Arizona

Supreme Court of the United States

384 U.S. 436 (1966)

[**Note**: For convenience of the reader, the following language is from the Syllabus of the case as provided by the U.S. Supreme Court Reporter of Decisions.]

[Ernesto Miranda] while in police custody was questioned by police officers . . . in a room in which he was cut off from the outside world. [He] was not given a full and effective warning of his rights at the outset of the interrogation process. [T]he questioning elicited . . . admissions . . . which were admitted at [his] trial. [He was convicted at trial. His conviction was affirmed on appeal.]

Held:

1. The prosecution may not use statements, whether exculpatory or inculpatory, stemming from questioning initiated by law enforcement officers after a person has been taken into custody or otherwise deprived of his freedom of action in any significant way, unless it demonstrates the use of procedural safeguards effective to secure the Fifth Amendment's privilege against self-incrimination.

(a) The atmosphere and environment of incommunicado interrogation as it exists today is inherently intimidating and works to undermine the privilege against self-incrimination. Unless adequate preventive measures are taken to dispel the compulsion inherent in custodial surroundings, no statement obtained from the defendant can truly be the product of his free choice.

(b) The privilege against self-incrimination, which has had a long and expansive historical development, is the essential mainstay of our adversary system and guarantees to the individual the "right to remain silent unless he chooses to speak in the unfettered exercise of his own will," during a period of custodial interrogation as well as in the courts or during the course of other official investigations.

. . .

(d) In absence of other effective measures the following procedures to safeguard the Fifth Amendment privilege must be observed: The person in custody must, prior to interrogation, be clearly informed that he has the right to remain silent, and that anything he says will be used against him in court; he must be clearly informed that he has the right to consult with a lawyer and to have the lawyer with him during interrogation, and that, if he is indigent, a lawyer will be appointed to represent him.

(e) If the individual indicates, prior to or during questioning, that he wishes to remain silent, the interrogation must cease; if he states that he wants an attorney, the questioning must cease until an attorney is present.

(f) Where an interrogation is conducted without the presence of an attorney and a statement is taken, a heavy burden rests on the Government to demonstrate that the defendant knowingly and intelligently waived his right to counsel.

(g) Where the individual answers some questions during in-custody interrogation he has not waived his privilege and may invoke his right to remain silent thereafter.

(h) The warnings required and the waiver needed are, in the absence of a fully effective equivalent, prerequisites to the admissibility of any statement . . . made by a defendant.

protections we have in the Bill of Rights. In other words, if we are accused of a crime, we cannot be forced to give testimony against ourselves. Notwithstanding this constitutional right, are police officers required to actually inform an individual of this right if the individual is being questioned? This issue led to the famous case of *Miranda v. Arizona*, as shown on the previous page (Illustrative Court Case 9.2), which addressed the rights of an individual who had been arrested, detained, and questioned regarding the rape of a teenage girl.

This case, of course, gave rise to the *Miranda* warning that law enforcement officers read to those who are taken into custody.

What Do You Think?

What should happen if a law enforcement officer reads someone his rights (i.e., right to remain silent, right to an attorney, etc.) in English but the person in custody does not understand English?

Sixth Amendment

The Sixth Amendment provides procedural protection to individuals accused of crimes.

SIXTH AMENDMENT TO THE UNITED STATES CONSTITUTION

In all criminal prosecutions, the accused shall enjoy the right to a speedy and public trial, by an impartial jury of the State and district wherein the crime shall have been committed, which district shall have been previously ascertained by law, and to be informed of the nature and cause of the accusation; to be confronted with the witnesses against him; to have compulsory process for obtaining Witnesses in his favor, and to have Assistance of Counsel for his defence.

As discussed in the *Miranda* case, an accused must be informed of his or her right to have a lawyer present. Notice the other rights provided in the Sixth Amendment, including the right to a speedy, public trial; a right to confront witnesses; and the right to an impartial jury. Regarding the right to an impartial jury, you may have heard of several incidents where a trial was moved from the city or town where the crime was committed because

ILLUSTRATIVE COURT CASE 9.3

Gideon v. Wainwright

Supreme Court of the United States

372 U.S. 335 (1963)

[**Note**: For convenience of the reader, the following language is from the Syllabus of the case as provided by the U.S. Supreme Court Reporter of Decisions.]

Charged in a Florida State Court with a noncapital felony, [Gideon] appeared without funds and with out counsel and asked the Court to appoint counsel for him, but this was denied on the ground that the state law permitted appointment of counsel for indigent defendants in capital cases only. [Gideon] conducted his own defense about as well as could be expected of a layman, but he was convicted and sentenced to imprisonment. Subsequently, he applied to the State Supreme Court on the ground that his conviction violated his rights under the Federal Constitution. The State Supreme Court denied all relief.

Held:

The right of an indigent defendant in a criminal trial to have the assistance of counsel is a fundamental right essential to a fair trial, and [Gideon's] trial and conviction without the assistance of counsel violated [his constitutional rights].

of a concern that the defendant could not obtain an impartial jury. Additionally, the importance of the Sixth Amendment right to have a lawyer present—even if the defendant cannot afford one—must not be overlooked. Consider the landmark United States Supreme Court case *Gideon v. Wainwright* (Illustrative Court Case 9.3). In this case, the defendant could not afford a lawyer and the trial court refused to appoint a lawyer for him. He represented himself the best he could, but nonetheless, a Florida jury convicted him of stealing $5.00 and a few beer bottles from a local pool hall/beer joint in Florida. He was sentenced to five years in prison.

As a result of this case, the government must make sure that public defenders are available to represent indigent defendants accused of a crime. This is costly to the public since the lawyers' salaries are paid by taxpayers.

What Do You Think?

Should taxpayers be required to cover the cost of an attorney and a public trial, even when it is obvious the defendant is guilty of the crime?

Eighth Amendment

The Eighth Amendment provides further protection to individuals finding themselves charged or even convicted of crimes.

EIGHTH AMENDMENT TO THE UNITED STATES CONSTITUTION

Excessive bail shall not be required, nor excessive fines imposed, nor cruel and unusual punishments inflicted.

A judge determines the amount of bail a person must pay in order to get out of jail before a pending trial. Sometimes, a judge may require that the defendant be held without bail if the defendant is a flight risk or poses a danger to society. Nevertheless, the amount of the bail cannot be excessive. The Eighth Amendment provision that gets significant attention, of course, is the "cruel and unusual punishments" clause. This is another phrase that is open to interpretation. The United States Supreme Court has grappled with this issue in several instances. Consider the *Graham v. Florida* case (Illustrative Court Case 9.4).

ILLUSTRATIVE COURT CASE 9.4

Graham v. Florida

Supreme Court of the United States

130 S. Ct. 2011 (2010)

Note: For convenience of the reader, the following language is from the Syllabus of the case as provided by the U.S. Supreme Court Reporter of Decisions.]

Petitioner Graham was 16 when he committed armed burglary and another crime. Under a plea agreement, the Florida trial court sentenced Graham to probation and withheld adjudication of guilt. Subsequently, the trial court found that Graham had violated the terms of his probation by committing additional crimes. The trial court adjudicated Graham guilty of the earlier charges, revoked his probation, and sentenced him to life in prison for the burglary. Because Florida has abolished its parole system, the life sentence left Graham no possibility of release except executive clemency. . . .

Held:

The [cruel and unusual punishment] Clause does not permit a juvenile offender to be sentenced to life in prison without parole for a nonhomicide crime.

(a) Embodied in the cruel and unusual punishments ban is the "precept . . . that punishment for crime should be graduated and proportioned to [the] offense." [Citation omitted.] The Court's cases

(*Continued*)

implementing the proportionality standard fall within two general classifications. In cases of the first type, the length of a term-of-years sentence is unconstitutionally excessive for a particular defendant's crime. The second classification comprises cases in which the Court has applied certain categorical rules against the death penalty. In a subset of such cases considering the nature of the offense, the Court has concluded that capital punishment is impermissible for nonhomicide crimes against individuals. [Citation omitted.] In a second subset, cases turning on the offender's characteristics, the Court has prohibited death for defendants who committed their crimes before age 18 . . . or whose intellectual functioning is in a low range. . . . In cases involving categorical rules, the Court first considers "objective indicia of society's standards, as expressed in legislative enactments and state practice" to determine whether there is a national consensus against the sentencing practice at issue. . . . Next, looking to "the standards elaborated by controlling precedents and by the Court's own understanding and interpretation of the Eighth Amendment's text, history, meaning, and purpose," . . . the Court determines in the exercise of its own independent judgment whether the punishment in question violates the Constitution. . . .

(b) Application of the foregoing approach convinces the Court that the sentencing practice at issue is unconstitutional.

. . .

(2) The inadequacy of penological theory to justify life without parole sentences for juvenile nonhomicide offenders, the limited culpability of such offenders, and the severity of these sentences all lead the Court to conclude that the sentencing practice at issue is cruel and unusual. . . . Moreover, defendants who do not kill, intend to kill, or foresee that life will be taken are categorically less deserving of such punishments than are murderers. . . . Serious nonhomicide crimes "may be devastating in their harm . . . but 'in terms of moral depravity and of the injury to the person and to the public,' . . . they cannot be compared to murder in their 'severity and irrevocability.'" . . . Thus, when compared to an adult murderer, a juvenile offender who did not kill or intend to kill has a twice diminished moral culpability. Age and the nature of the crime each bear on the analysis. As for the punishment, life without parole is "the second most severe penalty permitted by law," . . . and is especially harsh for a juvenile offender, who will on average serve more years and a greater percentage of his life in prison than an adult offender. . . . Because age "18 is the point where society draws the line for many purposes between childhood and adulthood," it is the age below which a defendant may not be sentenced to life without parole for a nonhomicide crime.

. . .

(4) Additional support for the Court's conclusion lies in the fact that the sentencing practice at issue has been rejected the world over; The United States is the only Nation that imposes this type of sentence. While the judgments of other nations and the international community are not dispositive as to the meaning of the Eighth Amendment, The Court has looked abroad to support its independent conclusion that a particular punishment is cruel and unusual.

The Fourth, Fifth, Sixth, and Eighth Amendments provide significant rights and protections to the people of the United States. While we have only briefly discussed these amendments in this chapter, their importance should not be overlooked. Although your immediate focus as a current or future businessperson may not be on the United States criminal justice system, a fundamental understanding of the system is essential to the legal environment in which businesses operate. In fact, Chapter 10 covers the more common crimes that are committed in the business context.

QUESTIONS FOR REVIEW

1. What are the rights and protections provided by the Fourth Amendment?

2. What is a warrant? How is one obtained?

3. What are the rights and protections provided by the Fifth Amendment?

4. What are the rights and protections provided by the Sixth Amendment?

5. What are the protections provided by the Eighth Amendment?

6. Why do you think so many of the amendments in the Bill of Rights focus on the rights of people accused of a crime?

7. Summarize the *Kyllo v. United States* case.

8. Summarize the *Miranda v. Arizona* case.

9. Summarize the *Gideon v. Wainwright* case.

10. Summarize the *Graham v. Florida* case.

INTERNET ACTIVITIES

1. Find the United States Supreme Court case *Arizona v. Gant*, 129 S. Ct. 1710 (2009).

   a. What was the issue or issues in the case?

   b. What was the holding of the Court?

   c. Summarize the analysis of the Court.

2. Find the United States Supreme Court case *Berghuis v. Thompkins*, 130 S. Ct. 2250 (2010).

   a. What was the issue or issues in the case?

   b. What was the holding of the Court?

   c. Summarize the analysis of the Court.

3. Find the United States Supreme Court case *Melendez-Diaz v. Massachusetts*, 129 S. Ct. 2527 (2009).

   a. What was the issue or issues in the case?

   b. What was the holding of the Court?

   c. Summarize the analysis of the Court.

4. Find the United States Supreme Court case *Lockyer v. Andrade*, 538 U.S. 63 (2003).

   a. What was the issue or issues in the case?

   b. What was the holding of the Court?

   c. Summarize the analysis of the Court.

5. Find the United States Supreme Court case *Riley v. California*, 134 S.Ct. 2473 (2014).

   a. What was the issue or issues in the case?

   b. What was the holding of the Court?

   c. Summarize the analysis of the Court.

Chapter 10

Criminal Law and Business

Now that we have covered the constitutional rights and protections relating to criminal law (Chapter 9), we can address more specifics in this area.

Classification of Crimes

Of course, the severity of crimes varies widely. In general, if the crime is subject to punishment of more than one year in prison, or death, the crime is classified as a **felony**. If the possible punishment is for one year or less, the crime is classified as a **misdemeanor**.

Evidence

As discussed in Chapter 7, the burden is on the government to show that a defendant is guilty beyond a reasonable doubt. Of course, in attempting to do this, the government's lawyers (called the **prosecution**) must be able to present evidence against the accused. The prosecution collects evidence relating to each element of the crime being charged. Not all evidence is admissible in court, however, so the parties must be familiar with the rules of evidence. Law enforcement officers must also be familiar with the rules of evidence so that they do not obtain evidence illegally, which will cause the evidence to be inadmissible at trial. We will discuss these issues in this section.

Elements of a Crime

Suppose you travel across the country by plane. When you arrive, you pick up some luggage that looks exactly like yours, but it turns out that it was someone else's luggage. Have you committed a crime? You likely have not committed a crime in this situation because you had no intent to steal the other person's luggage. Thus, a person's **intent** (or *mens rea*) is critical when determining if someone committed a crime. In other words, the person must have a "guilty mind." The person must also actually commit the wrongful **act** (or *actus reus*). The government must show that the defendant both committed the act and had the requisite intent.

Rules of Evidence

Since the prosecution has a high burden in convincing a jury that the defendant is guilty beyond a reasonable doubt, the credibility of the evidence is critical. Of course, if possible, the prosecution will want to have as much **direct** evidence as possible. The prosecution can also present **circumstantial** evidence, but such evidence is not as strong as direct evidence. Consider the following distinction regarding whether a defendant is guilty of breaking into a building to commit the crime of burglary:

Direct evidence: a witness saw the defendant break a window and climb through at 11:00 p.m.

Circumstantial evidence: a witness saw broken glass on the ground directly underneath the window at 11:10 p.m.

At a threshold level, to be admissible in court, any evidence must be **relevant** to the case. For example, if a defendant is currently on trial for theft, is it relevant to the case how many speeding tickets the defendant has had in the past five years? Probably not. Consequently, if the prosecution tries to admit that evidence, the judge would likely exclude it. In other words, the value of such information in deciding the defendant's guilt or innocence is outweighed by the potential prejudice it would have against the defendant.

All courts follow certain rules of evidence. In the federal courts, the Federal Rules of Evidence apply. State courts also have their own rules of evidence. These rules can be quite complex, as most law school students would attest. Consequently, judges and lawyers frequently review and study the rules of evidence in an attempt to ensure no material errors are made during a trial.

Exclusionary Rule

Some evidence, although relevant, may still be inadmissible. One major reason why it may be deemed inadmissible is because of the **exclusionary rule**. The exclusionary rule basically provides that if any evidence is collected illegally (*e.g.*, in violation of an individual's Fourth Amendment rights against unreasonable searches and seizures), then any additional evidence gathered that may have stemmed from the initial illegal gathering of evidence is excluded from evidence at trial. In other words, the "fruit of the poisonous tree" is not allowed in court. This puts law enforcement officers, forensics teams, and prosecuting attorneys under pressure to obtain and present evidence legally to avoid jeopardizing the government's case against the individual accused of a crime.

Consider the *Kyllo* case we covered in Chapter 9. In that case, law enforcement officers used thermal imaging technology to ascertain whether marijuana was being grown in a home. The officers did not have a warrant at the time of using the thermal imaging technology. Based upon the results of the thermal-imaging technology, the police subsequently obtained a warrant, entered the home, and found marijuana. As you may recall, the Supreme Court ruled that using the thermal-imaging

Bjoern Wylezich/Shutterstock.com

technology violated the defendant's Fourth Amendment rights against unreasonable searches and seizures, and the subsequent evidence (*i.e.*, marijuana) was inadmissible in court under the exclusionary rule. Some exceptions to the exclusionary rule apply, but such a discussion is beyond the scope of our discussion here.

What Do You Think?

Should evidence condemning a suspected criminal be inadmissible in court because of a simple mistake by law enforcement officers in gathering the evidence?

Specific Business Crimes

In addition to the "major" crimes we see in the news all the time (*e.g.*, murder, robbery, burglary, sexual offenses, kidnapping, etc.), other crimes are being committed that usually do not receive as much attention. This section briefly discusses various crimes that are more specifically related to business. Of course, this list is not intended to be exhaustive.

Fraud

Common law requires three elements for **fraud** to occur: (1) a material false statement or representation with the intent to deceive, (2) the victim's reasonable reliance on the statement or representation, and (3) damages. Fraud is a broad term that can include many different types of activities. For example, there is securities fraud, mail fraud, insurance fraud, health care fraud, etc.

Forgery

Forgery is a form of fraud. A forgery is when a person alters or creates a written document with the purpose to deceive or defraud another person. Of course, a common example is one person signing the name of another person on a check without authorization.

Embezzlement

Embezzlement is the taking of property of another while in lawful possession of the property. This crime is especially serious because of the existence of a trusting relationship, which does not exist in an ordinary theft case. For example, suppose the treasurer of a corporation has the responsibility to receive and deposit funds on behalf of the corporation. Instead, without authorization, the treasurer diverts funds from the corporation's bank account to his own bank account. Since the person is lawfully in control of the funds in his role as treasurer, his subsequent transfer of the funds to his personal account constitutes embezzlement.

Insider Trading

Chapter 28 is dedicated to securities law, regulations, and related crimes. Insider trading will be covered in that chapter.

Money Laundering

If a person obtains money through an illegal transaction, and then tries to conceal the fact that the money was obtained illegally (*e.g.*, setting up a business entity to make it look like the money was obtained through a legitimate activity), this is an example of **money laundering**. In other words, a person tries to "clean" the "dirty" money. A look at Illustrative Federal Statute 10.1 that makes this activity a crime is worth reviewing at this point.

The statute goes on to define the term "specified unlawful activity" very broadly. Examples of these activities include drug smuggling, murder, kidnapping, robbery, extortion, bribery, sex trafficking, violence at international airports, threatening public officials or their families, counterfeiting, smuggling goods into the United States, insurance fraud, certain lending transactions, and many more.

Bribery

In its basic form, **bribery** consists of offering a gift, payment, or other benefit, usually to a public employee, in exchange for some action or vote. For

---

ILLUSTRATIVE FEDERAL STATUTE 10.1

18 U.S.C. 1956

. . .

(a)(3) Whoever, with the intent—

(A) to promote the carrying on of a specified unlawful activity;

(B) to conceal or disguise the nature, location, source, ownership, or control of property believed to be the proceeds of specified unlawful activity; or

(C) to avoid a transaction reporting requirement under State or Federal law, conducts or attempts to conduct a financial transaction involving property represented to be the proceeds of specified unlawful activity, or property used to conduct or facilitate specified unlawful activity, shall be fined under this title or imprisoned for not more than 20 years, or both. . . .

example, suppose a person is a general contractor and has made a bid to a city council to build a new office building for the city government. The general contractor really needs to be awarded the bid to continue in business. Consequently, the general contractor tells one of the city council members that if the city council member votes in favor of awarding the contract to him, then the general contractor will hire the city council member's unemployed son to work on the project. This would be a bribe. In some countries, bribes are commonplace. Congress has recognized that some countries engage in forms of bribery or payoffs in order to transact business. Consequently, in 1977, Congress enacted the **Foreign Corrupt Practices Act (FCPA)** to address the issue. In substance, with some narrow exceptions, the FCPA prohibits bribery-like payments to foreign officials.

Business owners and managers should be very careful and well informed before engaging in these activities, even though bribery in some form may be culturally accepted in certain countries outside the United States. Moreover, even if forms of bribery are legal (or illegal, but the law is not enforced) in some countries, such activities may not survive ethical scrutiny.

What Do You Think?

You would like to get your product into Country X to sell to Country X residents. Before you can do that, however, you need the approval of Country X's customs officials. They expect a direct payment from you to them to get approval. This would be an illegal bribe if it were made to a U.S. customs official, but suppose such a transaction is commonplace in Country X. Do you make the payment?

Extortion

The crime of **extortion** is basically threatening someone so that he or she will give you money or property in exchange for your not carrying out the threat. Sometimes, the word "blackmail" is used instead of extortion. Suppose, for example, a religious leader with a very good reputation in the community is secretly having an affair. The religious leader would be very embarrassed if his affair became public. Suppose further that the person with whom the religious leader is having an affair gets upset at the religious leader and threatens to disclose the affair to the public if the religious leader does not give the person $10,000 to remain quiet. This would be extortion.

Racketeer Influenced and Corrupt Organizations (RICO)

The Racketeer Influenced and Corrupt Organizations Act (RICO) is a federal statute that is very broad in its scope. Its purpose is to punish those who engage in "prohibited activities" and engage in interstate commerce. See Illustrative Federal Statute 10.2 on the following page.

Of course, certain definitions are important relating to this statute. "Racketeering" is a very broad term that includes many criminal activities such as bribery, obstruction of justice, mail fraud, counterfeiting, financial institution fraud, etc. A "pattern of racketeering" basically means the person has committed more than one act of racketeering within the past 10 years. An "unlawful debt" for purposes of the RICO statute is one that is related to gambling activity that is a violation of state or federal law.

Obstruction of Justice

As the term implies, a person is guilty of the crime of **obstruction of justice** when the person avoids,

18 U.S.C. §1956

(a) It shall be unlawful for any person who has received any income derived, directly or indirectly, from a pattern of racketeering activity or through collection of an unlawful debt . . . to use or invest, directly or indirectly, any part of such income, or the proceeds of such income, in acquisition of any interest in, or the establishment or operation of, any enterprise which is engaged in, or the activities of which affect, interstate or foreign commerce. . . .

(b) It shall be unlawful for any person through a pattern of racketeering activity or through collection of an unlawful debt to acquire or maintain, directly or indirectly, any interest in or control of any enterprise which is engaged in, or the activities of which affect, interstate or foreign commerce.

(c) It shall be unlawful for any person employed by or associated with any enterprise engaged in, or the activities of which affect, interstate or foreign commerce, to conduct or participate, directly or indirectly, in the conduct of such enterprise's affairs through a pattern of racketeering activity or collection of unlawful debt.

. . .

evades, prevents or obstructs an investigation by law enforcement agencies. In addition, if a person willfully withholds, misrepresents, conceals, covers up, destroys, mutilates, alters, or falsifies any documents, or otherwise impedes the administration of the law, such actions are also an obstruction of justice.

Computer Crimes

Advances in technology also bring with it advances in computer crimes. Computer hackers continue to

leolintang/Shutterstock.com

find new ways to obtain confidential information or destroy or corrupt computer software and electronic data. This type of crime is broadly known as "cybercrime."

To combat cybercrime, Congress enacted the **Computer Fraud and Abuse Act (CFAA)**. The CFAA is broadly written and encompasses many different types of criminal activity involving computers, including extortion, fraud, destruction of data, and the unauthorized access to private financial information, among others. Some of these crimes involve the creation and transmission of viruses, malware, worms, etc.

Defenses

A defendant can certainly assert that he or she was not the one who committed the act. Sometimes, there is no doubt that the defendant committed the act, but the defendant can put forth certain reasons, or **affirmative defenses**, explaining why he or she committed the act. Some of these defenses are set forth below.

- **Mistake of Fact**. For example, a student picks up a laptop that he thought was his, even though it was, in fact, someone else's laptop. The student's defense is that there was no intent to commit a crime; rather, it was just an honest mistake. Importantly, a mistake of fact is different from a mistake of law, however. Mistake of law is no defense. If you thought the speed limit was 50 mph when in reality it was 30 mph, your misunderstanding of the applicable law is generally not a defense. In other words, a person's ignorance of the law is no defense.

- **Duress**. For example, a carjacker threatens a driver to drive 100 mph, run every red light, and not stop for police officers. The driver does so in fear for his or her life because the carjacker has a gun. If the driver is charged with speeding, running red lights, endangering others, and other related crimes, the driver could assert the defense that he or she was under duress at the time.

- **Justifiable Use of Force**. This is commonly known as "self-defense." For example, if your life is being threatened, you can defend yourself in a reasonable manner so as to protect your life. Of course, your greatest right to self-defense is in your own home.

- **Infancy**. This defense typically only applies to minors who may be so young that they do not understand the consequences to their actions.

- **Intoxication**. Someone may not have the requisite intent to commit a crime at the time the act occurred due to being mentally impaired because drugs or alcohol prevented him or her from fully understanding what he or she was doing or the consequences.

- **Insanity**. Similar to intoxication, the insanity defense goes to whether the person had the state of mind to understand what he or she was doing or the consequences. Of course, the defendant argues in these cases that he or she was insane at the time the act occurred.

- **Necessity**. This defense is based on the defendant's reasoning that the act was necessary in order to prevent another, more serious crime from being committed.

- **Consent**. If the alleged victim consented (and was capable of consenting), then the defendant asserts that no crime was committed. Of course, this defense is frequently asserted in sexual assault cases.

QUESTIONS FOR REVIEW

1. What is a felony?

2. What is a misdemeanor?

3. What is the meaning of *mens rea*? *Actus reus*?

4. What is the difference between "direct" and "circumstantial" evidence?

5. What is the "exclusionary rule"?

6. Name at least five business-related crimes.

7. Explain the FCPA.

8. What do the letters RICO stand for?

9. What is a "pattern of racketeering"?

10. Name at least five affirmative defenses.

INTERNET ACTIVITIES

1. Find a summary of the crimes committed by Bernie Madoff.

   a. Discuss briefly the crimes Bernie Madoff committed.

   b. How did law enforcement ultimately learn of Bernie Madoff's crimes?

   c. How long was Bernie Madoff sentenced to prison?

2. Some common financial crimes involve "Ponzi" schemes.

   a. In general, explain how a Ponzi scheme operates.

   b. Where did "Ponzi scheme" get its name?

Part V

Tort Law

Chapter 11

Intentional Torts

A tort is a wrongful act that causes harm to another person or to another person's property. A tort is sometimes called a "civil wrong" or a "private wrong." A tort does not include a breach of a contract, however. Torts may also constitute crimes.

The law consists of three broad categories of torts: (1) intentional torts, (2) negligent torts, and (3) strict liability torts. This chapter will discuss intentional torts. Chapter 12 will cover negligent and strict liability torts.

Elements of an Intentional Tort

To be liable for an intentional tort, a person first must have the requisite *intent* to engage in a certain action. Second, the person's *actions* must have been the *cause* of harm or damage to another person or the other person's property. Following is a discussion of some common intentional torts.

Assault

At common law, the tort of **assault** occurs when a person intentionally places another person in apprehension of imminent harmful or offensive contact. An assault is similar to a threat—no actual contact occurs. For example, suppose Alan clenches his fist two feet away from Alyssa's face and says, "If you don't give me that cell phone, I'll clobber you!" Suppose Alyssa is reasonably apprehensive about her physical safety because of Alan's actions. Alan has committed the tort of assault.

Battery

A **battery** occurs when a person intentionally contacts another person in a harmful or offensive manner. Although assault and battery often occur together, they are, in fact, separate torts. In a battery, the victim need not be in apprehension or fear of imminent harm. Thus, under common law, if Sebastian pushes Brody from behind when Brody is not looking, Sebastian is likely liable for battery, but not assault.

False Imprisonment

False imprisonment occurs when a person is unlawfully confined and the person's freedom of movement is restrained. In the business context, this issue arises frequently in shoplifting cases. Many states have a "merchant's statute" that provides certain rights to a business owner when the business owner suspects a customer of shoplifting. Consider the following Florida statute (Illustrative State Statute 11.1).

Notice in the Florida statute that the merchant must have "probable cause" that a person committed

SpeedKingz/Shutterstock.com

the theft and the merchant can only detain the person in a reasonable manner for a reasonable length of time. The obvious challenge here is to determine what "reasonable" means. In short, business owners should be familiar with applicable state laws and train employees on how to handle suspected shoplifters so as to avoid claims of false imprisonment.

What Do You Think?

Suppose you are the manager of a supermarket. A supermarket employee notices a customer putting a bottle in her purse. The employee confronts the customer and asks the customer what she put in her purse. The customer says, "Nothing." The employee immediately reports to you his suspicion that the customer was shoplifting. You then approach the customer and ask her to open her purse so you can see if she, in fact, shoplifted a product as the employee reported to you. The customer refuses to open her purse and again reaffirms that she has not shoplifted anything. Should you detain the customer by use of force?

ILLUSTRATIVE STATE STATUTE 11.1

Fla. Stat. § 812.015

. . .

(3)(a) A law enforcement officer, a merchant, a farmer, or a transit agency's employee or agent, who has probable cause to believe that a retail theft, farm theft, a transit fare evasion, or trespass, or unlawful use or attempted use of any antishoplifting or inventory control device countermeasure, has been committed by a person and, in the case of retail or farm theft, that the property can be recovered by taking the offender into custody may, for the purpose of attempting to effect such recovery or for prosecution, take the offender into custody and detain the offender in a reasonable manner for a reasonable length of time. . . . In the event the merchant, merchant's employee, farmer, or a transit agency's employee or agent takes the person into custody, a law enforcement officer shall be called to the scene immediately after the person has been taken into custody.

(b) The activation of an antishoplifting or inventory control device as a result of a person exiting an establishment or a protected area within an establishment shall constitute reasonable cause for the detention of the person so exiting by the owner or operator of the establishment or by an agent or employee of the owner or operator, provided sufficient notice has been posted to advise the patrons that such a device is being utilized. Each such detention shall be made only in a reasonable manner and only for a reasonable period of time sufficient for any inquiry into the circumstances surrounding the activation of the device.

(c) The taking into custody and detention by a law enforcement officer, merchant, merchant's employee, farmer, or a transit agency's employee or agent, if done in compliance with all the requirements of this subsection, shall not render such law enforcement officer, merchant, merchant's employee, farmer, or a transit agency's employee or agent, criminally or civilly liable for false arrest, false imprisonment, or unlawful detention.

Intentional Infliction of Emotional Distress

Assume that Samantha is terrified of snakes. In fact, whenever a snake is shown on television, she closes her eyes and turns her head to avoid seeing the snake. Suppose all of Samantha's friends and neighbors are aware of her fear of snakes. Raja, Samantha's friend, one day places a snake in Samantha's car as a practical joke. When Samantha comes out of her apartment, she opens her car door, gets in, closes the door, and drives away. A few seconds later, she sees the snake slither out from under the front passenger seat. Of course, Samantha screams, her heart races, and she is terrified the snake may harm her. She manages to quickly pull over and get out of the car.

Six months later, Samantha still suffers from nightmares and anxiety due to the "snake incident." She also learned that her now ex-friend Raja was the prankster. Samantha continues to have anxiety whenever she gets into a car, and her work performance has suffered since the incident. Does Samantha have a legal case against Raja? If so, under what legal theory? Samantha likely has a legitimate claim for **intentional infliction of emotional distress** (sometimes called "mental" distress) against Raja.

As a general rule, in order to be liable for intentional infliction of emotional distress, a person's conduct must be "extreme and outrageous" given the circumstances. Moreover, the victim must suffer *severe* mental or emotional distress. A person's free speech rights under the First Amendment may provide a viable defense, however. Consider the well-publicized *Snyder v. Phelps* United States Supreme Court case (Illustrative Court Case 11.1) regarding the balance between the First Amendment's right to free speech and the tort of intentional infliction of emotional distress.

Notice that an important part of the Court's analysis was that the Westboro church's speech was a matter of public concern rather than private concern.

ILLUSTRATIVE COURT CASE 11.1

Snyder v. Phelps

Supreme Court of the United States

131 S. Ct. 1737 (2011)

[**Note:** For convenience of the reader, the following language is from the Syllabus of the case as provided by the U.S. Supreme Court Reporter of Decisions.]

For the past 20 years, the congregation of the Westboro Baptist Church has picketed military funerals to communicate its belief that God hates the United States for its tolerance of homosexuality, particularly in America's military. The church's picketing has also condemned the Catholic Church for scandals involving its clergy. Fred Phelps, who founded the church, and six Westboro Baptist parishioners (all relatives of Phelps) traveled to Maryland to picket the funeral of Marine Lance Corporal Matthew Snyder, who was killed in Iraq in the line of duty. The picketing took place on public land approximately 1,000 feet from the church where the funeral was held, in accordance with guidance from local law enforcement officers. The picketers peacefully displayed their signs—stating, e.g., "Thank God for Dead Soldiers," "Fags Doom Nations," "America is Doomed," "Priests Rape Boys," and "You're Going to Hell"—for about 30 minutes before the funeral began. Matthew Snyder's father (Snyder), petitioner here, saw the tops of the picketers' signs when driving to the funeral, but did not learn what was written on the signs until watching a news broadcast later that night.

(Continued)

Snyder filed a[n] . . . action against Phelps, his daughters—who participated in the picketing—and the church (collectively Westboro) alleging, as relevant here, state tort claims of intentional infliction of emotional distress. . . . A jury held Westboro liable for millions of dollars in compensatory and punitive damages. Westboro challenged the verdict as grossly excessive and sought judgment as a matter of law on the ground that the First Amendment fully protected its speech. The District Court reduced the punitive damages award, but left the verdict otherwise intact. The Fourth Circuit reversed, concluding that Westboro's statements were entitled to First Amendment protection because those statements were on matters of public concern, were not provably false, and were expressed solely through hyperbolic rhetoric.

Held:

The First Amendment shields Westboro from tort liability for its picketing in this case.

(a) The Free Speech Clause of the First Amendment can serve as a defense in state tort suits, including suits for intentional infliction of emotional distress. . . . Whether the First Amendment prohibits holding Westboro liable for its speech in this case turns largely on whether that speech is of public or private concern, as determined by all the circumstances of the case. . . . Although the boundaries of what constitutes speech on matters of public concern are not well defined, this Court has said that speech is of public concern when it can "be fairly considered as relating to any matter of political, social, or other concern to the community," or when it "is a subject of general interest and of value and concern to the public." [Citations omitted.]

To determine whether speech is of public or private concern, this Court must independently examine the "content, form, and context," of the speech "as revealed by the whole record." [Citations omitted.] . . .

The "content" of Westboro's signs plainly relates to public, rather than private, matters. The placards highlighted issues of public import—the political and moral conduct of the United States and its citizens, the fate of the Nation, homosexuality in the military, and scandals involving the Catholic clergy—and Westboro conveyed its views on those issues in a manner designed to reach as broad a public audience as possible. Even if a few of the signs were viewed as containing messages related to a particular individual, that would not change the fact that the dominant theme of Westboro's demonstration spoke to broader public issues.

The "context" of the speech—its connection with Matthew Snyder's funeral—cannot by itself transform the nature of Westboro's speech. The signs reflected Westboro's condemnation of much in modern society. . . .

The "special protection" afforded to what Westboro said, in the whole context of how and where it chose to say it, cannot be overcome by a jury finding that the picketing was "outrageous" for purposes of applying the state law tort of intentional infliction of emotional distress. That would pose too great a danger that the jury would punish Westboro for its views on matters of public concern. For all these reasons, the jury verdict imposing tort liability on Westboro for intentional infliction of emotional distress must be set aside.

. . .

(d) Westboro addressed matters of public import on public property, in a peaceful manner, in full compliance with the guidance of local officials. It did not disrupt [the] funeral, and its choice to picket at that time and place did not alter the nature of its speech. Because this Nation has chosen to protect even hurtful speech on public issues to ensure that public debate is not stifled, Westboro must be shielded from tort liability for its picketing in this case.

In the business context, given the high "extreme and outrageous" standard, employees typically have a difficult time prevailing on claims against their employers for intentional infliction of emotional distress.

Trespass

Although many people think of **trespassing** primarily as a crime, trespassing is also a tort. As long as a person actually enters onto the real property of another and has the intent to enter onto the property without permission or other legal justification, trespassing occurs. "Entering" onto someone's real property is interpreted rather broadly. For example, throwing a rock onto someone's land could constitute trespassing. Mistakenly entering onto someone else's land is not a defense to trespassing.

In addition to trespassing with respect to real property, a person can also trespass against another person's *personal* property. Suppose your friend hides a textbook from you for a week, which deprives you of preparing for class and perhaps studying for an exam. Your friend has committed a trespass. This is sometimes called "trespass to

chattel" (*i.e.*, personal property). A severe trespass to chattel may constitute the tort of "conversion," and the trespasser must pay damages for the value of the personal property. If your friend hides your book for a week and then loses it, your friend has likely committed the tort of conversion. In other words, the trespass to the personal property is significant enough that the trespasser may need to pay damages to you for the full amount of the personal property.

A person may assert some defenses to a claim of trespassing. Of course, one defense may be that the defendant had permission to enter or take possession of the property. Another defense may be that the person entered the property to come to the aid of another person who was in danger.

Defamation

In some instances a person may say something about another person that is completely untrue and harms the other person's reputation. The law recognizes that a person's reputation has value, and a person can recover damages for another person's defamatory statements. In short, **defamation** occurs if a person makes a statement about a second person that is "published" (orally or in writing) to at least one third person and the statement injures the reputation of the second person. A defamatory statement is one that usually addresses the honesty, virtue, or integrity of the person about whom the comments were made. The defamatory statement typically must be an assertion of fact and not merely an opinion. For example, suppose Person A made a statement to Person B asserting as a fact that Person C had been convicted of a serious crime. If, in fact, this statement was untrue, the statement likely would constitute defamation. On the other hand, if Person A merely said that Person C is a "jerk," it is rather clear that such a statement is merely an opinion of Person A.

Defamation can be oral or written. If oral, this is called **slander**. If written, it is called **libel**. The tort of defamation can also be committed through plays, dramas, pictures, etc., as well. Defamation is more difficult to prove if the person about

Steve Design/Shutterstock.com

whom the statement was made is a **public figure** such as a celebrity or politician. Even if the statement is untrue about the public figure, the public figure must show that the defendant had "actual malice" in making the statement. "Actual malice" basically means that the person making the statement knew the statement was false (or at least acted with reckless disregard of the truth) but nevertheless intentionally published the defamatory statement.

The most common defense to defamation is that the statement was the truth. If the statement is, in fact, true, then the statement is not defamatory.

Invasion of Right to Privacy

The concept of a person's right to privacy is very broad. When a person's right to privacy has been violated is sometimes not very clear. A few subcategories of torts relating to invasion of right to privacy have developed over time. These are:

- **Intrusion** into the plaintiff's private affairs;
- **Appropriation** of the plaintiff's name or image for the defendant's personal commercial gain;
- Public disclosure of facts showing plaintiff in a **false light**; and
- Public disclosure of **private facts**

Remember that invasion of privacy most likely will not occur if you are at a public event or in a public place (*e.g.*, football game, concert, beach, etc.). Moreover, as with defamation, it is more difficult for a public figure to show that someone has invaded his or her right to privacy. Detailed coverage of each of these torts relating to invasion of

right to privacy is beyond the scope of our discussion here.

Fraud

Fraud exists when a person intentionally misrepresents a material fact to another person and the other person justifiably relies on the misrepresentation and suffers damages as a result. Fraud can occur in many different contexts, but a common example is falsely representing one's financial position to a lender. Other fraudulent activities often occur with respect to investment schemes. Victims of fraudulent activity often claim the defendant was also in breach of contract.

Although a person has no general duty to voluntarily disclose all facts relevant to a potential transaction, fraud can sometimes occur if a material fact is intentionally concealed.

Interference with Business Relations

Competition is at the heart of the free-market system. Nevertheless, when competition unfairly interferes with business relations of another enterprise, a tort may occur. The plaintiff must show, however, that the actions of the defendant went beyond mere competition. Consider the Utah Supreme Court case (Illustrative Court Case 11.2) that follows as an example.

Other torts related to interference with business relations are, for example, disparagement of products (*e.g.*, false statements about product title or quality) and interference with contractual relations (*e.g.*, directly inducing a party to breach an existing contract).

Eldridge v. Johndrow

Utah Supreme Court

345 P.3d 553 (2015)

. . .

INTRODUCTION

This appeal concerns claims for tortious interference with economic relations by Joseph and Lindsey Eldridge against David Johndrow. Johndrow moved for summary judgment, and the district court partially granted his motion, concluding there was no evidence that he had interfered with the Eldridges' economic relations through an improper means. But the court denied summary judgment for the Eldridges' claims based on the allegation that Johndrow had acted with an improper purpose.

. . .

BACKGROUND

Appellees Joseph and Lindsey Eldridge are the owners and operators of Harrison Companies, LLC, and Harrison Companies Property Management, LLC. Through these limited liability companies, the Eldridges manage residential property and provide various other services for wealthy homeowners in Summit County. Because providing these services means taking responsibility for clients' homes, the Eldridges' success depends a great deal on their reputation.

Appellant David Johndrow is a former friend and client of the Eldridges who used to recommend their services to his friends and other associates in the area. But the friendship lasted only a year. Lindsey Eldridge accused Mr. Johndrow of attacking her at a restaurant, and Mr. Johndrow accused the Eldridges of spreading false rumors and stealing his mobile phone. The once amicable relationship gave way to threats of legal action.

The action Johndrow actually took, however, did not involve a lawsuit. Instead, he "turned [the matter] over" to an "investigative team," which discovered various embarrassing facts about the Eldridges; liens, a foreclosure, an old felony conviction, and unflattering news reports from before they moved to Utah. Mr. Johndrow threatened that if the Eldridges refused to retract their accusations and compensate him for the allegedly stolen phone, he would have to protect his "credibility" by revealing what he had found to the people to whom he had recommended the Eldridges. When the Eldridges did not accede to his demands, he emailed embarrassing information to "at least nine" of the Eldridges' institutional clients and communicated it verbally to a number of their individual clients.

The Eldridges sued, asserting several theories of liability: tortious interference with economic relations, tortious interference with prospective economic relations, defamation, false light, and intentional infliction of emotional distress. The tortious interference theories each rested on two separate allegations: first, that by defaming the Eldridges, Mr. Johndrow had interfered with their economic relations through an improper means; and second, that because Mr. Johndrow's only goal was to hurt the Eldridges' business, he had interfered with their economic relations in pursuit of an improper purpose.

After preliminary discovery, [the court granted summary judgment in favor of Mr. Johndrow by rejecting the Eldridges' claims of intentional infliction of emotional distress and false light.]

. . .

(Continued)

. . .

ANALYSIS

The Eldridges' remaining tortious interference claims depend on the allegation that Mr. Johndrow interfered with their economic relations for an improper purpose. . . .

For reasons we articulate below, . . . , we hold that a claim for tortious interference may only succeed where the defendant has employed an improper means.

. . .

If we were convinced that the improper-purpose doctrine served important public purposes, we would uphold it despite its weak basis in precedent. But our conviction is the opposite: improper purpose, in the absence of any improper means, should not be a basis for tortious interference liability.

As our decisions have recognized, determining the predominant purpose behind a defendant's actions raises significant evidentiary problems. Because this inquiry is necessarily fact-intensive, appellate review has been limited, and little case law has developed to guide courts' and juries' work. The improper-purpose doctrine thus requires trial courts and juries to make decisions that are effectively without guidance.

This vagueness does more than lead to unpredictable verdicts. It also fails to give parties adequate notice of their rights and duties. If improper-purpose liability became commonplace, it would have a chilling effect on legitimate, socially beneficial competitive practices. Worse, it would chill speech, discouraging the free spread of information and opinion.

For these reasons, among others, other states have increasingly limited or rejected improper-purpose liability. . . . With both contemporary authority and our own reasoning opposed to improper-purpose liability, we conclude that it should be rejected.

. . .

Again, the trend on this point is not irresistible. But we are persuaded that our holding accords with the reasoned judgment of other jurisdictions that have considered the question.

. . . .

We therefore conclude that the improper-purpose doctrine has not worked well in practice, and that "more good than harm will come by departing from precedent." [Citation omitted.] It should therefore be abandoned.

. . .

CONCLUSION

For the foregoing reasons, we conclude that in the absence of any improper means, an improper purpose is not grounds for tortious interference liability. . . . In order to win a tortious interference claim under Utah law, a plaintiff must now prove "(1) that the defendant intentionally interfered with the plaintiff's existing or potential economic relations, (2) . . . by improper means, (3) causing injury to the plaintiff." [Citation omitted.]

The Eldridges' tortious interference claims fail the second prong of this test: they have failed to produce evidence of an improper means. The district court's denial of summary judgment on the tortious interference claims is therefore reversed, and the matter is remanded for further action consistent with this opinion.

QUESTIONS FOR DISCUSSION

1. What is a tort?

2. What are the elements of an intentional tort?

3. What is the distinction between the tort of assault and the tort of battery?

4. When does false imprisonment occur?

5. In order for a plaintiff to recover damages for the tort of intentional infliction of mental distress, the defendant's actions must be _____ and _____.

6. What is the tort of "trespass to chattel"?

7. What is "conversion"?

8. What is libel? Slander?

9. In order for a public figure to prevail for a claim of defamation, the public figure must show that the defendant acted with "_____" when publishing the defamatory statement.

10. What are the four generally accepted subcategories of the tort of invasion of privacy?

11. Define fraud.

12. Summarize the *Snyder v. Phelps* case.

13. Summarize the *Eldridge v. Johndrow* case.

INTERNET ACTIVITIES

1. Conduct a search to find a defamation case that has arisen because of "tweets" on the popular social network "Twitter." Summarize the situation and identify your source website.

2. Find the Ninth Circuit Court of Appeals case *White v. Samsung Electronics America, Inc.*, 971 F.2d 1395 (1992).

   a. What celebrity filed this lawsuit?

   b. Why did the celebrity file the lawsuit?

   c. Discuss the court's analysis and conclusion.

Chapter 12

Negligent and Strict Liability Torts

Negligent Torts

Remember from Chapter 11 that a "tort" is a civil wrong. Sometimes, unintentional events occur that cause harm to someone else. For example, a slip and fall at a grocery store is typically accidental and not an event that the business owner intended to cause. Nevertheless, if you are injured because of someone else's negligence, should you be able to recover the damages you suffered even though they did not *intend* to harm you?

Elements of Negligence

In order for a plaintiff to prevail in a negligence case, the plaintiff must show that the elements of a negligent tort exist. Those elements are that (1) the defendant had a **duty of care** toward the plaintiff, (2) the defendant **breached** the duty of care, (3) the defendant's actions were the **cause** of the plaintiff's injury, and (4) the plaintiff suffered **damages**. We will discuss each of these elements in the following sections.

Duty of Care

Suppose you are an excellent skier or snowboarder and that you are going down a steep slope enjoying your time away from studying. Assume further that toward the end of the run, the slope levels out and there are many beginners struggling to ski without falling down. As you approach the beginners, do you have a legal obligation to ski around them even if they are directly in your path?

When we engage in activities, the general standard of care is that we must act as a "reasonable person" would act under the circumstances. Failure to do so could cause accidents and a subsequent claim of negligence against us. The standard of care could vary, however, depending upon the relationship of the parties. For example, a physician performing a surgery is generally held to the level of skill and knowledge of other physicians performing surgeries. Other relationships where the duty of care standard may vary are landlord-tenant, school-student, employer-employee, common carrier-customer, innkeeper-guest, and homeowner-guest. A business owner obviously has a duty of care to the business owner's customers (*i.e.*, **"invitees"**) that come on the business premises. Generally, the business owner should use reasonable and ordinary care in maintaining the premises in a safe condition and should warn invitees of any risks to the invitees that may not be obvious. The owner should also inspect the premises to find and remove any potential hidden dangers that may potentially harm invitees.

With regard to a person's obligation to help another person, the law generally imposes no duty

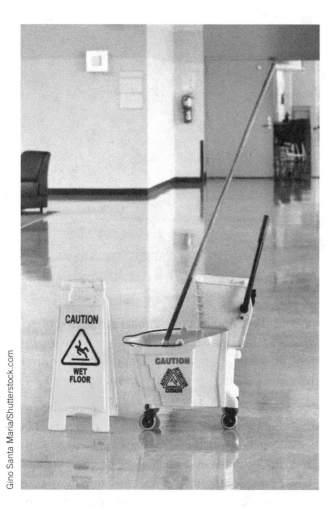

Gino Santa Maria/Shutterstock.com

to affirmatively act for the benefit of the other person. For example, suppose Jessica notices two individuals engaging in a fist fight. Does Jessica have a legal obligation to stop it? Although Jessica

has no legal obligation to get involved, if she does get involved she has a duty to act reasonably. Some states have **Good Samaritan** laws, which basically provide that doctors, nurses, and other professionals who voluntarily aid someone in an emergency situation are protected from ordinary negligence claims by the injured person. The injured person, however, may prevail if the medically trained volunteer was "grossly" negligent. Good Samaritan laws may also protect other people who may try to assist a person in danger.

Breach of Duty of Care

Once the plaintiff establishes that a defendant had a duty of care toward the plaintiff, the plaintiff must show that the defendant breached that duty. In some cases, it may be easy to show the breach of a duty of care. For example, if someone throws a bowling ball out of his or her car window onto a busy freeway, that action would likely be considered unreasonable and, consequently, a breach of the duty of care the person had to other drivers. One area of frequent litigation involves "slip and fall" cases. If someone slips and falls in a business establishment, is the owner of the establishment automatically liable to the plaintiff? State laws vary, but consider the following state statute from Florida (Illustrative State Statute 12.1).

In some situations, a plaintiff can show that the defendant breached his or duty of care to the plaintiff because the defendant violated a statute or ordinance. For example, suppose that a local ordinance establishes a 20 - m.p.h speed limit in a school zone. Failing to comply with this ordinance (*e.g.*, by speeding) would be evidence of a defendant's breach of his or her duty of care. The fact that a breach of duty can be shown by failure to comply with a statute or ordinance is called **negligence per se**.

Causation

Even if the plaintiff can show that the defendant had a duty of care to the plaintiff and the defendant did, in fact, breach that duty, the plaintiff must still show that the defendant *caused* the injury. The element of causation is typically broken down into two parts: (1) **cause-in-fact**, and (2) **proximate cause**. Both of these parts of causation must exist for a defendant to be considered the cause of plaintiff's injury.

Cause-in-Fact

But for the defendant's act would the accident have happened? For example, suppose Horton visits a bar on a Friday night. He gets out of his car and goes into the bar, but accidentally leaves his keys in the car's ignition and does not lock the car's doors. A stranger, Thad, walks out of the bar, notices the keys in Horton's car, and decides to go for a joy ride in Horton's car. While on the joy ride, Thad runs a stop sign and injures Alicyn, the driver of another car. Alicyn then sues both Thad and Horton. Alicyn's negligence case against Thad seems pretty clear. But is *Horton* liable to Alicyn for her injuries because of his negligence? Alicyn will try to show that "but for" Horton's leaving his keys in the car, the accident would not have happened. Nevertheless, for Alicyn to prevail against Horton, she would have to show that he was the "proximate cause" of her injury as well.

Proximate Cause

In determining whether a defendant was the proximate cause of the plaintiff's injury, a jury will look to determine if the harm to the plaintiff was *foreseeable*. Moreover, was there a *superseding cause* to the plaintiff's injury? To continue the example, Horton, of course, will raise the defense that Thad was the superseding cause to Alicyn's injury and that Alicyn was not a foreseeable plaintiff to Horton just because he left his keys in the car. Horton's negligence liability will likely be limited in this case because of the intervening actions of Thad, a third party.

ILLUSTRATIVE COURT CASE 12.1

Palsgraf v. Long Island Railroad Co 162 N.E. 99 (1928)

Court of Appeals of New York

[**Note:** For convenience of the reader, the following language is from the Syllabus of the court.]

A man carrying a package jumped aboard a car of a moving train and, seeming unsteady as if about to fall, a guard on the car reached forward to help him in and another guard on the platform pushed him from behind, during which the package was dislodged and falling upon the rails exploded, causing injuries to plaintiff, an intending passenger, who stood on the platform many feet away. There was nothing in the appearance of the package to give notice that it contained explosives. In an action by the intending passenger [Palsgraf] against the railroad company to recover for such injuries, the complaint should be dismissed. Negligence is not actionable unless it involves the invasion of a legally protected interest, the violation of a right, and the conduct of the defendant's guards, if a wrong in relation to the holder of the package, was not a wrong in its relation to the plaintiff standing many feet away.

A short excerpt from one of the most famous cases in the negligence area of tort law is presented in Illustrative Court Case 12.1.

Notice that the court in the *Palsgraf* case concluded that even if the railroad company's guards were negligent with regard to the person who held the package, the actions of the railroad's guards were not the proximate cause of the plaintiff's injuries.

A special legal doctrine that may apply in some cases is called **res ipsa loquitur**. This term, which basically means "the facts speak for themselves" is used in situations where the defendant is presumed negligent because it is obvious the accident would not have occurred without someone's negligence. For example, if a person walking on a sidewalk next to an office building is suddenly struck in the head by a falling coffeemaker, clearly someone in the office building was, at a minimum, negligent.

Damages

A plaintiff may be able to show that a defendant breached a duty of care and caused an event to occur, but to receive an award from a judge or jury, the plaintiff must show that damage has occurred to the plaintiff's person or property. For example, a plaintiff could be awarded damages for physical injury, pain and suffering, medical expenses, cost to repair or replace property, etc. Nevertheless, a plaintiff does have a duty to mitigate damages. This means, for example, a plaintiff should take reasonable steps to avoid aggravating an injury or allowing further damage to property to occur.

Defenses

One defense a defendant may raise is that there was a superseding cause to the plaintiff's injuries. Recall the example earlier in this chapter where Horton left his keys in the car, and a third-party stole the car and caused an accident. Horton could raise the "superseding cause" defense. Two other common defenses a defendant may assert are **comparative negligence** and **assumption of risk**.

Comparative Negligence

Suppose Marty is riding his bicycle outside the designated bike lane and weaving in and out of traffic on a busy street. Assume also that a driver of a car does not look into his rearview mirror nor does he properly signal that he is changing lanes. Marty collides into the car. Who is at fault for the accident? Are both partially at fault?

In situations where two or more parties may be at fault, the comparative negligence concept is applicable. Typically, a jury (or a judge if it is not a jury trial) will consider all the facts and can conclude that, for example, the defendant is 70% at fault and the plaintiff is 30% at fault. Thus, the total damages awarded to the plaintiff would be 70% of what would otherwise be awarded. Clearly, it is in the best interest of the defendant to raise this defense if there is any evidence that the plaintiff also engaged in negligent behavior.

Assumption of Risk

A defendant may also assert a defense that the plaintiff voluntarily assumed the risk of injury. For example, suppose you attend a baseball game with a friend, and you have really good seats along the third base line close to the dugout. During the game, a batter hits a hard line-drive foul ball that hits you and causes you injuries. If you sue the baseball team, the stadium owners, and/or the baseball player, what is the likely result? The defendant(s) would likely prevail with the argument that you assumed the risk of getting hit by a baseball by sitting that close to the field along the third base line. In short, a person

Jason Stitt/Shutterstock.com

"assumes the risk" if the person voluntarily participates in the activity and knows (or should know) the risk inherent in participating in the activity.

Strict Liability Torts

In addition to intentional torts and negligent torts, a third category is **strict liability** torts. Suppose you purchase an iron from a commercial retail store. The next morning when you are getting ready for work, you get out the iron to press your clothes. A few minutes after you plug in the iron, you properly pick up the iron by the handle, but the handle is so hot that it burns your hand. Obviously, such an injury should not occur. You could sue the retail store and manufacturer for your damages under the tort law of strict liability. In short, even though a

---

ILLUSTRATIVE COURT CASE 12.2

Pannu v. Land Rover North America, Inc. 191 Cal. App. 1298 (2011)

California Court of Appeals

[**Note:** For convenience of the reader, the following language is from the California Official Reports Summary.]

Plaintiff suffered a severe spinal injury, resulting in quadriplegia, when his sport utility vehicle rolled over following a chain of collisions. Plaintiff sued the vehicle's manufacturer alleging claims, among others, for strict liability based on defective design. Following a bench trial, the superior court entered a judgment in the amount of $21,654,000 in favor of plaintiff.

The Court of Appeal affirmed the judgment. The court concluded that the trial court's finding of strict liability under the risk-benefit test was amply supported by the record and fully justified the judgment in favor of plaintiff. With respect to stability design, plaintiff established that a comparable production vehicle would tip under evasive steering maneuvers and that slight modifications to the track width and center of gravity of the vehicle dramatically improved its rollover resistance. Similarly, modest enhancement of the roof support of the production vehicle yielded substantial gains in roof strength. Plaintiff proved these improvements could be achieved at a modest cost. The manufacturer did not rebut any of these showings. Moreover, the manufacturer's senior engineer acknowledged these modifications were available and could have been made at the time plaintiff's vehicle was manufactured. Substantial evidence supported the trial court's failure to warn finding. Rather than warn of the dangers of rollover or roof crush, the vehicle's window sticker informed plaintiff the vehicle had a steel inner body cage and a steel roof panel, among other things, leading him to believe the vehicle was not defectively designed. Substantial evidence also supported the award of economic damages. Plaintiff, who owned two convenience stores and two sandwich shops, introduced compelling evidence of the devastating impact of his injury on his ability to work and the length of time he was likely to be able to work. The ward of economic damages was based not on his stores' lost profits but on the unrebutted testimony of a vocational expert assessing plaintiff's lost earning capacity as a franchise owner/vice-president.

person or manufacturer exercises utmost care, some products may cause injury or some activities may be inherently ultrahazardous so as to cause liability to a defendant.

Product Liability

When a consumer is injured by a product sold by a commercial seller, the consumer has a number of potential arguments available against the seller and/or manufacturer of the product. The product may have a *design* defect, a *manufacturing* defect, or *inadequate warnings*. Any one of these arguments may be sufficient to prevail on a products liability claim. Consider the case from the California Court of Appeals on the previous page in which a plaintiff was severely injured when his SUV rolled over (Illustrative Court Case 12.2).

Whether a manufacturer failed to provide adequate warnings of potential harm that a product could cause is also a significant area of products liability. For example, many court cases address the issue of the adequacy of warnings on trampolines (*e.g.*, flips, multiple people jumping at once), swimming pools (*e.g.*, diving into shallow water, etc.), and other products.

Ultrahazardous Activities

Engaging in ultrahazardous activities can sometimes cause the tort of strict liability. For example, suppose your business engages in demolishing buildings in urban areas. No matter your using utmost care, if an injury occurs during the demolition, you will likely be subject to a strict liability claim. Also, suppose your neighbor has a wild tiger as a pet. Even if your neighbor uses utmost care to contain the animal, if the animal causes harm to someone else, your neighbor will likely be held liable under the theory of strict liability.

Defenses

Similar to the defenses in negligent torts, a defendant in a strict liability case may argue that the plaintiff was comparatively negligent and/or assumed the risk of injury. Related to these defenses is the argument that the plaintiff *misused* the product. Of course, with respect to warnings, the defendant can argue that the warnings of the risks were adequate and effective and that the plaintiff still voluntarily assumed the inherent risks.

QUESTIONS FOR REVIEW

1. What are the elements of negligence?
2. What is the general standard of care when evaluating a defendant's "duty of care"?
3. What is a Good Samaritan law?
4. Explain a business owner's general duty of care to invitees.
5. Explain the distinction between "cause-in-fact" and "proximate cause."
6. What is negligence per se? Res ipsa loquitur?
7. Name two defenses to a negligence claim.
8. Explain what a strict liability tort is.
9. Summarize the *Palsgraf v. Long Island Railroad* case.
10. Summarize the *Pannu v. Land Rover* case.

INTERNET ACTIVITIES

1. Conduct a search regarding your state's dog bite laws. Discuss whether a dog owner is automatically liable for injuries caused by the dog.
2. Conduct a search regarding your state's slip-and-fall laws. Discuss the obligations of business owners to invitees.

Part VI

Property Law

Chapter 13

Real Property

The right to own property is of significant importance in the United States. Property is generally classified into one of three categories: real property, personal property, and intellectual property. This chapter will focus on real property, while Chapters 14 and 15 will discuss personal property and intellectual property respectively.

Real property (also sometimes called **real estate** or **realty**) is land and improvements made on the land, such as buildings and roads. Real property also includes, generally, the rights to airspace above the land as well as water, minerals, and other subsurface rights.

Real property also includes **fixtures**. A fixture is originally personal property that is then attached in a permanent manner to real property. An example of a fixture would be a fireplace that is installed in a home. Compare this to a washer and dryer, which typically retain the status of personal property because they are movable and not affixed to the real property. In a landlord-tenant relationship, with some exceptions (*e.g.*, business fixtures), the tenant must usually leave fixtures behind when the tenant vacates the premises.

The law allows the ownership rights in real property to be held by one person or by many persons. Real property interests include the right to sell, lease, possess, subdivide, mine, gift, etc. These rights in real property can be thought of as a *bundle* of rights. Some or all of these rights can be transferred. For example, if you live in an apartment, the landlord has transferred to you the right to *possess*

Phillip Lange/Shutterstock.com

the property, but the landlord still *owns* the property. The next section discusses the major types of ownership interests a person can have in real estate.

Ownership Interests

Four of the most common ownership interests in real property are: (1) ownership in fee simple, (2) a life estate, (3) an easement, and (4) a leasehold estate.

Fee Simple

If a person owns all the bundle of rights, *e.g.*, right to sell, possess, use, lease, subdivide, mine, etc., in an unrestricted manner (other than zoning and other applicable laws), the person is said to own the real property in **fee simple absolute**. If the owner is restricted from exercising one or more of the bundle of rights because the prior owner placed such a restriction when the property was transferred, the current owner is said to have a **fee**

> ### EXAMPLE 13.1
>
> Suppose Omar transfers his fee simple owner-ship interest to Vanessa, but in the transfer document, Omar states the following:
>
> "I, Omar, hereby transfer all my right, title, and interest in this real property (described in detail) to Vanessa, but if Vanessa builds a liquor store on it, then the property shall revert to me or, if I am not alive, to my heirs."
>
> This example illustrates the fee simple defea-sible interest that Vanessa has. If she builds a liquor store on the property, she will lose her ownership interest in the property. Omar has a reversionary interest.

simple defeasible interest in the property, and the prior owner is said to have a **reversionary interest** (see Example 13.1).

A **deed** is the legal instrument used to transfer ownership of real property. A few of the different types of deeds are discussed later in this chapter.

Life Estate

A person can enjoy ownership of property during his life (or during the life of another person), but then have no control over where the property goes upon death. This ownership interest is called a **life estate** (see Example 13.2).

> ### EXAMPLE 13.2
>
> Suppose Omar wants his friend Earl to be able to live on his property while Earl is alive, but does not want Earl to be able to control where the property goes when Earl dies. Omar could include in the deed when transferring the property:
>
> "I, Omar, hereby transfer all my right, title, and interest in this real property to Earl for his life, then to me or, if I am not alive, to my heirs."
>
> In this example, Earl would have a life estate interest in the property, and Omar and his heirs would have a reversionary interest in the property.

If in Example 13.2 the property were to go to someone other than Omar or his heirs after Earl's life estate, the other person would be said to have a **remainder interest** in the property, rather than a reversionary interest.

Easements

An **easement** is a legal interest that runs with the land and is the legal right to use or cross over someone else's real property. Easements can take several forms. For example, an *express* easement arises when the parties specifically spell out the rights of one party to use or cross over the other person's property. An easement of *necessity* is another type of easement. Suppose someone owns property with no access to the property except by crossing over someone else's property. A judge may grant an easement of necessity to provide access to this property. Other forms of easements include easements by implication and easements by prescription, but a detailed explanation of these types of easements is beyond the scope of our discussion here.

If you have the legal right to go onto property and extract or remove something from the prop-erty, then you are said to have a **profits** interest in the property. This applies to rights to oil, coal, gas, timber, etc.

Suppose you have a ticket to a concert at a local arena. Further assume that the arena is privately owned. Do you have an easement to go to the arena (landowner's property) to attend the concert? Technically, what you have is not an easement, but a **license**. A license differs somewhat from an easement in that a license is typically temporary permission by the land-owner to come onto his or her property for a specific event or short-term project. Unlike an easement, a license is not a right in the land itself. For example, you would not be able to go to the next concert unless you had another ticket (*i.e.*, a license) to attend that specific concert. Owners of parking lots also grant you a license when you park your car there.

Leasehold Estate

Another right that a landowner has in his or her bundle of rights in real property is the right to lease the property. When the landowner does this, the landowner is then referred to as the **landlord** (or **lessor**) and the person leasing the property is referred to as the **tenant** (or **lessee**). The tenant has a **leasehold estate**.

The tenant typically has the right to occupy the premises for a *definite term*, such as six months or one year. Sometimes, a lease is structured in such a way that it exists from "month-to-month" or "year-to-year." This type of arrangement is called a **periodic tenancy**. Typically, the landlord or tenant must give the other sufficient notice when one of them wants to terminate the periodic tenancy. A **tenancy at will** is a lease arrangement that either the landlord or tenant can terminate anytime. If the tenant does not vacate the premises when the lease is over and occupies the property without the landlord's permission, the situation is called a **tenancy at sufferance**. Of course, in this situation, the landlord can evict the tenant.

Landlord-Tenant Relationships

In General

Many states have adopted the **Uniform Residential Landlord and Tenant Act** to govern landlord-tenant relationships. As the name implies, this Act governs rental properties used as residences. Importantly, this Act does not cover commercial leases, hotel or motel rooms, or mobile home parks. Such relationships are governed by other specific state laws. Of course, each state legislature is at liberty to modify landlord-tenant laws as it sees fit. Both landlords and tenants have specific rights and obligations. Those rights and obligations are discussed next.

Tenant's General Rights and Obligations

Tenants have the right to occupy, use, and enjoy the premises as contemplated in the lease agreement and that no third party will disturb the tenant or claim that the tenant's possession is wrongful. This right is called the right of **quiet enjoyment**. Of course, if a tenant breaches the lease agreement, a landlord may evict the tenant. An eviction may be an actual eviction or a "constructive" eviction. A constructive eviction could occur, for example, where the tenant is forced to move out because the landlord refuses to fix constantly ringing fire alarms or for other reasons that may make the property uninhabitable.

The tenant's primary obligation, of course, is to pay rent to the landlord for the period of the lease. Another obligation is to refrain from damaging the premises beyond normal wear and tear.

Andy Dean Photography/ Shutterstock.com

Landlord's Rights and Obligations

A landlord has the right to receive rents from the tenant. In return, the landlord is obligated to provide necessary repairs in common areas and to keep the property in livable condition (for residential leases). The law typically imposes **an implied warranty of habitability** upon the landlord in residential leases. In short, this means that adequate heat, water, electricity, weatherproofing, etc., is provided to maintain the property in habitable condition. The landlord also has an obligation to maintain the property adequately so that injury to tenants and third persons do not occur due to the landlord's negligence. Moreover, under federal law, the landlord cannot discriminate against tenants on the basis of race, color, gender, national origin, disability, religion, etc.

Remember that specific provisions in a lease between the landlord and tenant may in some situations alter the general rights and obligations discussed here.

Transfer of Interests in a Lease

What happens if a landlord sells the property when it is currently being leased? Additionally, what happens if the tenant wants to transfer his or her rights in the lease to someone else?

Landlord's Transfer Rights

A landlord typically has the right to sell or otherwise transfer the underlying property to another owner. The new owner would then be entitled to the rents from the tenant. In this situation the landlord is said to have **assigned** his rights in the lease. The new landlord then has the obligations to the tenant that the prior landlord had.

Tenant's Transfer Rights

A tenant's rights under the lease can be transferred also, unless the lease agreement restricts the exercise of these rights. If a tenant transfers all of his or her rights under the lease to someone else, the tenant is said to have assigned the rights. If the tenant transfers less than all of his or her rights, then the tenant is said to have **subleased** the property. Suppose, for example, you sign a lease for one year starting on January 1 and ending on December 31. You will be out of town the entire summer (three months) and would like to allow someone to lease the property for the months that you are gone so that you don't bear the full rent burden during that time. You find someone to rent the property for three months and pay rent equal to the rent you pay the landlord. This would be a sublease. Many lease contracts, however, prevent subleasing, so a tenant should double-check the specifics of the lease before attempting to sublease.

Limitations on Property Rights

One of the fundamental rights in the United States is the right to own property. Some people can get very passionate about their property rights when someone else infringes upon those rights or the government tries to restrict the activities that can be conducted on the property. Nevertheless, the government can place some restrictions on the use of property. Of course, an individual can also voluntarily agree to refrain from conducting certain activities on their property. The following paragraphs briefly discuss restrictions on ownership and use of property.

Zoning

All cities and counties have zoning ordinances. These ordinances govern, for example, where industrial, commercial, and residential areas (or "zones") are allowed within the city or county boundaries. Most cities, for example, likely have an ordinance that prohibits adult-oriented businesses from locating within a certain distance from a school. Additionally, restrictions may exist on a property owner's right to raise certain animals in a residential area. If a property owner desires to engage in an activity that would otherwise run afoul of a zoning ordinance, the property owner could apply for a **conditional use permit** or a **variance**. A hairdresser, for example, may be able to obtain permission to operate a hairstyling business out of a residence, even though the area is not zoned for commercial use.

Eminent Domain

The Fifth Amendment to the U.S. Constitution allows the government to take property from a private person for public use. Nevertheless, the Constitution provides that the government must provide "just compensation" to the property owner. Of course, this provision is often controversial because the value of property is often difficult to determine. Also, some property owners often argue with the government over the term "public use." Such was the issue in the U.S. Supreme Court case that follows (Illustrative Court Case 13.1).

Restrictive Covenants

A person's property may be subject to **restrictive covenants** established by deed or by homeowners'

Kelo v. City of New London

Supreme Court of the United States

545 U.S. 469 (2005)

[Note: For convenience of the reader, the following language is from the Syllabus of the case as provided by the U.S. Supreme Court Reporter of Decisions.]

After approving an integrated development plan designed to revitalize its ailing economy, respondent city, through its development agent, purchased most of the property earmarked for the project from willing sellers, but initiated condemnation proceedings when petitioners, the owners of the rest of the property, refused to sell. Petitioners brought this state-court action claiming . . . that the taking of their properties would violate the "public use" restriction in the Fifth Amendment's Takings Clause. The trial court granted a permanent restraining order prohibiting the taking of some of the properties, but denying relief as to others. [T]he Connecticut Supreme Court affirmed in part and reversed in part, upholding all of the proposed takings.

Held: The city's proposed disposition of petitioners' property qualifies as a "public use" within the meaning of the Takings Clause.

(a) Though the city could not take petitioners' land simply to confer a private benefit on a particular private party, . . . , the takings at issue here would be executed pursuant to a carefully considered development plan, which was not adopted "to benefit a particular class of identifiable individuals," . . . . Moreover, while the city is not planning to open the condemned land—at least not in its entirety—to use by the general public, this "Court long ago rejected any literal requirement that condemned property be put in to use for the . . . public." . . . Rather, it has embraced the broader and more natural interpretation of public use as "public purpose." . . . Without exception, the Court has defined that concept broadly, reflecting its longstanding policy of deference to legislative judgments as to what public needs justify the use of the takings power. . . .

(b) The city's determination that the area at issue was sufficiently distressed to justify a program of economic rejuvenation is entitled to deference. The city has carefully formulated a development plan that it believes will provide appreciable benefits to the community, including, but not limited to, new jobs and increased tax revenue. As with other exercises in urban planning and development, the city is trying to coordinate a variety of commercial, residential, and recreational land uses, with the hope that they will form a whole greater than the sum of its parts. To effectuate this plan, the city has invoked a state statute that specifically authorizes the use of eminent domain to promote economic development. Given the plan's comprehensive character, the thorough deliberation that preceded its adoption, and the limited scope of this Court's review in such cases, it is appropriate here . . . to resolve the challenges of the individual owners, not on a piecemeal basis, but rather in light of the entire plan. Because that plan unquestionably serves a public purpose, the takings challenged here satisfy the Fifth Amendment.

(c) Petitioners' proposal that the Court adopt a new bright-line rule that economic development does not qualify as a public use is supported by neither precedent nor logic. Promoting economic development is a traditional and long-accepted governmental function, and there is no principled way of distinguishing it from the other public purposes the Court has recognized. . . . Also rejected is petitioners' argument that for takings of this kind the Court should require a "reasonable certainty" that the expected public benefits will actually accrue. Such a rule would represent an even greater departure from the Court's precedent. . . . The disadvantages of a heightened form of review are especially pronounced in this type of case, where orderly implementation of a comprehensive plan requires all interested parties' legal rights to be established before new construction can commence.

associations to which the person may be a member. Restrictive covenants prevent a property owner from using the property in a certain way. For example, a homeowners' association may restrict homeowners in the development from painting their house bright orange or from having a basketball standard in the driveway. Other provisions might require a homeowner to include only certain types of trees in the yard. Commercial leases might include restrictive covenants also, such as prohibiting a tenant from selling pornography or operating a business that produces abundant pollution or noise, for example.

Acquiring Real Property

Real property can be acquired in several ways. The most common methods are by purchase, inheritance, or gift. A less common method of obtaining ownership in real property is by **adverse possession**. A person may be able to claim title to real property by adverse possession if the person possesses the land in an open, exclusive manner, which is "hostile" to the rights of the actual owner of the land. The person must possess the land for a certain period of time established by state law, which is typically several years or even over a decade. If the actual owner "sleeps on his rights" and does nothing to protect their property rights from the adverse possessor, state law may allow the adverse possessor to obtain title. State laws vary on this issue; some states, for example, require the adverse possessor to also pay property taxes on the real property that is the subject of the adverse possession attempt.

Transferring and Titling Real Property

Sales Contracts

A buyer and seller of real property will typically enter into a sales contract setting forth the terms and conditions of the agreement. States regulate the real estate brokerage industry and often require that real estate agents use state-approved forms in order to consummate a real estate sales transaction. Real estate sales contracts (sometimes also called "real estate purchase contracts" or REPC), frequently include contingencies that must be met before a party (typically the buyer) is bound by the contract. For example, a buyer may include a contingency in the contract that allows the buyer to withdraw from the contract if the buyer cannot find acceptable financing for the property or if the property fails a termite inspection.

The sales contract usually requires the buyer to place a certain sum of money into **escrow**, which is an account used to hold the money until the deal is closed. Real estate title companies are often used to handle the transaction and set up the escrow account. Depending upon the agreement, it is possible for the buyer to forfeit the money (often called "earnest" money) placed in escrow, so this gives the buyer an incentive to meet the terms of the contract. Finally, when all the contingencies have been satisfied, the deal is closed by the buyer's transferring the appropriate amount of funds to the

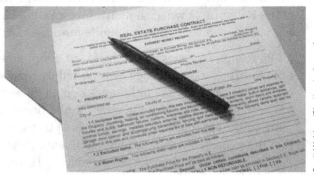

Scott Waldron/Shutterstock.com/Shutterstock.com

seller. As part of the transaction, a deed is recorded with a local government recording office formally transferring ownership (or "title") of the property to the buyer.

Deeds

A **deed** is the legal document that transfers ownership of real property from one person to another. Typically, a deed indicates in detail the specific real property that is being transferred, includes the transferor's (grantor's) signature, identifies the transferee (grantee), and may contain other information that may be required by state law. Deeds can take various forms. By executing a *general* **warranty deed**, for example, the grantor warrants that the property is free from any claims to ownership by third parties. By executing a *special* warranty deed, however, the grantor warrants that there are no claims to ownership by third parties that originated or occurred only during the time the grantor owned the property. Another type of deed, a **quit-claim deed**, is used by a grantor if the grantor desires to give no warranties at all to the grantee. Of course, the grantee may not agree to this and, as part of the transaction, require a warranty deed. A quit claim deed is frequently used, for example, when a real property owner wishes to transfer the property to a trust that the owner created for estate planning purposes or to a business entity that the owner controls.

Concurrent Ownership

When real property is acquired, the property must be "titled" so that the property can be recorded in the owner's name. When there is more than one owner, some different titling options are available. We will discuss three here.

Tenancy in Common

If the property is titled as **tenants in common**, each tenant (co-owner) has a right to use the entire property, subject to any agreement among the tenants. When a tenant dies, the tenant's ownership in the property is passed to the tenant's heirs according to the tenant's will or, if the tenant has no will, state law. (Keep in mind that the use of the term "tenant" in the concurrent ownership context has a different meaning than in the landlord/tenant context.)

Joint Tenancy

Just like tenancy in common, if the property is titled as a **joint tenancy**, the joint tenants each have a right to use the entire property, subject to any agreement among the joint tenants. In contrast to tenancy in common, however, when a tenant in a joint tenancy dies, the tenant's ownership in the property automatically is vested in the remaining joint tenant(s) rather than in the deceased tenant's heirs. Frequently, a joint tenancy is also called a "joint tenancy with right of survivorship" or "JTWROS." Joint tenancy is often the manner in which married individuals title property they co-own.

Community Property

A few states provide that, as a general rule, married couples are presumed to equally own any property that is acquired during the marriage (*i.e.*, **community property**). In other words, the property is owned by the marital "community" that exists between the two spouses. Of course, upon divorce, the property is divided and awarded to each spouse according to the state's divorce laws. It is possible, however, for a spouse to own property that is "separate" from the marital community. Such property is typically property that the spouse owned prior to the marriage or property that was inherited by or gifted to the spouse. Once a spouse commingles separate property with community property, however, the status of the property as "separate" may be lost. Arizona, California, Idaho, Louisiana, Nevada, New Mexico, Texas, Washington, and Wisconsin are community property states. All non-community property states are often called "common law" states.

QUESTIONS FOR REVIEW

1. What is a fixture?

2. What does it mean to own real property in "fee simple"?

3. What is the difference between a remainder interest and a reversionary interest?

4. What is an easement?

5. How does a license differ from an easement?

6. In a landlord-tenant relationship, what rights and obligations does each party have?

7. What is a sublease?

8. Discuss three possible restrictions on an owner of real property's right to do whatever the owner wants to do with the property.

9. Describe the term "adverse possession."

10. Describe the difference between a warranty deed and a quit-claim deed.

11. Explain the difference between owning real property as tenants in common versus owning real property as joint tenants.

12. Which states are community property states?

13. Summarize the *Kelo v. City of New London* case.

INTERNET ACTIVITIES

1. Locate the website of your county recorder's office (or other county department that records deeds).

   a. Does the website allow for the search of parcels of real property and the owners?

   b. What other services does the county recorder's office provide?

2. Locate the website of your state's association of Realtors (*e.g.*, California Association of Realtors).

   a. Summarize generally the information that the website provides.

   b. Does the website provide a standard form real estate purchase contract (or it may be called a real estate sales contract or a residential purchase contract or residential sales contract)? If so, discuss generally what provisions are included.

Chapter 14

Personal Property

Property other than real property is **personal property**. Personal property is either tangible or intangible. **Tangible** property can be touched, felt, moved (*e.g.*, car, hat, pencil, etc.). **Intangible** property, of course, cannot be touched or felt, but does represent something of value to the owner (*e.g.*, copyright, patent, trademark, and other types of intellectual property). We will discuss intellectual property in Chapter 15.

Acquiring Personal Property

Personal property can be acquired in several different ways. This includes acquisition by purchase, gift, and inheritance. In some cases, a person may also acquire ownership of personal property by finding it. These issues are discussed below.

Purchase, Gift, and Inheritance

Perhaps the most common method of acquiring personal property is by purchasing it. We engage in this activity nearly every day, such as when we purchase clothes, electronics, hair care products, etc. Upon purchase, we become the owners of such property even if we do not keep written documentation evidencing the purchase. Of course, we can subsequently sell or otherwise dispose of our ownership interest in the property.

Another way to acquire ownership in personal property is by receiving it as a gift. In order for the gift to be valid, however, the giver (sometimes called the "donor") must have the *intent* to make a gift. Sometimes what may appear to be a gift is actually intended to be a loan. In addition to intent, the giver must also *deliver* the property to the recipient and the recipient must *accept* the gift.

Personal property can also be acquired by inheritance if a person states in his or her will that certain property should go to a certain beneficiary. If a person dies without a will, then state law will determine who receives the deceased person's assets. Wills, trusts, and related issues are discussed further in Chapter 43.

Finders, Keepers?

If you find an item of personal property that someone else appears to have lost, do you own it? What if the true owner comes back looking for it? The answer may depend on whether the property is truly "lost" as opposed to "mislaid," or "abandoned."

Property is **lost** if the person did not intentionally set the property in a particular place (*e.g.*, a person's earring inadvertently falls off while the person is running, but the person doesn't realize it). By contrast, property is **mislaid** if the person intentionally set the item down in a particular place and then forgot to take it with them (*e.g.*, leaving a purse at a restaurant) or forgot where they set it. Property is **abandoned** if the person intentionally discards or manifests the intent that they no longer wish to own the property and will not reclaim it (*e.g.*, throwing it in the garbage).

At common law, a finder of lost property obtains ownership to the property superior to everyone except the true owner. A finder of abandoned property typically obtains ownership to the property superior to everyone including the true owner. A finder of mislaid property must turn the property over to the owner of the place where the mislaid property was found since there is a strong likelihood the true owner will come back to reclaim the mislaid property.

Consider the court case that follows from the Court of Appeals of Idaho (Illustrative Court Case 14.1). Notice this case's explanation of property that is lost, mislaid, abandoned, embedded, or treasure trove.

ILLUSTRATIVE COURT CASE 14.1

Corliss v. Wenner

Court of Appeals of Idaho

34 P.3d 1100 (2001)

OPINION BY: SCHWARTZMAN

. . .

In the fall of 1996, Jann Wenner hired Anderson Asphalt Paving to construct a driveway on his ranch in Blaine County. Larry Anderson, the owner of Anderson Asphalt Paving, and his employee, Gregory Corliss, were excavating soil for the driveway when they unearthed a glass jar containing paper wrapped rolls of gold coins. Anderson and Corliss collected, cleaned, and inventoried the gold pieces dating from 1857 to 1914. The coins themselves weighed about four pounds. Anderson and Corliss agreed to split the gold coins between themselves, with Anderson retaining possession of all coins. At some point Anderson and Corliss argued over ownership of the coins and Anderson fired Corliss. . . .

Corliss sued Anderson and Wenner for possession of some or all of the coins. Wenner, defending both himself and Anderson, filed a motion for summary judgment. The facts, except whether Corliss found all or just some of the gold coins without Anderson's help, are not in dispute. All parties agree that the coins were unearthed during excavation by Anderson and Corliss for a driveway on Wenner's ranch, that the coins had been protected in paper tube rolls and buried in a glass jar estimated to be about seventy years old. . . .

This is a case of first impression in Idaho, the central issue being the proper rule to apply in characterizing the gold coins found by Corliss and Anderson on Wenner's property.

. . .

At common law all found property is generally categorized in one of five ways. . . .

ABANDONED PROPERTY—that which the owner has discarded or voluntarily forsaken with the intention of terminating his ownership, but without vesting ownership in any other person. [Citation omitted.]

LOST PROPERTY—that property which the owner has involuntarily and unintentionally parted with through neglect, carelessness, or inadvertence and does not know the whereabouts. [Citation omitted.]

MISLAID PROPERTY—that which the owner has intentionally set down in a place where he can again resort to it, and then forgets where he put it. [Citation omitted.]

TREASURE TROVE—a category exclusively for gold or silver in coin, plate, bullion, and sometimes its paper money equivalents, found concealed in the earth or in a house or other private place. Treasure trove carries with it the thought of antiquity, i.e., that the treasure has been concealed for so long as to indicate that the owner is probably dead or unknown. [Citation omitted.]

EMBEDDED PROPERTY—that personal property which has become a part of the natural earth, such as pottery, the sunken wreck of a steamship, or a rotted-away sack of gold-bearing quartz rock buried or partially buried in the ground. [Citation omitted.]

Under these doctrines, the finder of lost or abandoned property and treasure trove acquires a right to possess the property against the entire world but the rightful owner regardless of the place of finding. [Citation omitted.] The finder of mislaid property is required to turn it over to the owner of the premises who has the duty to safeguard the property for the true owner. Possession of embedded property goes to owner of the land on which the property was found. [Citation omitted.]

One of the major distinctions between these various categories is that only lost property necessarily involves an element of involuntariness. [Citation omitted.] The four remaining categories involve voluntary and intentional acts by the true owner in placing the property where another eventually finds it. However, treasure trove, despite not being lost or abandoned property, is treated as such in that the right to possession is recognized to be in the finder rather than the premises owner.

. . .

On appeal, Corliss argues that the district court should have interpreted the undisputed facts and circumstances surrounding of the placement of the coins in the ground to indicate that the gold coins were either lost, abandoned, or treasure trove. Wenner argues that the property was properly categorized as either embedded or mislaid property.

As with most accidentally discovered buried treasure, the history of the original ownership of the coins is shrouded in mystery and obscured by time. The coins had been wrapped in paper, like coins from a bank, and buried in a glass jar, apparently for safekeeping. Based on these circumstances, the district court determined that the coins were not abandoned because the condition in which the coins were found evidenced an intent to keep them safe, not an intent to voluntarily relinquish all possessory interest in them. The district court also implicitly rejected the notion that the coins were lost, noting that the coins were secreted with care in a specific place to protect them from the elements and from other people until such time as the original owner might return for them. There is no indication that the coins came to be buried through neglect, carelessness, or inadvertence. Accordingly, the district court properly concluded, as a matter of law, that the coins were neither lost nor abandoned.

. . .

Corliss argues that the district court erred in deciding that the law of treasure trove should not apply in Idaho. However, the doctrine of treasure trove has never been adopted in this state. [The] Idaho Code . . . provides: "the common law of England, so far as it is not repugnant to, or inconsistent with, the constitution or laws of the United States, in all cases not provided for in these compiled laws, is the rule of decision in all courts of this state." Nevertheless, the history of the "finders keepers" rule was not a part of the common law of England at the time the colonies gained their independence. Rather, the doctrine of treasure trove was created to determine a rightful possessor of buried Roman treasures discovered in feudal times. [Citation omitted.] And while the common law initially awarded the treasure to the finder, the crown, as early as the year 1130, exercised its royal prerogative to take such property for itself. Only after the American colonies gained their independence from England did some states grant possession of treasure trove to the finder. Thus, it does not appear that the "finders keepers" rule of treasure trove was a part of the common law of England as defined by the

(*Continued*)

Idaho Code. We hold that the district court correctly determined that [Idaho statutory law] does not require the treasure trove doctrine to be adopted in Idaho.

Additionally, we conclude that the rule of treasure trove is of dubious heritage and misunderstood application, inconsistent with our values and traditions.

. . .

Land ownership includes control over crops on the land, buildings and appurtenances, soils, and minerals buried under those soils. The average Idaho landowner would expect to have a possessory interest in any object uncovered on his or her property. And certainly the notion that a trespassing treasure hunter, or a hired handyman or employee, could or might have greater possessory rights than a landowner in objects uncovered on his or her property runs counter to the reasonable expectations of present-day land ownership.

. . .

We hold that the owner of the land has constructive possession of all personal property secreted in, on or under his or her land. Accordingly, we adopt the district court's reasoning and conclusion melding the law of mislaid property with that of embedded property and conclude, as a matter of law, that the landowner is entitled to possession to the exclusion of all but the true owner, absent a contract between the landowner and finder.

What Do You Think?

If you find a wedding ring in the grass while you are enjoying a day at a public park, what would you do? What should you do? Would it matter if you found the ring on private property instead of public property?

Of course, state statutes can change these common law rules. Consider how the state of Illinois handles the issue of lost property (See Illustrative State Statute 14.1).

Most state and/or local governments now typically have some sort of established procedure that finders of property must comply with before the finder will legally be granted ownership of the item and protected against claims by others.

ILLUSTRATIVE STATE STATUTE 14.1

§765 ILCS 1020/27–28

Sec. 27. If any person or persons find any lost goods, money, bank notes, or other choses in action, of any description whatever, such person or persons shall inform the owner thereof, if known, and shall make restitution of the same, without any compensation whatever, except such compensation as shall be voluntarily given on the part of the owner. If the owner is unknown and if such property found is of the value of $100 or upwards, the finder or finders shall, within 5 days after such finding file in the circuit court of the county, an affidavit of the description thereof, the time and place when and where the same was found, that no alteration has been made in the appearance thereof since the finding of the same, that the owner thereof is unknown to the affiant and that the affiant has not secreted, withheld or disposed of any part thereof. . . .

Sec. 28. In all cases where such lost goods, money bank notes or other choses in action shall not exceed the sum of $100 in value and the owner thereof is unknown, the finder shall advertise the same at the court house, and if the owner does not claim such money, goods, bank notes or other choses in action within 6 months from the time of such advertisement, the ownership of such property shall vest in the finder and the court shall enter an order to that effect.

If the value thereof exceeds the sum of $100, the county clerk, within 20 days after receiving the certified copy of the court's order shall cause a notice thereof to be published for 3 weeks successively in some public newspaper printed in this county and if the owner of such goods, money, bank notes, or other choses in action does not claim the same and pay the finder's charges and expenses within one year after the advertisement thereof as aforesaid, the ownership of such property shall vest in the finder and the court shall enter an order to that effect.

Jamey Ekins/ Shutterstock.com

Bailments

Have you ever asked someone to watch some of your personal property while you are gone for a period of time? For example, suppose Julia asks her classmate Fiona to keep an eye on Julia's laptop for a few minutes while she steps out to make a phone call? If so, what liability would Fiona have to Julia if the laptop is gone or damaged when Julia returns? These situations raise issues relating to bailment law. A **bailment** is created when the owner of personal property delivers the property to another person with instructions on what to do with the personal property. In a bailment, the owner of the personal property does not give up ownership rights to the property. The owner of the property is called the **bailor** and the person to whom the property is delivered is called the **bailee**.

A bailment may be formed (1) as a mutual benefit bailment; (2) solely for the benefit of the bailor; or (3) solely for the benefit of the bailee.

Mutual Benefit Bailments

In a mutual benefit bailment arrangement, both the bailor and bailee benefit from the arrangement. For example, suppose you take your watch to a friend to be fixed. You agree to pay your friend $20 for the repair when she is finished. You (the bailor) benefit from this arrangement because your watch will get fixed, and your friend (the bailee) benefits from being paid the $20. Your friend has a duty to exercise ordinary care (sometimes called "reasonably prudent" care) while in possession of your watch.

Bailments for the Benefit of the Bailor

In a bailment arrangement for the benefit of the bailor, the bailor is basically asking the bailee for a favor (sometimes called a "gratuitous" bailment). Suppose you are going on vacation for a week, and you do not want to leave your coin collection in your apartment until you get back. Consequently, you take your coin collection to your friend's apartment and ask him to take care of it until you get back. Of course, your friend agrees to do this without any compensation from you. In this situation, your friend (the bailee) benefits very little or not at all. You are the sole benefactor. Consequently, the standard of care imposed on your friend is *lower* than the ordinary standard of care that is applicable to mutual benefit bailments.

Bailments for the Benefit of the Bailee

In a bailment arrangement for the benefit of the bailee, the bailee is basically asking the bailor for a favor. Suppose your lawnmower is broken, so you ask your neighbor if you can borrow his lawnmower for a few hours so you can mow your lawn. He allows you to do so without charging you anything.

Stephen Mcsweeny/Shutterstock.com

In this situation, you (the bailee) have a level of care that is *higher* than the ordinary standard of care that is applicable to mutual benefit bailments.

Consider the Supreme Court of Rhode Island court case that follows dealing with a dispute over a bailment (Illustrative Court Case 14.2).

Special rules apply to bailments involving common carriers (*e.g.*, UPS, FedEx, etc.), and innkeepers (*e.g.*, hotels) with regard to liability for loss or damage to personal property. A common carrier typically is strictly liable for loss or damage to goods shipped by a customer. Nevertheless, the law allows the common carrier to limit by contract the dollar amount of the common carrier's liability. The customer usually has the opportunity to purchase insurance on the article being shipped,

ILLUSTRATIVE COURT CASE 14.2

Don-Lin Jewelry Co., Inc. v. The Westin Hotel Company

Supreme Court of Rhode Island

877 A.2d 621 (2005)

OPINION

. . .

This dispute centers on whether a bailment was created between plantiff, Don-Lin Jewelry Co., Inc. (Don-Lin), and . . . The Westin Hotel Company [Westin], with respect to two boxes of jewelry prototypes . . . that Don-Lin left with Westin for inspection by a prospective buyer.

In March 1996, Richard St. Angelo (St. Angelo), acting as Don-Lin's vice president of sales, left two boxes of jewelry prototypes at the front desk of The Westin . . . with instructions to deliver the boxes to the hotel's guests from Dillards, Inc. (Dillard's), a national department store, who were using a conference room at the hotel. This delivery took place. After a representative from Dillard's notified Don-Lin that the boxes were ready to be retrieved by Don-Lin, St. Angelo returned to the hotel and requested the boxes. The boxes were missing and have not been seen again. After the Westin failed to return the boxes, Don-Lin filed suit . . . alleging breach of a bailment agreement, negligence, and conversion against The Westin, but not Dillard's.

St. Angelo also testified that, in accordance with Don-Lin's past practice with Dillard's, after performing the style-out, Dillard's was expected to pack the prototypes into the boxes and deliver them to The Westin to hold for Don-Lin to collect.

St. Angelo explained that a representative from Dillard's notified him that Dillard's was finished with the prototypes and the boxes were ready to be picked-up at The Westin but did not specify a location in the hotel where the boxes could be retrieved. When he reported to the front desk, the desk clerk directed a bellman to accompany St. Angelo to a locked room to search for the boxes. After a careful search, the boxes were not found. According to St. Angelo, the bellman recalled seeing the boxes but did not know where they were. The manager conducted an unsuccessful search of the conference room. St. Angelo repeatedly called and visited The Westin to check for the boxes without success. This lawsuit ensued.

At trial, Harry Jones (Jones), property manager and head of security of The Westin in Providence, testified that The Westin was unable to confirm or deny whether it had possession of [Don-Lin's] boxes. He testified that the hotel used a locked room off the lobby to store items at the request of its guests and that only employees of the hotel had access to that room. Jones acknowledged that it was not "unusual for the hotel to take a package from a guest for the benefit of someone who would pick it up at the front desk."

At the close of [Don-Lin's] evidence, [The Westin] moved to dismiss [the case]. The trial justice was satisfied that, by delivering the boxes to Dillard's, The Westin fulfilled any legal obligation it may have had to Don-Lin. The trial justice granted [The Westin's] motion and dismissed the action, finding that the evidence did not establish a gratuitous bailment, a bailment for hire, or any other legal obligation between Don-Lin and The Westin with regard to the return of the jewelry prototypes after The Westin delivered the boxes to Dillard's. The trial justice granted judgment for [The Westin], and [Don-Lin] appealed.

[Don-Lin] asks this Court to reverse the Superior Court's findings, contending that a bailment arose between the parties and that defendant breached the bailment. . . .

. . .

Discussion

Before this Court, [Don-Lin] argues that probative evidence demonstrating that a bailment relationship arose from the conduct of the parties is evident in the record, and by not delivering possession of the boxes to [Don-Lin] upon request, [The Westin] breached the bailment.

It is undisputed that [Don-Lin] was not a guest at The Westin. As such, any obligation The Westin assumed for the care of [Don-Lin's] boxes left in its possession was not as a hotelkeeper but, at best, was that of a bailee. [Citation omitted.] A bailment is "a delivery of personalty for some particular purpose, or on mere deposit, upon a contract, express or implied, that after the purpose has been fulfilled it shall be redelivered to the person who delivered it, or otherwise dealt with according to his directions, or kept until he reclaims it, as the case may be." [Citation omitted.] By delivering possession of the boxes to The Westin without giving any consideration, plaintiff and defendant entered into a gratuitous bailment.

St. Angelo, on behalf of [Don-Lin], surrendered possession of the personalty to [The Westin] with the sole instruction that the boxes be delivered to the conference room where the group from Dillard's was working. The record discloses that The Westin complied with that direction. A bailment terminates upon the surrender of possession in compliance with the bailment agreement. [Citation omitted.] By delivering the jewelry prototypes to Dillard's pursuant to [Don-Lin's] instructions, [The Westin] satisfied its obligations under the bailment with [Don-Lin]. [Don-Lin] cannot hold [The Westin] liable for loss of the bailed property that occurred after the hotel delivered possession of the bailed property to Dillard's under the terms of the bailment. . . .

[Don-Lin] alleges that the boxes were subject to a second bailment commencing when Dillard's returned the boxes to The Westin. We are satisfied that the evidence supported the trial justice's conclusion that "for the second part of the transaction, this is, the return of the goods, the bailor at

(*Continued*)

that time was Dillard's, and if there was a bailment relationship, it was between Dillard's and the hotel.

[Don-Lin] was not a party to that bailment, and therefore, it could only seek to hold The Westin liable as a third party beneficiary. However, whatever the merits of that claim, [Don-Lin] never pled this theory in its complaint nor otherwise raised it before the Superior Court. Consequently, this issue is not properly before us. [Citation omitted.]

For the foregoing reasons, we affirm the judgment of the Superior Court.

however, for an amount in excess of the default liability limitation established by the common carrier. Warehouses typically can also limit the dollar amount of liability on personal property stored there by customers (bailors). The customers may also purchase insurance to protect the property in excess of those limits.

Under common law, innkeepers also have strict liability to its guests for personal property of the guest. State law, however, typically allows the innkeeper to avoid strict liability if the innkeeper provides a safe in the room for the guest to use. Consider the Nevada statute relating to innkeeper liability (Illustrative State Statute 14.2).

ILLUSTRATIVE STATE STATUTE 14.2

Nev. Rev. Stat. Ann. § 651.010

§651.010. Civil liability of innkeepers limited.

1. An owner or keeper of any hotel, inn, motel, motor court, boardinghouse or lodging house in this State is not civilly liable for the theft, loss, damage or destruction of any property brought by a patron upon the premises or left in a motor vehicle upon the premises because of theft, burglary, fire or otherwise, in the absence of gross neglect by the owner or keeper.

2. An owner or keeper of any hotel, inn, motel, motor court, boardinghouse or lodging house in this State is not civilly liable for the theft, loss, damage or destruction of any property of a guest left in a guest room if:

a. The owner or keeper provides a fireproof safe or vault in which guests may deposit property for safekeeping;

b. Notice of this service is personally given to a guest or posted in the office and the guest's room; and

c. The property is not offered for deposit in the safe or vault by a guest, unless the owner or keeper is grossly negligent.

3. An owner or keeper is not obligated to receive property to deposit for safekeeping which exceeds $750 in value or is of a size which cannot easily fit within the safe or vault.

4. The liability of the owner or keeper does not exceed the sum of $750 for any property, including, but not limited to, property which is not deposited in a safe or vault because it cannot easily fit within the safe or vault, of an individual patron or guest, unless the owner or keeper receives the property for deposit for safekeeping and consents to assume a liability greater than $750 for its theft, loss, damage or destruction in a written agreement in which the patron or guest specifies the value of the property.

QUESTIONS FOR REVIEW

1. Explain the elements necessary to transfer ownership of personal property by gift.

2. Discuss the differences among lost, mislaid, and abandoned personal property.

3. What is a bailment? Who is the bailor? Who is the bailee?

4. Discuss the standard of care for bailees if the bailment is a (1) mutual benefit bailment; (2) bailment for the benefit of the bailor; and (3) bailment for the benefit of the bailee.

5. According to the Nevada innkeeper statute, when is a hotel in Nevada liable for the theft of personal property of a guest?

6. Summarize the *Corliss v. Wenner* case.

7. Summarize the *Don-Lin Jewelry v. Westin Hotel* case.

8. Summarize the Nevada Innkeeper statute.

INTERNET ACTIVITIES

1. Conduct a web search regarding the fact pattern that follows. Assume that Arnel surprises his girlfriend, Sheila, by kneeling down on one knee, holding out a ring and saying, "Sheila, will you marry me?" Assume Sheila says 'yes.' One month later Arnel and Sheila break off the engagement. Arnel wants the ring back.

   a. Legally, who owns the ring? Was the interaction between Arnel and Sheila a gift or a contract? Explain.

   b. If you conclude that Sheila legally owns the ring, should she give the ring back to Arnel for *ethical* or *moral* reasons?

2. Provide an example relating to each of the following situations other than the scenarios provided in the chapter. Identify your source website.

   a. Mutual benefit bailment

   b. Bailment for the benefit of the bailor

   c. Bailment for the benefit of the bailee

Chapter 15

Intellectual Property

An increasingly important asset to most businesses is intellectual property. Businesses often spend significant amounts of time and money, for example, in developing a new, innovative way of designing or manufacturing a product. Of course, the business does not want competitors stealing the inventions or creations. The Constitution recognizes the value in providing protection to people who invent or create things.

UNITED STATES CONSTITUTION

Article 1, Section 8. The Congress shall have the power to . . . promote the Progress of Science and useful Arts, by securing for limited Times to Authors and Inventors the exclusive Right to their respective Writings and Discoveries. . . .

In this chapter, we will discuss the law applicable to patents, trademarks, copyrights, and other intellectual property.

Patents

A **patent** is the government's granting of exclusive rights to an inventor to use and market the invention for a limited time. Unauthorized copying of the invention would be a patent **infringement**, which would give the patent holder the right to sue the infringing party for the damages the patent holder may have suffered. To obtain a patent, an inventor must apply to the Patent and Trademark Office (PTO) in Washington, D.C. The time the invention is protected by the patent is usually 20 years, although in some cases, the protected time period is only 14 years.

Federal law provides the scope of patentable subject matter, as shown in the statute that follows (Illustrative Federal Statute 15.1).

Notice that the statute lists processes, machines, manufactures, or compositions of matter as being patentable. This language is very broad and includes certain plants and genetic engineering, for example. As a result, a large number of patent applications are filed each year. In fact, it often takes the

---

ILLUSTRATIVE FEDERAL STATUTE 15.1

35 U.S.C. §101

§ 101. Inventions patentable

Whoever invents or discovers any new and useful process, machine, manufacture, or composition of matter, or any new and useful improvement thereof, may obtain a patent therefor, subject to the conditions and requirement of this title.

PTO several years to approve a patent because of the complexity and volume of applications.

To be patentable, the invention must also be **nonobvious**, **novel**, and **useful**. To be nonobvious, the invention must not be obvious to someone with ordinary skill in the trade or business related to the invention. To be novel, the invention must be new and not already invented by someone else. To be useful, the invention must have some utility to society.

The United States is a party to several international conventions that provide protection for patents and other intellectual property when the owner desires to protect the property in other countries. Of course, this is increasingly important in today's global economy for a business to protect its valuable intellectual property.

Trademarks

Many symbols and logos are instantly recognizable: the McDonald's golden arches, the Nike swoosh, and the cursive Coca-Cola writing on a soda can, just to name a few. Obviously, these companies have a very strong interest in protecting these symbols and names. The law allows them to do so. In short, a **trademark** is a distinctive symbol, logo, name, phrase, image, etc., used to distinguish a business or its products from the competition. A trademark is typically protected *intra*state by state statute or state common law. To be protected on an *inter*state basis, the trademark should be registered with the PTO.

Bertold Werkmann/ Shutterstock.com

You are likely familiar with the little notation of "TM" or "®" next to a logo or name on a product. The ® indicates that the trademark is, in fact, registered with the PTO. If the trademark has not yet been registered with the PTO, but the owner wants to put the world on notice that the owner is claiming rights in the trademark, then the TM symbol is used. Sometimes, you may also see an "SM" notation on a name. This indicates that the person is claiming ownership of a **servicemark**. A servicemark is appropriate for a business providing services rather than products.

Someone who uses a name, trademark, logo, etc., similar to someone else's is at risk of being sued for trademark **infringement** or trademark **dilution**.

ILLUSTRATIVE FEDERAL STATUTE 15.2

15 U.S.C. §1125

§1125. False designations of origin, false descriptions, and dilution forbidden. . .

(c) Dilution by blurring; dilution by tarnishment

(1) Injunctive relief

[T]he owner of a famous mark that is distinctive, inherently or through acquired distinctiveness, shall be entitled to an injunction against another person who, at any time after the owner's mark has become famous, commences use of a mark or trade name in commerce that is likely to cause dilution by blurring or dilution by tarnishment of the famous mark, regardless of the presence or absence of actual or likely confusion, of competition, or of actual economic injury.

. . .

Typically, to prevail on a trademark *infringement* claim, a plaintiff must demonstrate that there is customer confusion because of the similarity of the mark used by the defendant. Regarding trademark *dilution*, the owner of a *famous* trademark can prevail against a defendant, even without showing customer confusion, as Illustrative Federal Statute 15.2 provides.

Trademark protection is not given to generic names. For example, the courts have held that terms such as "aspirin," "zipper," and "refrigerator," among others, have all become *genericized* terms and not eligible to be trademarked. Consequently, businesses are wise to aggressively protect their trademarks to avoid becoming generic.

With regard to domain names, federal law prohibits "cybersquatting." Some people have tried

What Do You Think?

Have the terms "Jeep," "Google," "Xerox," and "Band-Aid" become generic terms, or have the companies done a good job protecting the distinctiveness of their trademarks?
If you were trying to maintain the distinctiveness of a mark so that it does not become genericized, how would you do it?

to profit by registering trademarked names in a website address and then selling the domain name to the trademark owner. What if a person's motive is for purposes of parody or to cause confusion? Consider the following Fourth Circuit Court of Appeals case (Illustrative Court Case 15.1).

ILLUSTRATIVE COURT CASE 15.1

People for Ethical Treatment of Animals v. Doughney

Fourth Circuit Court of Appeals

263 F.3d 359 (4th Cir. 2001)

OPINION

Gregory, Circuit Judge:

People for the Ethical Treatment of Animals ("PETA") sued Michael Doughney ("Doughney") after he registered the domain name *peta.org* and created a website called "People Eating Tasty Animals." PETA alleged claims of service mark infringement . . . unfair competition . . . and service mark dilution and cybersquatting. . . . Doughney appeals the district court's decision granting PETA's motion for summary judgment . . . . Finding no error, we affirm.

PETA is an animal rights organization with more than 600,000 members worldwide. PETA "is dedicated to promoting and heightening public awareness of animal protection issues and it opposes the exploitation of animals for food, clothing, entertainment. . . ." [Citation omitted.]

Doughney registered the domain name *peta.org* in 1995 with Network Solutions, Inc. ("NSI"). When registering the domain name, Doughney represented to NSI that the registration did "not interfere with or infringe upon the rights of any third party" and that a "nonprofit educational organization" called "People Eating Tasty Animals" was registering the domain name. Doughney made these representations to NSI despite knowing that no corporation, partnership, organization, or entity of any kind existed or traded under that name. Moreover, Doughney was familiar with PETA and its beliefs, and had been for at least 15 years before registering the domain name.

After registering the peta.org domain name, Doughney used it to create a website purportedly on behalf of "People Eating Tasty Animals." Doughney claims he created the website as a parody of PETA. A viewer accessing the website would see the title "People Eating Tasty Animals" in large,

(Continued)

bold type. Under the title, the viewer would see a statement that the website was a "resource for those who enjoy eating meat, wearing fur and leather, hunting, and the fruits of scientific research." The website contained links to various meat, fur, leather, hunting, animal research, and other organizations, all of which held views generally antithetical to PETA's views. Another statement on the website asked the viewer whether he or she was "Feeling lost? Offended? Perhaps you should, like, *exit immediately*." The phrase "*exit immediately*" contained a hyperlink to PETA's official website.

. . .

The district court found Doughney liable under the Anticybersquatting Consumer Protection Act ("ACPA). . . . To establish an ACPA violation, PETA was required to (1) prove that Doughney had a bad faith intent to profit from using the peta.org domain name, and (2) that the peta.org domain name is identical or confusingly similar to, or dilutive of, the distinctive and famous PETA Mark. [Citation omitted.]

. . .

None of Doughney's arguments are availing. . . .

Doughney's fourth argument—that he did not act in bad faith—also is unavailing. . . .

Doughney knowingly provided false information to NSI upon registering the domain name, knew he was registering a domain name identical to PETA's Mark, and clearly intended to confuse Internet users into accessing his website, instead of PETA's official website.

. . .

For the foregoing reasons, the judgment of the district court is affirmed.

Copyrights

The creators or authors of original works have an interest in ensuring other people do not copy or replicate the production. Copyright law provides that protection. A **copyright** is an exclusive right granted to the creator or author of the original work to use and market the creation for a specific time. Federal law provides the general categories of copyrightable subject matter (see Illustrative Federal Statute 15.3).

Obviously, the list of copyrightable subject matter is very broad. Although copyright protection

ILLUSTRATIVE FEDERAL STATUTE 15.3

17 U.S.C. §102

§102. Subject matter of copyright: In general

(a) Copyright protection subsists, in accordance with this title, in original works of authorship fixed in any tangible medium of expression, now known or later developed, from which they can be perceived, reproduced, or otherwise communicated, either directly or with the aid of a machine or device. Works of authorship include the following categories:

1. literary works;

2. musical works, including any accompanying words;

3. dramatic works, including any accompanying music;

4. pantomimes and choreographic works;

5. pictorial, graphic, and sculptural works;

6. motion pictures and other audiovisual works;

7. sound recordings; and

8. architectural works.

...

can arise under the common law without identifying that the work is copyrighted, it is much more prudent to indicate that the work is copyrighted. This can be done simply by affixing the "©" symbol to the work. This mark puts the world on notice that someone is claiming copyright protection for the work. Most copyrights are protected for the life of the author plus 70 years.

Someone who infringes upon copyrighted materials may face both civil and criminal penalties. Nevertheless, the law contains some exceptions to the general copyright statutes and allows some uses by others without having to compensate the copyright owner. Likely the most common exception to copyright laws is the "fair use" exception (see Illustrative Federal Statute 15.4).

Notice that the **fair use** exception is really a matter of degree. This, of course, can lead to debate on what does or does not constitute a copyright infringement.

New technologies continue to appear in the marketplace, and it can take some time for lawmakers to implement laws addressing unique issues raised by advancing technologies. When the internet became prominent in the 1990s, for example, new copyright laws were necessary to regulate downloading copyrighted material. Internet service providers (ISPs) also were at some risk in "enabling" a person to illegally download copyrighted material. Currently, federal law provides that the ISPs are not liable for the copyright violations of their subscribers as long as the ISP follows certain strict regulations.

ILLUSTRATIVE FEDERAL STATUTE 15.4

17 USC §107

§107. Limitation on exclusive rights: Fair use

Notwithstanding the provisions of sections 106 and 106A, the fair use of a copyrighted work simply for purposes such as criticism, comment, news reporting, teaching (including multiple copies for classroom use), scholarship, or research, is not an infringement of copyright. In determining whether the use made of a work in any particular case is a fair use the factors to be considered shall include—

1. the purpose and character of the use, including whether such use is of a commercial nature or is for nonprofit educational purposes;

2. the nature of the copyrighted work;

3. the amount and substantiality of the portion used in relation to the copyrighted work as a whole; and

4. the effect of the use upon the potential market for or value of the copyrighted work.

The fact that a work is unpublished shall not itself bar a finding of fair use if such finding is made upon consideration of all the above factors.

What Do You Think?

Should a person who illegally downloads or "pirates" copyrighted material, such as music and movies from the internet, face criminal charges? Is it justifiable to illegally download music because so many people seem to be doing it? Should educational institutions have written copyright policies regarding illegal music or movie downloads by students?

Other Intellectual Property

Many businesses have expended a lot of money and employee hours in diligent research to create a product, process, or method of operation. These creations or processes could also include financial or marketing strategies, internal business policies, and a myriad of other potential confidential information relating to the particular employer, etc. Businesses clearly have an interest in keeping these **trade secrets** confidential. In fact, most employers with trade secrets will require every employee to sign a contract promising not to disclose any trade secrets, particularly if the employee resigns and is hired by some other employer.

Trade secrets do not have to be registered with the government like a patent does. Common law protects the trade secret as long as the business makes diligent efforts to keep the secret a secret. The trade secret owner can seek an injunction to prevent others from disclosing the secret. If the business casually allows the secret to be disclosed or fails to closely guard the secret, then the courts will likely not rule that someone obtained the trade secret illegally.

Another type of intellectual property is **trade dress**. This is basically the design, shape, color, and overall appearance or image of a place or product. For example, most franchises (*e.g.*, McDonalds, Starbucks, etc.) require that each store be designed in a certain way and have a similar "feel" in order to maintain consistency at each location throughout the country or world. Certain products are marketed with certain colors and designs in the packaging and labeling that could be considered trade dress. Federal law protects these unique features as part of a business's intellectual property.

QUESTIONS FOR REVIEW

1. Where does an inventor register a patent?

2. What is patentable subject matter?

3. Explain trademark dilution.

4. What do the symbols "TM" and "®" mean?

5. What does it mean for a trademark to become "genericized"?

6. What types of works may be copyrighted?

7. How long does copyright protection generally last?

8. Explain the "fair use" exception to copyright infringement.

9. How does a business keep a trade secret a secret?

10. What is trade dress?

11. Summarize the *People for Ethical Treatment of Animals v. Doughney* case.

INTERNET ACTIVITIES

1. Visit the United States Patent and Trademark Office website at www.uspto.gov. Click on the Learning and Resources tab then the General FAQs link and find answers to the following questions:

   a. Summarize the role of the USPTO.

   b. Is there such thing as an international trademark?

   c. What is intellectual property?

2. Visit the United States Copyright Office website at www.copyright.gov. Click on the About Us link, then the Resources and Education link, and then the Frequently Asked Questions link and find answers to the following questions:

   a. Does a copyright have to be registered to be protected? Explain.

   b. What does a copyright protect?

   c. Are copyrights in the United States valid in other countries? Explain.

Part VII
Contract Law

Chapter 16

Fundamentals of Contract Formation

When was the last time you entered into a contract? You likely have entered into multiple contracts over the past week, or even in the past day or two. Did you buy any gasoline, groceries, snacks, or soda? All of these transactions represent the formation and execution of a contract. In other words, you exchanged (or promised to exchange) something of value (*e.g.*, money) for something else of value (*e.g.*, a product or service). In short, a **contract** is a legally binding agreement between two or more people. If a party to the contract fails to perform his or her obligations, then the other party may sue for damages.

Perhaps the most frequent area of law a businessperson encounters is that of contract law. Imagine if the law did not provide for contract enforcement. Would there be any predictability or confidence in business transactions? Understanding the fundamentals of contracts not only will be beneficial for you in business transactions, but also in your personal life.

Fundamentals of Contract Formation

The common law has established five "elements" that must be present for a contract to be validly formed and enforceable. These elements are:

- Offer
- Acceptance
- Consideration
- Capacity
- Legality

We will discuss each of these elements in the paragraphs following.

Offer

Basically, an **offer** is a commitment or promise to do something (or refrain from doing something) at a later time. The person making the offer is referred to, in legal terms, as the **offeror**. The person to whom the offer is made is called the **offeree**. For the offer to be valid, the offeror must: (1) communicate the offer to the offeree, (2) make the offer with definite enough

Feng Yu/ Shutterstock.com

terms so a court could enforce it, and (3) make the offer in a manner that evidences the offeror's intent to be bound by it if the offeree accepts it (*e.g.*, the offer was not a joke). Consider the following scenarios.

Scenario 1. Alan states to his friend, Ben, when they are both attending a professional baseball game together, "If you act like a fool when you are shown on the stadium's jumbo-tron, I will eat 75 hotdogs before the game is over."

Scenario 2. Alan states to his friend, Ben, when they are both attending a professional baseball game together, "I will buy you a bunch of nachos if you buy me a bunch of hotdogs."

Scenario 3. Alan states to his friend, Ben, when they are both attending a professional baseball game together, "If you buy me a hotdog, I will pay the fee for parking."

Which of Alan's offer(s) are valid? The offer in Scenario 1 does not appear to be a serious offer. Alan likely is not intending to be contractually bound to eat 75 hotdogs by the end of the game. Thus, Alan is most likely joking and will not be bound by the offer if Ben accepts it. The offer in Scenario 2 may seem like a valid offer, but only if the term "bunch" is definite enough. What does the term "bunch" mean in this context? Three? Six? Ten? Unlike Scenario 1, this statement does not appear to be a joke, but it may lack definiteness to constitute a valid offer to which Alan could be bound. The offer in Scenario 3 is likely a valid offer. There is no indication that the offer is a joke, and the offer is definite.

As indicated, a critical part of determining whether an offer is valid is the offeror's intent. The context in which the statement is made must also be considered. For example, advertisements (*e.g.*, newspaper, radio, television, etc.) are usually considered invitations to negotiate rather than offers to which the offeror intends to be bound. In many instances, however, the person advertising will accept an offer that you make that contains the terms of the advertisement.

A person's mere opinion is not an offer. Suppose your car needs to be fixed and you take it to a mechanic. You ask the mechanic how long it will take for the car to be fixed. The mechanic says, "I should have it fixed in about two hours." You say, "Ok." Three hours later, the car is fixed. You are upset that it took three hours instead of two. Did the mechanic's statement "About two hours" constitute an offer to which the mechanic was bound?

An offer may terminate in several ways. First, the offeror may **revoke** the offer prior to the offeree's acceptance of the offer. Second, the offeree may **reject** the offer. Doing so terminates the original offer. Third, the offeree may make a **counteroffer**. Doing so rejects the original offer and creates an offer that the original offeror can now accept. Fourth, the offer may terminate due to a **lapse of time**. Generally, an offer will terminate if the offer is not accepted within a *reasonable* amount of time. Fifth, the **death of the offeror or offeree** will terminate the offer. Finally, the **destruction of the subject matter** involved in the offer will terminate the offer.

Acceptance

Once a valid offer has been made, the offeree then has the "power" of **acceptance**. An acceptance is when the offeree voluntarily agrees to the terms set forth by the offeror in the offer. An offer and an acceptance constitute an **agreement**. The acceptance by the offeree could be in the form of words or by performance, depending upon the circumstances. If an offeror promises to do something and the offeree accepts the offer by return promise, this arrangement is considered a **bilateral** contract (assuming all other elements of a contract are present). For example, Juan states to Melissa, "I offer to sell you 100 shares of my XYZ Corporation stock for $5,000." Melissa, then states, "I accept your offer." This is a bilateral contract since both parties exchanged promises to perform. It is possible for a contract to be a **unilateral** contract. This occurs when the offeror promises something of value in return for an action rather than a return promise. For example, Ahmad states specifically to Derek, "If you fix my roof, I will pay you $3,000." Even if Derek does not express his agreement verbally or in writing, Derek can accept the offer by performing the action contained in Ahmad's offer (*i.e.*, fixing the roof).

A very important concept relating to the acceptance of an offer is the **mirror image rule**. This rule established by common law states that unless the acceptance exactly mirrors the offer, then the acceptance is not an acceptance at all; rather, it is a counteroffer. Consider the following exchange between Olivia and Brigette.

Olivia: "I will purchase your television for $300 if you will deliver it to my house by 3:00 p.m. today."

Brigette: "I accept your offer, but I won't be able to deliver it until 6:00 p.m. today because I have to work until 5:30 p.m."

Did Brigette accept Olivia's offer, or was it a counteroffer? Under the mirror image rule, Brigette made a counteroffer. This terminates Olivia's initial offer *in its entirety*. Olivia can now accept or reject the counteroffer made by Brigette. The mirror image rule is critical for you to remember when you receive an offer from a potential employer. Consider the following exchange between an employer and Nick during a job interview.

Employer: "Nick, we really like your qualifications, and we think you will fit in nicely with our firm. We hereby offer you $80,000 per year to come to work for our firm."

Nick: "Thank you very much for your kind offer. I would really love to work for your firm. Nevertheless, I believe the market rate for someone with my knowledge, skills, and experience is $100,000 per year."

Employer: "Thank you for your response, Nick. Given the tight economic conditions, however, we regret that we cannot pay you $100,000."

Nick: "Ok. Then I will accept your offer for $80,000."

At this point, is there an agreement between the employer and Nick? No. Nick made a counteroffer, which terminated the employer's original offer. The employer did not accept Nick's counteroffer, which terminated Nick's counteroffer. Nick's apparent acceptance for $80,000 is not a valid acceptance because at that point in time *there was no offer to accept*. In reality, Nick's last statement is a new offer by Nick for the employer to consider whether to accept. In short, Nick faces some risk by making a counteroffer because the counteroffer extinguishes the original offer, and the employer could altogether walk away from the negotiation.

Denisenko/ Shutterstock.com

Usually, an offeror will specify the time and manner in which the offeree must manifest acceptance of the offer (*e.g.*, fax, email, mail, telephone, etc.). Under common law, when the offer is silent about timing and manner of acceptance, however, the offeree has a *reasonable* time to accept the offer in a manner that is *reasonable* under the circumstances. Another important concept is determining when an offer is accepted. For example, is an offer accepted when the offeree sends the acceptance, or is the offer accepted when the offeror receives the acceptance? The common law **mailbox rule** provides that an offer is accepted when the offeree places the acceptance "in the mailbox." Thus, the offeror can no longer revoke the offer if the offeree has already dispatched the acceptance, even if the offeror has not yet received the acceptance. If, however, the offeree sends the acceptance in a slower manner than the offer was made or if the acceptance was not sent in a commercially reasonable manner, then the acceptance is effective upon receipt by the offeror.

Some offers and acceptances are communicated, either orally or in writing, wherein the terms of the agreement are explicitly set forth. These types of situations are known as **express** contracts. Other offers and acceptances that are not discussed either orally or verbally can still legally constitute an agreement between the parties. For example, suppose you walk into a restaurant and order a meal. You have **implied** that you will pay for such meal, even though perhaps you did not specifically say so. Thus, implied contracts can be created by the conduct of the parties.

An offer usually is not considered accepted if an offeree is silent. In other words, an offeror generally cannot bind an offeree by stating, "By your silence, you accept my offer." In some unique situations, however, the offeree's silence may be enough to constitute an acceptance and cause the offeree to have to pay for services provided when the offeree knows that the person providing the services expects to be paid for the services.

Consideration

Once an agreement (*i.e.*, offer and acceptance) exists, then consideration (in addition to capacity and legality) must also be present to constitute an enforceable contract. **Consideration** is basically an exchange of value between the parties. Suppose that Manny states to his grandson, "I promise to pay you $500 on your next birthday." The grandson says, "Great!" Is this a contract? No, because the grandson gave no consideration to Manny. Thus, Manny is not contractually bound by his statement. His intent is to make a *gift*, not enter into a contract.

Sometimes, what constitutes sufficient consideration is the subject of litigation. For example, can *refraining* from doing something be sufficient consideration? Consider the following landmark court case decided by the highest state court in New York regarding this issue (Illustrative Court Case 16.1).

Thus, as the court held in *Hamer v. Sidway*, a **legal detriment** (*e.g.*, refraining from doing

---

ILLUSTRATIVE COURT CASE 16.1

Hamer v Sidway

New York Court of Appeals

124 N.Y. 538 (1891)

Opinion by: Parker

The question . . . is whether by virtue of a contract [uncle] became indebted to his nephew . . . on his twenty-first birthday in the sum of five thousand dollars. The trial court found as a fact that "on the 20th day of March, 1869, [uncle] agreed to and with [nephew] that if he would refrain from drinking liquor, using tobacco, swearing, and playing cards or billiards for money until he should become 21 years of age then he, [uncle], would at that time pay [nephew] the sum of $5,000 for such refraining, to which [nephew] agreed." . . .

The defendant contends that the contract was without consideration to support it, and, therefore, invalid. He asserts that the promisee by refraining from the use of liquor and tobacco was not harmed but benefited; that that which he did was best for him to do independently of his uncle's promise, and insists that it follows that unless the promisor was benefited, the contract was without consideration. A contention, which if well founded, would seem to leave open for controversy in many cases whether that which the promisee did or omitted to do was, in fact, of such benefit to him as to leave no consideration to support the enforcement of the promisor's agreement. Such a rule could not be tolerated, and is without

(Continued)

foundation in the law. The Exchequer Chamber, in 1875, defined consideration as follows: "A valuable consideration in the sense of the law may consist either in some right, interest, profit or benefit accruing to the one party, or some forbearance, detriment, loss or responsibility given, suffered or undertaken by the other." Courts "will not ask whether the thing which forms the consideration does in fact benefit the promissee or a third party, or is of any substantial value to anyone. It is enough that something is promised, done, forborne or suffered by the party to whom the promise is made as consideration for the promise made to him." [citation omitted.]

. . .

Now applying this rule to the facts before us, the promissee used tobacco, occasionally drank liquor, and he had a legal right to do so. That right he abandoned for a period of years upon the strength of the promise of the [uncle] that for such forbearance he would give him $5,000. We need not speculate on the effort which may have been required to give up the use of those stimulants. It is sufficient that he restricted his lawful freedom of action within certain prescribed limits upon the faith of his uncle's agreement, and now having fully performed the conditions imposed, it is of no moment whether such performance actually proved a benefit to the promisor, and the court will not inquire into it. . . .

something that a person has a legal right to do) can constitute sufficient consideration to form a contract. The important distinction between what may constitute a gift and what may constitute legally enforceable consideration is whether the agreement was a **bargained-for exchange**.

Another important concept with regard to consideration is the **pre-existing duty** rule. Basically, if a person promises to perform what someone already has a pre-existing duty to perform, the additional promise does not constitute additional consideration. For example, suppose a lawn-care company promises to mow your lawn for $40. You agree to that amount. When the lawn-care company arrives at your house, you find the company has changed its mind and offers to mow your lawn for no less than $50. Even if you paid them $50 so they would mow the lawn, most courts would hold the lawn-care company to the agreed-upon $40 price because the company had a pre-existing duty to do so before the demand for $50 (*i.e.*, you could sue to recover the extra $10 you paid). Not surprisingly, there are some exceptions to the pre-existing duty rule, but we will not discuss them here.

Capacity

To be contractually bound, a person must understand the nature of what he or she is doing. In other words, a person must have the **capacity** to enter into a contract. Some situations in which a person may lack contractual capacity include when the person is a minor, mentally incompetent, or intoxicated.

A minor (*i.e.*, an individual younger than 18 years old) can enter into a valid contract. Nevertheless, a minor can usually **disaffirm** the contract. This means the contract is **voidable** by the minor. In these situations, the minor must manifest his or her intent to not be bound by the contract within a reasonable time after the contract is formed. If the other party is an adult, the adult is generally bound by the terms of the contract and cannot disaffirm a contract with a minor. In many states, if the minor disaffirms the contract, the minor must return the goods purchased or do what is necessary to return the other party to the same position the other party was in before the contract. Obviously, a minor's right to disaffirm a contract makes many individuals and businesses hesitant to enter into contracts with minors.

What Do You Think?

Should a minor be able to disaffirm a contract?

Contracts entered into by intoxicated persons are **void** if the person was intoxicated at the time the contract was entered into and did not understand the legal consequences of what they were doing. Contracts entered into by mentally incompetent persons are *void* if a judge has previously declared the person as mentally incompetent. The contract is *voidable* by the mentally incompetent person if, even though a judge had not previously declared the person incompetent, the person was in fact incompetent at the time the contract was entered into.

Legality

The courts will not enforce an illegal contract. For example, suppose Camille enters into a contract with Jered for Jered to supply Camille with illegal drugs. Camille promises to pay Jered $10,000 upon delivery of the drugs. Suppose Jered supplies the drugs to Camille, but Camille fails to pay $10,000 to Jered. Since this is an illegal contract, the courts would not enforce the contract by ordering Camille to pay Jered $10,000, even though Jered fulfilled his end of the agreement. In short, contracts to commit crimes are not enforceable. Other contracts that may be against public policy could also be considered illegal by a court. For example, suppose a retail store sells a dishwasher to a customer. Suppose further that the contract is in English and the customer does not read or speak English. The contract states a selling price of $8,000 payable in installments over 10 years at an interest rate of 35%. Notwithstanding these terms, the customer signs the contract. Should the customer be bound by the contract? The courts may likely rule in this case that the contract is **unconscionable**, which means that the terms are so grossly unfair to one party that the contract should not be enforced. This is a relatively rare occurrence, however, because the courts are usually hesitant to second-guess the fairness of a contract.

Must a Contract Be in Writing?

Some people believe that *every* contract must be in writing to be enforceable. Of course, this is not correct. *Some* contracts, however, must be in writing to be enforceable.

Statute of Frauds

England established a law in 1677 that required some agreements be reduced to writing in an effort to prevent fraudulent transactions. This law became known as the **statute of frauds**. The statute of frauds still applies in certain transactions today. Basically, the statute of frauds requires that, for someone to be bound contractually regarding certain transactions, that person must have signed a written document.

The most common types of contracts that must be in writing to satisfy the statute of frauds are as follows:

- Contracts involving an interest in land. This includes contracts for the sale of land, mortgages, easements, etc.

- Promises to pay the debt of another. Suppose your friend owes a bank $1,000. You tell the bank that if your friend does not pay the money back, you will. For the bank to enforce this agreement against you, your promise must be in writing.

- Contracts that cannot be performed within one year. If a contract cannot possibly be performed within one year, the contract must be in writing to be enforced. Suppose that you contract with a photographer to take 1,000 pictures of exotic animals at various places around the world. You both agree that the photographer will complete the project no later than 18 months from now. Must your agreement be in writing? No. Even though the artist has 18 months to complete the project, it is *possible* that the artist could finish the project within one year. Contrast this with a situation where you hire the photographer for a term of exactly 18 months, and the photographer will take direction from you on what photographs to take during the 18 months. This contract must be in writing to be enforceable since it is not possible to fulfill the contract within one year.

- Sale of goods for more than $500. This rule will be discussed further in Chapter 20, which addresses the Uniform Commercial Code.

Exceptions to the Statute of Frauds

In some situations, an oral contract may be enforced, even though it technically should have been in writing under the statute of frauds. For example, one party of the contract could have already partially performed the contract. This **partial performance** could provide enough evidence for a court to rule that a contract was, in fact, in place, notwithstanding the lack of a written document.

Other exceptions exist to the statute of frauds, including when two *merchants* deal with each other. Some of these exceptions will be discussed in Chapter 20, but more detailed coverage of other exceptions is beyond the scope of our discussion here.

Parol Evidence Rule

As a general rule, once an agreement is reduced to writing, the terms of the writing control. Under the **parol evidence rule**, extraneous evidence such as oral discussions, pre-contract negotiations, etc., is not allowed in court. Some outside evidence may be presented in some cases, such as when the terms of the contract are unclear, a typographical error exists, or when evidence of prior dealings or usage of trade common in the industry would help a judge interpret the meaning of the contract terms.

Third Parties' Rights

Two parties may enter into a contract with the intent to benefit a third party. The benefited party, called a **third-party beneficiary**, may have the right to sue one of the contracting parties for failure to fulfill the contract. For example, your uncle enters into a contract with a car dealership to deliver to you a new car as a graduation gift. The contract specifies that the dealer is to deliver the car to you when you contact the dealer. If the dealer fails to deliver to you, you can sue the dealer even though you were not a party to the signed contract. In this case, you would be a *donee* beneficiary with a legal right to benefit from the contract entered into by the dealer and your uncle. Thus, *intended* beneficiaries, including donee and creditor beneficiaries, may have a claim against parties of the contract. *Incidental* beneficiaries (*i.e.*, third parties not specifically intended to benefit from the contract between others) have no such claim.

As we discussed in Chapter 13, a landlord may assign his or her rights in a lease. As a general rule, this ability to **assign** rights in a contract applies to all contracts, not just lease agreements. This is only true if the contract does not prohibit assignment, however. The party assigning the rights is called the **assignor**, while the party being assigned the rights is called the **assignee**. The assignee generally has the same rights in the contract as the assignor did. Also, a party that has an obligation to perform a duty under a contract may **delegate** that duty. Exceptions exist, of course, to the general ability of someone to assign their rights or delegate their duties under a contract. For example, suppose you wish to have a certain person paint a portrait of you. You carefully select the artist because of the artist's reputation, knowledge, and unique skills. The artist with whom you contract will unlikely be able to delegate their duty to perform the contractual obligation because you are relying specifically on that particular artist's skill to perform a unique service. In cases where a duty may be delegated, the person who delegated the duty is still obligated under the contract if the delegatee fails to perform (unless you agree to enter into a whole new contract with the delegatee—called a contract **novation**— and release the initial person from his or her obligations).

QUESTIONS FOR REVIEW

1. What are the five elements necessary to form a contract?

2. If an offer is silent regarding how long the offer is open, how long does the offeree have to accept the offer?

3. What constitutes an agreement?

4. Explain the mirror image rule.

5. What is the mailbox rule?

6. Explain the meaning of the term "consideration."

7. What is the risk of entering into a contract with a minor?

8. What does "unconscionable" mean in the context of contracts?

9. Give three examples of contracts that must be in writing to comply with the the statute of frauds.

10. What is the parol evidence rule?

11. What is a third-party beneficiary? What rights does a third-party beneficiary have?

12. When might a person be prohibited from delegating a contractual duty?

13. Summarize the *Hamer v. Sidway* case.

INTERNET ACTIVITIES

1. Find the Louisiana Court of Appeal case *Century 21 Shackelford-French Real Estate, Inc. v. Ealy*, 71 So. 3d 429 (2011).

   a. What was the issue or issues in the case?

   b. What was the holding of the court?

   c. Summarize the court's analysis.

2. Find the United States Court of Appeals for the First Circuit case *The Capability Group, Inc. v. American Express Travel Related Services Company, Inc.*, 658 F.3d 75 (2011).

   a. What was the issue or issues in the case?

   b. What was the holding of the court?

   c. Summarize the court's analysis.

Chapter 17

Performance and Discharge

Once a valid contract is in place, the parties must then perform their respective obligations. A contract where both parties have performed their obligations is called an **executed** contract. A contract that is not yet fully performed by one or more parties is called an **executory** contract. In this chapter, we focus on executory contracts and a party's obligations to perform the party's duties under the contract. We also discuss how a party may successfully discharge those duties to perform.

Performance

In many day-to-day situations, parties perform their contractual obligations at the same time. For example, when you go to the grocery store and present the goods you want to purchase to the cashier, you make an implied offer to purchase the goods for the stated price. The grocery store accepts the offer, places the goods in a bag, and delivers them to you. At the same time, you pay for the goods. Both parties basically fulfill their performance obligation under the implied contract at the same time.

Some contracts place conditions on the timing of performance. For example, consider the following two scenarios:

Scenario 1. Suppose David signs a valid contract to sell his home to Jude. In the contract, however, a provision states that Jude only has to perform his obligation to purchase the home if the home passes a termite inspection conducted by a licensed inspector. This is an example of a contract that contains a **condition precedent**. In other words, some event must occur before a party has an obligation to perform.

Scenario 2. Suppose Marcus signs a contract wherein he agrees to remove snow from Jill's sidewalks and driveway for $20 each time. The contract provides, however, that if gas prices exceed $4.00 per gallon, Marcus no longer has an obligation to remove the snow for that price. This is an example of a contract that contains a **condition subsequent**. In other words, a party has the obligation to perform until a particular event occurs.

jabiru/ Shutterstock.com

Payment and delivery terms are also an important part of most contracts. The parties usually will agree on these terms, but in situations where payment or method and time of delivery of goods is not specified, then the Uniform Commercial Code (discussed in Chapter 20) will likely apply. If the contract is not for the sale of goods, then *reasonable* terms under the circumstances will apply.

Discharge

A party to a contract is said to have **discharged** their obligation once performance occurs. If a party fails to perform and discharge the party's obligations, the party may be in **breach** of contract. The non-breaching party may then seek damages from the breaching party (discussed further in Chapter 18). The most straightforward way to discharge a party's obligations under a contract is by **complete performance**. In some cases, when a party cannot completely perform, the courts will often view **substantial performance** as satisfying the contractual obligation. Of course, the other party may be entitled to some payment from the party that only substantially performed to make up the difference between substantial performance and complete performance. As you might suspect, parties often argue over whether a party has "substantially" performed.

If a party **materially breaches** a contract (*e.g.*, the party fails to completely or substantially perform), the breach discharges the non-breaching party's obligation to perform. In some situations, a party to a contract may decide not to perform, even before the time of performance arrives. By notifying the other party of this intent, this refusal to perform is called an **anticipatory repudiation**. An anticipatory repudiation is a breach of contract, and the non-breaching party may sue for damages or find another party with whom to enter into a similar contract. The anticipatory repudiation discharges the non-breaching party from performance. The non-breaching party, however, may allow the repudiating party to change their mind and actually perform the contractual obligation.

What Do You Think?

Is it ever ethical to anticipatorily repudiate a contract?

Another way to discharge performance obligations is for the parties to agree to cancel or **rescind** the contract. Moreover, a party may **waive** performance by the other party or **release** the other party from any remaining contractual obligations.

In some situations, a party can be legally excused from the obligation to perform. For example, a party to the contract may die, which, of course, would excuse performance (*e.g.*, a professional athlete signs a three-year contract but dies one year into the contract). In addition, a performance may be **impossible** (*e.g.*, a person contracted to fix a roof of a house is excused from performance if the house burns down before the performance can occur). Consider the following old case from England (Illustrative Court Case 17.1) establishing the discharge of an obligation due to impossibility.

Another excuse from performing may be **commercial impracticability**. This is similar to impossibility, but basically means that the contemplated

---

ILLUSTRATIVE COURT CASE 17.1

Taylor v. Caldwell

England and Wales High Court

122 ER 309 (1863)

Blackburn J. In this case, the plaintiffs and defendants had, on the 27th May, 1861, entered into a contract by which the defendants agreed to let the plaintiffs have the use of The Surrey Gardens and Music Hall on four days then to come, viz., the 17th June, 15th July, 5th August and 19th August, for the purpose of giving a series of four grand concerts . . . and the plaintiffs agreed to take the Gardens and Hall on those days, and pay 100 [pounds] for each day. . . . The agreement then proceeds to set out various stipulations between the parties as to what each was to supply for these concerts and entertainments, and as to the manner in which they should be carried on. The effect of the whole is to [show] that the existence of the Music Hall in the Surrey Gardens in a state fit for a concert was essential for the fulfillment of the contract, such entertainments as the parties contemplated in their agreement could not be given without it. After the making of the agreement, and before the first day on which a concert was to be given, the Hall was destroyed by fire. This destruction, we must take it on the evidence, was without the fault of either party, and was so complete that in consequence the concerts could not be given as intended. And the question we have to decide is whether, under these circumstances, the loss which the plaintiffs have sustained is to fall upon the defendants. The parties when framing their agreement evidently had not present to their minds the possibility of such a disaster, and have made no express stipulation with reference to it, so that the answer to the question must depend on the general rules of law applicable to such a contract. There seems no doubt that where there is a positive contract to do a thing, not in itself unlawful, the contractor must perform it or pay damages for not doing it, although in consequence of unforeseen accidents, the performance of his contract has become unexpectedly burthensome or even impossible.

. . .

There is a class of contracts in which a person binds himself to do something which requires to be performed by him in person; and such promises, e.g. promises to marry, or promises to serve for a certain time, are never in practice qualified by an express exception of the death of the party; and therefore in such cases the contract is in terms broken if the promisor dies before fulfillment. Yet it was very early determined that, if the performance is personal, the executors are not liable. . . . "Where a contract depends upon personal skill, and the act of God renders it impossible, as, for instance, in the case of a painter employed to paint a picture who is struck blind, it may be that the performance might be excused." [Citation omitted.]

. . .

The principle seems to us to be that, in contracts in which the performance depends on the continued existence of a given person or thing, a condition is implied that the impossibility of performance arising from the perishing of the person or thing shall excuse the performance. . . . In the present case, looking at the whole contract, we find that the parties contracted on the basis of the continued existence of the Music Hall at the time when the concerts were to be given; that being essential to their performance.

We think, therefore, that the Music Hall having ceased to exist, without fault of either party, both parties are excused, the plaintiffs from taking the gardens and paying the money, the defendants from performing their promise to give the use of the hall and Gardens and other things.

performance has become extremely and unreasonably difficult or expensive. Suppose, for example, you own a music store and sell pianos that you import from a foreign country. You enter into contracts with high schools to provide certain foreign-made grand pianos by the beginning of the school year. Unfortunately, an earthquake significantly damages the supplier's manufacturing plant, and you are informed that only a few pianos will be made or delivered for several months. You may be excused from performing under the contract (*i.e.*, not in breach) due to commercial impracticability, but, at a minimum, you likely would be expected to see if you could find the pianos from another supplier to fulfill your obligations under the contract. Consider the following New York case addressing the issue of commercial impracticability (Illustrative Court Case 17.2).

Maple Farms, Inc. v. City School District of Elmira

Supreme Court of New York

352 N.Y.S.2d 784 (1974)

Opinion by: Startwood

Opinion

This is a motion for summary judgment . . . whereby the plaintiff seeks . . . a determination that the contract wherein the plaintiff agreed to supply milk to the defendant school district at an agreed price be terminated without further liability on the grounds of legal "impossibility" or "impracticality" because of the occurrence of events not contemplated by the parties which makes performance impracticable. . . .

The background of this dispute is that the price of raw milk at the farm site is and has been controlled for many years in this area by the United States Department of Agriculture. . . . The president of the plaintiff milk dealer has for at least 10 years bid on contracts to supply milk for the defendant school district and is thoroughly conversant with prices and costs. Though the plaintiff avers that the defendant was aware of the prices of raw milk and the profit picture, the fiscal officer of the defendant denies that either the price of raw milk or the profit structure of suppliers was known or of any concern to him or the defendant. The defendant's only concern was the assurance of a steady supply of milk for the school lunch program at an agreed price on which the school's budget had to be based.

The mandated price of raw milk has in the past fluctuated from a cost of $6.73 cwt in 1969 to a high of $7.58 cwt in 1972, or 12%, with fluctuation within a calendar year ranging from 1% to 4.5%. The plaintiff agreed to supply milk to the defendant for the school year 1973–1974 by agreement of June 15, 1973 at a price of $.0759 per half pint, at which time the mandated price of raw milk was $8.03 cwt. By November of 1973 the price of raw milk had risen to $9.31 cwt. and by December 1973 to $9.89 cwt., an increase of 23% over the June 1973 price. However, it should be noted that there was an increase from the low price in 1972 to the June 1973 price (date of the contract) of 9.5%. Because of considerable increase in the price of raw milk, the plaintiff, beginning in October 1973, has requested the defendant to relieve the plaintiff of its contract and to put the contract out for rebidding. The defendant has refused.

The plaintiff spells out in detail its costs based on the June and December prices of raw milk and shows that it will sustain a loss of $7,350.55 if it is required to continue its performance on the same volume with raw milk at the December price. Its contracts with other school districts where it is faced with the same problem will triple its total contemplated loss.

. . .

The plaintiff goes to great lengths to spell out the cause of the substantial increase in the price of raw milk, which the plaintiff argues could not have been foreseen by the parties because it came about in large measure from the agreement of the United States to sell huge amounts of grain to Russia and to a lesser extent to unanticipated crop failures.

. . .

The common-law rule is . . . as follows: ". . . [I]mpossibility means not only strict impossibility but impracticability because of extreme and unreasonable difficulty, expense, injury or loss involved." [Citation omitted.]

> "When the issue is raised, the court is asked to construct a condition of performance based on the changed circumstances, a process which involves at least three reasonably definable steps. First, a contingency—something unexpected—must have occurred. Second, the risk of the unexpected occurrence must not have been allocated either by agreement or by custom. Finally, occurrence of the contingency must have rendered performance commercially impracticable." [Citation omitted.]
>
> . . .
>
> There is no precise point, though such could conceivably be reached, at which an increase in price of raw goods above the norm would be so disproportionate to the risk assumed as to amount to "impracticality" in a commercial sense. However, we cannot say on these facts that the increase here has reached the point of "impracticality" in performance of this contract in light of the risks that we find were assumed by the plaintiff.
>
> . . .
>
> The plaintiff's motion is denied and the defendant is granted summary judgment dismissing the complaint.

In summary, once a person has a contractual obligation, the person must discharge that obligation either by performance or by satisfying the requirement for discharge as a matter of law (*e.g.,* death of a party, impossibility, commercial impractability, etc.).

QUESTIONS FOR REVIEW

1. What is the difference between an executed contract and an executory contract?

2. Give an example of a condition precedent.

3. Give an example of a condition subsequent.

4. If a party cannot "completely" perform obligations under a contract, what significance does "substantially" performing have?

5. What is anticipatory repudiation?

6. Give an example of a contractual obligation that may be commercially impracticable or impossible to perform.

7. Summarize the *Taylor v. Caldwell* case.

8. Summarize the *Maple Farms v. City School District of Elmira* case.

INTERNET ACTIVITIES

1. Find the Supreme Court of Idaho case *Perception Construction Management, Inc. v. Bell*, 254 P.3d 1246 (2011).

   a. What was the issue or issues in the case?

   b. What was the holding of the court?

   c. Summarize the court's analysis.

2. Find the Supreme Court of the United States case *Mobil Oil Exploration & Producing Southeast, Inc. v. United States*, 530 U.S. 604 (2000).

   a. What is the issue or issues in the case?

   b. What was the holding of the Court?

   c. Summarize the Court's analysis.

Chapter 18

Contract Remedies

I f one party is in breach of contract, the other party may seek a **remedy** for the harm suffered. Typically, the remedy sought by the non-breaching party will be in the form of monetary **damages**. The non-breaching party potentially has a number of different remedies that may be pursued, depending upon the particular circumstances surrounding the breach of contract. This chapter addresses many of these potential contractual remedies.

Monetary Damages

Except in unique cases, the typical remedy sought by a non-breaching party is monetary damages. There are several categories of monetary damages. Compensatory, punitive, and liquidated damages are discussed here.

Compensatory Damages

If a party can persuade a court that another party to the contract was in breach, the court will likely award the non-breaching party **compensatory** damages. The purpose of compensatory damages is, of course, to place the non-breaching party in as good a position as the non-breaching party would have been in had the breaching party performed the contractual obligations (*i.e.*, to *compensate* the party for the loss suffered). Compensatory damages also include **consequential** damages and **incidental** damages. Consequential damages may include, for example, a claim by the plaintiff that, as a consequence of the breach of contract by the defendant, the plaintiff also suffered some personal physical injuries (*e.g.*, because

of a product malfunction). Incidental damages may occur if the non-breaching party incurs additional cost to deal with the breaching party's breach. Suppose Art and Zane enter into a valid contract where Art agrees to sell Zane a set of golf clubs. They agree that Art will deliver the clubs and then Zane will pay for the clubs when he receives them. After Art ships the clubs, but before Zane receives them, Zane calls Art and informs Art that he has changed his mind and no longer wants the clubs and will not pay for them. Zane is in breach of contract and, in addition to any other damages Art may be entitled to, Art may incur *incidental* damages by stopping shipment of the golf clubs to Zane.

A non-breaching party typically has a duty to try to **mitigate** damages. In other words, if a non-breaching party can subsequently enter into a contract with someone else to accomplish the same result, then the non-breaching party should do so.

For example, Debra orders 500 soccer balls from Maria at $5 each. Suppose Maria fails to deliver and is in breach of contract. Debra is able to find 500 soccer balls from Shay for $5.25 per ball. In this situation, Debra has mitigated the damages so that she only suffered a loss of 25 cents per soccer ball (plus any incidental damages).

What Do You Think?

Is it ethical for a non-breaching party to fail to mitigate damages to the fullest extent possible?

Punitive Damages

In addition to awarding compensatory damages to a plaintiff, a court may award additional damages to the plaintiff as a means to punish the defendant for willful and malicious conduct. These damages are called **punitive** damages. The purpose of a judge or jury awarding these damages is to discourage the defendant (and others) from engaging in this type of behavior. Note that in contract cases where punitive damages are awarded, it may be because the defendant has also committed a tort in addition to a breach of contract. Consider the following case from the Supreme Court of Virginia (Illustrative Court Case 18.1).

ILLUSTRATIVE COURT CASE 18.1

Dunn Construction Company, Inc v. Cloney

Supreme Court of Virginia

278 Va. 260, 682 S.E.2d 943 (2009)

Opinion By Justice Larwrence L. Koontz, Jr.

This appeal arises from a contract dispute between a building contractor and a property owner involving the construction of a new house. During the construction of the house the contractor made allegedly fraudulent representations concerning certain repairs made by the contractor to the foundation wall of the house. Ultimately at the trial of the case, in addition to a breach of contract claim, the circuit court permitted the property owner's claim for compensatory and punitive damages based on fraud to be submitted to the jury. The dispositive issue we consider with regard to the jury's award of punitive damages is whether the fraudulent representations arose out of the contract or constituted an independent tortious breach of a common law duty.

Background

On September 12, 2005, Bill G. Dunn, part owner and as president of Dunn Construction Company, Inc. (collectively, "Dunn"), and Richard M. Cloney entered into a contract for the partial construction of a house. . . . Dunn was to perform all the major construction, leaving some of the interior finishing to be done by Cloney or another contractor. The contract stated that "[a]ll work was to be completed in a workmanlike manner according to standard practices." The contract further stated that because Dunn was not completing the house, only a partial certificate of occupancy permit could be obtained when the contract was completed. The contract provided a schedule of specific progress payments and further provided that "any balance left on this contract will be paid" when the work specified in the contract was completed.

It is not disputed that Dunn initially failed to properly construct the front foundation wall in accord with standards required by the applicable Virginia building code. As a result, while the house was still under construction, cracks appeared in the wall and a portion of it bowed out several inches. Dunn undertook remedial efforts to repair the wall, adding additional steel reinforcing bars, commonly called "rebar," into the interior of the wall, which was constructed of concrete two-celled masonry units, commonly called "cinderblocks." Dunn placed the rebar in one cell of each cinderblock along the face of the wall, approximately every 16 inches, and filled these cells with concrete to the level of where the wall had cracked.

After Dunn performed these repairs, Dunn told David Hash, the Mecklenburg County building inspector, that "the wall had been filled with concrete and rebar" but did not specify the amount of concrete or placement of rebar within the wall. During his post-repair inspection Hash identified a new hairline crack in the repaired foundation wall and directed that a structural engineer inspect the foundation and prepare a report as a condition of obtaining a temporary certificate of occupancy.

After completing repairs to satisfy various other conditions of obtaining the temporary certificate of occupancy, Dunn presented Cloney with a final bill. Cloney disputed certain items in the bill and indicated that he would prefer to place any final payment in escrow until after the inspection of the foundation wall. A heated exchange between Dunn and Cloney ensued, with Dunn insisting that he had completed the contract and was entitled to be paid. Eventually, Cloney gave Dunn a check for the amount Dunn claimed was due, and Dunn gave Cloney a written statement guaranteeing the wall's stability for ten years and averring that the wall had been repaired by placing rebar in every cell of the cinderblocks and filling the wall to its top with concrete.

When Dunn refused to pay for the inspection Hash had called for, Cloney hired Leon Morris, a structural engineer, who determined that the wall had not been filled with reinforced concrete or adequately reinforced with rebar, as Dunn had represented to Hash and Cloney. Morris found that between one-third to one-half of the cells had no reinforcement and that, as a result, the wall, both as originally constructed and following the attempted repair, did not meet the requirements of the building code. In Morris' opinion, the defect in the foundation wall could cause the house to collapse because this wall was "a candidate for a catastrophic failure."

On August 21, 2006, Cloney filed a complaint in the Circuit Court of Mecklenburg County against Dunn seeking damages under theories of breach of contract, negligence, and fraud. Cloney alleged that the total cost to repair the foundation was $31,813.27 and that an additional $2,225 would be required to complete other obligations Dunn had neglected to perform under the contract. Thus, for the alleged breach of the contract, Cloney claimed damages of $34,038.27. Likewise, Cloney sought to recover the same amount as compensatory damages for the alleged negligence and fraud. Additionally, Cloney sought $100,000 in punitive damages for the alleged fraud. Dunn filed an answer admitting the general factual allegations of the complaint, but denying liability to Cloney under any theory of recovery.

A jury trial was held in the circuit court beginning on April 7, 2008 at which evidence in accord with the above-recited facts was received. At the conclusion of the evidence, the court reviewed the proffered instructions including instructions 21, 23 and 24 addressing the availability of punitive damages. Instruction 21 read, in relevant part:

> If you find that Richard M. Cloney is entitled to be compensated for his damages, and if you further believe by clear and convincing evidence that Billy G. Dunn and Dunn Construction Co., Inc. acted with actual malice toward Richard M. Cloney or acted under circumstances amounting to a willful and wanton disregard to Richard Cloney's rights, then you may also award punitive damages to Richard M. Cloney to punish Billy G. Dunn and Dunn Construction Co., Inc. for their actions and to serve as an example to prevent others from acting in a similar way.

The jury returned its verdict for Cloney, awarding him $33,838.27 in compensatory damages . . . and $25,000 in punitive damages. The jury also awarded interest on the compensatory damages of 6%

(*Continued*)

from August 21, 2006 until the judgment was paid. Dunn objected to all aspects of the verdict and made a motion that it be set aside, which motion the circuit court overruled.

Prior to entry of a final order confirming the jury's verdict, Dunn filed a motion for reconsideration. As relevant to the issues raised in this appeal, Dunn contended that the award of punitive damages was impermissible because "any misrepresentation, if any were demonstrated, arose out of contract, not tort." This was so, Dunn contended, because there was no evidence that Dunn did not intend to fulfill the obligations of the contract, but only that there may have been a misrepresentation as to the manner of performance. By permitting the jury to award punitive damages for fraud, Dunn contended that the circuit court impermissibly permitted Cloney to convert his breach of contract action into a tort action.

. . .

Discussion

The dispositive issue in this appeal is whether the circuit court erred in determining that there was sufficient evidence to permit the jury to find that Dunn had committed an act of fraud independent of the contractual relationship between Dunn and Cloney such that Cloney could maintain an action both for breach of contract and fraud. . . . [W]e conclude that there was insufficient evidence of an independent act of fraud and, for the reasons that follow, we hold that the circuit court erred in permitting the jury to consider awarding punitive damages to Cloney.

"As a general rule, damages for breach of contracts are limited to the pecuniary loss sustained." [Citation omitted.] However, a single act or occurrence can, in certain circumstances, support causes of action both for breach of contract and for breach of a duty arising in tort, thus permitting a plaintiff to recover both for the loss suffered as a result of the breach and traditional tort damages, including where appropriate, punitive damages. [Citation omitted.] To avoid turning every breach of contract into a tort, however, we have consistently adhered to the rule that, in order to recover in tort, "the duty tortiously or negligently breached must be a common law duty, not one existing between the parties solely by virtue of the contract." [Citation omitted.]

. . .

Under the contract, Dunn had a duty to construct the foundation wall "in a workmanlike manner according to standard practices." Clearly, the original wall was not constructed in accord with this duty, and Dunn was required to make repairs to bring the wall in compliance with the applicable building code under that same duty. Dunn's false representation that he had made adequate repairs thus related to a duty that arose under the contract. The fact that the representation was made in order to obtain payment from Cloney does not take the fraud outside of the contract relationship, because the payment obtained was also due under the original terms of the contract. . . .

Dunn's conduct in failing to properly construct the wall initially could be attributed to negligence. His subsequent misrepresentations to Cloney and Hash regarding the repairs undertaken, however, were unquestionably deliberate and false. We do not condone such misrepresentations. Nonetheless . . . we cannot permit "turning every breach of contract into an actionable claim for fraud" simply because of misrepresentations of the contractor entwined with a breach of the contract.

Conclusion

For these reasons, the judgment of the circuit court confirming the award of punitive damages for fraud will be reversed and final judgment for Cloney limited to the award of compensatory damages with interest from August 21, 2006 will be entered here.

Liquidated Damages

Sometimes parties to a contract will actually insert a provision in the contract that states the amount of damages a potential breaching party will pay. These are called **liquidated** damages. For example, suppose Ned contracts with Jory to construct a restaurant on some land Ned owns. The contract provides that if the project is not completed on time, then Jory owes Ned $1,000 per day until construction is complete. Of course, Ned may want this provision in the contract because any delay in finishing construction of the restaurant may cause Ned to lose anticipated profits.

Restitution

In addition to monetary damages, another remedy a non-breaching party may seek is **restitution**. This is simply putting the non-breaching party back in the same position the party was in before the parties entered into the contract. Perhaps the non-breaching party merely seeks a return of the consideration paid to the breaching party.

Equitable Remedies

Occasionally, a non-breaching party does not want to be compensated monetarily for the breach. Rather, the non-breaching party may wish to force the breaching party to fulfill the contract's terms or perhaps the non-breaching party may wish to stop the other party from engaging in certain behavior contrary to the contractual provisions. These two situations are discussed next.

Specific Performance

Suppose you are looking to open an amusement park. You find the perfect location for the park and enter into a contract with the landowner to sell you the land. Further suppose that the landowner later backs out of the contract and refuses to deed the land to you. One remedy you might seek is for a court to order **specific performance** from the landowner. In other words, given the uniqueness of the land and your purpose for acquiring it, you believe monetary damages will not be a sufficient remedy for you. Instead, you seek a court order forcing the landowner to transfer the land to you according to the contract. Specific performance is an appropriate remedy when the subject matter of the contract is real property, but a court generally will not order specific performance as a remedy when the subject matter is personal property, unless the personal property is sufficiently rare or unique (*e.g.*, a famous painting). A court also will not order specific performance with respect to personal services contracts. Consider the Appellate Court of Illinois case on the issue of specific performance (Illustrative Court Case 18.2).

ILLUSTRATIVE COURT CASE 18.2

Short v. Hankins

Appellate Court of Illinois, Third District

2015 IL App (3d)

Opinion

Plaintiffs William Short and Jim Maloof Realty Inc. brought actions against defendant William Hankins for specific performance and breach of a commission provision in a real estate listing contract executed between Short as buyer and Hankins as seller. Maloof Realty represented Short in the transaction. The closing did not take place on the contracted closing date and Hankins thereafter sought to declare

(Continued)

the contract null and void. The trial court ruled in favor of Short on his claim for specific performance and in favor of Maloof Realty on its commission claim. Hankins appealed both rulings. We affirm.

Facts

On August 1, 2011, defendant William Hankins entered into a listing agreement with [Maloof Realty]. Hankins sought to sell a vacant parcel of 83.54 acres he owned in Gladsford in Peoria County. . . . Plaintiff William Short expressed an interest in buying the property. . . .

Hankins and Short entered into a vacant land sales contract. Short signed the sales contract on October 22, 2011, and Hankins signed it on November 4, 2011. The contract specified the following terms: a purchase price of $300,000; no financing contingency; and a December 2, 2011, closing date. A repair amendment to the contract required the removal of some 55-gallon drums on the property at least five days before the closing. . . . The closing did not take place on December 2 [because Short thought the parties had agreed to extend the closing date. On December 15, 2011, Short was notified by Hankins that he no longer wished to sell his property to Short.] On December 22, 2011, Short sent notice that Hankins had breached the sales contract and had 10 days to cure the breach. Short thereafter filed a complaint for specific performance and Maloof Realty filed a complaint seeking the commission owed by Hankins. The cases were consolidated and a bench trial took place.

. . .

Analysis

The issues on appeal are whether the trial court erred when it awarded specific performance to Short and awarded a commission to Maloof Realty.

We [now] consider Hankins' challenge to the award of specific performance. He argues that Short was not entitled to specific performance and the trial court erred in granting it. He maintains that Short was not ready, willing and able to buy the property on the December 2 closing date; Short's inability to timely close was not based on any affirmative conduct by Hankins; Hankins was not required to provide Short notice and an opportunity to cure Short's default; and the statute of frauds negates any oral agreement to extend the closing date.

Specific performance is appropriate as a matter of right and enforceable in equity "where the parties have fairly and understandingly entered into a valid contract for the sale of real property." [Citation omitted.] A party is entitled to specific performance if it establishes either that the party has performed according to the contract terms or that the party was ready, willing and able to perform the contract but was prevented, and excused, from doing so by the other party's conduct. [Citation omitted.] A buyer is ready, willing and able to perform when he has agreed to buy the property and has sufficient funds to make the purchase or can obtain the necessary funds within the contractual time limit. [Citation omitted.]

. . .

The contract required Hankins to give Short written notice of the breach within 10 days and an opportunity to cure. As found by the trial court, "assuming, *arguendo*, that Short was in breach," Hankins failed to provide notice and an opportunity to cure.

Paragraph 5 of the land sales contract provides:

"CLOSING. *** If the closing is delayed past the closing date due to the fault of either party, even if this transaction is subsequently closed, the defaulting party shall pay damages as provided in the Contract. The non-defaulting party will be entitled to collect damages as soon as the default occurs

(*Continued*)

and the notice and cure provisions provided for in Paragraph 13, Default, are not applicable to this paragraph."

Paragraph 13 provides:

"DEFAULT. If either party does not perform any obligation under this Contract (a "default"), the non-defaulting party shall give written notice of the default to the defaulting party. Notice must be given no later than seven (7) days after the scheduled closing date (or any written extension thereof) or possession. Failure to provide the notice shall limit available remedies of the non-defaulting party to recovery of the earnest money deposit. If notice is properly given, and the defaulting party does not cure the default within ten (10) days of the notice, the non-defaulting party may pursue any remedy available in law or equity, including specific performance."

. . .

The land sales contract required written notice of default and opportunity to cure be provided within seven days of a missed closing. The notice and cure provisions under paragraph 13 apply to all aspects of default, contrary to Hankins proposed interpretation that the inapplicability of notice and cure to the non-defaulter's ability to collect damages under paragraph 5 negates the applicability of paragraph 13's notice and cure provisions. Hankins did not comply with the notice requirements and failed to give Short an opportunity to cure the breach. Despite the December 2, breach, Short was ready, willing and able to perform the contract but was prevented from doing so by Hankins' failure to give him notice of default and the opportunity to cure it. The breach was not material and did not preclude an award of specific performance. Accordingly, we find the trial court did not abuse its discretion in granting specific performance to Short.

. . .

For the foregoing reasons, the judgment to the circuit court of Peoria County is affirmed.

Injunctions

When a party seeks a court order to stop another party from engaging in a certain action, the remedy sought is an **injunction**. For example, you sign an option contract, which gives you the right to purchase some rare artwork within 30 days. A couple of days later, you learn that the owner intends to sell the artwork to another buyer next week. You may be able to obtain an injunction prohibiting the owner of the rare art from selling to the other buyer during your option period.

QUESTIONS FOR REVIEW

1. Explain the difference between compensatory and punitive damages.

2. A non-breaching party to a contract generally has an obligation to mitigate damages. What does this mean?

3. What are liquidated damages?

4. In what situations might a court award specific performance as a remedy?

5. What is an injunction?

6. Summarize the *Dunn Construction v. Cloney* case.

7. Summarize the *Short v. Hankins* case.

INTERNET ACTIVITIES

1. Find the Supreme Court of Utah case *TruGreen Companies, LLC v. Mower Brothers, Inc.*, 199 P.3d 929 (2008).

   a. What is the issue or issues in the case?

   b. What was the holding of the court?

   c. Summarize the court's analysis.

2. Find the Supreme Court of California case *Lewis Jorge Construction Management, Inc. v. Pomona Unified School District*, 102 P.3d 257 (2004).

a. What is the issue or issues in the case?

b. What was the holding of the court?

c. Summarize the court's analysis.

Chapter 19

Mistakes, Misrepresentation, Duress, and Undue Influence

Sometimes when parties enter into contracts, a mistake might be made by one or both parties. One party may also engage in some form of fraud or misrepresentation. Additionally, a party may enter into a contract under duress or because of the undue influence of another party. This chapter addresses the impact of these situations on the validity of a contract and whether there truly was a "genuine agreement" between the parties.

Mistakes

Suppose Lena has a painting for sale. She believes it was painted by a famous artist. Sheila wants to purchase the painting, and she believes it is a painting by a famous artist as well. Lena and Sheila then enter into a contract wherein Sheila agrees to pay Lena $500,000 for the painting. After the contract is signed, they discover that the painting is really not by a famous artist, but one painted by an imposter. Is Sheila still required to pay $500,000 to Lena? What if, at the time the contract was signed, Sheila thought it was a painting by a famous artist, but Lena knew that it was not? Should Sheila still have to pay Lena $500,000?

In contract law, mistakes are classified as either **mutual** (or "bilateral") or **unilateral**. In general,

if both parties are mistaken about a material fact contained in the contract, a judge may allow the contract to be rescinded by either party. Notice that the mistake must be a mistake of *fact*. A court will typically not allow the rescission of a contract due to a mistake of *value*, however.

If only one party is mistaken about a material fact in the contract, then that party generally is not entitled to rescind the contract. Of course, exceptions exist to these general rules, and state laws can vary somewhat also. Consider the United States Eight Circuit Court of Appeals case (Illustrative Court Case 19.1) relating to a party's argument that the contract they entered into should be rescinded because of a mistake.

Obviously, care should be taken before one enters into a contract. An argument that the contract should be rescinded because of a mistake may not prevail in court.

Misrepresentation

As was discussed in Chapter 16, an essential element of a contract is for the parties to agree to the terms (*i.e.*, offer and acceptance). What happens if one party lies or misrepresents to the other party to induce the party to enter into the contract? In such cases, the innocent party may be able to rescind the contract.

Generally, a person commits a **fraudulent misrepresentation** when the person (1) misrepresents a *material* fact, (2) intends to deceive the other person, and (3) the other person justifiably relies on the misrepresentation. While fraud is also a tort (and possibly a crime), it often is claimed as a reason to rescind a contract. Notice that for fraud to occur, the person must have the intent to deceive.

ILLUSTRATIVE COURT CASE 19.1

Health East Bethesda Hospital v. United Commercial Travelers of America

Eighth Circuit Court of Appeals

596 F.3d 986 (8th Cir. 2010)

OPINION

BENTON, Circuit Judge.

In this diversity case, HealthEast Bethesda Hospital ("HealthEast") sued United Commercial Travelers of America ("UCT") for breach of an insurance settlement contract. The district court granted summary judgment to HealthEast. Having jurisdiction . . . this court affirms.

I.

In June 2005, Nels J. Hansen purchased a Medicare supplement policy from UCT. That October, he was admitted to HealthEast. Before his admission, UCT informed HealthEast that Hansen was covered by its policy. HealthEast cared for Hansen until his death in April 2006.

In October HealthEast billed UCT $331,893.40 for Hansen's care. UCT offered to settle for $265,514.72, which HealthEast accepted in November.

Days after settling, UCT obtained Hansen's health records. Reviewing them, UCT concluded that Hansen misrepresented his medical history on the insurance application. UCT rescinded the policy and refused to pay HealthEast. Months after rescinding, UCT hired an expert who determined that its maximum potential liability for Hansen's care was $134,985.44.

HealthEast sued UCT for breach of contract. Both moved for summary judgment. The district court granted summary judgment to HealthEast, ruling that the contract was not voidable because UCT bore the risk of any mistake. The district court awarded HealthEast the full settlement amount, plus interest. UCT appeals.

II.

. . .

In a diversity suit, this court applies the substantive law of the forum state, here Minnesota. [Citation omitted.]

A.

UCT asserts it properly rescinded the settlement based on its unilateral mistake. Under Minnesota law, rescission of a contract for mistake is ordinarily founded on either mutual mistake or a "mistake by one [party] induced or contributed to by the other." [Citation omitted.] Generally, a party cannot avoid a contract on the basis of a unilateral mistake unless there is ambiguity, fraud, or misrepresentation. [Citation omitted.] Even if there is no ambiguity, fraud, or misrepresentation, relief from a unilateral mistake is available where enforcement is an "oppressive burden" and rescission would impose no substantial hardship on the other party. [Citation omitted.] A party may not, however, escape contract liability based on unilateral mistake if the party bears the risk of that mistake. [Citations omitted.]

The district court denied relief to UCT, ruling that it was a sophisticated party that bore the risk of mistake and could have avoided it by investigating Hansen's policy. A party bears the risk of mistake if it is aware, at the time of contracting, that it has limited knowledge of facts to which the mistake relates, but treats that knowledge as sufficient. [Citation omitted.] A court may also allocate risk to a party where reasonable. [Citation omitted.]

UCT contends that because HealthEast's claim was substantially larger than its rare high claims, it is not a sophisticated party in this case. This court disagrees. UCT had significant experience in handling and negotiating claims with healthcare providers. A UCT officer estimated that in 2006, the year of the HealthEast claim, UCT handled more than 495,000 claims and had premium revenue exceeding $25 million. According to the record, UCT reimbursed claims of varying amounts, including some exceeding $100,000, and has sufficient knowledge and experience to evaluate claim settlement issues. Although the HealthEast demand was atypical, the district court reasonably allocated the risk of mistake to UCT. [Citations omitted.]

UCT also maintains that its inaction does not reach the degree of fault required to deny relief. [Citation omitted.] The fact that a party could have avoided a mistake by reasonable care neither commands nor precludes rescission. . . . In this case, UCT did not exercise anything approaching ordinary care. One month elapsed between HealthEast's billing and the finalizing of the settlement agreement. During that time, UCT sought clarification only of hospital coinsurance information and lifetime reserve days. UCT did not investigate Hansen's health history despite having billing information showing Hansen's medical treatment, including that he entered HealthEast shortly after the policy became effective. UCT also failed to investigate the "exceptionally large" amount HealthEast billed. UCT did not investigate Hansen's medical records until three days *after* settling with HealthEast. Under these facts, UCT's pre-settlement inaction is an easily avoidable mistake. [Citation omitted.] Because UCT bore the risk of mistake, the district court properly denied rescission based on unilateral mistake. [Citation omitted.]

   B.

UCT next asserts that the district court erred in granting summary judgment by applying principles of mutual mistake to its claim of unilateral mistake. UCT contends that an allocation-of-risk analysis is relevant only to a mutual mistake. This assertion is without merit. [Citations omitted.]

The outcome is the same, however, under principles of mutual mistake. As with unilateral mistake, an adversely effected party may not avoid a contract based on mutual mistake if it bears the risk of the mistake. [Citation omitted.] As discussed, UCT possessed the facts necessary to challenge the validity of the policy and the amount of the demand before settling. Nevertheless, it merely subtracted 20% from the total HealthEast demand and offered the settlement amount. UCT failed to investigate Hansen's health history until after the settlement, and did not calculate what it now claims is its maximum liability until 15 months after settling the claim. This record of inaction strongly supports the denial of relief under both unilateral and mutual mistake.

   C.

On appeal, UCT also contends that the judgment is a windfall to HealthEast, because it exceeds UCT's maximum liability under its policy. UCT's lone authority, however, provides no support. In *Ferguson v. Cotler* [citation omitted], the appellate court reduced a trial court's award after finding that the parties operated under a mutual mistake. The appellate court noted that relief would be granted for a mistake so long as the mistake was not the result of a lack of due care. . . . Here, to the contrary, UCT's inaction and lack of due care preclude equitable relief.

   III.

The judgment of the district court is affirmed.

Notice also that the misrepresentation must be with regard to a *fact* (*e.g.*, "My car has never been in an accident."). This means that if someone gives you their *opinion* on a matter (*e.g.*, "I think my car is worth $10,000"), misrepresentation generally does not occur.

Sometimes a misrepresentation can occur without the intent to deceive. In these cases, **negligent** misrepresentation (*i.e.*, lack of due care) or **innocent** misrepresentation may have occurred. Many courts will not allow a contract to be rescinded for negligent or innocent misrepresentation. For example, suppose your car was in an accident before you purchased it, but you were not aware that it had been in an accident. Later, you represent to a potential buyer that the car has never been in an accident. In this situation, you clearly did not have the intent to deceive, but your statement was still a misrepresentation because it was not, as a matter of fact, true. Of course, a party harmed by the misrepresentation may sue for any damages suffered.

Is it possible to make a misrepresentation by remaining silent? Generally, a person has no duty to speak regarding information he or she knows if the other party could reasonably find out or inquire about the pertinent facts. If the other person could not reasonably discover the facts, however, then remaining silent about the facts could constitute misrepresentation by silence.

Duress and Undue Influence

If a person does not enter into a contract voluntarily, the person may be able to rescind the contract. This may be a situation, for example, where a person is threatened physically by the other person to sign the contract. In such a situation, the threatened person can argue that they signed the contract under **duress** and should be excused from performing the obligations set forth in the contract. **Undue influence** may exist in situations, for example, where a close family member or friend is in a dominant position in a relationship and exerts significant

Dariush M/ Shutterstock.com

pressure on the other person to enter into a contract, even though the pressure may not rise to the level of duress. In most of the undue influence cases, the dominant person also benefits significantly from the provisions in the contract at the expense of others.

What Do You Think?

Suppose you offer your car for sale. Your car was submerged up to the windows in a flood three years ago, but the car currently seems to be operating fine for you. A potential buyer asks you, "Has your car ever been in an accident?" If you say "no," have you committed a misrepresentation? Suppose the person instead asks you "Has your car ever been damaged?" If a potential buyer does not ask you any questions regarding the condition of your car, must you voluntarily disclose that your car has been in a flood? Should you?

QUESTIONS FOR REVIEW

1. Explain generally the situation(s) in which a person may be able to rescind a contract due to a mistake.

2. What must happen for a fraudulent representation to occur? What other types of misrepresentation are there?

3. Discuss a factual situation where you believe that misrepresentation could occur by remaining silent.

4. Discuss a factual situation where someone may sign a contract or engage in a transaction as a result of the undue influence of another person.

5. Summarize the *Health East v. United Commercial Travelers* case.

INTERNET ACTIVITIES

1. Find the Court of Appeals of Michigan case *Roberts v. Saffell*, 760 N.W.2d 715 (2008).

   a. What is the issue or issues in the case?

   b. What was the holding of the court?

   c. Summarize the court's analysis.

2. Find the Supreme Court of Idaho case *O'Connor v. Harger Construction, Inc.*, 188 P.3d 846 (2008).

   a. What is the issue or issues in the case?

   b. What was the holding of the court?

   c. Summarize the court's analysis.

Chapter 20

The Uniform Commercial Code: Scope, Contract Formation, and Performance and Breach

The previous chapters covering contracts addressed the fundamental common law rules. Of course, federal and state laws can change the common law rules. In an attempt to make state laws more uniform regarding certain business transactions, states have adopted the **Uniform Commercial Code** (UCC). The UCC contains nine "articles," with each article addressing a different area of business transaction (*e.g.*, sale and lease of goods, secured transactions, negotiable instruments, etc.). If the UCC is silent on a particular issue, then common law controls. If the UCC and common law are in conflict, the UCC controls. Provisions of the UCC relating to the *sale* of goods are found in Article 2. Provisions of the UCC relating to the *lease* of goods are found in Article 2A, but we will focus on the sale of goods.

Scope of Article 2

Article 2 of the UCC applies to the sale of **goods**. A good is tangible personal property that is **movable**. If the goods are associated with real estate (*e.g.*, crops, timber, etc.), then whether the UCC applies or common law applies may be an issue. Generally, the UCC applies on the sale of growing crops no matter who harvests them or severs them from the real property. If a structure or minerals are being sold independent of the land and the structure or minerals will be severed by the seller, then the UCC applies. In the situation where both goods and services are provided, the UCC applies if the sale of goods is the "predominant factor" in the transaction as opposed to the provision of services.

In some situations throughout Article 2 the law may differ depending upon whether the parties involved in a transaction are **merchants**. Section 104 of the UCC defines a merchant as

> "a person who deals in goods of the kind or otherwise by his occupation holds himself out as having knowledge or skill peculiar to the practices or goods involved in the transaction or to whom such knowledge or skill may be attributed by his employment of an agent or broker or other intermediary who by his occupation holds himself out as having such knowledge or skill."

Vagabondivan/ Shutterstock.com

As you can probably surmise, merchants are usually held to a higher standard than a person who does not have the knowledge or skill that a merchant has in relation to the goods being sold.

Contract Formation

The same basic elements of contract formation apply under the UCC (*i.e.*, offer, acceptance, consideration, capacity, legality), but with a few modifications.

Offer

Remember under common law that an offer can generally be revoked by the offeror any time before the offeree accepts the offer. Under the UCC the same rules apply, but if a *merchant* makes a "firm" offer, the offer is irrevocable for the time stated, or up to a maximum of three months. A firm offer is an offer in writing by a merchant stating that the offer will remain open.

Acceptance

The UCC modifies some rules regarding valid acceptances also. For example, unlike the mirror image rule under common law, an acceptance can be made even though the acceptance varies somewhat from the offer. Between *merchants*, sometimes the offeree will accept the offer by sending a document that adds additional terms to the offeror's offer. Basically, in these situations, the offeree's terms become part of the contract unless (a) the offer expressly limits acceptance to the terms of the offer or (b) the offeree's terms materially alter the offeror's terms. This back-and-forth of different terms is often called the "battle of the forms." Under the UCC a seller can also manifest acceptance by a prompt promise to ship or by promptly shipping the goods to the buyer. In some situations when a judge interprets a contract for the sale of goods, the parties' "course of performance" with each other over time can be relevant.

Consideration

One important element of contract formation is that consideration must be present. Under the UCC, this requirement is modified slightly in some situations. For example, no consideration is necessary for a merchant's firm offer to be irrevocable or when parties modify a contract that is for the sale of goods.

Statute of Frauds

As you may recall from Chapter 16, the statute of frauds requires that some contracts be in writing. One contract that must generally be in writing to enforce against a nonperforming party is a contract for the sale of goods for the price of $500 or more. Consider Illustrative UCC Provision 20.1 on the next page with regard to when a sale of goods must be in writing to satisfy the statute of frauds.

Notice that one of the exceptions to the statute of frauds under the UCC is if the goods are specially manufactured.

Missing Terms

Another important contribution of the UCC is that it provides gap-fillers if a contract leaves out certain terms. For example, if the contract leaves out the *price*, the UCC provides that the contract is still valid, but a reasonable price can be determined in good faith by the parties at a later time, usually at time of delivery. If the *payment terms* are omitted, then the buyer must generally pay at the time and place where the buyer receives the goods. If *delivery terms* are omitted, then delivery is generally deemed to have occurred when the seller makes the goods available to the buyer to pick up at the seller's place of business. If the buyer and seller know that the goods are at another location already, however, then the delivery is deemed made when those goods are available for pick up at the other location (*e.g.*, a warehouse).

In some contracts for the sale of goods, the exact quantity of goods is unknown. For example, suppose Andria enters into an agreement with Shana

UCC Section 2-201

§2-201. Formal Requirements; Statute of Frauds

1. Except as otherwise provided in this section a contract for the sale of goods for the price of $500 or more is not enforceable by way of action or defense unless there is some writing sufficient to indicate that a contract for sale has been made between the parties and signed by the party against whom enforcement is sought or by his authorized agent or broker. . . .

. . .

3. A contract which does not satisfy the requirements of subsection (1) but which is valid in other respects is enforceable

(a) if the goods are to be specially manufactured for the buyer and are not suitable for sale to others in the ordinary course of the seller's business and the seller, before notice of repudiation is received and under circumstances which reasonably indicate that the goods are for the buyer, has made either a substantial beginning of their manufacture or commitments for their procurement; . . .

promising to purchase "all of the corn that Shana produces." This is known as an **output** contract. Conversely, if Andria enters into an agreement with Shana promising to purchase "all of the corn that I require," then that is a **requirements** contract. In these situations, the parties must act in good faith, and no quantity unreasonably disproportionate to any stated estimate may be delivered (in an output contract) or demanded (in a requirements contract).

Performance and Breach

If a party to a contract meets the obligations under the contract, the party is considered to have **performed**. Failure to so perform could result in a **breach** of the contract.

Cristi Kerekes/ Shutterstock.com

Performance

To successfully perform, both the seller and buyer have certain obligations to meet. This, of course, includes proper delivery of goods that conform to the contract, proper payment by the buyer, etc.

Unless otherwise agreed to by the parties, the seller must tender delivery at the seller's place of business. In a situation where the parties agree that the goods should be shipped by the seller via common carrier, the agreement can be in one of two forms. First, the contract can be a **shipment contract**, which requires the seller to deliver the goods to the shipping company. Second, the contract can be a **destination contract**, which requires the seller to guarantee delivery to the buyer at a particular destination. In a destination contract, the seller must tender delivery at a reasonable hour and at a reasonable time.

Title (*i.e.*, ownership) to the goods generally follows the shipping rules (*i.e.*, the seller has title until seller tenders delivery to the shipper in a shipment contract or until the goods are delivered in a destination contract), but this is not always the case. Some other issues relating to title can sometimes arise. For example, suppose a bank loans money to a business that sells tractors. To protect itself, the bank retains a security interest (discussed more in Chapter 35) in the inventory of tractors so that if the business does not pay the loan back, the bank can recover the tractors. If a farmer purchases a tractor from the business, however, the bank no longer can recover that particular tractor if the tractor was sold in the **ordinary course of business**. This, of course, protects the farmer so that the farmer can obtain title. Another unique situation dealing with transfer of title is the **entrustment rule**. Suppose you take a diamond ring to a jewelry store to be fixed and cleaned. By accident, the jewelry store (a merchant) sells the diamond ring to Paula. Can you recover the ring from Paula, or does Paula have title? Under the entrustment rule, Paula has title. This protects customers who in good faith purchase goods from merchants. You, of course, could sue the jewelry store for selling the ring.

What happens if the goods are lost or spoiled while being shipped? Who bears the risk of loss?

Generally, if the contract is a shipment contract, the buyer bears the **risk of loss** once the seller has successfully made delivery to the shipper. If the contract is a destination contract, the seller bears the risk of loss until the goods are tendered to the buyer at the specific destination. Of course, parties can purchase insurance to protect against the risk of loss. A party has an **insurable interest** in the goods once the goods to which the contract refers are identified. Consider the Court of Appeals of Ohio case relating to risk of loss (Illustrative Court Case 20.1).

Breach

A seller is required to meet the requirements of the contract by delivering **conforming** goods. This is known as the **perfect tender** rule. If the seller delivers **nonconforming** goods, then the seller is in breach of contract unless the seller can **cure** the

---

ILLUSTRATIVE COURT CASE 20.1

Capshaw v. Hickman

Court of Appeals of Ohio

880 N.E.2d 118 (2007)

OPINION

BRYANT, J.

Defendant-appellant, Rachel Hickman, appeals from a judgment of the Franklin County Municipal Court granting judgment on the pleadings . . . to . . . Charles W. Capshaw . . . . Because the pleadings do not entitle [Capshaw] to judgment as a matter of law, we reverse.

According to the allegations in the parties' pleadings, [Capshaw] entered into a written contract with [Hickman] to purchase [Hickman's] 1996 Honda Civic EX for the purchase price of approximately $5,025. According to the contract, "the title will be surrendered upon the new owner's check clearing." After making a cash payment of $80, [Capshaw] gave [Hickman] a personal check for the balance. [Hickman] provided [Capshaw] with the keys to the vehicle. She also complied with [Capshaw's] request to sign the certificate of title over into the name of [Capshaw's] father. They agreed the vehicle was to remain parked in [Hickman's] driveway until the check cleared.

Unfortunately, before [Hickman] was notified that the check cleared, a hailstorm heavily damaged the vehicle. Due to the damage the vehicle sustained, [Capshaw] decided [he] no longer wanted the vehicle and requested that [Hickman] return [his] money. [Hickman] refused, believing the sales transaction was complete and the vehicle belonged to [Capshaw]. [Hickman] requested that [Capshaw] remove the vehicle from her driveway.

. . .

[Capshaw] filed a motion and an amended motion for judgment on the pleadings, and [Hickman] filed a response to both. [Capshaw] asserted the risk of loss remained with [Hickman] until the check cleared; because it had not cleared at the time the hail damaged the car, [Hickman] sustained the loss. Relying on [Ohio statutory law], [Hickman] maintained the risk-of-loss for non-merchant sellers such as her passes to the buyer after a non-merchant seller tenders delivery. [Hickman] contended that because a material issue of fact exists as to whether she tendered delivery of the vehicle to [Capshaw], judgment on the pleadings was improper.

Based upon the pleadings, the trial court found the parties agreed to the following facts: (1) [Capshaw] offered to purchase the vehicle for $5,025, minus an $80 down payment; (2) [Capshaw] tendered a check to [Hickman] for the remaining balance due; (3) until the check cleared the vehicle would remain on [Hickman's] property; (4) before the check cleared, hail damaged the vehicle while it still was in [Hickman's] driveway; and (5) because of the damage, [Capshaw] never took possession of the vehicle, no longer wanted it, and asked [Hickman] to return the purchase price.

Premised on those facts, the trial court concluded the parties agreed the transfer of title and delivery of the vehicle would occur only after the successful transfer of funds. In reaching its decision, the trial court applied [Ohio statutory law] which provides that "[u]nless otherwise explicitly agreed, title passes to the buyer at the time and place at which the seller completes performance with reference to the physical delivery of the goods, despite any reservation of security interest and even though a document of title is to be delivered at a different time or place." Because the agreed facts demonstrated no delivery of the title or vehicle occurred at the time of the hailstorm, the trial court granted [Capshaw's] motion and entered judgment for [Capshaw] on [his] complaint and on [Hickman's] counterclaims.

[Hickman] appeals. . . .

Where a motor vehicle identified to a purchase contract is damaged, lost or destroyed prior to the issuance of a certificate of title in the buyer's name, the risk of such damage, loss or destruction lies with either the seller or buyer as determined under the rules set forth in [Ohio statutory law]. In relevant part, [the statute] states "the risk of loss passes to the buyer on his receipt of the goods if the seller is a merchant; otherwise the risk passes to the buyer on tender of delivery." The parties here agree that [Hickman] is not a merchant. Thus, if [Hickman] tendered delivery, [Capshaw] bore the risk of the loss; if [Hickman] did not tender delivery, the risk of loss remained with her.

Although the trial court concluded [Hickman] did not tender delivery, it incorrectly focused on ownership and legal title in reaching its decision. Title is no longer "of any importance in determining whether a buyer or seller bears the risk of loss." [Citation omitted.] Rather, tender of delivery "requires that the seller put and hold conforming goods at the buyer's disposition and give the buyer any notification reasonably necessary to enable him to take delivery." [Citation omitted.] In this context, disposition means "doing with as one wishes: discretionary control." Delivery does not consist in the mere transfer of location or custody of property. [Citation omitted.] The parties concurring to a transfer per the contract must intend one to deliver and the other to receive.

When tendering delivery, the seller must not limit the buyer's disposition of the goods. [Citation omitted.] . . .

When, however, limitations upon a buyer's disposition of personal property do not result from the seller's activity, then the requirements for tender of delivery are met. . . .

(Continued)

[Hickman] contends she fulfilled the statutory requirements for tendering delivery by turning over the keys to the vehicle and, after signing the certificate of title over to [Capshaw's] father per [Capshaw's] request, by placing the certificate of title in the vehicle's glove box. She asserts [Capshaw] chose to leave the vehicle at her residence in order to induce her to take a personal check. [Hickman] argues that "for all intents and purposes" [Capshaw] "possessed and controlled the vehicle when the keys were given to them." [Citation omitted.] She thus claims not only that she tendered delivery of the vehicle, but also that [Capshaw was] in actual possession of the vehicle at the time it was damaged. Describing the fact that the vehicle remained parked in her driveway as a "red herring," [Hickman] asserts she could have done "absolutely nothing else" to complete her performance with respect to physical delivery of the vehicle. [Citation omitted.]

The vehicle's continued presence in [Hickman's] driveway is not a red herring. Under Ohio law, a purchaser's performance under a contract generally is complete when the purchaser tenders the check. [Ohio statutory law] states "[t]ender of payment is sufficient when made by any means or in any manner current in the ordinary course of business unless the seller demands payment in legal tender and gives any extension of time reasonably necessary to procure it." Thus, upon tendering the check, [Capshaw] ordinarily would be free to drive away in the vehicle. Understanding why the car remained in the driveway is central to determining whether [Hickman] tendered delivery.

The difficulty in applying the law to this case lies in determining why the car remained on [Hickman's] property, as the pleadings do not disclose that information. If [Capshaw] paid by check but [Hickman] refused to consider payment made until the check cleared, then [Capshaw was] not free to remove the vehicle from [Hickman's] driveway until the check cleared. Under those circumstances, [Hickman] did not tender delivery . . . as [Capshaw] lacked the discretionary control over the vehicle. As a result, the risk of loss would not have passed to [Capshaw]. By contrast, if to induce [Hickman] to accept payment by check [Capshaw] offered to allow the vehicle to remain on [Hickman's] driveway until the check cleared, then the risk of loss passed to [Capshaw] who in [his] discretion volunteered to leave the car on [Hickman's] driveway in order to pay in tender most convenient to them. Because the pleadings do not reveal the underlying reasons for leaving the car in the driveway until [Capshaw's] check cleared, judgment on the pleadings is inappropriate.

In the final analysis, the pleadings do not entitle [Capshaw] to judgment as a matter of law as to whether [Hickman] tendered delivery of the vehicle, including why the vehicle remained on [Hickman's] property. . . . [W]e reverse the judgment of the trial court granting judgment on the pleadings to [Capshaw], and we remand for further proceedings in accordance with this opinion.

delivery. Both the seller and buyer have certain rights when nonconforming goods are tendered, however, that may save the contract.

The buyer has a reasonable time to inspect the goods. But if the goods are nonconforming, the buyer must inform the seller within a reasonable time. If nonconforming goods are delivered, the buyer has the right to reject the entire shipment, accept the entire shipment, or reject part and accept part. If the time for delivery still has not passed, the seller also has the right to cure the delivery and deliver conforming goods to the buyer. In some situations, the seller can even cure the delivery after the time for delivery has passed if the seller has "reasonable grounds" to believe that the buyer will accept them. Consider the Supreme Court of Nebraska case that follows (Illustrative Court Case 20.2) addressing a buyer's rights when nonconforming goods are delivered.

Another exception to the perfect tender rule is if it is "commercially impracticable" to satisfy the terms of the contract (*e.g.*, the seller's city's transportation infrastructure is shut down due to an impending hurricane and there is no way to timely ship the goods). The commercial impracticability defense is usually a difficult one to prevail on, however. Another exception to the perfect tender rule is if the goods are destroyed (fire, natural disaster, etc.).

ILLUSTRATIVE COURT CASE 20.2

Fitl v. Strek

Supreme Court of Nebraska

690 N.W.2d 605 (2005)

OPINION BY: WRIGHT

James G. Fitl purchased a baseball card from Mark Strek, doing business as Star Cards of San Francisco. When Fitl discovered that the baseball card had been altered and was of no value, he sued Strek for what he argued was the current fair market value of an unaltered version of the same card. Following a bench trial, judgment was entered against Strek in the amount of $17,750 plus costs. Strek appeals.

. . .

In September 1995, Fitl attended a sports card show in San Francisco, California, where Strek was an exhibitor. Fitl subsequently purchased from Strek a 1952 Mickey Mantle Topps baseball card for $17,750. According to Fitl, Strek represented that the card was in near mint condition. After Strek delivered the card to Fitl in Omaha, Nebraska, Fitl placed it in a safe-deposit box.

In May 1997, Fitl sent the baseball card to Professional Sports Authenticators (PSA), a grading service for sports cards that is located in Newport Beach, California. PSA reported to Fitl that the baseball card was ungradable because it had been discolored and doctored.

On May 29, 1997, Fitl wrote to Strek and indicated that he planned to pursue "legal methods" to resolve the matter. Strek replied that Fitl should have initiated a return of the baseball card in a timely fashion so that Strek could have confronted his source and remedied the situation. Strek asserted that a typical grace period for the unconditional return of a card was from 7 days to 1 month.

In August 1997, Fitl sent the baseball card to ASA Accugrade, Inc. (ASA), in Longwood, Florida, for a second opinion. ASA also concluded that the baseball card had been refinished and trimmed.

On September 8, 1997, Fitl sued Strek, alleging that Strek knew the baseball card had been recolored or otherwise altered and had concealed this fact from him. Fitl claimed he had reasonably relied upon Strek's status as a reputable sports card dealer. Strek's answer generally denied Fitl's allegations.

In a trial to the court, Fitl appeared with counsel and offered evidence. Strek was represented by counsel but did not appear or offer any evidence. Fitl testified that he was in San Francisco over the Labor Day weekend of 1995, where he met Strek at a sports card show. Fitl subsequently purchased from Strek a 1952 Mickey Mantle Topps baseball card and placed it in a safe-deposit box. In 1997, Fitl retrieved the baseball card and sent it to PSA, a sports card grading service.

(Continued)

Steve Orand testified that he had been a sports card collector for 27 years and that he bought, sold, and traded cards. He testified that PSA originated in 1996 or 1997 and was a leader in the sports card grading industry. He stated that PSA would not grade an altered card because alteration would totally devalue the card. He opined that any touchup or trimming of a card would render the card valueless and that an altered card is worth no more than the paper on which it is printed.

Orand examined the baseball card in question the week before trial and said that the edges of the card had been trimmed and reglued. One spot on the front of the baseball card and a larger spot on the back had been repainted, which left the card with no value. He testified that the standard for sports memorabilia was a lifetime guarantee and that a reputable collector would stand behind what he sold and refund the money if an item were fake or had been altered.

The district court entered judgment for Fitl in the amount of $17,750 and costs. The court found that Fitl had notified Strek as soon as he realized the baseball card was altered and worthless and that Fitl had notified Strek of the defect within a reasonable time after its discovery. The court rejected Strek's theory that Fitl should have determined the authenticity of the baseball card immediately after it had been purchased.

. . .

[O]ur review is whether the district court's finding as to the reasonableness of the notice was clearly erroneous.

[Nebraska statutory law] states: Where a tender has been accepted . . . the buyer must within a reasonable time after he discovers or should have discovered any breach notify the seller of breach or be barred from any remedy." [Citation omitted.]

The notice requirement . . . serves three purposes. It provides the seller with an opportunity to correct any defect, to prepare for negotiation and litigation, and to protect itself against stale claims asserted after it is too late for the seller to investigate them. [Citation omitted.] "Whether the notice given is satisfactory and whether it is given within a reasonable time are generally questions of fact to be measured by all the circumstances of the case." [Citation omitted.]

The most important [policy relating to giving notice] is to enable the seller "to make efforts to cure the breach by making adjustments or replacements in order to minimize the buyer's damages and the seller's liability." [Citation omitted.] . . .

Fitl purchased the baseball card in 1995 and immediately placed it in a safe-deposit box. Two years later, he retrieved the baseball card, had it appraised, and learned that it was of no value. Fitl testified that he had relied on Strek's position as a dealer of sports cards and on his representations that the baseball card was authentic. [This court has] stated that a party is justified in relying upon a representation made to the party as a positive statement of fact when an investigation would be required to ascertain its falsity. In order for Fitl to have determined that the baseball card had been altered, he would have been required to conduct an investigation. We find that he was not required to do so. Once Fitl learned that the baseball card had been altered, he gave notice to Strek.

. . .

Strek claimed via his correspondence to Fitl that if Strek had received notice earlier, he could have contacted the person who sold him the baseball card to determine the source of the alteration, but there is no evidence to support this allegation. In fact, Strek offered no evidence at trial. His letter is merely an assertion that is unsupported. Earlier notification would not have helped Strek prepare for negotiation or defend himself in a suit because the damage to Fitl could not be repaired. Thus, the policies behind the notice requirement, to allow the seller to correct a defect, to prepare for negotiation and litigation, and to protect against stale claims at a time beyond which an investigation can be completed, were not unfairly prejudiced by the lack of an earlier notice to Strek. Any problem Strek may have had with the party from whom he obtained the baseball card was a separate matter from his transaction with Fitl, and an investigation into the source of the altered card would not have minimized Fitl's damages.

Strek represented himself as a sports card dealer at a card show in San Francisco. After Fitl expressed interest in a specific baseball card, Strek contacted Fitl to sell him just such a card. Orand stated that a reputable dealer will stand behind what he sells and refund the money if an item is fake or has been altered. In the context of whether a rejection of goods was made in a reasonable amount of time, we have stated that "when there is no precise rule of law which governs, the question of what, under the circumstances of a particular case, is a reasonable amount of time is usually a question for the jury." [Citation omitted.]

The district court found that it was reasonable to give Strek notice of a defect 2 years after the purchase. This finding was not clearly erroneous. . . .

The judgment of the district court is affirmed.

If the seller refuses to deliver the goods and is, therefore, in breach, the buyer has certain remedies available. Among the remedies available are: (1) the right to cancel the contract, (2) sue to recover damages incurred, (3) purchase the goods from a third party (*i.e.*, "cover") and sue the seller for damages if, for example, the purchase price from the third party is higher than it was under the contract with the seller that breached the contract, and (4) sue for specific performance if the goods were so unique as to not be obtainable anywhere else. As mentioned earlier, if the goods are already delivered, but the goods are nonconforming, then the buyer can reject the goods in whole or in part. A rejection may be possible even if the buyer already accepted the goods, but it was difficult to determine that the goods were conforming. This is technically called a **revocation of acceptance** rather than a rejection.

If the buyer refuses to pay and is, therefore, in breach, the seller has certain remedies available. If the goods are still at the seller's place of business, then among the remedies of the seller are (1) the right to cancel the contract, (2) sell the goods to some other party, and sue the buyer for the difference, if for example the seller has to sell the goods to another party at a lower price, (3) withhold delivery, (4) sue for the purchase price. If the goods are in transit, the seller can stop delivery. If the goods are already in the hands of the buyer, then the seller can sue for the purchase price plus incidental damages incurred to recover the purchase price.

QUESTIONS FOR REVIEW

1. If common law and the UCC conflict, which controls?

2. Who is a "merchant"?

3. What is the significance of a merchant making a "firm" offer?

4. Explain the concept of the "battle of the forms" and how it applies in the context of whether an offer has been accepted.

5. What is an output contract? A requirements contract?

6. What is a shipment contract? A destination contract?

7. When does the risk of loss transfer from the seller to the buyer? If so, explain.

8. What is the entrustment rule?

9. If a seller delivers nonconforming goods to the buyer, what options does the buyer have?

10. What is a right to cure?

11. If a buyer breaches the contract, what rights does the seller have?

12. Summarize the *Capshaw v. Hickman* case.

13. Summarize the *Fitl v. Strek* case.

INTERNET ACTIVITIES

1. Find the Superior Court of Connecticut case *Epstein v. Giannattasio*, 197 A.2d 342 (1963).

   a. What is the issue or issues in the case?

   b. Did the court hold that the transaction constituted a sale of goods?

   c. Summarize the court's analysis.

2. Find the Supreme Court of South Carolina case *Columbia Hyundai, Inc. v. Carll Hyundai, Inc.*, 484 S.E.2d 468 (1997).

   a. What is the issue or issues in the case?

   b. What was the holding of the court?

   c. Summarize the court's analysis.

Chapter 21

The Uniform Commercial Code: Warranties

Sellers of most new products (and some used products) will provide certain **express** warranties so that customers will have confidence that the product will work as intended. The law also imposes **implied** warranties on sales of goods. Sellers of goods can often disclaim these warranties, however. This chapter covers both express and implied warranties, and a seller's ability to limit or disclaim those warranties.

Express Warranties

An express warranty can be made either orally or in writing. If a salesperson describes a product's features, how it functions, its durability, quality, etc., and the customer relies on the representations by the salesperson, then those representations become part of the terms of the contract in the form of an express warranty. The UCC more specifically provides how an express warranty

---

ILLUSTRATIVE STATE STATUTE 21.1

13 Pa.C.S. § 2313

§ 2313. Express warranties by affirmation, promise, description or sample.

a. General rule. —Express warranties by the seller are created as follows:

1. Any affirmation of fact or promise made by the seller to the buyer which relates to the goods and becomes part of the basis of the bargain creates an express warranty that the goods shall conform to the affirmation or promise.

2. Any description of the goods which is made part of the basis of the bargain creates an express warranty that the goods shall conform to the description.

3. Any sample or model which is made part of the basis of the bargain creates an express warranty that the whole of the goods shall conform to the sample or model.

b. Formal words or specific intent unnecessary. —It is not necessary to the creation of an express warranty that the seller use formal words such as "warrant" or "guarantee" or that he have a specific intention to make a warranty, but an affirmation merely of the value of the goods or a statement purporting to be merely the opinion of the seller or commendation of the goods does not create a warranty.

is created. Consider the related Pennsylvania UCC statute (Illustrative State Statute 21.1).

Of course, business owners must be careful in their communications with customers if they do not intend to create express warranties. Consider the court case from the Superior Court of New Jersey, Appellate Division (Illustrative Court Case 21.1) regarding a dispute over whether an express warranty was created.

Gupta v. Asha Enterprises, L.L.C.

Superior Court of New Jersey

2011 N.J. Super. LEXIS 141 (2011)

OPINION BY: PAYNE

Plaintiffs, sixteen Hindu vegetarians, appeal from an order of summary judgment entered against them dismissing their action premised upon allegations of negligence, negligent infliction of emotional distress, consumer fraud, products liability, and breach of express and implied warranties arising when defendant Asha Enterprises, L.L.C. d/b/a Moghul Express & Catering Co. (Moghul Express), an Indian restaurant, filled their order for vegetarian samosas with meat-filled samosas causing spiritual injuries resulting in damages. Plaintiffs explain their injuries and damages as follows:

"Hindu vegetarians believe that if they eat meat, they become involved in the sinful cycle of inflicting pain, injury and death on God's creatures, and that it affects the karma and dharma, or purity of the soul. Hindu scriptures teach that the souls of those who eat meat can never go to God after death, which is the ultimate goal for Hindus. The Hindu religion does not excuse accidental consumption of meat products. One who commits the religious violation of eating meat, knowingly or unknowingly, is required to participate in a religious ceremony at a site located along the Ganges River in . . . India, to purify himself. The damages sought by plaintiffs included compensation for the emotional distress they suffered, as well as economic damages they would incur by virtue of having to participate in the required religious cleansing ceremony in India."

. . .

According to the certification of plaintiff Durgesh Gupta, filed in opposition to summary judgment, on August 10, 2009, he and [another plaintiff] placed an order for vegetarian samosas at Moghul Express, a restaurant located in Edison, New Jersey. At the time that the order was placed, [the plaintiffs] advised Mogul Express's employee that they required vegetarian samosas, because they were being purchased for a group of individuals who were strict vegetarians. The two men were informed that they should not be concerned because the restaurant did not make meat-filled samosas. One-half hour later, the men returned to the restaurant to pick up their order and were handed a tray that had written on its top "VEG samosas," and they were again assured of the vegetarian nature of the food.

After plaintiffs had consumed some of the samosas, some plaintiffs became concerned that the samosas might contain meat. They called Moghul Express to verify the food's content, and they were again assured that Moghul did not make meat-filled samosas. Although the plaintiffs continued eating for a time, eventually they determined to return the remaining samosas to Moghul Express to verify their content. Once there, Moghul Express's employee advised them that the samosas, indeed, contained meat. As a consequence of eating the meat-filled samosas, plaintiffs were spiritually injured.

. . .

As a final matter, we turn to plaintiffs' claims of breach by Moghul Express of its express warranty of fitness of the samosas sold to plaintiffs.

The Uniform Commercial Code provides:

1. "Express warranties by the seller are created as follows:

a. Any affirmation of fact or promise made by the seller to the buyer which relates to the goods and becomes part of the basis of the bargain creates an express warranty that the goods shall conform to the affirmation or promise.

b. Any description of the goods which is made part of the basis of the bargain creates an express warranty that the goods shall conform to the description.

. . .

2. It is not necessary to the creation of an express warranty that the seller use formal words such as "warrant" or "guarantee" or that he have a specific intention to make a warranty. . . . " [Citation omitted.]

Our review of the record in summary judgment leads us to conclude that plaintiffs have presented prima facie evidence of a warranty by employees of Moghul Express that the samosas sold to them were vegetarian.

. . .

Because discovery has not commenced in this matter, we cannot determine what consequential damages were foreseen at the time of the sale of the samosas in the event of a breach. We thus reverse summary judgment . . . and remand for further proceedings.

What Do You Think?

If you were a judge (or on the jury) in a case like the Gupta v. Asha Enterprises *case, how would you go about calculating a monetary award for "spiritual damages" suffered by the plaintiffs?*

Express warranties are not created by a typical "sales pitch" like, for example, "This is a great price!" or "This is a popular car." On the other hand, if a sales person states that "This car has never been in an accident," then an express warranty is likely created because it clearly is an assertion of fact rather than an opinion or mere "puffery" (*e.g.*, exaggerations).

Implied Warranties

The law imposes certain warranties on goods sold even if the seller does not give an express warranty. We will discuss three of these implied warranties here. They are (1) the implied warranty of merchantability, (2) the implied warranty of fitness for a particular purpose, and (3) the implied warranty of title.

Implied Warranty of Merchantability

If the seller is a merchant, the goods sold are deemed to have the **implied warranty of merchantability**. This basically means that the good sold will function for the purpose for which it is made (*e.g.*, a lawnmower will cut grass). Consider the North Carolina statute that follows (Illustrative State Statute 21.2) with regard to the implied warranty of merchantability.

N.C. Gen. Stat. §25-2-314

§ 25-2-314. Implied warranty: Merchantability; usage of trade

1. Unless excluded or modified, a warranty that the goods shall be merchantable is implied in a contract for their sale if the seller is a merchant with respect to goods of that kind. Under this section the serving for value of food or drink to be consumed either on the premises or elsewhere is a sale.

2. Goods to be merchantable must be at least such as

a. pass without objection in the trade under the contract description; and

b. in the case of fungible goods, are of fair average quality within the description; and

c. are fit for the ordinary purposes for which such goods are used; and

d. run, within the variations permitted by the agreement, of even kind, quality and quantity within each unit and among all units involved; and

e. are adequately contained, packaged, and labeled as the agreement may require; and

f. conform to the promises or affirmations of fact made on the container or label if any.

3. Unless excluded or modified other implied warranties may arise from course of dealing or usage of trade.

In evaluating the applicability of the implied warranty of merchantability, several issues can arise. For example, is the seller a "merchant"? Is the product sold a "good"? Consider the following court case from the Supreme Court of Montana (Illustrative Court Case 21.2).

Rothing v. Kallestad

Supreme Court of Montana

159 P.3d 222 (2007)

OPINION BY: James C. Nelson

Peter and Tanya Rothing (the Rothings) brought this action to recover damages resulting from the death of nineteen horses owned by the Rothings that they alleged were fed botulism contaminated hay purchased from Arnold Kallestad (Kallestad). The Rothings sought recovery under theories of strict liability in tort, negligence and breach of contract. The District Court . . . granted Kallestad's Motions for Summary Judgment thereby dismissing the Rothings' . . . Complaint.

. . .

The Rothings conducted business near Belgrade, Montana, under the name Diamond R Enterprises. . . . [The business] is primarily involved in breeding, raising and selling of horses. . . .

Kallestad owns a ranch in Gallatin County where he primarily raises hay and a small amount of grain. . . . Each year since he began ranching in 1984, Kallestad has sold some of the hay he raised, and at times, he has advertised his hay for sale in the Bozeman Daily Chronicle. Kallestad estimated that he sells between 300 and 1,000 tons of hay annually.

[T]he Rothings purchased hay from Kallestad for $90.00 a ton. . . .

Kallestad later testified that his hay was a second-cutting of alfalfa taken from a field that had been re-seeded approximately two years earlier. The hay was cut with a swather and allowed to dry for two to four days depending on the temperature. The hay was then twin-raked (wherein two rows are turned and combined so that the bottom portion can also dry) and baled with a mid-size square baler a day or two after being raked. The bales were then stacked outside on a raised bed of gravel and fly ash from August 2000 until April 2001 when it was sold to the Rothings.

Kallestad further testified that the hay was exposed to moisture during the winter months and that, one winter, a ditch near the stacked hay overflowed causing water to go along the west side of the stack of hay and then onto a road. Kallestad was unsure whether the ditch water came in contact with the hay, but he indicated that the water "may have been up there an inch or so."

On April 23, 2001, the Rothings received 45 to 48 large bales of hay from Kallestad. Some of the hay was fed to the Rothings' horses the same day it was delivered. On May 2, 2001, nine days after the delivery of the hay, one of the Rothings' yearling colts was found "down." That afternoon, the colt was taken to the Hardaway Veterinary Hospital . . . where the colt had to be euthanized. The body was transported to the Marsh Laboratory at Montana State University where a post mortem was performed by Dr. Bill Layton. The other yearling colt was treated with charcoal, but died two days later.

On May 3, 2001, Dr. Layton contacted Dr. Robert Whitlock at the University of Pennsylvania. Dr. Whitlock is an Associate Professor of Medicine and the Director of the Botulism Laboratory at the University. Dr. Layton inquired about sending diagnostic samples to be tested for botulism.

On May 4, 2001, three mares with foals exhibited symptoms similar to the others. They were taken to the [animal hospital] and treated with charcoal and other medications. One of the foals died during the night. The treating veterinarians . . . suspected that the hay purchased from Kallestad may be the cause of the problem, hence the remaining hay was removed from the feeding area.

Shortly thereafter, Dr. Whitlock shipped botulism antitoxin to the Rothings and their veterinarians, but by the time the outbreak was over, nineteen animals had died. Dr. Whitlock concluded that the hay purchased from Kallestad and fed to the Rothings' horses was contaminated with botulism. . . .

The Rothings filed suit against Kallestad on July 26, 2001. In their suit, the Rothings pursued theories of recovery based upon strict liability, negligence and breach of contract. As a result of this incident, the Rothings claimed that they suffered significant damages, including veterinarian bills for services and antitoxin in the amount of $38,549.28; the value of the nineteen dead horses in the amount of $40,000; and the loss of income as a result of the deaths of nineteen horses in excess of $100,000. They also sought damages for emotional distress from watching their horses die and the resulting economic devastation to their business.

. . .

The District Court concluded that . . . foreseeability is a factor in breach of contract claims in Montana. Hence, the court granted Kallestad's Motion for Summary Judgment on the Rothings' breach of contract claim on the basis that the injuries to the Rothings' horses were not foreseeable.

. . .

In [this] case, the Rothings' purchase of hay from Kallestad was a transaction in goods, thus it may be governed by Montana's Uniform Commercial Code (UCC) pertaining to sales. . . .

. . .

(*Continued*)

In addition to the requirement that the transaction consist of the sale of "goods," the seller must meet the definition of a "merchant." A "merchant" under the UCC "means a person who deals in goods of the kind or otherwise by his occupation holds himself out as having knowledge or skill peculiar to the practices or goods involved in the transaction. . . ." [Citation omitted.]

. . .

Thus, in this case, if the trial court determines that Kallestad was a merchant for purposes of the sale of his hay to the Rothings, then the provisions of the UCC, and more specifically, the Implied Warranty of Merchantability, would apply to this transaction. . . . [Citation omitted.]

[U]nder the UCC, goods to be merchantable must be "fit for the ordinary purposes for which such goods are used." [Citation omitted.]

. . .

Here, Kallestad would have breached the implied Warranty of Merchantability if the trial court determines that the goods were not "fit for the ordinary purposes for which such goods are used," i.e., as feed for livestock. . . .

Thus, contrary to the District Court's conclusion that all breach of contract actions in Montana require foreseeability, a breach of contract action under the UCC does not require foreseeability if injury to person or property proximately results from any breach of warranty.

Accordingly, we hold that the District Court erred in granting Kallestad's Motion for Summary Judgment on the Rothings' breach of contract claim.

Implied Warranty of Fitness for a Particular Purpose

Suppose you are in need to move an upright piano out of your apartment or home. You go to a hardware store to look for some straps to use for wrapping around the piano to assist you in the move. The hardware store does not have any straps specifically made for moving pianos so you ask the clerk if the store has "anything that you could use to move an upright piano." The clerk shows you some general purpose straps that he says "should work fine if you wrap the piano in a blanket, then wrap the piano with the straps, and then lift the piano with the straps." You take the clerk's advice and purchase the general purpose straps. When you get home you follow the instructions that the clerk told you, but when you and your friend who is helping you lift up on the straps, one of the straps breaks, causing the piano to tilt one way and crash, which causes damage to the piano and the floor. Should you be able to recover damages from the hardware store that recommended you use the general purpose straps to move an upright piano?

If, in fact, the seller has represented that a good is fit for a particular purpose, then the seller is in breach if the good does not perform in accordance with the purpose intended. The UCC provides how an **implied warranty of fitness for a particular purpose** is created. Consider the Iowa UCC statute that follows (Illustrative State Statute 21.3).

Implied Warranty of Title

In addition to the implied warranties of merchantability and fitness for a particular purpose is the **warranty of title**. This basically provides that the seller warrants that he or she has good title to the product being sold (*e.g.*, that a third party will not claim ownership of the good after the sale). Some exceptions exist to this warranty, such as if the purchaser is *aware* that a third party may eventually make a claim to title of the goods.

Limitations on Warranties

A seller can exclude, modify, or limit warranties on the sale of goods. In fact, written contracts for the sale of goods often state that all express warranties are excluded unless specifically identified in the written contract. The UCC provides that sellers must meet certain specific criteria in order exclude or modify an implied warranty. Consider the Tennessee UCC statute that follows (Illustrative State Statute 21.4).

Notice in the statute that implied warranties can be excluded by stating that the product is sold "as is" or "with all faults" and the notice must be conspicuous. It may seem relatively straightforward to disclaim implied warranties, but sellers can often get tripped up in their attempts. Consider the case from the Supreme Court of New Mexico that follows (Illustrative Court Case 21.3).

ILLUSTRATIVE COURT CASE 21.3

Salazar v. D.W.B.H. Inc. d/b/a Santa Fe Mitsubishi

Supreme Court of New Mexico

192 P.3d 1205 (2008)

OPINION BY: EDWARD L. CHAVEZ

Defendant D.W.B.H., Inc., d/b/a Santa Fe Mitsubishi (Mitsubishi), installed a used engine in Plaintiff Sandra Salazar's car. Salazar sued Mitsubishi, alleging that the used engine smoked and lost oil from the moment the car was retrieved from Mitsubishi until it ultimately ceased to work approximately three months after its installation. Following a bench trial, the trial court found that Mitsubishi had breached express and implied warranties. . . . Mitsubishi appealed this adverse judgment to the Court of Appeals, which reversed the trial court. We granted certiorari and conclude that there is substantial evidence to support the trial court's award of compensatory damages under the theories of breach of implied warranty of merchantability. . . . We therefore reverse the Court of Appeals and remand for its consideration of the issues concerning punitive damages, attorney's fees, and loss of use damages.

I. BACKGROUND

Salazar sought Mitsubishi's services after having engine problems with her 1993 Mitsubishi Eclipse. A Mitsubishi employee informed Salazar that her car's engine needed to be replaced. Salazar initially wanted her car's engine to be replaced with a new engine, but after speaking with a Mitsubishi employee about the cost of a new engine, she opted to have a used engine installed instead. She left her car with Mitsubishi in December 2000. Mitsubishi installed a used replacement engine that it purchased from Coronado Auto Recyclers (Coronado). Unbeknownst to Salazar, Coronado provided a 90-day warranty on the used engine.

Salazar picked up her car from Mitsubishi in April 2001. She testified that the car was smoking when she drove it home from Mitsubishi and that two days later, after the car's oil light went on, a service attendant at a gas station checked the oil and found the car was completely out of oil. A few days later, Salazar took the car back to Mitsubishi. Mitsubishi was unable to find a problem with the engine, so it sent the car to Coronado for further troubleshooting. Coronado was also unable to find anything wrong with the engine.

Salazar retrieved her car from Coronado and drove it until mid-July. She testified that during this time, the car continued to smoke and lose oil rapidly. After the engine completely stopped working, it was towed to Mitsubishi, and Mitsubishi advised Salazar that the engine needed to be replaced. Salazar asked Mitsubishi to replace the engine based on her belief that Mitsubishi had warranted the engine. At this point, the 90-day warranty that Coronado provided on the engine had expired. According to Salazar, Mitsubishi informed her that, while their labor was warranted, they did not provide a warranty on the engine itself, and thus Salazar would have to pay for another replacement engine.

Salazar then filed suit against Mitsubishi alleging . . . breach of express and implied warranty . . . and breach of contract. After a two-day bench trial, the trial court found in Salazar's favor on each count and awarded her compensatory damages, punitive damages, and attorney's fees. . . . Mitsubishi appealed the trial court's judgment. . . . The Court of Appeals filed an unpublished opinion reversing the trial court because it concluded that the evidence was insufficient to support the trial court's judgment.

. . .

II. DISCUSSION

A. BREACH OF EXPRESS WARRANTY

Under the Uniform Commercial Code . . . a warranty can be created in one of three ways: (1) "any affirmation of fact or promise made by the seller to the buyer which relates to the goods and becomes part of the basis of the bargain," (2) "any description of the goods which is made part of the basis of the bargain," or (3) "any sample or model which is made part of the basis of the bargain." [Citation omitted.] Common to all three types of express warranty is the requirement that an express warranty must be made as part of the basis of the bargain. This does not mean, however, that an express warranty must be specifically bargained for or even included as part of a written contract. [Citation omitted.] The UCC specifically provides that use of formal words such as "warrant" or "guarantee" are not necessary for the creation of an express warranty. [Citation omitted.] Nor is it necessary for the seller to have the specific intention to make an express warranty. While the law does not require such specificity and formality in creating an express warranty, the fact still remains that at the very least, an express warranty must be made as part of the basis of the bargain.

. . .

After reviewing the record, we do not find evidence that would indicate that the employee's statement was made as part of the basis of the bargain. The employee testified that he made the statement as part of "[g]ood customer service." Salazar testified that she believed that the statement constituted a warranty. The testimony that Salazar believed the statement to be a warranty is not enough to conclude that the statement was an express warranty. Finding no other evidence that would support such a conclusion, we find that the trial court's determination that the used engine was expressly warranted is not supported by substantial evidence. The breach of warranty review, however, does not end here.

B. BREACH OF IMPLIED WARRANTY

Unlike express warranties, implied warranties are not bargained for; they are imposed by law. [Citation omitted.] Under the UCC, "[u]nless excluded or modified, a warranty that the goods shall be merchantable is implied in a contract for their sale." [Citation omitted.] The trial court found that "[Mitsubishi] did not provide [Salazar] with a written statement of warranty or statement that there was no warranty." In so finding, the trial court concluded that "[p]ursuant to [the UCC], the engine and installation [Salazar] purchased was warranted. . . . The Court of Appeals disagreed and held that Mitsubishi effectively excluded the implied warranty of merchantability by including an "Exclusion of Warranties" provision, which is typed in extremely small print in a document Salazar allegedly signed when she picked up her car from Mitsubishi. The "Exclusion of Warranties" provision reads:

"[a]ny warranties on the parts and accessories sold hereby are made by the manufacturer. The undersigned purchaser understands and agrees that dealer makes no warranties of any kind, express or implied, and disclaims all warranties, including warranties of merchantability or fitness for a particular purpose, with regard to the parts and/or accessories purchased; and that in no event shall dealer be liable for incidental or consequential damages or commercial losses arising out of such purchase. The undersigned purchaser further agrees that the warranties excluded by dealer include, but are not limited to, any warranties that such parts and/or accessories are of merchantable quality or that they will enable any vehicle or any of its systems to perform with reasonable safety, efficiency, or comfort."

(Continued)

For such a written exclusion to be effective, the UCC provides that it must mention merchantability and it must be conspicuous. [Citation omitted.] While the exclusion mentions merchantability, whether it is conspicuous requires further analysis. . . .

The UCC defines conspicuous as "so written, displayed or presented that a reasonable person against whom it is to operate ought to have noticed it." [Citation omitted.] For example, a heading in all capital letters "equal to or greater in size than the surrounding text" is considered to be conspicuous. [Citation omitted.] The Court of Appeals relied on these two examples in determining that, as a matter of law, Mitsubishi's exclusion provision was conspicuous and thus constituted a valid exclusion of warranties. [Citation omitted.] The provision is set off to one side of the page with the heading "Exclusion of Warranties" in all capital letters. The heading's capital letters are greater in size than the provision's extremely small lettering, but they are smaller than other capitalized words on the page. Indeed, the heading is smaller than the word "Signed," which follows the provision and calls for Salazar's signature, noting her agreement that warranties are excluded. As discussed below, Salazar did not sign her acknowledgment of this provision, and therefore did not agree that the warranties could be excluded.

Although we do not conclude as a matter of law that the "Exclusion of Warranties" on this document is conspicuous, even if it was conspicuous, the exclusion is without force. The exclusion provision explicitly calls for an affirmative act; it requires that the customer agree to the exclusion of warranties. The exclusion provision states that "[t]he *undersigned* purchaser understands and agrees that dealer makes no warranties of any kind, express or implied, and disclaims all warranties, including warranties of merchantability." Directly under the provision are lines for date and signature. Both lines are blank. A signature does appear on another portion of the document that specifically authorizes repairs. However, while Salazar may have signed the document to authorize repairs, she did not sign agreeing to exclude warranties from the transaction.

. . .

In requiring such an affirmative agreement, a seller ensures that a buyer is not taken by surprise. We realize that actual consent is not mandated by the UCC in this area. The requirements and examples provided in the UCC, however, set the minimum criteria to protect buyers. Sellers are free to supplement the standards established in the UCC, and in doing so, make certain that buyers are aware of an exclusion of warranties. . . .

In this case, without an effective exclusion, the implied warranty of merchantability remained intact. Therefore, the used engine was guaranteed to be merchantable. Under the UCC, for goods to be merchantable, they must at least be "fit for the ordinary purposes for which such goods are used." [Citation omitted.] . . .

. . .

[T]he implied warranty of merchantability, as applied to a used engine, does not guarantee that the engine will operate as would a brand-new engine. Nonetheless, the used engine at the very least must be fit for its ordinary purpose.

After reviewing the evidence, we conclude that there is sufficient evidence to support a finding that the used engine did not operate properly when Mitsubishi delivered the car to Salazar, and thus that Mitsubishi breached the implied warranty of merchantability. . . .

. . .

Salazar was not required to prove the existence of a specific defect in the used engine. Rather, it was incumbent on Salazar to show only that the used engine was not fit for its ordinary purpose.

While this may be proven with evidence of a specific defect, it can also be proven by circumstantial evidence. In this case, the trial court found the circumstantial evidence sufficient to find a breach of the implied warranty of merchantability, and the record supports such a finding.

. . .

III. CONCLUSION

We . . . reverse the Court of Appeals . . . and reinstate Salazar's compensatory damage award. . . .

Suppose you purchase a toaster and give it to some newlyweds as a wedding present. Then suppose the toaster does not work. Do the warranties on the toaster extend to the newlyweds, or are the warranties only effective with respect to you, the purchaser? In other words, is it possible to have the product warranties apply to **third-party beneficiaries**? This has been an area of some controversy. As a result, the UCC provides some alternatives for states to adopt. For example, states could allow the warranty to extend to other persons in the household or household guests that may be injured by the product even though such person did not actually purchase the product. Alternatively, states could allow the warranty to extend to all persons who it is reasonable to expect would use the product.

Another common practice for sellers is to provide a **limited warranty**. Federal law provides that if a seller does provide a limited warranty and not a full warranty, then the seller must conspicuously disclose that fact in the warranty information provided to the consumer.

alexskopje/ Shutterstock.com

QUESTIONS FOR REVIEW

1. How is an express warranty created?

2. Explain the difference between "puffery" and an express warranty.

3. Name three implied warranties.

4. How is the implied warranty of merchantability created? How is it disclaimed?

5. How is the implied warranty of fitness for a particular purpose created? How is it disclaimed?

6. Summarize the *Gupta v. Asha Enterprises* case.

7. Summarize the *Rothing v. Kallestad* case.

8. Summarize the *Salazor v. Mitsubishi* case.

INTERNET ACTIVITIES

1. Find the Appellate Court of Illinois case *Mitsch v. General Motors Corp.*, 833 N.E.2d 936 (2005).

   a. What is the issue or issues in the case?

   b. What was the holding of the court?

   c. Summarize the court's analysis.

2. Find the Supreme Judicial Court of Massachusetts case *Webster v. Blue Ship Tea Room, Inc.*, 198 N.E.2d 309 (1964).

   a. What is the issue or issues in the case?

   b. What was the holding of the court?

   c. Summarize the court's analysis.

Part VIII
Business Entities

Chapter 22

Sole Proprietorships and Business Formation Issues in General

When an individual decides to start up a business, but does not specifically form a separate entity, the person is operating a **sole proprietorship**. Business organizations other than sole proprietorships will be discussed in the next few chapters. In this chapter we will first discuss the sole proprietorship form of doing business, and then we will address common business formation issues that apply to sole proprietorships, partnerships, limited liability companies, and corporations as well.

Sole Proprietorships

In this chapter and in the following chapters discussing different business organizational forms we will address four major issues common to each form of business: (1) formation; (2) management and operation; (3) taxation; and (4) owner liability.

Formation

Sole proprietorships are easy to form. Generally, since a sole proprietorship is not an entity separate from its owner, no organizational documents must be submitted to a state agency to form the sole proprietorship.

Management and Operation

One of the greatest advantages of being a sole proprietor is that the sole proprietor is in control of managing the business and has no boss to "answer" to. The sole proprietor also benefits from having no other person to share profits with, but also takes on all the risk of losses as well.

Taxation

The profits of a sole proprietorship are reported by the owner on the owner's individual income tax return (typically on Schedule C of IRS Form 1040). The business itself is not separately taxed apart from the individual owner. These profits are added to whatever other income the individual may have from other sources (*e.g.*, wages from a part-time job, etc.). The sole proprietor generally cannot wait until she files her tax return to pay all her income taxes for the year. Rather, she must comply with IRS regulations regarding the "estimated tax" payment system that requires a sole proprietor to make quarterly installments based upon the individual's estimated tax liability for the year.

Owner Liability

Most people would agree that the biggest disadvantage of the sole proprietorship form of doing business is that the owner is personally liable for all the debts of the business. Thus, if the business fails to pay its creditors, the creditors can file suit against the owner and cause the owner to pay off the business's debts from her personal assets. Consider the court case from the Supreme Judicial Court of Maine that follows (Illustrative Court Case 22.1).

Steve Heap/ Shutterstock.com

Business Formation Issues in General

Some issues are common to all forms of business, whether sole proprietorship, partnership, limited liability company, or corporation. The following discussion addresses these common issues such as selecting a name for the business, obtaining applicable licenses, hiring employees, etc.

Business Name Availability

Given other forms of doing business in today's marketplace that do provide liability protection to the owner(s), a sole proprietorship is likely not the optimal business organizational form.

How do you know whether the name you have chosen for your business is available or already taken by someone else? Typically, each state has a website that you can check to see if there is another business that has registered that name or one very

---

ILLUSTRATIVE COURT CASE 22.1

Bank of America, N.A. v. Barr

Supreme Judicial Court of Maine

9 A.3d 816 (2010)

OPINION BY: ALEXANDER, J.

Constance H. Barr appeals from a judgment entered in the Superior Court . . . following a non-jury trial in which Barr was found to be personally liable for debt incurred on a small business line of credit. Barr argues that the evidence was insufficient to support several findings key to the court's judgment. We affirm the judgment.

In 2004, Barr was the 100% owner of The Stone Scone, a business operating as a sole proprietorship. On January 7, 2004, Fleet Bank approved a $100,000 unsecured small business line of credit for The Stone Scone, conditioned upon receipt of a properly signed and witnessed authorization/personal guaranty.

Acting on behalf of The Stone Scone, Barr executed and delivered to Fleet Bank a properly signed and witnessed authorization agreement/personal guaranty portion of the Fleet Bank small business services credit application, dated January 7, 2004. . . .

Two years after the line of credit was approved, The Stone Scone filed articles of organization with the State, registering itself as a limited liability company (LLC) and naming Barr as the manager. [Citation omitted.] BoA was not notified of the change in The Stone Scone's status. Had BoA been informed that The Stone Scone had organized as an LLC, it would have asked for documentation and a new line of credit agreement under the entity's name.

The last payment made to the line of credit account was on October 28, 2008. . . . As of the last monthly statement, the principal owed on the account was $91,444.09.

On November 4, 2008, BoA sent a past due notice addressed to Barr and The Stone Scone. No payments were made on the account thereafter. Barr admitted that, pursuant to the terms of the line of credit, interest on the unpaid principal balance continued to accrue at a rate of 6.5% per annum.

In March 2009, BoA filed a complaint against Barr and The Stone Scone in the District Court. . . . The only issue for trial was Barr's personal responsibility for the debt.

. . .

II. Legal Analysis

. . .

B. Sufficiency of the Evidence

. . .

The trial record . . . contains sufficient evidence that Barr is personally liable for the debt owed to BoA. The evidence demonstrates that, at the time Barr acted on The Stone Scone's behalf to procure the small business line of credit, she was the owner of The Stone Scone and the sole proprietor of that business. [Citations omitted.]

An individual doing business as a sole proprietor, even when business is done under a different name, remains personally liable for all of the obligations of the sole proprietorship. [Citations omitted.]

As the sole proprietor of The Stone Scone when that sole proprietorship entered into the agreement for a line of credit with Fleet Bank, Barr became personally liable for the debts incurred on that line of credit account. The fact that The Stone Scone subsequently converted to an LLC, a fact of which Fleet Bank/BoA was not made aware, does not alter Barr's individual liability in this regard. . . .

similar to it. A person starting a business can usually reserve or register an available business name for a relatively small fee.

Local Business License

Local governments require that a business obtain and maintain a license to do business in the city. As an example, consider the following city ordinance from Colorado Springs, Colorado with respect to obtaining a business license (Illustrative City Ordinance 22.1).

If the business is not located in an incorporated city, then the business usually obtains the business license from the county government instead. The city or county charges a fee for the license upon application. Other licenses—in addition to a business license—may need to be obtained as well depending upon the type of business. Licensing is typically required for child care businesses, restaurants (*e.g.*, food handling, liquor, etc.), and adult-oriented businesses, to name a few. Moreover, the business owners may need to have occupational licenses (*e.g.*, lawyers, CPA, engineers, doctors, dentists, etc.)

Employer Identification Number

Businesses other than sole proprietorships typically must obtain an **employer identification number** (EIN) from the IRS. This unique number must be stated on the business's income tax return and is usually required by financial institutions to open a bank account. This number is obtained by filing IRS Form SS-4 with the IRS, which now can be accomplished online. A business may also need to obtain a number from the state similar to an EIN, particularly if the business has employees and must withhold payroll taxes.

Colorado Springs, Colorado

2.1.301: License Required:

It shall be unlawful for any person, either directly or indirectly or through an agent or employee, to conduct any business, or to use in connection with the business any vehicle, premises, machine or device, in whole or in part, for which a license is required by this General Licensing Code without first obtaining a license.

2.1.302: For the purpose of this General Licensing Code, one act of any of the following activities within the City limits constitutes doing business:

(a) Soliciting business or selling any goods or services for which a license is required;

(b) Acquiring or using any vehicle or any premises in the City for purposes requiring a license.

. . .

2.1.401: Qualifications of Applicants:

Every applicant for a license or renewal of a license must meet the general standards and qualifications set out in this part.

A. Good Moral Character: Each applicant shall be of good moral character. In determining good moral character, the Deputy Licensing Officer must consider:

1. License History: The license history of the applicant; whether in previously conducting business in this or another locality, any license has been revoked or suspended, the reasons for any administrative action and the demeanor of the applicant subsequent to the action. The Deputy Licensing Officer shall also consider whether, when previously conducting business, the applicant engaged in false or misleading advertising, falsified any business records or participated in any unlawful business practice.

2. General Personal History: Each applicant shall have a satisfactory general personal history. The Deputy Licensing Officer shall investigate other facts relevant to the general personal history of the applicant as necessary to fairly determine the applicant's qualifications and ability to conduct the business in a lawful manner. Relevant facts may include, but not be limited to, the applicant's criminal history, knowing or willful deception in any phase of the application or licensing process, fraud in obtaining any license or registration, addition to alcohol, habit-forming drugs or controlled substances or complaints received by the City Clerk's Office.

B. No Obligations To City: Each applicant shall not be indebted or obligated in any manner to the City.

C. Compliance With All City Regulations: Each applicant shall, to the extent applicable, present certificates furnished by the appropriate City departments to the effect that the proposed use of any premises is in compliance with all applicable City regulations including, but not limited to, Zoning, Building and Fire Codes.

Hiring Employees

Once a business hires employees, regulatory compliance issues increase significantly. For example, the business must decide about offering health care plans, retirement plans, and other employee benefits. Moreover, employee safety, tax, and various labor laws and regulations come into play. These regulations governing employers and their relationship with employees are why many businesses try to classify workers as "independent contractors" rather than employees. In many cases, certain government regulations do not apply to independent contractors. The federal government has set forth a number of factors that are relevant in the analysis of whether someone working for the business is an employee or an independent contractor. These factors include, among others:

- Does the business have the right to direct or control how the work is done?
- Does the worker provide his or her own equipment and tools?
- Does the worker have a permanent relationship with the business?
- How does the business pay the worker?
- Does the business reimburse the worker for expenses incurred?

An employer's misclassification of workers is an issue that is at the fore-front for government regulators. Consequently, businesses must consider all the factors and make an informed decision when classifying a worker as either an employee or independent contractor.

Obtaining Capital

Is it better for a business to borrow money or to obtain equity contributions from investors? The answer to this question may differ based upon the business's objectives and the owner's desire

for control. Of course, the advantage to borrowing money is that the owner does not give up voting control of the business and still can manage the business without answering to third parties (other than the lender). A major disadvantage is that the borrowed money must usually be repaid on a regular schedule, which could lead to cash-flow problems. If the business wants to attract very large amounts of money, then finding investors may be the only option. This may have drawbacks also, like complying with federal and state securities laws and giving up some voting power and control, for example. Nevertheless, obtaining needed capital through investors relieves to some extent the cash-flow problem that borrowing money presents.

QUESTIONS FOR REVIEW

1. Discuss some advantages and disadvantages of organizing a business as a sole proprietorship.

2. Explain generally how a sole proprietorship is treated for federal income tax purposes.

3. What state agency website would you go to in your state to see whether a proposed business name is already taken?

4. What is an EIN?

5. Discuss the reasons why classifying a worker as an employee or independent contractor is so important.

6. Discuss the advantages and disadvantages of borrowing compared to attracting capital through investors.

7. Summarize the *Bank of America v. Barr* case.

INTERNET ACTIVITIES

1. Visit your state agency's website and determine whether the following business names are available.

   a. Lake View Investment Company

   b. Fifth Avenue Tuxedos

    c. Bridal Fashion Outlet

    d. AAA Locksmiths

2. Visit your local city or county website.

    a. How much does it cost for a standard business license?

    b. Does the cost of a license depend upon the nature of the business?

3. Visit the IRS website at www.irs.gov. Click on the "Forms and Publications" link. Find Form SS-4.

    a. What information does Line 9a ask for?

    b. What information does Line 10 ask for?

Chapter 23

Partnerships

P artnership law has evolved over a long period of time. Currently there are two major forms of partnerships under state law: general partnerships and limited partnerships. Each of these is discussed below.

General Partnerships

Formation

A general partnership is easy to form. A **general partnership** is formed by two or more persons entering into a business relationship with the intent to make a profit. No formal organizational document is typically necessary to file with a state agency. In other words, a mere handshake may be enough to create a general partnership. This can pose certain challenges, however, such as documenting to some third party (*e.g.*, a bank) that a person is really a partner in a partnership. Most states have adopted the **Uniform Partnership Act** (or revised versions thereof) as the law governing partnerships in their state.

Operation

Under state law, each general partner has the right to manage the partnership. Additionally, each partner can bind the partnership by entering into a contract on behalf of the partnership. Consider the Illinois statute that follows (Illustrative State Statute 23.1).

Mangostock/ Shutterstock.com

Partners also have the right to inspect the books and require the partnership to provide an accounting of income and expenses. Other internal matters governing the partnership are typically set forth in a **partnership agreement** signed by all the partners. This agreement would include allocation of profits and losses among the partners, the right to vote on partnership matters, the process of admitting new partners, the process of withdrawing from the partnership, and partnership dissolution.

Taxation

A partnership is not subject to federal income taxation. This is readily apparent from reading Section 701 of the Internal Revenue Code (Illustrative Federal Statute 23.1).

A partnership reports its income on IRS Form 1065, but does not pay income taxes on

805 ILC 206/301

Section 301. Partner agent of partnership. Subject to the effect of a statement of partnership authority under Section 303 of this Act:

(1) Each partner is an agent of the partnership for the purpose of its business. An act of a partner, including the execution of an instrument in the partnership name, for apparently carrying on in the ordinary course the partnership business or business of the kind carried on by the partnership binds the partnership, unless the partner had no authority to act for the partnership in the particular matter and the person with whom the partner was dealing knew or had received a notification that the partner lacked authority.

(2) An act of a partner which is not apparently for carrying on in the ordinary course the partnership business or business of the kind carried on by the partnership binds the partnership only if the act was authorized by the other partners.

26 U.S.C. §701

Section 701. Partners, not partnership, subject to tax

A partnership as such shall not be subject to the income tax imposed by this chapter. Persons carrying on business as partners shall be liable for income tax only in their separate or individual capacities.

the income. Rather, the information from Form 1065 is furnished to each partner, and each partner reports their share of the income (or loss) on their individual income tax return. Since partnerships are not subject to income tax, partnerships are often called "flow-through" or "pass-through" entities from an income tax standpoint. Most *state* income tax laws typically follow federal income tax laws and also treat partnerships as flow-through entities.

Owner Liability

Partners in a general partnership are personally liable for the actions of the other partners within the scope of doing business for the partnership and are also personally liable for the debts of the partnership. Consider the Ohio statute that follows (Illustrative State Statute 23.2).

Notice in the Ohio statute that if a general partnership registers to be a limited liability partnership (LLP), then partners can enjoy liability protection. Most states allow general partnerships to register as an LLP and provide liability protection to the partners.

Limited Partnerships

Formation

To form a limited partnership, the partners must decide who is going to be the general partner(s) and who will be the limited partner(s). A limited partnership is required to have at least one general partner and at least one limited partner. State law requires that the partnership file a document with the appropriate state agency identifying the partnership as a limited partnership and who the general partners

Ohio R.C. §1776.36

(a) Except as otherwise provided in divisions (b) and (c) of this section, all partners are liable jointly and severally for all obligations of the partnership unless otherwise agreed by the claimant or provided by law.

(b) A person admitted as a partner into an existing partnership is not personally liable for any partnership obligation incurred before the person's admission as a partner.

(c) An obligation of a partnership incurred while the partnership is a limited liability partnership, whether arising in contract, tort, or otherwise, is solely the obligation of the partnership. A partner is not personally liable, directly or indirectly, by way of contribution or otherwise, for such an obligation solely by reason of being or acting as a partner. This division applies notwithstanding anything inconsistent in the partnership agreement that existed before any vote required to become a limited liability partnership under division (b) of section 1776.81 of the Revised Code.

are. This document is usually called a "certificate of limited partnership," or some name similar to that. If a partnership fails to file this document, or fails to renew its status as a limited partnership as required by state law, the partnership may then be considered a general partnership causing the limited partners to lose liability protection.

Operation

The general partner in a limited partnership typically has all the authority to manage the day-to-day operations of the partnership. Limited partners do have the right to vote on partnership matters and to inspect the books of the partnership. As with all forms of partnerships, the partnership agreement is important in setting forth the rights, powers, and limitations of the partners.

Taxation

For federal income tax purposes, a limited partnership is treated as a partnership. As mentioned previously, partnerships are not separately subject to income taxes; rather, the income earned or the loss incurred by the partnership flows through to the partners and is reported on the partners' income tax returns.

Owner Liability

Unlike general partners, limited partners in a limited partnership are typically not personally liable for the debts of the partnership. Consider the following case from the United States Court of Appeals for the Ninth Circuit (Illustrative Court Case 23.1). Some states provide liability protection to a general partner in a limited partnership if the partnership registers as a limited liability limited partnership (LLLP). Many states now have statutes allowing a limited partnership to register as an LLLP.

What Do You Think?

Why would someone agree to be a general partner in a limited partnership when the general partner is personally liable for the debts of the partnership?

What Do You Think?

Assuming a general partnership is eligible to register as an LLP in a particular state, is there any reason why the partnership would not do so?

Shimko v. Guenther

Court of Appeals for the Ninth Circuit

505 F.3d 987 (2007)

OPINION BY: Milan D. Smith, Jr., Circuit Judge:

[Guenther] appeals a judgment awarding $359,668.00 in attorneys' fees to [Shimko and his law firm] in payment for certain legal services allegedly provided to Arizona limited partnerships (collectively the "CORF" partnerships) and their limited partners. The [organizational] documents of both the CORF entities list Guenther as a limited partner, not as a general partner.

On appeal, Shimko argues that it reasonably believed Guenther to be a general, rather than a limited partner, and that, as a result, Guenther is liable for the legal fees of the CORF entities under [Arizona law]. We disagree. Shimko is not an ordinary creditor. Shimko is a law firm hired to defend the CORF entities and its limited partners against a significant number of multimillion dollar claims filed across the country, primarily alleging fraud. We hold that because Shimko owed a fiduciary duty of care to its clients, [Shimko] is chargeable under the facts of this case with knowledge of the contents of the CORF entities' [organizational documents], whether or not it actually examined them, and consequently, that it was not reasonable for Shimko to believe that Guenther was a general partner of either of the CORF entities. Accordingly, Shimko may not recover from the Guenthers the legal fees owed by the CORF entities to Shimko.

. . .

I. Background and Prior Proceedings

The CORF entities offered clients consulting and management services to help them establish and operate Medicare-compliant outpatient treatment facilities. Upon commencement of the CORF entities' operations, Guenther was in charge of field operations, actively lectured at CORF marketing seminars, and helped find locations and medical directors for CORF clients.

During the period from late 2001 to 2003, a number of the CORF entities' clients located in various parts of the country threatened to file or did file complaints against the CORF entities, as well as against the [the CORF partners] in their individual capacities, alleging fraud and other causes of action.

. . .

Following a one day bench trial, the district court held that Guenther, as a limited partner in control [was] liable for the entirety of Shimko's unpaid attorneys' fees.

In its Findings and Conclusions, the district court found that Shimko was retained to represent the CORF entities as well as its individual principals. It found that the Guenthers were personally represented by Shimko, that they personally agreed to this representation, and that they were liable for legal services performed for them personally. The district court also found that Guenther participated in the control of the CORF entities as a general partner, along with his colleagues, and that due to his substantial involvement in the operations of the CORF entities, "it was reasonable for Shimko to believe that he was dealing with a general partner." The court then found in favor of Shimko . . . and found the Guenthers liable for all unpaid legal fees charged to the CORF entities. . . .

. . .

III. Discussion

[Arizona law] states, in pertinent part:

[A] limited partner is not liable for the obligations of a limited partnership unless he is also a general partner or, in addition to the exercise of his rights and powers as a limited partner, he participates in the control of the business. However, if the limited partner participates in the control of the business, he is liable only to persons who transact business with the limited partnership reasonably believing, based on the limited partner's conduct, that the limited partner is a general partner.

Thus, a limited partner may be held liable to a third party for the debts of the partnership if the limited partner is either a general partner or a participant in the control of the business and the third party reasonably believes that the limited partner is a general partner. [Arizona law] defines a general partner as "a person who has been admitted to a limited partnership as a general partner in accordance with the partnership agreement and named in the certificate of limited partnership as a general partner." [Citation omitted.] Guenther was not a general partner, as defined by [Arizona law], of either CORF entity. The district court found, however, that Guenther participated in the control of the business. We review this factual finding for clear error, and we find none.

This determination, however, does not complete our inquiry. Guenther can only be held liable as a general partner to persons who "transact business with the limited partnership reasonably believing, based on the limited partner's conduct, that the limited partner is a general partner." [Citation omitted.] . . .

Were a different creditor involved, Guenther's conduct may have been enough to support the conclusion that a third party reasonably believed that he was a general partner of the CORF entities. Here, however, such a holding would be perverse because Shimko acted as legal counsel to both the CORF entities and the Guenthers, and owed a fiduciary duty of care to each.

. . .

In this case, [Shimko's] Response Brief states: "Shimko was asked to advise Dr. Guenther and the other owners on the extent of their individual and personal exposure, if any, beyond the protection offered to them by the limited partnership structure under which they owned and operated [the CORF entities]." One of the first acts of any competent lawyer or law firm hired under those circumstances should have been to review the [organizational] documents of the potentially liable limited partnerships to determine whether all legal formalities had been followed and whether any limited partner, by his previous or current actions, might have exposed himself to liability under [Arizona law]. Had Shimko examined the CORF entities' [organizational] documents, [Shimko] would have observed that Guenther was listed as a limited partner, not as a general partner.

. . .

We reverse the district court's finding that Guenther is liable as a general partner of either of the CORF entities. Accordingly, Guenther and his spouse are not personally liable for those attorneys' fees properly chargeable to the CORF entities.

QUESTIONS FOR REVIEW

1. Explain how a general partnership is formed.

2. Are all the partners in a general partnership liable for the debts of the partnership?

3. Explain broadly how general partnerships and limited partnerships are treated for federal income tax purposes.

4. How is a limited partnership formed?

5. What are the advantages and disadvantages of being a limited partner in a limited partnership?

6. Explain what an LLP is and why a partnership would want to register as an LLP.

7. Summarize the *Shimko v. Guenther* case.

INTERNET ACTIVITIES

1. Explain the difference between a limited partnership (LP) and a limited liability limited partnership (LLLP). Does your state recognize LLLP's?

2. If a general partnership in your state desired to register as a LLP, what document would it need to file with the appropriate state agency?

Chapter 24

Limited Liability Companies

One of the most popular forms of doing business is the **limited liability company** (LLC). Compared to partnerships and corporations, LLCs have not been around very long. Wyoming was the first state to allow the LLC form of doing business (1977). Now all 50 states have passed LLC statutes.

Formation

A limited liability company is formed by filing **Articles of Organization** (or some other similarly named document such as "Certificate of Formation") with the appropriate state agency. The articles of organization state, among other things, the company's name, address, and whether the LLC is "member-managed" or "manager-managed." The owners of an LLC are called **members** (similar to "partners" of a partnership and "stockholders" of a corporation). If an LLC is member-managed, then all the members typically have authority to engage in every-day management of the company, and can bind the LLC contractually. If the LLC is manager-managed, then only the designated manager or managers can engage in management and bind the LLC contractually. A manager-managed LLC may be preferred when there are a lot of members of the LLC.

Operation

A member's rights to engage in management decisions is significantly impacted by whether the LLC is member-managed or manager-managed.

Furthermore, members of an LLC typically enter into an **operating agreement** (similar to a partnership agreement for partnerships) wherein the members set forth their agreement for sharing profits and losses, admitting new members, dissolving the company, etc. LLCs are popular because of their flexibility in management, profit sharing, and generally favorable income tax treatment. State laws also allow for an LLC to have only one owner, which is not possible for a partnership.

Your image/Shutterstock.com

Taxation

An LLC that has more than one member is treated as a partnership for federal income tax purposes. Thus, a "multi-member" LLC is governed by the same sections of the Internal Revenue Code as are general partnerships and limited partnerships. An LLC that has only one owner (*i.e.*, a "single-member" LLC) is treated as a "disregarded entity" for federal income tax purposes. This means that for *federal income tax purposes* the LLC is not treated as separate from its owner and all items of income, expense, gain, loss, etc., are reported on the sole member's income tax return and no income tax return is required to be filed for the single-member LLC. With some exceptions, most *states* treat LLCs in the same manner as federal law for income tax purposes.

ILLUSTRATIVE COURT CASE 24.1

Breen v. Judge

Connecticut Court of Appeals

124 Conn. App. 147 (2010)

OPINION BY: BISHOP

This appeal stems from an action by the plaintiffs, Robert V. Breen and Susan Breen, to hold the defendant, Craig T. Judge, the managing member of Patriot Truck Equipment, LLC (Patriot), personally liable on a judgment previously recovered against Patriot. The plaintiffs, appealing from the judgment in favor of the defendant, claim that the court improperly (1) failed to pierce Patriot's corporate veil under either the identity rule or the instrumentality rule, (2) required proof of intent to defraud in order to find certain transfers of assets to be fraudulent under [Connecticut law] and (3) failed to find that the defendant was unjustly enriched by the transfers he received from Patriot. We affirm the judgment of the trial court.

Susan Breen was employed as a bookkeeper at Patriot from February, 2003, to March, 2004. Beginning in March, 2003, she deposited funds, which she had borrowed from credit card accounts in the name of [the plaintiffs], into Patriot's checking account. At the time Susan Breen made these deposits, Patriot was unable to pay its current liabilities, including vendor payments. She testified [that] she made these deposits to help Patriot avoid having to cease operation. Neither [the defendant], who was the managing member of Patriot, nor anyone else at Patriot solicited these deposits. Patriot did acknowledge the deposits, which were carried on the books of Patriot as a loan from Susan Breen. She left employment at Patriot in March, 2004. In August, 2005, the plaintiffs . . . sued Patriot to recover the money they loaned, plus interest. . . . [O]n January 8, 2006, judgment entered in the plaintiffs' favor, against Patriot, in the total amount of $ 58,495.35. . . . On May 14 and June 27, 2007, the plaintiffs conducted an examination of judgment debtor by examining [the defendant], who appeared as the representative of Patriot.

On November 8, 2007, the plaintiffs filed a complaint against the defendant, seeking to hold him personally liable on the judgment previously obtained against Patriot. . . .

. . .

The plaintiffs first claim that the court improperly denied their request to pierce Patriot's corporate veil in order to hold the defendant personally liable for the judgment against Patriot. Specifically, the plaintiffs claim that under either the instrumentality rule or the identity rule, the court should have found that the defendant had complete unity of interest with Patriot and should not be allowed to avoid liability. We are not persuaded.

The following additional facts, as found by the court, are relevant to the plaintiffs' claim. "Much of the evidence and testimony at trial concerned the books and records of Patriot, and money received by [the defendant] and his mother, Shirley Judge. Shirley Judge was a member of Patriot . . . for a period of time and made capital contributions to Patriot. She also performed bookkeeping services at Patriot for no salary. . . . Patriot was in the business of outfitting trucks with snow plows and truck bodies. Patriot commenced operation in January, 2002, and it filed articles of dissolution with

(Continued)

the secretary of the state on September 16, 2005. At the trial, the accountant for Patriot and [the defendant] . . . testified at length as to information contained in the tax returns filed by Patriot and [the defendant] for the years 2002 through 2005. The court found his testimony credible and of assistance."

. . .

The court also found that "[d]uring the time Patriot was in existence, [the defendant] worked at the business full-time as its managing member. While Patriot was in business, [the defendant] received money from Patriot in the form of draws and by way of payment of his personal expenses. These draws and personal expenses were noted on the books of the business. . . .

In response to the plaintiffs' quest to pierce the corporate veil in order to hold the defendant personally liable for Patriot's debt to them, the court stated: "In applying the instrumentality test to the facts of this case, the court cannot find that [the defendant] exerted such control over Patriot that it had no existence of its own. As noted earlier, [the defendant] shared ownership of Patriot, at various times, with Clark and Shirley Judge. The business did not exist only for [the defendant's] benefit but was a going business with average annual sales of approximately $ 660,000 for the four years it was in operation. Furthermore, Patriot kept books and records, filed tax returns and gave notice of its dissolution to the secretary of the state. . . ."

"As to the identity test, the court is not persuaded that there was such unity of interest between [the defendant] and Patriot that Patriot's independence never began or ceased. This case does not present the exceptional circumstances that justify piercing the corporate veil."

. . .

"When determining whether piercing the corporate veil is proper, our Supreme Court has endorsed two tests: the instrumentality test and the identity test. The instrumentality rule requires, in any case but an express agency, proof of three elements: (1) Control, not mere majority or complete stock control, but complete domination, not only of finances but of policy and business practice in respect to the transaction attacked so that the corporate entity as to this transaction had at the time no separate mind, will or existence of its own; (2) that such control must have been used by the defendant to commit fraud or wrong, to perpetrate the violation of a statutory or other positive legal duty, or a dishonest or unjust act in contravention of plaintiff's legal rights; and (3) that the aforesaid control and breach of duty must proximately cause the injury or unjust loss complained of." [Citation omitted.]

"The identity rule has been stated as follows: If [the] plaintiff can show that there was such a unity of interest and ownership that the independence of the corporations had in effect ceased or had never begun, an adherence to the fiction of separate identity would serve only to defeat justice and equity by permitting the economic entity to escape liability arising out of an operation conducted by one corporation for the benefit of the whole enterprise. . . ."

"Courts, in assessing whether an entity is dominated or controlled, have looked for the presence of a number of factors. Those include: (1) the absence of corporate formalities; (2) inadequate capitalization; (3) whether funds are put in and taken out of the corporation for personal rather than corporate purposes; (4) overlapping ownership, officers, directors, personnel; (5) common office space, address, phones; (6) the amount of business discretion by the allegedly dominated corporation; (7) whether the corporations dealt with each other at arm's length; (8) whether the corporations are treated as independent profit centers; (9) payment or guarantee of debts of the dominated corporation; and (10) whether the corporation in question had property that was used by other of the corporations as if it were its own. . . . The concept of piercing the corporate veil is equitable in nature. . . . No hard and fast rule, however, as to the conditions under which the entity may be disregarded can be stated

(Continued)

as they vary according to the circumstances of each case. . . . Ordinarily the corporate veil is pierced only under exceptional circumstances, for example, where the corporation is a mere shell, serving no legitimate purpose, and used primarily as an intermediary to perpetuate fraud or promote injustice. . . . The improper use of the corporate form is the key to the inquiry, as [i]t is true that courts will disregard legal fictions, including that of a separate corporate entity, when they are used for fraudulent or illegal purposes. Unless something of the kind is proven, however, to do so is to act in opposition to the public policy of the state as expressed in legislation concerning the formation and regulation of corporations." [Citation omitted.]

Upon our review of the record, we conclude that the court's determination that the facts in this case did not present exceptional circumstances to justify piercing the corporate veil was not clearly erroneous. . . .

The judgment is affirmed.

Owner Liability

Similar to limited partners in a limited partnership and partners in an LLP, state law provides that members of an LLC are not personally liable for the debts of the LLC. In some situations, a member may be personally liable for a tort that he or she committed in their capacity as a member or if a plaintiff can successfully persuade a judge to **pierce the LLC veil** and allow the plaintiff to recover damages from the LLC members. Piercing the LLC veil is not easy to do, but plaintiffs often try it. Consider the preceding court case from the Connecticut Court of Appeals (Illustrative Court Case 24.1).

ILLUSTRATIVE COURT CASE 24.2

Sturm v. Harb Development, LLC

Connecticut Supreme Court

298 Conn. 124 (2010)

OPINION BY: VERTEFEUILLE

The plaintiffs, Chris K. Sturm and Tammy Sturm, brought this action against the defendants, Harb Development, LLC (Harb Development), and its principal, John J. Harb, alleging that their poor workmanship in the construction of the plaintiffs' new home constituted . . . negligence and fraud, and violated both the Connecticut Unfair Trade Practices Act (CUTPA), and the New Home Construction Contractors Act (New Home Act). The trial court granted the defendant's motion to strike all counts of the complaint against him in his individual capacity, concluding that the plaintiffs had failed to plead sufficient facts to warrant piercing the corporate veil . . . . The plaintiffs now appeal, claiming that the trial court improperly: (1) required the pleading of facts sufficient to pierce the corporate veil for all counts against the defendant; and (2) determined that they failed to plead sufficient facts to support the causes of action against the defendant in three counts of the complaint. We agree with the plaintiffs that the trial court misconstrued all of the counts of the complaint against the defendant and improperly required the plaintiffs to plead facts sufficient to pierce the corporate veil in order to establish the defendant's personal liability. We conclude, however, that the motion to strike counts three and four of the complaint alleging the CUTPA violation and negligence properly was granted because the plaintiffs failed to adequately state a cause of action for the defendant's individual liability on those counts. . . .

(Continued)

The complaint alleges the following facts. On March 17, 2005, the plaintiffs and Harb Development entered into a contract for the construction of a new home in Bristol. After the house was built, the plaintiffs found that the house had not been built in accordance with the contract and that the workmanship was poor. Specifically, the plaintiffs claimed that: the foundation lacked an adequate concrete slab; the lot was not properly sloped, which resulted in water pooling against the foundation; the dormer was built incorrectly; the first and second floors varied from the construction plans; two adjacent windows were not installed symmetrically; the windows throughout the house were improperly installed, resulting in noticeable drafts; the stairway was installed on an uneven floor and without proper trim; the shutters, beam details and floor adjacent to the fireplace were negligently installed; and the interior painting was deficient.

The plaintiffs alleged several causes of action arising from these defects against both Harb Development and the defendant. Against Harb Development, the plaintiffs alleged: breach of contract in the first count; violation of CUTPA in the second count; and failure to comply with the New Home Act in the fifth count. Against the defendant in his individual capacity, the plaintiffs alleged: individual liability for Harb Development's violation of CUTPA in the third count; negligence in the fourth count; failure to comply with the New Home Act in the sixth count; fraudulent misrepresentation in the seventh count; and negligent misrepresentation in the eighth count.

The defendant filed a motion to strike all counts against him in his individual capacity. The defendant claimed that because the plaintiffs had asserted fundamentally similar claims against both Harb Development and himself, the plaintiffs were required to allege facts sufficient to pierce the corporate veil in order to state a valid claim against him in his individual capacity. In the plaintiffs' opposition to the motion to strike, they responded that they were not making a claim to pierce the corporate veil, but instead were bringing an action against the defendant for his own personal liability in tort. The trial court agreed with the defendant and granted the motion to strike, ruling, first, that, because the counts against the defendant in his individual capacity arose out of his management of Harb Development, the plaintiffs were required, but failed, to allege facts sufficient to warrant piercing the corporate veil. In addition, the trial court further concluded that there were additional reasons for striking the sixth, seventh and eighth counts of the complaint, namely, the plaintiffs' failure to plead properly the required elements for each cause of action. This appeal followed.

TORT LIABILITY OF A MEMBER OF A LIMITED LIABILITY COMPANY

We first address whether the trial court properly struck all counts of the complaint against the defendant on the basis that, in order to establish the defendant's personal liability, the plaintiffs were required to plead facts sufficient to pierce the corporate veil. The plaintiffs contend that the trial court improperly required them to plead facts sufficient to warrant piercing the corporate veil in order to hold the defendant personally liable. Put another way, the plaintiffs claim that the trial court misconstrued the complaint, failing to understand that their claim is that the defendant is personally and individually liable in tort despite being a member or manager of Harb Development, and it therefore is not necessary to pierce the corporate veil in order to establish his personal liability. The defendant responds that he is immune from liability on these grounds because of the protection against personal liability found in [Connecticut statutory law]. More specifically, because the allegations against him not only arise from his membership in or management of Harb Development but also appear to be substantially similar to the allegations against Harb Development, the defendant contends that the plaintiffs must allege facts sufficient to warrant piercing the corporate veil. We agree with the plaintiffs.

We begin our analysis with a brief review of Connecticut law concerning the individual liability in tort of a corporate agent or officer. "It is well established that an officer of a corporation does not incur personal liability for its torts merely because of his official position. Where, however, an agent

(Continued)

or officer commits or participates in the commission of a tort, whether or not he acts on behalf of his principal or corporation, he is liable to third persons injured thereby. . . . Thus, a director or officer who commits the tort or who directs the tortious act done, or participates or operates therein, is liable to third persons injured thereby, even though liability may also attach to the corporation for the tort." [Citations omitted.] . . .

[T]he defendant contends that we should follow the trial court's reasoning and construe as requiring the plaintiffs to allege facts sufficient to pierce the corporate veil. . . .

The defendant's analysis fails, however, to acknowledge our well established common-law exception to individual liability in a corporate context for an individual's tort liability. . . . According to [Connecticut statutory law], "a member or manager of a limited liability company is not liable, *solely* by reason of being a member or manager . . . ." (Emphasis added.). Thus, although being a member or manager does not impose liability, the statute's use of the term "solely" opens the door to other types of liability, such as common-law liability.

. . .

The trial court thus improperly concluded that the plaintiffs were required to allege facts sufficient to pierce the corporate veil with regard to all of the counts of the complaint alleged against the defendant in his individual capacity. The trial court improperly failed to consider the common-law tort exception that the plaintiffs chose to invoke as the basis for their individual claims against the defendant. The trial court therefore improperly struck all of the counts against the defendant in his individual capacity for the plaintiffs' failure to make allegations sufficient to pierce the corporate veil. . . .

Keep in mind that whenever a court discusses "piercing the corporate veil," the same principles generally apply to "piercing the LLC veil." Consider another Connecticut court case—this one from the Connecticut Supreme Court—relating to whether an LLC member was liable for his *tortious* conduct (Illustrative Court Case 24.2).

QUESTIONS FOR REVIEW

1. What document must an organizer of an LLC file with the appropriate state agency in order to legally form an LLC?

2. Explain the difference between a manager-managed LLC and a member-managed LLC.

3. What is an operating agreement?

4. If an LLC has more than one member, how is the LLC treated for federal income tax purposes?

5. If an LLC has only one member, how is the LLC treated for federal income tax purposes.

6. Explain what it means to "pierce the LLC veil."

7. Even though a member of an LLC may generally be protected from the debts of the LLC and claims against the LLC, is it possible for the LLC member to be liable for committing torts?

8. Summarize the *Breen v. Judge* case.

9. Summarize the *Sturm v. Harb Development* case.

INTERNET ACTIVITIES

1. Determine the amount of the filing fee in your state to file Articles of Organization (or Certificate of Formation) for an LLC in your state.

2. At what address would the formation document for an LLC be filed in your state?

Chapter 25

Corporations

Most large businesses are organized as corporations. Many new businesses also choose the corporate form of doing business. Being familiar with the fundamental laws relating to corporations is important for every businessperson.

Formation

A person forms a corporation by filing **Articles of Incorporation** with the appropriate state agency. The person filing the Articles of Incorporation is called the **incorporator**. The Articles of Incorporation including the name, address, and purposes and powers of the corporation (which are usually stated very broadly). Moreover, the Articles of Incorporation identify who is the corporation's **statutory agent** (or **registered** agent). The statutory agent's responsibility is to receive legal documents on behalf of the corporation in the event the corporation is sued. The incorporator also engages in pre-incorporation activities and may appoint the initial board of directors and hire accountants and lawyers to help with the incorporation process. The incorporator should act with care, however, to protect against the possibility that the incorporator could be personally liable for actions taken before the corporation is legally formed.

The corporation issues shares of stock in return for capital contributions by investors. The owners of stock, of course, are called **stockholders** or **shareholders**. The corporation may issue stock certificates to the stockholders to evidence ownership of the corporation. Issuing certificates is not required, but a corporation nevertheless should maintain a stock register to keep track of the stockholders' names, address, and number of shares held.

Olivier Le Queinec/Shutterstock.com

The incorporator(s) or initial members of the board of directors first hold an organizational meeting. At this meeting the incorporators or board members adopt the **bylaws**. The bylaws contain important provisions regarding how the board of directors is constituted, when board meetings and shareholder meetings will take place, voting rights of board members and shareholders, when a board member's term ends, the duties of the officers, etc.

In addition to obtaining initial capital from investors, a corporation may seek financing by issuing **bonds** or borrowing from financial institutions.

The **capital structure** of a corporation (*i.e.*, its mix of equity and debt) is an important strategic decision made early on by the corporation's officers. Corporations have the flexibility of issuing multiple classes of stock, including preferred stock. **Preferred** stockholders have priority over **common** stockholders as to dividends and to assets of the corporation upon liquidation.

Operations

The day-to-day operations of a corporation are entrusted to **officers**. A corporation can have many officers, but typically has at least a president, vice-president, treasurer, and secretary. The officers are typically hired by the **board of directors**. Members of the board of directors oversee the corporation's affairs and provide approval and/or recommendations to the shareholders to approve major policies (*e.g.*, conflicts of interest, employee policies, etc.) and transactions that the corporation may engage in (*e.g.*, mergers and acquisitions, etc.) Members of the board of directors are usually elected by the shareholders, although different arrangements may exist in the bylaws to provide for how a person becomes a member of the board, remains on the board, or is removed from the board.

hxdbzxy/Shutterstock.com

Relationships between and among the shareholders may be governed by an agreement entered into by the shareholders. Such agreement typically is in place for closely held corporations, but not publicly traded corporations. The **shareholders'**

agreement will typically cover issues such as the admission of new shareholders and restrictions on selling stock.

In larger corporations, the board of directors usually establishes subcommittees. These committees may include a compensation committee, audit committee, litigation committee, and executive committee. The audit committee, for example, reviews reports from the public accounting firm that audits the corporation's financial statements and complies with other laws and regulations relating to internal controls, auditor independence, etc.

The law imposes on directors and officers certain duties. For example, directors and officers have a **duty of care** toward the corporation. In other words, members of the board should attend meetings, understand the contents of corporate reports and records, and make informed decisions. If board members exercise the duty of care and make informed decisions, a court will typically not second-guess the board of directors even if a decision turns out to be a bad decision. This notion is called the **business judgment rule**. In other words, a member of the board of directors typically will not be personally liable merely because he or she in good faith voted for a particular course of action that turned out to be less than ideal for the corporation.

Directors and officers also have a **duty of loyalty**. This means, for example, that they should not engage in activities in direct competition to the corporation, nor **usurp** (*i.e.*, personally take advantage of) opportunities that may come to the corporation. Corporations should have a conflict of interest policy in place that directors and officers are made aware of (or preferably sign) to help prevent breaches of the duty of loyalty. Directors and officers may face personal liability for breaching the duties of care and loyalty. Consider the Supreme Court of Delaware case that follows (Illustrative Court Case 25.1).

When a corporation is harmed by a third party, board members and officers typically will initiate a lawsuit against the third party. If the board or officers do not cause a lawsuit to be filed, the shareholders

Guth v. Loft, Inc.

Supreme Court of Delaware

5 A.2d 503 (1939)

LAYTON, Chief Justice, delivering the opinion of the Court:

. . .

As stated by [Guth], there were certain questions before the Chancellor for determination:

1. Was Guth at the time the Pepsi-Cola opportunity came to him obligated, in view of his official connection with Loft, to take the opportunity for Loft rather than for himself?

. . .

2. Was Guth, nevertheless, estopped from denying that the opportunity belonged to Loft; and was he rightfully penalized to the extent of his whole interest therein, merely because resources borrowed from Loft had contributed in some measure to its development; and did Loft's contributions create the whole value behind the interests of Guth . . . in Pepsi, thereby constituting Loft the equitable owner of those interests? These questions were answered in the affirmative; and because of the answers, the Chancellor, it is said, did not answer the last question before him, that is, upon what theory and to what extent should Loft share in the proceeds of the Pepsi-Cola enterprise?

. . .

In these circumstances of contention, certain questions suggest themselves for consideration, and some of them for answer: Did the Chancellor make an explicit finding that the Pepsi-Cola opportunity belonged in equity to Loft, and if so, was such finding justifiable in fact and in law? If the Chancellor made no such explicit finding, should he have done so, or should this court make such finding? . . .

. . .

Corporate officers and directors are not permitted to use their position of trust and confidence to further their private interests. While technically not trustees, they stand in a fiduciary relation to the corporation and its stockholders. A public policy, existing through the years, and derived from a profound knowledge of human characteristics and motives, has established a rule that demands of a corporate officer or director, peremptorily and inexorably, the most scrupulous observance of his duty, not only affirmatively to protect the interests of the corporation committed to his charge, but also to refrain from doing anything that would work injury to the corporation, or to deprive it of profit or advantage which his skill and ability might properly bring to it, or to enable it to make in the reasonable and lawful exercise of its powers. The rule that requires an undivided and unselfish loyalty to the corporation demands that there shall be no conflict between duty and self-interest. The occasions for the determination of honesty, good faith and loyal conduct are many and varied, and no hard and fast rule can be formulated. The standard of loyalty is measured by no fixed scale.

If an officer or director of a corporation, in violation of his duty as such, acquires gain or advantage for himself, the law charges the interest so acquired with a trust for the benefit of the corporation, at its election, while it denies to the betrayer all benefit and profit. The rule, inveterate and uncompromising in its rigidity, does not rest upon the narrow ground of injury or damage to the corporation resulting from a betrayal of confidence, but upon a broader foundation of a wise public policy that, for the purpose of removing all temptation, extinguishes all possibility of profit flowing from a breach of the confidence imposed by the fiduciary relation. . . .

(Continued)

The rule, referred to briefly as the rule of corporate opportunity, is merely one of the manifestations of the general rule that demands of an officer or director the utmost good faith in his relation to the corporation which he represents.

It is true that when a business opportunity comes to a corporate officer or director in his individual capacity rather than in his official capacity, and the opportunity is one which, because of the nature of the enterprise, is not essential to his corporation, and is one in which it has no interest or expectancy, the officer or director is entitled to treat the opportunity as his own, and the corporation has no interest in it, if, of course, the officer or director has not wrongfully embarked the corporation's resources therein. [Citations omitted.]

On the other hand, it is equally true that, if there is presented to a corporate officer or director a business opportunity which the corporation is financially able to undertake, is, from its nature, in the line of the corporation's business and is of practical advantage to it, is one in which the corporation has an interest or a reasonable expectancy, and, by embracing the opportunity, the self-interest of the officer or director will be brought into conflict with that of his corporation, the law will not permit him to seize the opportunity for himself. And, if, in such circumstances, the interests of the corporation are betrayed, the corporation may elect to claim all of the benefits of the transaction for itself, and the law will impress a trust in favor of the corporation upon the property, interests and profits so acquired. [Citations omitted.]

. . .

Duty and loyalty are inseparably connected. Duty is that which is required by one's station or occupation; is that which one is bound by legal or moral obligation to do or refrain from doing; and it is with this conception of duty as the underlying basis of the principle applicable to the situation disclosed, that the conduct and acts of Guth with respect to his acquisition of the Pepsi-Cola enterprise will be scrutinized. Guth was not merely a director and the president of Loft. He was its master. It is admitted that Guth manifested some of the qualities of a dictator. The directors were selected by him. Some of them held salaried positions in the company. All of them held their positions at his favor. . . .

Prior to May, 1931, Guth became convinced that Loft was being unfairly discriminated against by the Coca-Cola Company of whose syrup it was a large purchaser, in that Loft had been refused a jobber's discount on the syrup, although others, whose purchases were of far less importance, had been given such discount. He determined to replace Coca-Cola as a beverage at the Loft stores with some other cola drink, if that could be accomplished. So, on May 19, 1931, he suggested an inquiry with respect to desirability of discontinuing the use of Coca-Cola, and replacing it with Pepsi-Cola at a greatly reduced price. Pepsi-Cola was the syrup produced by National Pepsi-Cola Company. As a beverage it had been on the market for over twenty-five years, and while it was not known to consumers in the area of the Loft stores, its formula and trademark were well established. Guth's purpose was to deliver Loft from the thraldom of the Coca-Cola Company, which practically dominated the field of cola beverages, and, at the same time to gain for Loft a greater margin of profit on its sales of cola beverages. Certainly, the choice of an acceptable substitute for Coca-Cola was not a wide one, and, doubtless, his experience in the field of bottled beverages convinced him that it was necessary for him to obtain a cola syrup whose formula and trademark were secure against attack. Although the difficulties and dangers were great, he concluded to make the change. Almost simultaneously, National Pepsi-Cola Company, in which [Mr.] Megargel was predominant and whom Guth knew, went into bankruptcy; and Guth was informed that the long established Pepsi-Cola formula and trademark could be had at a small price. Guth, of course, was Loft; and Loft's determination to replace Coca-Cola with some other cola beverage in its many stores was practically co-incidental with the opportunity to acquire the Pepsi-Cola formula and trademark. . . .

It is urged by [Guth] that Megargel offered the Pepsi-Cola opportunity to Guth personally, and not to him as president of Loft. . . .

It was incumbent upon Guth to show that his every act in dealing with the opportunity presented was in the exercise of the utmost good faith to Loft; and the burden was cast upon him satisfactorily to prove that the offer was made to him individually. Reasonable inferences, drawn from acknowledged facts and circumstances, are powerful factors in arriving at the truth of a disputed matter, and such inferences are not to be ignored in considering the acts and conduct of Megargel. He had been for years engaged in the manufacture and sale of a cola syrup in competition with Coca-Cola. He knew of the difficulties of competition with such a powerful opponent in general, and in particular in the securing of a necessary foothold in a new territory where Coca-Cola was supreme. He could not hope to establish the popularity and use of his syrup in a strange field, and in competition with the assured position of Coca-Cola, by the usual advertising means, for he, himself, had no money or resources, and it is entirely unbelievable that he expected Guth to have command of the vast amount of money necessary to popularize Pepsi-Cola by the ordinary methods. He knew of the difficulty, not to say impossibility, of inducing proprietors of soft drink establishments to use a cola drink utterly unknown to their patrons. . . .

Leaving aside the manner of the offer of the opportunity, certain other matters are to be considered in determining whether the opportunity, in the circumstances, belonged to Loft; and in this we agree that Guth's right to appropriate the Pepsi-Cola opportunity to himself depends upon the circumstances existing at the time it presented itself to him without regard to subsequent events, and that due weight should be given to character of the opportunity which Megargel envisioned and brought to Guth's door.

The real issue is whether the opportunity to secure a very substantial stock interest in a corporation to be formed for the purpose of exploiting a cola beverage on a wholesale scale was so closely associated with the existing business activities of Loft, and so essential thereto, as to bring the transaction within that class of cases where the acquisition of the property would throw the corporate officer purchasing it into competition with his company. This is a factual question to be decided by reasonable inferences from objective facts.

It is asserted that, no matter how diversified the scope of Loft's activities, its primary business was the manufacturing and selling of candy in its own chain of retail stores, and that it never had the idea of turning a subsidiary product into a highly advertised, nationwide specialty. Therefore it had never initiated any investigation into the possibility of acquiring a stock interest in a corporation to be formed to exploit Pepsi-Cola on the scale envisioned by Megargel, necessitating sales of at least 1,000,000 gallons a year. It is said that the most effective argument against the proposition that Guth was obligated to take the opportunity for Loft is to be found in the [Loft's] own assertion that Guth was guilty of an improper exercise of business judgment when he replaced Coca-Cola with Pepsi-Cola at the Loft stores. Assuming that [Loft's] argument in this respect is incompatible with its contention that the Pepsi-Cola opportunity belonged to Loft, it is no more inconsistent than is the position of [Guth] on the question. In the court below, [Guth] strove strenuously to show, and to have it believed, that the Pepsi-Cola opportunity was presented to Loft by Guth, with a full disclosure by him that if the company did not embrace it, he would. This, manifestly, was a recognition of the necessity for his showing complete good faith on his part as a corporate officer of Loft.

. . .

The manufacture of syrup was the core of the Pepsi-Cola opportunity. The manufacture of syrups was one of Loft's not unimportant activities. It had the necessary resources, facilities, equipment,

(*Continued*)

technical and practical knowledge and experience. The tie was close between the business of Loft and the Pepsi-Cola enterprise. [Citations omitted.] Conceding that the essential of an opportunity is reasonably within the scope of a corporation's activities, latitude should be allowed for development and expansion. To deny this would be to deny the history of industrial development.

. . .

Although the facts and circumstances disclosed by the voluminous record clearly show gross violations of legal and moral duties by Guth in his dealings with Loft, [Guth] makes bold to say that no duty was cast upon Guth hence he was guilty of no disloyalty. The fiduciary relation demands something more than the morals of the market place. . . .

Upon a consideration of all the facts and circumstances as disclosed we are convinced that the opportunity to acquire the Pepsi-Cola trademark and formula, goodwill and business belonged to [Loft], and that Guth, as its president, had no right to appropriate the opportunity to himself.

can file suit on behalf of the corporation through what is called a shareholders' **derivative suit**. These lawsuits can often be brought against members of the board of directors or executive officers. State law provides the procedures for which a derivative suit can be initiated.

If the board of directors of a corporation decides to issue more corporate stock in order to obtain additional capital, existing shareholders of the corporation may suffer a dilution of their percentage ownership of the corporation. Consequently, existing shareholders typically have **preemptive rights** to purchase an amount of newly issued stock that will allow them to maintain the same percentage ownership in the corporation as they had before the issuance of the new stock.

Shareholders also have the right to inspect the books. The inspection request must be for a proper purpose, however, and not for reasons such as to obtain access to confidential information or trade secrets or to harass the corporation. Moreover, the shareholder typically has to give advance notice to the corporation of the desire to inspect the books.

A corporation terminates by filing **Articles of Termination** (or **Articles of Dissolution**) with the appropriate state agency. The officers wind up the affairs of the corporation by liquidating assets, paying creditors, and distributing any remaining assets to the shareholders.

Taxation

Unlike a partnership or LLC, a corporation is itself subject to federal income tax on its taxable income. It is not a "flow-through" entity. Consequently, when the corporation distributes profits to the shareholders in the form of a dividend, the shareholders must also pay income taxes on the dividend. As a result, people often refer to corporations as being "double-taxed"—once at the entity level and once at the shareholder level.

What Do You Think?

Why might someone form a corporation instead of a partnership or LLC given that a corporation is subject to income taxation and partnerships and LLCs are not?

Tax issues often play an important part in structuring corporate transactions and in financing decisions. For example, payments of interest are tax deductible to the corporation; payments of dividends are not tax deductible. This may have an impact on whether the corporation's management decides to borrow money or to instead seek capital contributions from investors.

O.C.G.A. § 14-2-622

. . .

(b) Unless otherwise provided in the articles of incorporation, a shareholder of a corporation is not personally liable for the acts or debt of the corporation except that he may become personally liable by reason of his own acts or conduct.

Regular corporations that are subject to income tax are often referred to by tax professionals as **"C" corporations**. The "C" refers to the place in the Internal Revenue Code where the tax law governing corporations is found (*i.e.*, Subchapter C). Congress realized that a "C" corporation can be a disadvantageous form of doing business from an income tax standpoint. Consequently, Congress has allowed for some corporations to obtain special **"S" corporation** status. An "S" corporation is generally not subject to federal income taxes and is often referred to as a "pass-through" or "flow-through" entity much like a partnership. In order to obtain this special tax treatment, however, the corporation must meet certain strict requirements. For example, the corporation:

- must have 100 or fewer shareholders (family members are combined to count as only one shareholder);
- cannot have more than one class of stock;
- cannot have a nonresident alien, corporation, or partnership as a shareholder; and
- the corporation must timely make the "S" election

A corporation must meet a few other requirements also in order to qualify for "S" status. As you might suspect, the tax law governing "S" corporations is found in Subchapter S of the Internal Revenue Code.

Owner Liability

Shareholders of corporations are not personally liable for the debts of the corporation. Consider the Georgia statute (Illustrative State Statute 25.1) as an example.

Some exceptions exist, of course, to this general rule of shareholder liability protection. A corporation's protection for shareholders can be "pierced" (*i.e.*, **piercing the corporate veil**), for example, if the corporate entity is not properly respected as separate from the shareholders. Recall the discussion of piercing the LLC veil in Chapter 24. The same principles apply to corporations. For example, shareholders should not commingle their personal funds with the corporation's, and the officers of the corporation should engage in transactions in their capacity as officers rather than in their own individual capacity or in the capacity as a shareholder (if the officer is also a shareholder). In other words, the corporate entity should be respected as a truly separate entity by the officers, board members, and shareholders to protect against a "piercing-the-corporate veil" attack from potential plaintiffs. Shareholders of closely held corporations are particularly vulnerable to this attack if they are not careful.

QUESTIONS FOR REVIEW

1. What document is filed with the appropriate state agency to legally form a corporation?

2. What is the role of a corporation's statutory (or registered) agent?

3. Explain the primary differences between preferred stock and common stock.

4. Discuss the organizational structure of a corporation and the relationship among shareholders, board of directors, and officers.

5. Explain the duty of care, duty of loyalty, and the business judgment rule.

6. What is a shareholders' derivative suit?

7. What are shareholders' preemptive rights?

8. How is a corporation treated for federal income tax purposes? How does a corporation qualify for "S" corporation status? What is the primary benefit of qualifying for "S" status?

9. Explain some of the facts that might be present to allow a plaintiff to successfully "pierce the corporate veil" of a corporation.

10. Summarize the *Guth v. Loft* case.

INTERNET ACTIVITIES

1. Visit the IRS website at www.irs.gov. Click on the "Forms and Publications" link. Find Form 2553.

    a. What is the purpose of this form?

    b. In Part I of the form, what information does Line G ask for?

    c. In Part I of the form, what information does Column J ask for?

    d. In Part I of the form, what information does Column M ask for?

2. Some businesses provide registered agent services for an annual fee. Conduct a search of businesses that provide registered agent services in your state. Name at least two such businesses and cite your source website.

Chapter 26

Franchises, Joint Ventures, and Nonprofit Corporations

In addition to the forms of doing business we have discussed in previous chapters, certain other business forms and arrangements exist. We will discuss three here: (1) franchises; (2) joint ventures; and (3) nonprofit corporations.

Franchises

You are likely familiar with the idea of franchising. McDonald's, Subway, and Baskin Robbins are a few of the many popular franchises. A **franchise** is basically an agreement by the **franchisor** (*e.g.*, McDonald's headquarters) with a **franchisee** (*e.g.*, someone looking to open a local McDonald's restaurant) wherein the franchisor licenses the rights to a trade name, trademark, etc., to a franchisee. Of course, the franchisee must pay a fee—sometimes a substantial fee—to the franchisor in return for the right to use the franchisor's name and marks. The franchisee typically organizes his or her own separate entity (*e.g.*, LLC or corporation) to enter into the franchise agreement with the franchisor.

Federal regulations govern many aspects of the franchisor/franchisee relationship. For example, the franchisor must disclose certain material facts to the franchisee. The Federal Trade Commission has issued what has become known as the **Franchise Rule**, which governs franchisors and their relationships with franchisees. Consider the selection from the federal regulations on the next page (Illustrative Federal Regulation 26.1) as an example.

The franchisor usually has significant control over how the franchisee operates the business, of course. For example, the "look" and "feel" (*e.g.*, colors, interior design, exterior design, etc.) of the franchise must be consistent with franchisor requirements. Moreover, product quality must be consistent, and the franchisee likely must follow other strict requirements mandated by the franchisor.

Sorbis/Shutterstock.com

Suppose a franchisee commits a tort or violates federal law regarding employee rights (*e.g.*, discrimination, minimum wage, etc.). What is the liability

16 CFR §436.2

§ 436.2 Obligation to furnish documents.

In connection with the offer or sale of a franchise to be located in the United States of America or its territories, unless the transaction is exempted . . ., it is an unfair or deceptive act or practice in violation of Section 5 of the Federal Trade Commission Act:

(a) For any franchisor to fail to furnish a prospective franchisee with a copy of the franchisor's current disclosure document . . . at least 14 calendar-days before the prospective franchisee signs a binding agreement with or makes any payment to, the franchisor or an affiliate in connection with the proposed franchise sale.

(b) For any franchisor to alter unilaterally and materially the terms and conditions of the basic franchise agreement or any related agreements attached to the disclosure document without furnishing the prospective franchisee with a copy of each revised agreement at least seven calendar-days before the prospective franchisee signs the revised agreement. Changes to an agreement that arise out of negotiations initiated by the prospective franchisee do not trigger this seven calendar-day period.

. . .

of the franchisor? As a general rule, the franchisor is not liable for the torts, crimes, etc., of the franchisee. Nevertheless, if the franchisor so closely controls the day-to-day management and activities of the franchisee, it is possible the franchisor could be held liable for actions of the franchisee. Consider the following court case from the Court of Appeals of Mississippi (Illustrative Court Case 26.1).

Allen v. Choice Hotels International

Court of Appeals of Mississippi

942 So. 2d 817 (2006)

OPINION

IRVING, J., FOR THE COURT:

This appeal arises out of an action filed by Darlene Allen, individually, and as the wrongful death heir of her husband, William Allen, for his death and her injuries at a Gulfport Comfort Inn. The action was filed against R.C.P. Enterprises d/b/a Comfort Inn, the franchisee, and R.D. Patel, its managing partner, (collectively, the Comfort Inn) and against Choice Hotels International (Choice), the franchisor. This appeal is against Choice only. Darlene claims that Choice failed to provide reasonable security to protect guests at the hotel and, as a result, she and her husband were harmed by the criminal acts of an intruder. The trial court entered summary judgment on behalf of Choice, finding that the franchisor was not vicariously liable because it did not control or have the right to control the day-to-day operation of the hotel.

. . .

Finding no error, we affirm.

FACTS

On October 25, 1996, the Allens, who were from Galveston County, Texas, finished visiting a Gulfport casino and returned to their room at the Comfort Inn. Unbeknownst to them, a trio of individuals from Montgomery, Alabama, was surveilling the casino parking lot looking for someone to rob. The three had decided to visit the Mississippi Gulf Coast and rob a non-Mississippian at one of the casinos. Upon seeing a Texas tag on the Allens' van, the trio followed the Allens back to the Allens' hotel. Presumably by pretense, one robber got William to answer the door. After the door was opened, the robber and an accomplice pushed their way into the Allens' room and struggled with William over his wallet. During the struggle, William was fatally shot, and Darlene was injured.

. . .

ANALYSIS AND DISCUSSION OF THE ISSUES

. . .

Liability in the Franchise Context

. . .

Other jurisdictions that have addressed the question of a franchisor's vicarious liability have noted that a franchise relationship is far different from contract of employment where the rules of master/servant are typically applied. [Citation omitted.] Because of this difference, courts have held the franchisor vicariously liable only when it had the right to control the specific instrumentality or aspect of the business that was alleged to have caused the harm. We find this application of the law to be consistent with Mississippi law, which has consistently refused to hold the employer of an independent contractor liable unless the employer was maintaining a "right of control over the performance of that aspect of work which gave rise to the injury." [Citation omitted.] Furthermore, the Mississippi Supreme Court has stated that "the main element required to constitute the relationship of master and servant is that the servant be subject to the control of the master in carrying on the business at the time of the injury." [Citation omitted.]

With these principles in mind, we turn to the specific facts of the case at hand. Because the Allens were harmed by an alleged deficiency in the Comfort Inn's security, we must look to whether Choice exercised control over, or had the right to control, the hotel's security. At oral argument, Darlene's counsel urged this Court to find that Choice's requirements about motel doors show that choice exercises control over the safety system at the hotel. Choice requires that a guest room entry door be a minimum of two inches in width and have a 180-degree door viewer, commonly called a peephole. A deadbolt lock is also required on the door, and security bars must be placed on any sliding doors. We are not persuaded that these requirements show enough control to shift responsibility for safety to Choice. We note again that it is not only results that a franchisor must control, but also the means to those ends. These few requirements regarding hotel doors do not show that Choice had the right to control both the means and the ends of security at the Comfort Inn.

Our review of this issue is consistent with that of other courts, which have generally granted summary judgment for a franchisor after finding the franchisor did not control the franchisee's day-to-day operation. . . . A general summation of the relationship between a franchisor and its franchisee in a vicarious liability setting is found in *Kerl*, where summary judgment was granted to the franchisor, Arby's, Inc., on a claim of negligent failure to supervise a work-release inmate who was temporarily employed at an Arby's restaurant. [Citation omitted.] The inmate left Arby's without permission and went to another location, where he shot his former girlfriend and killed her fiancé.

The court said that, in the typical franchise arrangement, the franchisee operates "an independent business pursuant to a license to use the franchisor's trademark or trade name." [Citation omitted.]

(*Continued*)

Usually the franchise arrangement involves a detailed agreement "designed to protect the integrity of the trademark by setting 'uniform quality, marketing, and operational standards.'" [Citation omitted.] . . .

In our case, the eighteen-page franchise agreement grants the franchisee, R.C.P. Enterprises, use of "the system." The agreement defines "the system" as "a plan and system for providing to the traveling public lodging of a high standard of service, courtesy, and cleanliness, utilizing distinctive identification schemes, standards, specifications, and Proprietary Marks and information." . . .

Our review of the franchise agreement in this case indicates that the agreement, like the agreements discussed in other cases, is meant to provide a system of uniformity for Choice franchisees. . . . In other words, the franchisee is operating a hotel that is designed to look like other Comfort Inns, so that customers feel as though they are not staying in a completely different hotel.

Darlene's central argument is that the agreement, along with the imposition of extensive rules and regulations upon R.C.P. by Choice, proves that Choice retains the right of control. . . . Choice presented the deposition testimony of a Choice corporate representative, Robert Kerr. When questioned regarding different aspects of the operation of a Comfort Inn by a franchisee, Kerr insisted at every turn that Choice did not control the hotel's daily operations. The plaintiffs presented no sworn testimony to contradict or dispute Kerr's testimony, and there was no admission in Kerr's testimony that Choice controlled customer safety on the franchised premises.

. . .

THE JUDGMENT OF THE CIRCUIT COURT OF HARRISON COUNTY IS AFFIRMED.

What Do You Think?

In the *Allen v. Choice Hotels International* case, the court addressed the issue of whether the franchisor was liable for the wrongful death of Darlene's husband. Should the *franchisee* be liable for the wrongful death of Darlene's husband?

Joint Ventures

A **joint venture** is when two or more parties join together to participate in a business project that is usually of a short-term nature. For example, two construction companies may join together to build a large-scale shopping center. The companies may form an LLC or other entity for operating purposes during the joint venture. The joint venturers agree upon their respective shares of profits and losses of the joint venture. Once the project is complete, the LLC (or other entity) typically winds up and terminates. A joint venture is typically treated as a general partnership if the joint venturers do not form a separate entity for the joint venture. Of course, the joint venturers usually have a sophisticated contract between them, thus bringing contract law into play as well. For federal income tax purposes, a joint venture is treated a partnership unless the joint venturers create a corporation in which to house the joint venture.

Nonprofit Corporations

People desiring to form charities and other organizations intent on promoting the "public good" may also form an entity under state law. The most common entity for these purposes is a **nonprofit corporation**. A nonprofit corporation is formed by filing Articles of Incorporation for a nonprofit corporation under applicable state law. Nonprofit corporations (also sometimes called "not-for-profit" corporations) do not typically have shareholders like a for-profit corporation does. Although a group of persons may identify themselves as "members" of the nonprofit corporation, their function is not to seek profits or maximize personal wealth from the activities of the nonprofit corporation.

Nonprofit organizations usually qualify as being **tax-exempt** under federal income tax law, although organizing as a nonprofit corporation does not guarantee tax-exempt status. Rather, the nonprofit corporation must qualify as tax-exempt as provided in Section 501 of the Internal Revenue Code, as partially provided in Illustrative Federal Statute 26.1.

Section 501 lists many types of organizations that qualify as tax-exempt. Notice that credit unions, chambers of commerce, religious organizations, charitable organizations, etc., all qualify. Organizations listed in Section 501(c)(3) (*e.g.*, religious, charitable, scientific, literary, etc.) are a special type of tax-exempt entity. In short, a person that donates money or property to an organization that qualifies as a "501(c)(3)" organization receives a charitable contribution deduction on the person's income tax return. Donations to organizations other than "501(c)(3)" organizations typically are not deductible for income tax purposes as charitable contributions.

ILLUSTRATIVE FEDERAL STATUTE 26.1

26 U.S.C. §501

§501. Exemption from tax on corporations, certain trusts, etc.

(a) Exemption from taxation.—An organization described in subsection (c) . . . shall be exempt from taxation under this subtitle . . .

. . .

(c) List of exempt organizations.—The following organizations are referred to in subsection (a):

(1) Any corporation organized under Act of Congress which is an instrumentality of the United States . . .

. . .

(3) Corporations, and any community chest, fund, or foundation, organized and operated exclusively for religious, charitable, scientific, testing for public safety, literary, or educational purposes, or to foster national or international amateur sports competition . . . , or for the prevention of cruelty to children or animals, no part of the net earnings of which inures to the benefit of any private shareholder or individual, no substantial part of the activities of which is carrying on propaganda, or otherwise attempting, to influence legislation . . ., and which does not participate in, or intervene in . . ., any political campaign on behalf of (or in opposition to) any candidate for public office.

(4) Civic leagues or organizations not organized for profit but operated exclusively for the promotion of social welfare . . .

(5) Labor, agricultural, or horticultural organizations.

(6) Business leagues, chambers of commerce, real-estate boards . . .

(7) Clubs organized for pleasure, recreation, and other nonprofitable purposes, substantially all of the activities of which are for such purposes and no part of the net earnings of which inures to the benefit of any private shareholder.

. . .

(14) (A) credit unions . . .

. . .

Joseph Sohm/Shutterstock.com

Consider the United States Tax Court case that follows (Illustrative Court Case 26.2).

Consider the United States Tax Court case that follows (Illustrative Court Case 26.2).

What Do You Think?

Should the federal government be in the business of subsidizing charitable activities by allowing income tax deductions to those people who donate to charities? Should people who donate to religious organizations receive income tax deductions? Why or why not?

Of course, it would be unfair for a tax-exempt organization to engage in the same activity as a for-profit corporation, but not have to pay tax like the for-profit corporation does. Thus, the IRS may revoke an organization's tax-exempt status if the organization does not conduct a substantial part of its activities consistent with its stated tax-exempt purposes.

ILLUSTRATIVE COURT CASE 26.2

New Faith, Inc. v. Commissioner of Internal Revenue

United States Tax Court

T.C. Memo 1992-601

OPINION BY: FAY

In 1985, after examining the records and activities of New Faith, Inc., for the period ended December 31, 1982, [the IRS] revoked [New Faith's] tax-exempt status for the tax year ended December 31, 1982, and all subsequent years. [New Faith] challenges [the IRS's] determination. . . .

The issue presented to us is whether [New Faith] is operated exclusively for charitable purposes within the meaning of Section 501(c)(3) [of the Internal Revenue Code].

Background

[New Faith] is a nonprofit . . . corporation organized under the laws of the State of California. . . .

[New Faith's] articles of incorporation provide that New Faith's specific purpose is "to supply money, goods, and services for the poor." The articles of incorporation further declare that "This corporation is organized and operated exclusively for charitable purposes within the meaning of Section 501(c)(3) of the Internal Revenue Code."

On March 3, 1981, [New Faith] filed a Form 1023, Application for Recognition of Exemption under Section 501(c)(3) of the Internal Revenue Code (application), with [the IRS]. . . . In its application, [New Faith] represented that its "sole source of financial support will be its fund-raising activities" which [New Faith] described as "raffles, bingo and donations."

In its application, [New Faith] further described its charitable activities as follows:

"Essentially, the programs and activities of the corporation will be to supply money, goods and services to the poor.

The corporation intends to keep a supply of such necessities as food and clothing in stock so that when a qualified person comes to New Faith he can be supplied with such necessities immediately. If a person needs a place to sleep, we want to be able to immediately provide a place to sleep. There will be no cost for these services. In this way the corporation hopes to provide *immediate* assistance to the poor without forcing them to spend money they either do not have or cannot afford to spend.

. . .

The corporation also plans on conducting such "social" activities as picnics for the poor. Food would be provided free of charge.

The key to any activity planned by the corporation would be its ability to immediately assist, without cost, the truly poor people."

[New Faith] also represented in its application that there would be no cost for these services, and that services would be limited to persons with referrals from ministers or lawyers certifying the individual's need for assistance.

[B]ased on the information supplied in [New Faith's] application, [the IRS] issued an advance letter ruling to [New Faith] recognizing it as an exempt organization.

For the years at issue, [New Faith's] primary activity and source of income was the operation of several lunch trucks, which provided food items to the general public in exchange for scheduled "donations". . . .

[The IRS] conducted an examination of [New Faith's] activities . . . and . . . advised [New Faith] that [New Faith] did not qualify as an exempt organization since [New Faith's] primary purpose or activity was determined to be the conduct of a trade or business.

On September 3, 1985, following consideration of a protest filed by [New Faith], [the IRS] issued a final determination revoking [New Faith's] status as an exempt organization described under section 501(c)(3).

The final adverse determination letter stated as grounds for revocation:

The organization failed to meet the requirements of I.R.C. section 501(c)(3) and related Treasury Regulations, in that: 1) It was not operated exclusively for a tax-exempt purpose. 2)(a) A primary purpose of the organization was a trade or business (lunch truck) which constituted a substantial part of its operations, and (b) this business was carried on for profit, and was not in furtherance of nor related to the organization's tax exempt purposes. . . .

Discussion

Under section 501(c)(3), an organization which is organized and operated exclusively for an exempt purpose (and meets the other requirements of the provisions) qualifies as a tax-exempt organization. In order for an organization to be exempt from Federal income taxes under section 501(a) and (c)(3), it must satisfy both the organizational and operational tests of [the Treasury Regulations].

[The Treasury Regulations] provide:

"(c) Operational test – (1) Primary activities. An organization will be regarded as "operated exclusively" for one or more exempt purposes only if it engages primarily in activities which accomplish one or more of such exempt purposes specified in section 501(c)(3). An organization will not be so regarded if more than an insubstantial part of its activities is not in furtherance of an exempt purpose.

The word "exclusively" as used in section 501(c)(3) does not mean "solely" or "without exception." [Citation omitted.] An organization which engages in nonexempt activities can obtain and maintain exempt status so long as such activities are only incidental and insubstantial." [Citation omitted.]

(Continued)

The purpose toward which an activity is directed, rather than the nature of the activity itself, determines whether the operational test is satisfied. The fact that an organization's activity constitutes a trade or business does not, in itself, disqualify that organization under section 501(c)(3). [Citation omitted.] The critical inquiry is whether [New Faith's] activity encompasses a substantial nonexempt purpose irrespective of the presence of other exempt purposes. . . .

[New Faith's] main activity is the operation of a number of canteen-style lunch trucks. This type of activity is normally carried on by commercial profit-making enterprises. [New Faith's] practice of collecting cash in exchange for food items is indistinguishable from the commercial activities of other for-profit commercial ventures engaged in the food retailing business. The extent of [New Faith's] commercial activities is reflected in [New Faith's tax return for 1982]. During 1982, [New Faith's] commercial activity accounted for approximately 80 percent of its gross expenditures and nearly 100 percent of its gross revenues. It is incumbent on [New Faith] to show that this activity somehow furthered an enumerated exempt purpose.

[New Faith's] sole argument . . . is that food items were routinely provided to needy travelers on California highways on a donation or "love offering" basis and that the needy traveler could determine what amount, if any, he could pay. We find, however, that the evidence . . . does not support [New Faith's] argument.

At the outset, we find no credible evidence in the record to support the position that food items were routinely offered to anybody for free or at below-cost prices. [Citation omitted.]

Furthermore, there is no evidence in the record showing that people, if any, who received food items from [New Faith] for free or at below-cost prices were impoverished or needy persons. [New Faith] provided no evidence that the alleged charitable activities were tailored to serve the poor, nor did [New Faith] limit its alleged assistance to those with referrals from ministers or lawyers, as was represented in [New Faith's] application filed with [the IRS].

. . .

[New Faith's] submission of a newspaper article that contains its founder's own statements relating to [New Faith's] activities does not substitute for specific documentation in the form of checks, invoices, receipts, contemporaneous journals, and other documentation necessary to substantiate [New Faith's] alleged charitable activities.

Accordingly, based on all the evidence contained in the administrative record, we hold that [New Faith] has not carried its burden of proof in showing that [New Faith's] lunch trucks were operated exclusively in furtherance of one or more exempt purposes.

QUESTIONS FOR REVIEW

1. What is a franchise? Who is the franchisor? Franchisee?

2. What is the Franchise Rule?

3. Are franchisors typically liable for the crimes and/or torts committed by franchisees? Explain your answer.

4. What is a joint venture?

5. Are the terms "nonprofit" and "tax-exempt" and "charitable" synonyms? Explain.

6. What is unique about an organization that qualifies as tax-exempt under Section 501(c)(3) of the Internal Revenue Code?

7. In the *New Faith* Tax Court case, what were the reasons why New Faith lost its tax-exempt status?

8. Summarize the *Allen v. Choice Hotels* case.

INTERNET ACTIVITIES

1. Conduct a search for a "Consumer Guide to Buying a Franchise" or "Buying a Franchise: A Consumer Guide" published by the Federal Trade Commission.

   a. Summarize the contents of the guide (*i.e.*, what topics are discussed?)

   b. What is your source website?

2. Visit the IRS website at www.irs.gov. Click on the "Forms and Publications" link. Find Form 1023. What is the purpose of the form? Summarize generally the information the IRS asks for on the form.

Part IX

Securities Law and Accounting Regulation

Chapter 27

Securities Law: Issuances of Securities

Congress saw a need for much stronger regulation of the securities markets after the stock market crash in 1929. Consequently, Congress passed the Securities Act of 1933 and the Securities Act of 1934. The 1933 Act governs the initial issuance of securities and the 1934 Act governs securities trading on secondary markets. This chapter will discuss the law relating to the initial issuance of securities and Chapter 28 will discuss the law applicable to subsequent trading of securities.

The Securities and Exchange Commission

Congress created the Securities and Exchange Commission as an independent regulatory agency to monitor and enforce laws governing the securities markets. The mission of the SEC is to "protect investors, maintain fair, orderly, and efficient markets, and facilitate capital formation." The SEC has five commissioners, and the Chairman of the SEC is appointed by the President of the United States. Some of the responsibilities of the SEC include interpreting federal securities laws, issuing regulations, and overseeing brokerages, investment advisers, and, to some extent, public accounting firms.

Of course, the threshold issue regarding securities regulation is the definition of "security."

Definition of "Security"

You are likely somewhat familiar with different types of securities already, such as common stock, preferred stock, bonds, convertible bonds, etc. But federal law defines the term "security" very broadly. Consider Illustrative Federal Statute 27.1 that follows.

ktasimar/Shutterstock.com

Given the definition of "security," consider the United States Supreme Court's application of the term in Illustrative Court Case 27.1 that follows.

Registration Process

If a security is governed by federal securities law (and is not an "exempt" security), then the issuer of the security must comply with the securities registration process. An issuer must provide the SEC

15 U.S.C. §77b

§77b. Definitions

(a) Definitions. When used in this title unless the context otherwise requires—

(1) The term "security" means any note, stock, treasury stock, security future, bond, debenture, evidence of indebtedness, certificate of interest or participation in any profit-sharing agreement, collateral-trust certificate, preorganization certificate or subscription, transferable share, investment contract, voting-trust certificate, certificate of deposit for a security, fractional undivided interest in oil, gas, or other mineral rights, any put, call, straddle, option, or privilege on any security, certificate of deposit, or group or index of securities (including any interest therein or based on the value thereof), or any put, call straddle, option, or privilege entered into on a national securities exchange relating to foreign currency, or, in general, any interest or instrument commonly known as a "security," or any certificate of interest or participation in, temporary or interim certificate for, receipt for, guarantee of, or warrant or right to subscribe to or purchase, any of the foregoing. . . .

SEC v. Edwards

Supreme Court of the United States

540 U.S. 389 (2004)

[**Note:** For convenience of the reader, the following language is from the Syllabus of the case as provided by the U.S. Supreme Court Reporter of Decisions]

[Edwards] was the chairman, chief executive officer, and sole shareholder of ETS Payphones, Inc., which sold payphones to the public via independent distributors. The payphones were offered with an agreement under which ETS leased back the payphone from the purchaser for a fixed monthly payment, thereby giving purchasers a fixed 14% annual return on their investment. Although ETS' marketing materials trumpeted the "incomparable pay phone" as "an exciting business opportunity," the payphones did not generate enough revenue for ETS to make the payments required by the leaseback agreements, so the company depended on funds from new investors to meet its obligations. After ETS filed for bankruptcy protection, the Securities and Exchange Commission (SEC) brought this civil enforcement action, alleging, among other things, that [Edwards] and ETS had violated registration requirements and antifraud provisions of the Securities Act of 1933 and the Securities Exchange Act of 1934, and Rule 10b–5 thereunder. The District Court concluded that the sale-and-leaseback arrangement was an "investment contract" within the meaning of, and therefore subject to, the federal securities laws. The Eleventh Circuit reversed, holding that (1) this Court's opinions require an "investment contract" to offer either capital appreciation or a participation in an enterprise's earnings, and thus exclude schemes offering a fixed rate of return; and (2) those opinions' requirement that the return on the investment be derived solely from the efforts of others was not satisfied when the purchasers had a contractual entitlement to the return.

Held: An investment scheme promising a fixed rate of return can be an "investment contract" and thus a "security" subject to the federal securities laws. Section 2(a)(1) of the 1933 Act and § 3(a)(10) of the 1934 Act define "security" to include an "investment contract," but do not define "investment contract." This Court has established that the test for determining whether a particular scheme is an investment contract is "whether the scheme involves an investment of money in a common enterprise with profits to come solely from the efforts of others." [Citation omitted.] This definition embodies a flexible, rather than a static, principle that is capable of adaptation to meet the countless and variable schemes devised by those seeking to use others' money on the promise of profits. The profits this Court was speaking of . . . are profits—in the sense of the income or return—that investors seek on their investment, not the profits of the scheme in which they invest, and may include, for example, dividends, other periodic payments, or the increased value of the investment. There is no reason to distinguish between promises of fixed returns and promises of variable returns for purposes of the test, so understood. In both cases, the investing public is attracted by representations of investment income. Moreover, investments pitched as low risk (such as those offering a "guaranteed" fixed return) are particularly attractive to individuals more vulnerable to investment fraud, including older and less sophisticated investors. Under the reading [Edwards] advances, unscrupulous marketers of investments could evade the securities laws by picking a rate of return to promise. This Court will not read into the securities laws a limitation not compelled by the language that would so undermine the laws' purposes. [Edwards'] claim that including investment schemes promising a fixed return among investment contracts conflicts with precedent is mistaken. . . . The SEC has consistently maintained that a promise of a fixed return does not preclude a scheme from being an investment contract. The Eleventh Circuit's alternative holding, that [Edwards'] scheme falls outside the definition because purchasers had a contractual entitlement to a return, is incorrect and inconsistent with this Court's precedent.

Reversed and remanded.

with a **prospectus** and a **registration statement**. The prospectus is a document required to be given to potential investors that discloses pertinent information about the company, its financial statements, the particular securities being offered, and the risks of investing in the securities. As you might expect, the law requires that the prospectus be written in an understandable manner even for unsophisticated investors. Together the registration and prospectus must disclose all information required by SEC regulations. Sometimes this is a controversial issue. Consider Illustrative Court Case 27.2.

Once the registration statement and prospectus are filed, the SEC reviews these documents. During the SEC review the issuing company can advertise the securities for sale, but cannot actually sell them. If the SEC does not reject the registration, then after the waiting period the issuing company can sell the securities. Of course, if this is the first time the company is issuing securities to the public the issuance is called an **initial public offering (IPO)**.

The SEC has established an online database where the public can access companies' registration statements, quarterly reports (Form 10-Q), annual reports (Form 10-K), and other information. This is

called the **Electronic Data Gathering, Analysis, and Retrieval (EDGAR)** database.

Exemptions from Registration

Suppose you decide to form a corporation where you will be the only person to contribute capital to the corporation and you will be the only shareholder. Must you register with the SEC the securities that your corporation issues? No. That transaction would fall under one of the several exemptions from registration. We will discuss briefly here certain transactions and certain securities that are exempt from registration.

Exempt Transactions

Following are examples of transactions that are exempt from the registration requirements under the Securities Act of 1933.

Intrastate Offerings

If the issuance will be solely within the state in which the company is organized and doing business, then no registration with the SEC is necessary. Some strict requirements must be met such

Omnicare, Inc. v. Laborers District Council Construction Industry Pension Fund

Supreme Court of the United States

135 S. Ct. 1318 (2015)

[**Note:** For convenience of the reader, the following language is from the Syllabus of the case as provided by the U.S. Supreme Court Reporter of Decisions]

The Securities Act of 1933 requires that a company wishing to issue securities must first file a registration statement containing specified information about the issuing company and the securities offered. [Citation omitted.] The registration statement may also include other representations of fact or opinion. To protect investors and promote compliance with these disclosure requirements, . . . the Act creates two ways to hold issuers liable for a registration statement's contents: A purchaser of securities may sue an issuer if the registration statement either "contain[s] an untrue statement of a material fact" or "omit[s] to state a material fact . . . necessary to make the statements therein not misleading." [Citation omitted.] In either case, the buyer need not prove that the issuer acted with any intent to deceive or defraud. [Citation omitted.]

Petitioner Omnicare, a pharmacy services company, filed a registration statement in connection with a public offering of common stock. In addition to the required disclosures, the registration statement contained two statements expressing the company's opinion that it was in compliance with federal and state laws. After the Federal Government filed suit against Omnicare for allegedly receiving kickbacks from pharmaceutical manufacturers, respondents, pension funds that purchased Omnicare stock (hereinafter Funds), sued Omnicare . . . . They claimed that Omnicare's legal-compliance statements constituted "untrue statement[s] of . . . material fact" and that Omnicare "omitted to state [material] facts necessary" to make those statements not misleading.

The District Court granted Omnicare's motion to dismiss. Because the Funds had not alleged that Omnicare's officers knew they were violating the law, the court found that the Funds had failed to state a . . . claim. The Sixth Circuit reversed. Acknowledging that the statements at issue expressed opinions, the court held that no showing of subjective disbelief was required. In the court's view, the Funds' allegations that Omnicare's legal-compliance opinions were objectively false sufficed to support their claim.

Held:

1. A statement of opinion does not constitute an "untrue statement of . . . fact" simply because the stated opinion ultimately proves incorrect. The Sixth Circuit's contrary holding wrongly conflates facts and opinions. A statement of fact expresses certainty about a thing, whereas a statement of opinion conveys only an uncertain view as to that thing. [The law] incorporates that distinction . . . by exposing issuers to liability only for "untrue statement[s] of . . . *fact*." [Citation omitted.] Because a statement of opinion admits the possibility of error, such a statement remains true–and thus is not an "untrue statement of . . . fact"–even if the opinion turns out to have been wrong.

But opinion statements are not wholly immune from liability . . . . Every such statement explicitly affirms one fact; that the speaker actually holds the stated belief. A statement of opinion thus qualifies as an "untrue statement of . . . fact" if *that fact* is untrue—*i.e.*, if the opinion expressed was not sincerely held. In addition, opinion statements can give rise to false-statement liability . . . if they contain embedded statements of untrue facts. Here, however, Omnicare's sincerity is not contested and the statements at issue are pure opinion statements. The Funds thus cannot establish liability . . . .

2. If a registration statement omits material facts about the issuer's inquiry into, or knowledge concerning, a statement of opinion, and if those facts conflict with what a reasonable investor, reading the statement fairly and in context, would take from the statement itself, then . . . the omissions [create] liability.

(a) [W]hether a statement is "misleading" is an objective inquiry that depends on a reasonable investor's perspective. [Citation omitted.] Omnicare goes too far by claiming that no reasonable person, in any context, can understand a statement of opinion to convey anything more than the speaker's own mindset. A reasonable investor may, depending on the circumstances, understand an opinion statement to convey facts about the speaker's basis for holding that view. Specifically, an issuer's statement of opinion may fairly imply facts about the inquiry the issuer conducted or the knowledge it had. And if the real facts are otherwise, but not provided, the opinion statement will mislead by omission.

An opinion statement, however, is not misleading simply because the issuer knows, but fails to disclose, some fact cutting the other way. A reasonable investor does not expect that every fact known to an issuer supports its opinion statement. Moreover, whether an omission makes an expression of opinion misleading always depends on context. Reasonable investors understand opinion statements in light of the surrounding text, and [the law] creates liability only for the omission of material facts that cannot be squared with a fair reading of the registration statement as a whole. Omnicare's arguments to the contrary are unavailing.

(b) Because neither court below considered the Funds' omissions theory under the right standard, this case is remanded for a determination of whether the Funds have stated a viable omissions claim. On remand, the court must review the Funds' complaint to determine whether it adequately alleges that Omnicare omitted from the registration statement some specific fact that would have been material to a reasonable investor. If so, the court must decide whether the alleged omission rendered Omnicare's opinion statements misleading in context.

[V]acated and remanded.

as the investor cannot sell the security to someone else out-of-state for a period of at least nine months. Although federal securities laws may not apply to intrastate offerings, issuing companies should consult *state* securities laws.

What Do You Think?

Why would federal securities law exempt from SEC registration requirements those issuances that occur intrastate only?

Regulation A Offerings

The SEC has issued various regulations necessarily more specific than federal statutory law. Among these regulations is **Regulation A**. This regulation exempts "small" public offerings. A small public offering is one where the issuing company does not offer securities exceeding a value of over $50 million over a 12-month period. Certain information must still be filed with the SEC, but the process is more streamlined.

Regulation D Offerings

Several transactions are exempted under **Regulation D**. These exemptions include issuances by "noninvestment companies" (*i.e.*, the company does not primarily engage in the business of trading or investing in securities) for up to $1 million over a 12-month period, and issuances up to $5 million in any 12-month period if the issuance is only to **accredited investors** (*i.e.*, sophisticated investors such as banks, investment companies, insurance companies, and others).

Regulation D also allows **private placements**. As the name implies, offerings that are made without advertising to or soliciting the public may fall within the private placement exemption. Basically, the number of non-accredited investors must not be more than 35, but there can be an unlimited number of accredited investors. The non-accredited investors must still be sophisticated and capable of evaluating the risks involved, however.

Exempt Securities

Securities exempt from registration under the Securities Act of 1933 include the following, for example:

- short-term notes and drafts (maturing in nine months or less)
- securities issued by federal or state governments
- securities issued by nonprofit organizations and charities

Other exemptions exist also, but are beyond the scope of our discussion here.

Violations

Failure to comply with the Securities Act of 1933 could bring both civil and criminal penalties to the violators. Consider Illustrative Federal Statute 27.2 regarding civil liability and criminal liability.

State Securities Laws

Even though some securities offerings may be exempt from federal registration, state securities laws often fill in the gaps. State securities laws are often referred to as "blue sky" laws. This interesting term is indicative of the state's interest in preventing securities issuers from selling potential investors a piece of "the big blue sky." Fraudulent

Ruslan Iventsov/Shutterstock.com

transactions involving securities do occur, and state and federal officials work together to try to prevent securities fraud.

As this chapter has discussed, securities law can be quite complicated, and issuers should be careful to obtain competent advice both on federal law and state law securities matters.

QUESTIONS FOR REVIEW

1. Explain generally what the Securities Act of 1933 governs.

2. What is the mission of the SEC?

3. What is a "security"?

4. What is a prospectus? Registration statement?

5. What does EDGAR stand for? What is its function?

6. Give examples of securities that may be exempt from registration with the SEC.

7. Discuss three transactions involving the issuance of securities that are exempt from registration with the SEC.

8. What is an accredited investor?

9. What is a private placement?

10. What are "blue sky" laws?

11. Summarize the *SEC v. Edwards* case.

12. Summarize the *Omnicare v. Laborers* case.

15 U.S.C. §77l, §77x

§77l. Civil liabilities arising in connection with prospectuses and communications

(a) In general. Any person who—

. . .

(2) offers or sells a security (whether or not exempted . . .), by the use of any means or instruments of transportation or communication in interstate commerce or of the mails, by means of a prospectus or oral communication, which includes an untrue statement of a material fact or omits to state a material fact necessary in order to make the statements, in the light of the circumstances under which they were made, not misleading (the purchaser not knowing of such untruth or omission), and who shall not sustain the burden of proof that he did not know, and in the exercise of reasonable care could not have known, of such untruth or omission, . . .

shall be liable . . . to the person purchasing such security from him, who may sue either at law or in equity in any court of competent jurisdiction, to recover the consideration paid for such security with interest thereon, less the amount of any income received thereon, upon the tender of such security, or for damages if he no longer owns the security.

. . .

§77x. Penalties

Any person who willfully violates any of the provisions of [the Securities Act of 1933], or the rules and regulations promulgated by the Commission under authority thereof, or any person who willfully, in a registration statement filed under [the Securities Act of 1933], makes any untrue statement of a material fact or omits to state any material fact required to be stated therein or necessary to make the statements therein not misleading, shall upon conviction be fined not more than $10,000 or imprisoned not more than five years, or both.

INTERNET ACTIVITIES

1. Visit the SEC website at www.sec.gov and click on the "Filings" link and then the "Company Filing Search". Search for the company "Ford Motor".

   a. Find the most recently filed 8-K report that Ford Motor filed with the SEC. When was it filed?

   b. Find the most recently filed 10-Q report that Ford Motor filed with the SEC. When was it filed?

2. Find the website of the state agency that regulates securities law in your state.

   a. What is the agency's name?

   b. What is the agency's website address?

   c. What is the name of the person (*e.g.*, commissioner) who heads the agency?

Chapter 28

Securities Law: Secondary Markets

Once a public company issues a security, a subsequent sale of that security would be on a "secondary" market like the New York Stock Exchange or NASDAQ, etc. The Securities Act of 1934 governs securities transactions on secondary markets.

The Securities Exchange Act of 1934

The 1934 Act requires certain securities being traded after the initial public offering to be registered with the SEC and informational reports to be filed periodically. Remember the primary goal

BEST-BACKGROUNDS/Shutterstock.com

ILLUSTRATIVE FEDERAL STATUTE 28.1

15 U.S.C. §78j(b)

§78j(b). Manipulative and deceptive devices

It shall be unlawful for any person, directly or indirectly, by the use of any means or instrumentality of interstate commerce or of the mails, or of any facility of any national securities exchange—

. . .

(b) To use or employ, in connection with the purchase or sale of any security registered on a national securities exchange or any security not so registered, . . . any manipulative or deceptive device or contrivance in contravention of such rules and regulations as the Commission may prescribe as necessary or appropriate in the public interest or for the protection of investors. . . .

(c) (1) To effect, accept, or facilitate a transaction involving the loan or borrowing of securities in contravention of such rules and regulations as the Commission may prescribe as necessary or appropriate in the public interest or for the protection of investors. . . .

of the 1933 Act as well as the 1934 Act is to ensure investors have adequate information to evaluate investments, and to provide punishment for those who may try to manipulate markets by acting on information not available to the public. Consider the federal statute on the previous page (Illustrative Federal Statute 28.1), which is Section 10(b) of the 1934 Act (codified in the United States Code in Title 15, Section 78).

Congress has delegated authority to the SEC to issue regulations and rulings. The SEC has, in fact, issued many regulations and rulings. Pertinent to our discussion here regarding securities regulation is an oft-referenced promulgation by the SEC called **Rule 10b-5** (Illustrative SEC Rule 28.1).

Insider Trading

One of the most talked about violations of securities law is **insider trading**.

Notice the similar language in Rule 10b-5 (see Illustrative SEC Rule 28.1 below) as is contained in Section 10(b) of the Act quoted earlier (see Illustrative Federal Statute 28.1). As you can see, the language is very broad and can be applied in many different factual situations, including insider trading. Consider the following case from the United States Court of Appeals for the Second Circuit (Illustrative Court Case 28.1).

One important question to ask in relation to insider trading is, "Who is an 'insider'"? The law provides that members of the board of directors,

---

ILLUSTRATIVE SEC RULE 28.1

17 C.F.R. §240.10b-5

§ 240.10b-5 Employment of manipulative and deceptive devices.

It shall be unlawful for any person, directly or indirectly, by the use of any means or instrumentality of interstate commerce, or of the mails or of any facility of any national securities exchange,

(a) To employ any device, scheme, or artifice to defraud,

(b) To make any untrue statement of a material fact or to omit to state a material fact necessary in order to make the statements made, in the light of the circumstances under which they were made, not misleading, or

(c) To engage in any act, practice, or course of business which operates or would operate as a fraud or deceit upon any person,

in connection with the purchase or sale of any security.

ILLUSTRATIVE COURT CASE 28.1

Securities and Exchange Commission v. Texas Gulf Sulphur Co.

Court of Appeals for the Second Circuit

401 F.2d 833 (1968)

OPINION BY: WATERMAN

This action was commenced in the United States District Court for the Southern District of New York by the Securities and Exchange Commission (the SEC) pursuant to . . . the Securities Exchange Act of 1934 (the Act) . . . against Texas Gulf Sulphur Company (TGS) and several of its officers, directors and employees, to enjoin certain conduct by TGS and the individual defendants said to violate Section 10(b) of the Act, and Rule 10b-5 (the Rule), promulgated thereunder, and to compel the rescission by the

---

individual defendants of securities transactions assertedly conducted contrary to law. The complaint alleged . . . that defendants . . .Clayton [and] Crawford . . . had either personally or through agents purchased TGS stock or calls thereon from November 12, 1963 through April 16, 1964 on the basis of material inside information concerning the results of TGS drilling in Timmins, Ontario, while such information remained undisclosed to the investing public generally or to the particular sellers. . . . Judge Bonsal in a detailed opinion decided . . . that the insider activity prior to April 9, 1964 was not illegal because the drilling results were not "material" until then; that Clayton and Crawford had traded in violation of law because they traded after that date. . . . Defendants Clayton and Crawford appeal from that part of the decision below which held that they had violated Sec. 10(b) and Rule 10b-5. . . .

. . .

For reasons which appear below, we decide the various issues presented as follows:

(1) As to Clayton and Crawford, as purchasers of stock on April 15 and 16, 1964, we affirm the finding that they violated [Sec. 10(b)] and Rule 10b-5 and remand, pursuant to the agreement by all the parties, for a determination of the appropriate remedy.

. . .

THE FACTUAL SETTING

This action derives from the exploratory activities of TGS begun in 1957 on the Canadian Shield in eastern Canada. In March of 1959, aerial geophysical surveys were conducted over more than 15,000 square miles of this area. . . . The group included . . . defendant Clayton, an electrical engineer and geophysicist. . . . These operations resulted in the detection of numerous anomalies, *i.e.*, extraordinary variations in the conductivity of rocks, one of which was on the Kidd 55 segment of land located near Timmins, Ontario.

On October 29 and 30, 1963, Clayton conducted a ground geophysical survey on the northeast portion of the Kidd 55 segment which confirmed the presence of an anomaly and indicated the necessity of diamond core drilling for further evaluation. Drilling of the initial hole, K-55-1, at the strongest part of the anomaly was commenced on November 8 and terminated on November 12 at a depth of 655 feet. Visual estimates . . . of the core of K-55-1 indicated an average copper content of 1.15% and an average zinc content of 8.64% over a length of 599 feet. This visual estimate convinced TGS that it was desirable to acquire the remainder of the Kidd 55 segment, and in order to facilitate this acquisition TGS President Stephens instructed the exploration group to keep the results of K-55-1 confidential and undisclosed even as to other officers, directors, and employees of TGS. The hole was concealed and a barren core was intentionally drilled off the anomaly. Meanwhile, the core of K-55-1 had been shipped to Utah for chemical assay which, when received in early December, revealed an average mineral content of 1.18% copper, 8.26% zinc, and 3.945 ounces of silver per ton over a length of 602 feet. These results were so remarkable that neither Clayton, an experience geophysicist, nor four other TGS expert witnesses, had ever seen or heard of a comparable initial exploratory drill hole in a base metal deposit. So, the trial court concluded, "There is no doubt that the drill core of K-55-1 was unusually good and that it excited the interest and speculation of those who knew about it." By March 27, 1964, TGS decided that the land acquisition program had advanced to such a point that the company might well resume drilling, and drilling was resumed on March 31.

During this period, from November 12, 1963 when K-55-1 was completed, to March 31, 1964 when drilling was resumed, certain of the individual defendants . . . purchased TGS stock or calls thereon. Prior to these transactions these persons had owned 1135 shares of TGS stock and possessed no calls; thereafter they owned a total of 8235 shares and possessed 12,300 calls.

. . .

(*Continued*)

Meanwhile, rumors that a major ore strike was in the making had been circulating throughout Canada. . . . [TGS issued] a press release designed to quell the rumors, which release . . . was issued at 3:00 p.m. on Sunday, April 12, and which appeared in the morning newspapers of general circulation on Monday, April 13. . . .

. . .

While drilling activity ensued to completion, TGC officials were taking steps toward ultimate disclosure of the discovery. . . .

Between the time the first press release was issued on April 12 and the dissemination of the TGS official announcement on the morning of April 16, the only defendants before us on appeal who engaged in market activity were Clayton and Crawford. . . .

During the period of drilling in Timmins, the market price of TGS stock fluctuated but steadily gained overall. On Friday, November 8, when the drilling began, the stock closed at 17 3/8. . . . On April 16, the day of the official announcement of the Timmins discovery, the price climbed to a high of 37 and closed at 36 3/8. By May 15, TGS stock was selling at 58 1/4.

I. THE INDIVIDUAL DEFENDANTS

A. *Introductory*

Rule 10b-5 . . . on which the action is predicated, provides:

"It shall be unlawful for any person, directly or indirectly, by the use of any means or instrumentality of interstate commerce, or of the mails, or of any facility of any national securities exchange,

(1) to employ any device, scheme, or artifice to defraud,

(2) to make any untrue statement of a material fact or to omit to state a material fact necessary in order to make the statements made, in the light of the circumstances under which they were made, not misleading, or

(3) to engage in any act, practice, or course of business which operates or would operate as a fraud or deceit upon any person,

in connection with the purchase or sale of any security."

Rule 10b-5 was promulgated pursuant to the grant of authority given the SEC by Congress in Section 10(b) of the Securities Exchange Act of 1934. By that Act Congress purposed to prevent inequitable and unfair practices and to insure fairness in securities transactions generally, whether conducted face-to-face, over the counter, or on exchanges. . . . Insiders, as directors or management officers are, of course, by this Rule, precluded from so unfairly dealing, but the Rule is also applicable to one possessing the information who may not be strictly termed an "insider" within the meaning of Sec. 16(b) of the Act. Thus, anyone in possession of material inside information must either disclose it to the investing public, or, if he is disabled from disclosing it in order to protect a corporate confidence, or he chooses not to do so, must abstain from trading in or recommending the securities concerned while such inside information remains undisclosed. So, it is here no justification for insider activity that disclosure was forbidden by the legitimate corporate objective of acquiring options to purchase the land surrounding the exploration site; if the information was, as the SEC contends, material, its possessors should have kept out of the market until disclosure was accomplished.

B. *Material Inside Information*

An insider is not, of course, always foreclosed from investing in his own company merely because he may be more familiar with company operations than are outside investors. An insider's duty to disclose information or his duty to abstain from dealing in his company's securities arises only in "those situations which are essentially extraordinary in nature and which are reasonably certain to have a substantial effect on the market price of the security if [the extraordinary situation is] disclosed." [Citation omitted.]

. . .

[W]hether facts are material within Rule 10b-5 when the facts relate to a particular event and are undisclosed by those persons who are knowledgeable thereof will depend at any given time upon a balancing of both the indicated probability that the event will occur and the anticipated magnitude of the event in light of the totality of the company activity. Here, notwithstanding the trial court's conclusion that the results of the first drill core, K-55-1, were "too 'remote' . . . to have had any significant impact on the market, *i.e.*, to be deemed material," . . . knowledge of the possibility, which surely was more than marginal, of the existence of a mine of the vast magnitude indicated by the remarkably rich drill core located rather close to the surface . . . within the confines of a large anomaly . . . might well have affected the price of TGS stock and would certainly have been an important fact to a reasonable, if speculative, investor in deciding whether he should buy, sell, or hold. After all, this first drill core was "unusually good and . . . excited the interest and speculation of those who knew about it." [Citation omitted.]

Finally, a major factor in determining whether the K-55-1 discovery was a material fact is the importance attached to the drilling results by those who knew about it. In view of other unrelated recent developments favorably affecting TGS, participation by an informed person in a regular stock-purchase program, or even sporadic trading by an informed person, might lend only nominal support to the inference of the materiality of the K-55-1 discovery; nevertheless, the timing by those who knew of it of their stock purchases . . . virtually compels the inference that the insiders were influenced by the drilling results. . . .

. . .

The core of Rule 10b-5 is the implementation of the Congressional purpose that all investors should have equal access to the rewards of participation in securities transactions. It was the intent of Congress that all members of the investing public should be subject to identical market risks,—which market risks include, of course the risk that one's evaluative capacity or one's capital available to put at risk may exceed another's capacity or capital. The insiders here were not trading on an equal footing with the outside investors. They alone were in a position to evaluate the probability and magnitude of what seemed from the outset to be a major ore strike; they alone could invest safely, secure in the expectation that the price of TGS stock would rise substantially in the event such major strike should materialize, but would decline little, if at all, in the event of failure, for the public, ignorant at the outset of the favorable probabilities would likewise be unaware of the unproductive exploration, and the additional exploration costs would not significantly affect TGS market prices. Such inequities based upon unequal access to knowledge should not be shrugged off as inevitable in our way of life, or, in view of the congressional concern in the area, remain uncorrected.

We hold, therefore, that all transactions in TGS stock or calls by individuals apprised of the drilling results of K-55-1 were made in violation of Rule 10b-5.

executive officers, and some stockholders as insiders. These insiders are subject to strict rules, including rules governing **short swing** profits. A short swing profit occurs if an insider purchases and sells stock of the company within a six month period. Such profits must be returned to the company.

Other people, even if they are not directors, employees, or shareholders of the company may also be subject to the penalties of violating insider trading laws. These "outsiders" could be, for example, the corporation's lawyers, accountants, consultants, and other third-parties that may come across inside information as part of their jobs. These individuals may try to profit by **misappropriating** information they come across while performing their contracted projects for the company (*e.g.*, an auditor from a public accounting firm conducting an audit). Moreover, friends of insiders may also violate insider trading laws if an insider gives them a "tip" and the friend then trades based on the tip (*e.g.*, there is a **tipper** and a **tippee**).

"Pump" and "Dump" Schemes

Some traders have used technology to "pump" up a corporation's stock by touting the virtues of the stock in online chatrooms, etc. The intent, of course, is for a person to purchase the stock, pump up the stock, and then profit from selling the stock (*i.e.*, "dumping" the stock) after the artificial pumping of the stock's price has occurred. This violates federal securities laws as a form of manipulating a stock's price.

Violations of the 1934 Act

If a person violating the 1934 Act does so willfully, the person could face criminal prosecution which could result in prison time, significant fines, or both. To the extent the action does not constitute a crime, the person could still be liable for damages in a civil suit. The SEC itself could bring a civil suit as well as other investors who suffered damages because of the person's violation of the securities laws. With some exceptions, a plaintiff must typically show that (1) the defendant made a material misstatement (or omission), (2) had the intent to deceive (often called **scienter**), and (3) that the plaintiff relied on the defendant's misstatement.

Publicly traded companies may also be subject to fines for failure to file the appropriate reports (annual 10-K reports and quarterly 10-Q reports, for example), or to properly register with the SEC the securities being traded. Remember also that state securities laws may apply whenever federal securities laws do not.

QUESTIONS FOR REVIEW

1. What is the purpose of the Securities Exchange Act of 1934?

2. Explain briefly Section 10(b) of the 1934 Act.

3. Explain briefly Rule 10b-5.

4. Regarding insider trading, generally who is an insider?

5. Can "outsiders" violate insider trading laws? If so, how?

6. What are short swing profits?

7. Explain pump and dump schemes.

8. What is "scienter"?

9. Summarize the *SEC v. Texas Gulf Sulphur* case.

INTERNET ACTIVITIES

1. Visit the SEC website at www.sec.gov and click on the "Education" tab and then on the "Publications" link. Then click on the "Insider Trading" link. "Insiders" must file certain forms when engaging in stock transactions. What forms are they? What is reported on each form?

2. Conduct a search for news stories on "pump and dump" schemes. Select a story.

   a. What is the person's name that was accused or convicted of a pump and dump scheme?

   b. Summarize the particulars of the scheme.

   c. What is your source website?

Chapter 29

Accounting Regulation

JohnKwan/Shutterstock.com

Accountants engage in important information gathering, reporting, and auditing activities that impact the confidence investors have in a company's financial statements. Thus, the public has a vested interest that accountants perform their professional obligations in an independent, trustworthy manner. Given some well-publicized accounting failures in the early 2000s (*e.g.*, Enron, WorldCom, etc.), Congress reacted with much stronger laws and oversight of the accounting profession. The primary legislation to result from the accounting failures is known as the **Sarbanes-Oxley Act of 2002** (also known as the Public Company Accounting Reform and Investor Protection Act of 2002).

Sarbanes-Oxley Act of 2002

The Sarbanes-Oxley Act of 2002 (SOX) contains significant regulation of public accounting firms that audit publicly traded companies. Moreover, the Act imposes strict rules regarding a corporation's internal controls and a corporation's responsibility for the accuracy of its own financial statements. We discuss these issues in the following sections.

Creation of the Public Company Accounting Oversight Board

A major part of SOX is the creation of the **Public Company Accounting Oversight Board** (the PCAOB). The PCAOB is an independent board that

the SEC oversees. Consider the following statute contained within SOX that explains the duties of the PCAOB (Illustrative Federal Statute 29.1).

Registration of Public Accounting Firms with the PCAOB

Accounting firms that provide audit reports for publicly traded companies must be registered with the PCAOB. The PCAOB is charged with regulating these accounting firms to ensure compliance with SOX. For example, the PCAOB inspects the audit processes of these audit firms and to the extent the firm fails to comply with SOX, SEC rules or PCAOB rules, the firms will likely face fines and penalties. The PCAOB has an extensive website that lists registered firms, provides access to PCAOB rules, discloses fines and disciplinary orders against violating firms, among other information.

15 U.S.C. § 7211

§ 7211. Establishment; administrative provisions

. . .

(c) Duties of the Board. The Board shall . . .

(1) register public accounting firms that prepare audit reports for issuers, brokers, and dealers . . .;

(2) establish or adopt, or both, by rule, auditing, quality control, ethics, independence, and other standards relating to the preparation of audit reports for issuers, brokers, and dealers . . .;

(3) conduct inspections of registered public accounting firms . . .;

(4) conduct investigations and disciplinary proceedings concerning, and impose appropriate sanctions where justified upon, registered public accounting firms and associated persons of such firms . . .;

(5) perform such other duties or functions as the Board . . . determines are necessary or appropriate to promote high professional standards among, and improve the quality of audit services offered by, registered public accounting firms and associated persons thereof, or otherwise to carry out this Act, in order to protect investors, or to further the public interest;

(6) enforce compliance with this Act, the rules of the Board, professional standards, and the securities laws relating to the preparation and issuance of audit reports and the obligations and liabilities of accountants with respect thereto, by registered public accounting firms and associated persons thereof; and

(7) set the budget and manage the operations of the Board and the staff of the Board.

Conflicts of Interest

One of the actual and perceived problems with audits of publicly traded companies before the passage of SOX was whether the accounting firms were truly independent and objective when conducting the audit. For example, suppose an accounting firm were to provide business consulting services and recommend certain transactions that the company should engage in. Then, the same accounting firm audits the company. What is the likelihood the auditors will criticize or seriously question the activities or financial reporting of the company when it was the auditors' own firm that gave the company the advice? SOX and PCAOB rules address these conflict-of-interest situations. Basically, the auditing firm cannot also simultaneously provide certain nonaudit services to the company such as bookkeeping services, management consulting services, appraisal or valuation services, etc. Additionally,

the firm's partner(s) in charge of conducting the audit must rotate off the audit typically every five years so that the partner's independence is not compromised by being involved in the same audit for a substantial number of years.

Corporate Responsibility for Financial Reports

According to SOX, a publicly traded company's management must establish an **internal control**

What Do You Think?

Is it possible for an auditor to truly be objective and independent when the company the auditor is auditing pays the auditor's fee?

structure and procedures for financial reporting. Then, the auditing firm must attest to and report on the representations of management regarding internal control and the effectiveness of the internal control structure and financial reporting procedures. Senior officers of the company must also "sign off" on the reports prepared by the auditors certifying, among other things, that they have reviewed the reports and that the reports do not contain any untrue statements of material fact or omissions of material facts.

A company subject to SOX must also establish and maintain an **audit committee**. The audit committee must consist of board members who are not also employees of the company and at least one board member must be a financial expert that can readily understand financial reports and accounting issues that may be raised by the auditors. The auditors work with the audit committee in making sure the auditors have access to information they need to perform and complete the audit.

SOX requires the company to disclose whether the company has a **code of ethics** policy for senior financial officers. A code of ethics is defined in SOX to be "standards as are reasonably necessary to promote . . . honest and ethical conduct [and] full, fair, accurate, timely, and understandable disclosure in the [financial] reports."

Violations of SOX could bring penalties, fines, and other possible sanctions against both the accounting firms and senior management of the publicly traded company.

Civil Liability of Accountants

Accountants provide a broad range of services to the public and to private enterprise. Of course, a vast number of businesses and individuals need accounting services that are not subject to SOX (*e.g.*, the business is not publicly traded). Accountants can still be held liable to clients and third parties for various reasons as we discuss next.

Liability to Clients

Most any business engagement for accounting services is a contractual arrangement. A client will promise to pay a certain amount (or amount per hour) in return for the accountant's services. If the accountant fails to perform the services according to the contract, then, of course, the client could sue for *breach of contract*. If the accountant fails to perform in the expected professional manner, then the client may file a suit for *negligence* (*i.e.*, professional "malpractice"). An accountant may also be sued for *fraud* if the accountant has the requisite intent to deceive a client.

Liability to Third Parties

Suppose you read a company's prospectus and based upon the information provided in the prospectus you invest in that particular company. You later find out that the financial statements in the prospectus were misleading. Should you be able to sue the accounting firm that audited the company's financial statements and concluded that the financial statements accurately reflected the company's financial position in all material respects? Would it matter whether or not you actually *relied* on the financial statements in question? What if you just "glossed over" the details in the financial statements?

State and federal courts have not adopted a uniform standard in analyzing this issue. Thus, the outcome may depend on which jurisdiction hears the case. One approach holds that the third party must be in a "privity of contract" relationship with the accountant. This approach is called the **Ultramares** approach, which got its name from a landmark court case involving the Ultramares Corporation. The privity of contract requirement as applied in this approach basically means that the accountant prepared or audited the financial statement for a specific purpose or person (*e.g.*, so the company could get a loan from a particular bank), and the third party (*e.g.*, bank) relied on the accountant's representations as to the reliability of the financial statements.

A second approach to analyzing an accountant's liability to third parties is the **Restatement** approach. This adopts a position where an accountant could be liable to a broader class of third parties, not just one specific third party of which the accountant is aware (*e.g.*, several potential banks or other lenders will review the financial statements to determine whether to loan the company money). A third approach is even broader than the Restatement approach. This is called the **foreseeability standard**. Under the foreseeability standard, an accountant could be liable to any foreseeable third party that may use and rely on the financial statements prepared or audited by the accountant. This broad standard would include, for example, numerous potential investors in the company.

Accountants may face civil lawsuits for violation of securities laws also. In Chapter 28, we briefly mentioned that a defendant could be held liable to a plaintiff if the defendant possessed "scienter," which references the defendant's state of mind or intent to deceive or reckless disregard. Consider the following court case from the United States Court of Appeals for the Ninth Circuit, which addresses the issue of whether the defendant had the requisite scienter (Illustrative Court Case 29.1).

ILLUSTRATIVE COURT CASE 29.1

New Mexico State Investment Council v. Ernst & Young LLP

Court of Appeals for the Ninth Circuit

641 F.3d 1089 (2011)

OPINON BY: Jack Zouhary, District Judge

INTRODUCTION

Lead Plaintiff New Mexico State Investment Council, individually and on behalf of all others similarly situated ("Plaintiffs"), appeals the district court's grant of Defendant Ernst & Young's ("EY") Motion to Dismiss. The claims against EY stem from a securities class action complaint against Broadcom Corporation ("Broadcom"), certain Broadcom officers and directors, and Broadcom's auditor EY (collectively, "Defendants"), for a fraudulent $2.2 billion stock options backdating scheme. Plaintiffs specifically allege that EY, as Broadcom's auditor, knew of, or recklessly disregarded, Broadcom's fraudulent backdating actions yet issued unqualified audit opinions attesting to the validity of Broadcom's financial statements. The district court granted EY's Motion to Dismiss, finding the Consolidated Amended Class Action Complaint ("Complaint") failed to adequately plead scienter against EY.

Plaintiffs contend on appeal that the Complaint contains well-pled factual allegations sufficient to survive a motion to dismiss. EY argues dismissal was proper and, in the alternative, the district court's judgment should be affirmed based on Plaintiffs' failure to sufficiently plead loss causation, a ground the district court explicitly did not reach.

Procedural History

This case finds its roots in a large accounting fraud related to stock option backdating. Broadcom, a semiconductor company with revenues in excess of $2.5 billion in 2006, fraudulently overstated its net earnings, and understated its compensation expense, by more than $2.2 billion between 2000 and 2006 due to improper accounting of backdated stock options.

The Complaint seeks damages under Section 10(b) of the Securities Exchange Act of 1934 . . . and Securities Exchange Commission Rule 10b-5 for Defendants' fraudulent accounting practices, alleging they caused Broadcom's stock price to be artificially inflated.

. . .

The Complaint

The lengthy Complaint includes nearly thirty-five pages of allegations that EY, as Broadcom's auditor, was complicit in a stock option backdating scheme involving options to purchase over 239 million shares of Broadcom stock between 1998 and 2005. Broadcom used options as part of a compensation package for officers, directors, and key employees. The recipient of the option was given the opportunity to purchase a certain number of shares of company stock at a given price on or after a predetermined date. Broadcom's option plan provided for a vesting schedule of four years, meaning an employee could only exercise his or her option over a four-year period.

Backdating of options is akin to betting on a horse race after the horse has already crossed the finish line. Backdating of options occurs when a company's officers or directors responsible for administering the stock option plan monitor the price of the company stock and then award a stock option grant as of a certain date in the past when the share price was lowest, thus locking in the largest possible gain for the option recipient.

A backdated option is not in and of itself improper under the law or accounting principles. [Citation omitted.] However, when a company chooses to issue such "in the money" options (so called because the options represent an immediate paper profit), accounting principles require the company to record an expense for the "profit," treated as compensation to the option recipient over the vesting period. If the company does not properly record the backdated options, then the company's reported net income is overstated for each of the years the options vest, potentially deceiving the market and investors.

The Restatement and EY Opinion

Broadcom engaged in an improper stock option backdating scheme that required the company to restate its financial statements in January 2007 for fiscal years 1998 to 2005 (the "Restatement"). The Restatement acknowledged that Broadcom had improperly accounted for $2.2 billion in income, largely due to improper option backdating. Additionally, every financial statement, and quarterly and annual report issued during the time period covered by the Restatement, was false and misleading. As a result, Broadcom agreed to a civil penalty of $12 million in connection with a SEC civil securities fraud investigation, and various Broadcom officers and directors face civil and criminal charges.

The crux of Plaintiffs' claim is that EY, in its role of auditor issuing the unqualified 2005 Opinion, knew of, or was deliberately reckless in not knowing, that the 2005 Opinion was materially false and misleading due to Broadcom's stock option backdating scheme. The 2005 Opinion covered three years of Broadcom's financial statements (2003-05), stating that the financial statements "present fairly, in all material respects, the consolidated financial position of Broadcom Corporation at December 31, 2005 and 2004, and the consolidated results of its operations and its cash flows for each of the three years in the period ended December 31, 2005, in conformity with generally accepted accounting principles ("GAAP")." The 2005 Opinion also stated that EY had performed the audit in accordance with generally accepted auditing standards ("GAAS").

Allegations Against EY

Plaintiffs' allegations that EY had the required scienter for a fraud claim, namely that EY knew, or was deliberately reckless in not knowing, about the fraudulent option backdating, are as follows:

- EY knew the material consequences of a May 2000 backdated option grant that would have resulted in a $700 million charge to Broadcom's financial results but, despite violations of GAAS, signed off on the grant without obtaining documentation;

(Continued)

- EY knew that several significant option grants were approved on dates when Broadcom's compensation committee was not legally constituted due to the death of one of the two committee members;

- EY presided over corrective reforms in 2003 to prevent and detect any future instances of improper stock option awards without questioning the integrity of Broadcom's accounting for options granted prior to the corrective reforms;

- EY knew that there was insufficient documentation for nearly half of the $2.2 billion in backdated option grants in violation of GAAS;

- EY knew that Broadcom's internal controls were weak and failed to expand the scope of its audit procedures as required under GAAS; and

- EY was deliberately reckless in ignoring a number of "red flags" that should have alerted them to the potential for material misstatements related to stock-based compensation.

The Complaint includes additional details with respect to each of the above allegations, and Plaintiffs argue that these detailed allegations, both individually and collectively, support a strong inference that EY had the necessary scienter to survive a Motion to Dismiss.

ALLEGATIONS OF SCIENTER

To adequately plead scienter, a securities fraud complaint must "state with particularity facts giving rise to a strong inference that the defendant acted with the required state of mind." [Citation omitted.] A complaint can plead scienter by raising a strong inference that the defendant possessed actual knowledge or acted with deliberate recklessness. [Citation omitted.] . . .

. . .

Under . . . Ninth Circuit law, we conduct a two-part inquiry for scienter: first, we determine whether any of the allegations, standing alone, are sufficient to create a strong inference of scienter; second, if no individual allegation is sufficient, we conduct a "holistic" review of the same allegations to determine whether the insufficient allegations combine to create a strong inference of intentional conduct or deliberate recklessness. [Citation omitted.]

We hold that these factual allegations were each sufficient to support an inference of scienter by EY. While a holistic review is therefore unnecessary, these primary allegations certainly support an inference of scienter when viewed collectively with other claims that EY received no documentation for many option grants, knew Broadcom's internal controls were weak, and ignored other red flags.

. . .

When assessing GAAP violations in connection with auditor scienter, the violations should generally be more than "minor or technical in nature" and "constitute widespread and significant inflation" to contribute to a strong inference of scienter. [Citation omitted.] While a violation of GAAP, standing alone, is not sufficient, allegations of recklessness have been sufficient where defendants "failed to review or check information that they had a duty to monitor, or ignored obvious signs of fraud." [Citation omitted.]

With respect to allegations of GAAS violations and how an audit is conducted, "[a]lleging a poor audit is not equivalent to alleging an intent to deceive. [Citation omitted.] Rather, just as with GAAP, the more likely an auditor would have discovered the truth if a reasonable audit had been conducted, the stronger the scienter inference. [Citation omitted.]

. . .

EY would lead this Court to believe that its failure to further investigate amounts to, at most, negligence. However, an auditor, in fulfilling duties of public trust, should take a long hard look at a transaction of $700 million, roughly a quarter of Broadcom's reported revenue in 2006 of $2.5 billion. This Complaint alleges more than negligence. EY, as Broadcom's auditor, owes its ultimate allegiance to the company creditors and stockholders, as well as to the investing public. [Citation omitted.] By offering an "unqualified" or "clean" audit opinion, as EY did in its 2005 Opinion, EY provided the "highest level of assurance." [Citation omitted.] "Accountants will 'qualify' their opinion where discrepancies are identified in a client's financial statements." [Citation omitted.]

. . .

Here, the allegations strongly suggest EY knew of and participated in the corrective reforms to address improper stock option grants, but made no communication and took no action until Broadcom announced its Restatement several *years* later. This scenario survives a motion to dismiss.

. . .

CONCLUSION

For the reasons set forth above, we REVERSE the ruling granting Defendant EY's Motion to Dismiss, and REMAND the case for further proceedings consistent with this Opinion.

In summary, an accountant could be liable to a client or third party in a variety of circumstances. In some situations, ordinary negligence may be all that a plaintiff has to prove. In other cases, a plaintiff may have to show that the defendant accountant had scienter. Yet in other situations, the plaintiff would just have to show the accountant was in breach of contract.

What Do You Think?

Should accounting firms be liable to third parties (e.g., investors) for not fully complying with professional auditing standards when conducting an audit of a publicly traded company?

Robyn Mackenzie/Shutterstock.com

Criminal Liability of Accountants

Accountants are not immune from being prosecuted for criminal conduct in addition to whatever civil liability they may have to clients or third parties. Of course, securities laws, tax laws, and other general criminal statutes may apply to an accountant that has the requisite intent to willfully violate the law.

Needless to say, accountants should be aware of the potential criminal penalties and civil liability that they may face for professional malpractice and other activities. Although this chapter has focused on SOX and accountant liability, other professionals are subject to civil and criminal liability as well. Doctors, lawyers, dentists, engineers, etc., are wise to understand the civil and criminal laws relating to professional liability in their respective areas of expertise.

QUESTIONS FOR REVIEW

1. Explain generally the purpose of the Sarbanes-Oxley Act of 2002.

2. What are the duties of the PCAOB?

3. Discuss specific aspects of SOX, including the requirement for auditing firms to register with PCAOB, ethics issues, and corporate responsibility for its financial statements.

4. Explain how an accountant may be civilly liable to a client.

5. Discuss the three major approaches adopted by the courts to analyze whether an accountant is liable to a third party.

6. As discussed in the case against Ernst & Young provided in this chapter, what did the plaintiffs argue that E&Y did (or did not do) to establish liability to third party investors?

7. Summarize the *New Mexico v. Ernst & Young* case.

INTERNET ACTIVITIES

1. Visit the PCAOB website at www.pcaob.org. Click on the "Enforcement" tab. Click on the "Adjudicated Final Board Disciplinary Actions" link. Select a Respondent.

   a. What is the name of the accounting firm or accountant that you selected?

   b. Summarize why the PCAOB investigated the respondent and what the outcome was.

2. Conduct a search for news articles or other information where an accountant or CPA was accused or convicted of a crime relating to the accountant's profession.

   a. What is the accountant's name?

   b. What was the crime the accountant was accused or convicted of committing?

   c. Summarize the alleged criminal activity of the accountant.

   d. What is your source website?

Part X
Agency, Employment, and Labor Law

Chapter 30

Agency

Many business transactions involve one person (*i.e.*, the **agent**) who is negotiating on behalf of another person (*i.e.*, the **principal**). This relationship occurs frequently in real estate transactions, for example. To what extent can an agent legally bind the principal? What if the agent does something that was not pre-approved by the principal? Suppose you are a business owner and your employee agrees to sell a product to a customer well below a price that you would approve. Are you liable to the customer if you refuse to sell it for the price your employee negotiated? These questions all involve the legal principle of agency.

agent agreements to be in writing depending upon the terms of the agreement or upon the subject matter (*e.g.*, real estate). Employees are considered agents of their employers. Independent contractors can be agents, but generally are not automatically assumed to be agents. Sometimes the issue arises as to whether a person is an employee or independent contractor. This can be an important distinction for many reasons, especially in determining whether a principal/agent relationship exists. When a dispute arises as to whether an employer/employee relationship exists, the courts use a number of different factors to analyze the relationship. The factors include the amount of control the employer has over the work, whether the person uses his or her own tools, the extent of supervision of the project, the method and timing of payment (*e.g.*, is it structured like an employee's?), etc.

Some agency relationships may be created as a matter of law (*e.g.*, parents on behalf of children). In other situations, a principal may **ratify** the actions of a purported agent even if the agent acted outside the scope of the agent's authority or if the principal did not pre-approve the agent's actions. Once a principal/agent relationship exists, then the agent must know his or her expected duties.

Stephen Colburn/Shutterstock.com

Formation of a Principal/ Agent Relationship

Typically, the principal and agent enter into the relationship on terms both agree on. The agreement usually does not have to be in writing. The Statute of Frauds, however, may require some principal/

An Agent's Duties to the Principal

In general, the law imposes certain duties upon an agent (sometimes referred to as "fiduciary" duties). These duties include:

- The duty of loyalty
- The duty of accounting
- The duty of performance
- The duty of obedience
- The duty of notification

In short, the agent must not take advantage of an opportunity that could compete against the principal (*i.e.*, duty of loyalty). In fact, the agent must inform the principal of information relevant to the agency relationship (*i.e.*, duty of notification). The agent must perform the acts required by the principal in accordance with the agency agreement and account for the property and funds received and disbursed on the principal's behalf (*i.e.*, the duties of performance, obedience, and accounting).

A Principal's Duties to the Agent

The principal's duties to the agent include:
- The duty of compensation
- The duty of reimbursement and indemnification
- The duty of cooperation
- The duty of safe working conditions

These duties appear to be relatively straight forward. The principal must compensate the agent, unless the agent agreed to no compensation. If the agent incurs expenses or incurs liability acting within the scope of the agent's responsibilities, the principal has a duty to reimburse or indemnify the agent. Of course, the principal must cooperate with the agent so the agent can fulfill the agent's duties in accordance with the

What Do You Think?

Would there ever be a situation where a principal would not be inclined to cooperate with the agent?

agreement. This also includes providing safe working conditions for the agent to fulfill the agent's duties.

An Agent's Authority

If a principal explains to the agent in a clear, direct, manner what authority the agent has, then the agent has **express** authority to accomplish those tasks directed by the principal. A principal will sometimes give an agent a **power of attorney** to evidence the authority the agent has to act on behalf of the principal. A power of attorney is simply a document signed by the principal explaining the authority the principal is granting to another person (*i.e.*, the agent) to act on the principal's behalf. The power of attorney can grant broad authority to an agent (*i.e.*, a "general" power of attorney) or narrow authority to conduct specifically identified acts (*i.e.*, a "special" power of attorney).

An agent often has **implied** authority to enter into transactions on behalf of the principal. Suppose, for example, you own a business and hire several employees. One employee, the manager, goes to an office supply store to purchase copy paper for the business. Does the manager have the authority to do this? Likely so. Given the position as manager, it would be reasonable for the manager to assume that he or she has the authority to purchase copy paper on behalf of the business even if you did not specifically direct the manager to do so.

Another type of authority an agent could have is **apparent** authority. Apparent authority can arise when a principal leads a third party to believe (usually because of a pattern of conduct over time) that a person is acting in the capacity as the principal's agent. If the third party reasonably believes that a person is an agent of the principal, the principal is likely bound to the third party by the agent's actions. Consider the following case from the Supreme Court of Connecticut (Illustrative Court Case 30.1) involving the issue of apparent authority.

Ackerman et al v. Sobol Family Partnership, LLP, et al

Supreme Court of Connecticut

298 Conn. 495, 4 A.3d 288 (2010)

OPINION

ZARELLA, J. The principal issue in this consolidated appeal, which arises out of a series of disputes concerning the management and oversight of a family partnership and various family trusts, is whether the plaintiffs' attorney had apparent authority to make settlement proposals, engage in settlement discussions and bind the plaintiffs to a global settlement agreement with the defendants. The plaintiffs claim that the trial court's enforcement of a settlement agreement between the parties, based on a finding of apparent authority on the part of the plaintiffs' attorney to bind the plaintiffs to the agreement, was clearly erroneous in the absence of conduct by the plaintiffs (1) manifesting that their attorney had authority to settle the pending litigation, and (2) leading the opposing defense attorneys reasonably to believe that the plaintiffs' attorney had full and final authority to settle the litigation, as distinguished from authority only to negotiate. . . . The defendants respond that the trial court's finding that the plaintiffs' counsel had apparent authority to settle the litigation was not clearly erroneous. . . . We affirm the judgment of the trial court.

. . .

The cases were scheduled for a combined jury and court trial to commence on July 8, 2008, after the completion of jury selection. On July 3, 2008, however, the Sobol defendants and the defendant Bank of America each filed a motion to enforce a settlement agreement purportedly reached with the plaintiffs on July 1, 2008. On July 8, 2008, the trial court . . . conducted a hearing . . . to determine whether the settlement agreement was enforceable, at which the plaintiffs argued that there was no agreement and the defendants argued that there was. On July 9, 2008, the court issued an oral decision from the bench containing the following findings of fact and conclusions of law.

"[T]he parties met for a mediation, which was held on May 29, 2008, before the Honorable Michael Sheldon. The plaintiffs' attorney, Glenn Coe, represented the plaintiffs at this mediation.

. . .

"[Coe] had been speaking on behalf of all [the] plaintiffs regarding settlement with the knowledge and authority of his own client[s], as well as [the attorney] who [represented] the other two plaintiffs. . . . During [settlement negotiations, Coe] expressly assured [the] defendants' attorneys on separate occasions in response to direct questioning on the issue that the settlement offer proposed by him at that time was fully authorized by his client[s] . . . [and] that if accepted by the defendants, [it] would resolve the litigation in all respects.

. . .

"At no time prior to the acceptance of the settlement proposal on July 1, 2008, were [the] defendants or their attorneys notified that the offer had been withdrawn, unauthorized, or otherwise ineffective. During that same period . . . Ackerman never manifested to [the] defendants or their attorneys that the settlement authority of her attorney was limited or had been terminated.

. . .

"Having found the agreements to be clear and unambiguous, the court next moves to what is really the crux of the issue in this particular matter and that is the apparent authority of [Coe] to make the

(*Continued*)

settlement proposals and to accept the settlement on behalf of all the plaintiifs. Connecticut law is clear to the extent that under the ordinary rules of a contract, an agent who has apparent authority, but not express authority, can bind his principal especially as to parties who act in good faith. . . .

"[T]he court's inquiry as to the doctrine of apparent authority is now refined to a two part analysis. Apparent authority exists, one, where the principal held the agent out as possessing sufficient authority to embrace the act in question and knowingly permitted him to act as having such authority; and, two, in consequence thereof, the person dealing with the agent acting in good faith reasonably believed under all the circumstances that the agent had the necessary authority. . . ."

. . .

I

The plaintiffs first claim that the trial court improperly granted the defendants' motions to enforce the purported settlement agreement. They specifically claim that the trial court's finding that their lead attorney, Coe, had apparent authority to settle the pending litigation was clearly erroneous because it was lacking in evidentiary support. The defendants respond that the trial court's finding of apparent authority was not clearly erroneous because it was properly supported by the evidence. We agree with the defendants.

. . .

"[A]pparent authority is that semblance of authority which a principal, through his own acts or inadvertences, causes or allows third persons to believe his agent possesses. . . . Consequently, apparent authority is to be determined, not by the agent's own acts, but by the acts of the agent's principal. . . . The issue of apparent authority is one of fact to be determined based on two criteria. . . . First, it must appear from the principal's conduct that the principal held the agent out as possessing sufficient authority to embrace the act in question, or knowingly permitted [the agent] to act as having such authority. . . . Second, the party dealing with the agent must have, acting in good faith, reasonably believed, under all the circumstances, that the agent had the necessary authority to bind the principal to the agent's action. . . .

"Apparent authority terminates when the third person has notice that: (1) the agent's authority has terminated; (2) the principal no longer consents that the agent shall deal with the third person; or (3) the agent is acting under a basic error as to the facts. . . ." [Citations omitted.]

. . .

The same principles apply to the relationship between attorneys and their clients. . . . In the context of settlement agreements, the authority to determine whether and on what terms to settle a claim is reserved to the client except when the client has validly authorized the attorney to make such decisions. . . . Thus, an attorney with apparent authority may enter into a settlement agreement that is binding on the client. . . .

. . .

We conclude that the trial court's finding that the plaintiffs clothed Coe with apparent authority to settle the litigation is supported by evidence of a course of dealing involving the plaintiffs, Coe, the defendants and the parties' attorneys that was well established before the Sobol defendants and the Bank of America accepted the global settlement offer.

Liability of Principal and Agent

Liability of Principal to Third Party

A principal is legally bound with respect to a third party if the agent is acting within the scope of the agent's authority (whether express, implied, or apparent) when dealing with the third party. This includes liability for tort actions committed by the agent. The concept of the principal being liable for the actions of an agent is called **respondeat superior** (also sometimes referred to as "vicarious liability"). An employer, for example, is generally liable for the intentional and negligent torts of an employee (*e.g.*, car accident), unless the employee was acting outside the scope of employment (*i.e.*, the employee was on a "frolic and detour"). Consider the following case from the Supreme Court of Mississippi (Illustrative Court Case 30.2).

ILLUSTRATIVE COURT CASE 30.2

Akins v. Golden Triangle Planning & Development District, Inc.

Supreme Court of Mississippi

34 So. 3d 575 (Miss. 2010)

CARLSON, PRESIDING JUSTICE, FOR THE COURT:

Walter Akins d/b/a Akins Construction Company (Akins) filed suit in the Circuit Court of Oktibbeha County against Golden Triangle Planning and Development District, Inc. (Golden Triangle) under the theory of *respondeat superior*, seeking . . . $80,628, an amount that he claimed represented profits owed to him for constructing homes under the federal government's HOME Investment Partnerships Program (HOME), which was administered locally by Golden Triangle. According to Akins, the profits to which he was entitled were embezzled by a Golden Triangle employee, Phyllis Tate. Upon both parties filing motions for summary judgment, the trial court denied Akins's motion for summary judgment and granted summary judgment in favor of Golden Triangle. Consistent with these actions, the trial court entered final judgment in favor of Golden Triangle. . . . Aggrieved by the trial court's judgment, Akins timely filed this appeal.

. . .

FACTS AND PROCEEDINGS IN THE TRIAL COURT

. . .

Eventually, Tate began a scheme in which she colluded with her daughter and her daughter's then-boyfriend, Jason Clark, to divert HOME funds by transferring profits from the building projects to the checking account of a shell corporation, J-Max Construction Company, purportedly owned by Clark. In reality, J-Max was created for the fraudulent purpose of receiving the illegally diverted HOME funds. Tate convinced future homeowners to contract with builders with whom she purportedly had been working. Tate then requested cash allotments for J-Max Construction Company. The county or municipality receiving the grant funds wrote checks to J-Max. Tate, Clark, or Tate's daughter would withdraw the necessary funds to pay the subcontractors. When building was complete, Tate incorporated into the withdrawals the profits which should have been paid to the general contractor who actually had performed the work.

Akins was one of the general contractors who built homes under the HOME program administered by Golden Triangle. Akins was paid a total of $820,000 with HOME funds for various construction projects. Akins contracted with prospective homeowners to construct their residences. Golden Triangle approved these contracts. Akins requested periodic payments and a final payment upon completion. At Golden Triangle's request, Akins was paid for his services.

(Continued)

In August 2005, Golden Triangle suspected that Tate and/or Akins was involved in fraudulent activity after learning that Akins was charging building supplies to an account opened by Tate on behalf of a county at an area building supply warehouse, thereby avoiding sales tax on the building supplies. A forensic certified public accountant, hired by Golden Triangle, investigated and determined that Tate was embezzling HOME funds.

Upon receiving this information from the forensic CPA, Golden Triangle reported Tate's actions to the local district attorney, the Mississippi State Auditor, and the Mississippi Development Authority. In due course, the Federal Bureau of Investigation conducted its own investigation, ultimately resulting in a forty-seven-count federal grand jury indictment. . . .

. . .

On December 12, 2006, Akins filed suit against Golden Triangle. . . . In his complaint Akins alleged that the amount of $80,628 was embezzled by Tate, but actually owed to him for his services, and that Golden Triangle was vicariously liable under the doctrine of *respondeat superior*. Akins alleged that payments made to J-Max were for construction that he completed.

In due course, both Akins and Golden Triangle filed motions for summary judgment. The Circuit Court . . . denied Akins's motion for summary judgment and granted Golden Triangle's motion for summary judgment on the grounds that Tate was acting outside the scope of her duties in stealing government money and that Golden Triangle did not receive any benefit from Tate's illegal actions. From the trial court judgment entered in favor of Golden Triangle, Akins appeals to us.

DISCUSSION

Akins presents to us the single issue of whether the circuit court erroneously granted Golden Triangle's motion for summary judgment.

. . .

The trial court relied on the test . . . for determining whether an employee was acting within the scope of employment. [T]his Court [has] defined an employee's conduct as being in the scope of employment if:

(a) it is of the kind he is employed to perform;

(b) it occurs substantially within the authorized time and space limits;

(c) it is actuated, at least in part, by a purpose to serve the master, and

(d) if force is intentionally used by the servant against another, the use of force is not unexpectable by the master.

. . .

From the record before us, we find that the trial court did not err in granting Golden Triangle's motion for summary judgment, notwithstanding that genuine issues of a fact exist, because Akins's claims fail as a matter of law. The trial court was correct in finding that Tate's misdeeds were for her own personal gain and were of no benefit to Golden Triangle. She took government money and funneled it into the J-Max account. Later, this money was put into Tate's personal account. Even if this money was earmarked for Akins, as a matter of law, Akins cannot be granted relief under a theory of *respondeat superior*. . . .

CONCLUSION

As a matter of law, Akins was not entitled to recover any funds from Golden Triangle, given that Golden Triangle's employee, Tate, embezzled money for her own personal gain and did not serve to mutually benefit Golden Triangle. Rather, such actions were to the detriment of Golden Triangle. For all the reasons stated, the trial court did not err in granting Golden Triangle's motion for summary judgment; therefore, the . . . final judgment entered in favor of Golden Triangle . . . is affirmed.

Liability of Principal to Agent

A principal is liable to the agent if the principal breaches the principal's duties discussed earlier in the chapter. For example, if the principal fails to compensate the agent in accordance with the agreement, then the agent may sue the principal for damages.

Liability of Agent to Third Party

If the agent acts outside the scope of the agent's authority when dealing with a third party, the principal is typically not liable for the agent's actions. Consequently, the agent is liable to the third party.

Liability of Agent to Principal

An agent is liable to the principal if the agent fails to perform according to the agreed upon duties. For example, the agent would likely be liable to the principal if the agent failed to account for some monies that belonged to the principal.

QUESTIONS FOR REVIEW

1. Explain the duties that an agent has to a principal.

2. Explain the duties that a principal has to an agent.

3. What is the difference between implied authority and apparent authority?

4. What is a power of attorney? What is the difference between a "general" power of attorney and a "special" power of attorney?

5. Explain the doctrine of *respondeat superior*?

6. Summarize the *Ackerman v. Sobol* case.

7. Summarize the *Akins v. Golden Triangle* case.

INTERNET ACTIVITIES

1. Find the Supreme Court of Utah case *Clover v. Snowbird Ski Resort*, 808 P.2d 1037 (1991).

   a. What is the issue or issues in the case

   b. What was the holding of the court?

   c. Summarize the court's analysis.

2. Find the Supreme Court of Washington case *Rahman v. State of Washington*, 246 P.3d 182 (2011).

   a. What is the issue or issues in the case?

   b. What was the holding of the court?

   c. Summarize the court's analysis.

Chapter 31

Employment and Labor Law

Federal and state laws regulate many aspects of employer-employee relationships. For example, the law addresses issues such as minimum wage, workers' compensation, safety in the work place, pension benefits, unions, strikes and lockouts, among several others. This chapter discusses issues related to employment and labor law.

Employment Law

The industrial revolution in the United States created the need for some companies to have hundreds if not thousands of workers. Some employers hired workers for very low wages, long hours, and provided unsafe working conditions. Consequently, the government has stepped in and passed many laws regulating the employer-employee relationship.

Minimum Wage

The Fair Labor Standards Act (FLSA) requires employers to pay a minimum wage. In 2009, the minimum wage was raised to $7.25 per hour. Many states also have minimum wage laws. In cases where the federal and state minimum wage laws differ, the employee is entitled to the higher rate.

Overtime Pay

The FLSA also governs when an employer must include overtime pay to an employee. An employee who is not an "exempt" employee is entitled to overtime pay (*i.e.*, "time-and-a-half") for a week during which the employee works more than 40 hours. An exempt employee is generally an employee that is "salaried" and whose pay is not directly tied to the number of hours worked. The FLSA includes technical definitions of who is and who is not an exempt employee. Consider the following case decided by the United States Court of Appeals for the Second Circuit (Illustrative Court Case 31.1).

ILLUSTRATIVE COURT CASE 31.1

Davis v. J.P. Morgan Chase & Co.

Court of Appeals for the Second Circuit

587 F.3d 529 (2009)

OPINION

GERARD E. LYNCH, *Circuit Judge*:

This appeal requires us to decide whether underwriters tasked with approving loans, in accordance with detailed guidelines provided by their employer, are administrative employees exempt

---

(Continued)

from the overtime requirements of the Fair Labor Standards Act. Andrew Whalen was employed by J.P. Morgan Chase ("Chase") for four years as an underwriter. As an underwriter, Whalen evaluated whether to issue loans to individual loan applicants by referring to a detailed set of guidelines, known as the Credit Guide, provided to him by Chase. The Credit Guide specified how underwriters should determine loan applicant characteristics such as qualifying income and credit history, and instructed underwriters to compare such data with criteria, also set out in the Credit Guide, prescribing what qualified a loan applicant for a particular loan product. Chase also provided supplemental guidelines and product guidelines with information specific to individual loan products. An underwriter was expected to evaluate each loan application under the Credit Guide and approve the loan if it met the Guide's standards. If a loan did not meet the Guide's standards, certain underwriters had some ability to make exceptions or variances to implement appropriate compensating factors. Whalen and Chase provide different accounts of how often underwriters made such exceptions.

Under the Fair Labor Standards Act (FLSA), employers must pay employees overtime compensation for time worked in excess of forty hours per week. . . . Whalen claims that he frequently worked over forty hours per week. A number of categories of employees are exempted from the overtime pay requirement. The exemptions are drawn along a number of lines demarcating the type of profession, job function, and other characteristics. One categorical exemption is for employees who work in a "bona fide executive, administrative, or professional capacity." [Citation omitted.]

At the time of Whalen's employment by Chase, Chase treated underwriters as exempt from the FLSA's overtime requirements. Whalen sought a declaratory judgment that Chase violated the FLSA by treating him as exempt and failing to pay him overtime compensation. Both Whalen and Chase filed motions for summary judgment. The district court denied Whalen's motions and granted Chase's motion, dismissing Whalen's complaint. This appeal followed.

. . .

The statute specifying that employees who work in "bona fide executive, administrative, or professional capacit[ies]" are exempt from the FLSA overtime pay requirements does not define "administrative." . . . Federal regulations specify, however, that a worker is employed in a bona fide administrative capacity if she performs work "directly related to management policies or general business operations" and "customarily and regularly exercises discretion and independent judgment." [Citation omitted.] Regulations further explain that work directly related to management policies or general business operations consists of "those types of activities relating to the administrative operations of a business as distinguished from 'production' or, in a retail or service establishment, 'sales' work." [Citation omitted.] Employment may thus be classified as belonging in the administrative category, which falls squarely within the administrative exception, or as production/sales work, which does not.

. . .

The line between administrative and production jobs is not a clear one, particularly given that the item being produced . . . is often an intangible service rather than a material good. Notably, the border between administrative and production work does not track the level of responsibility, importance, or skill needed to perform a particular job. The monetary value of the loans approved by Whalen as an underwriter, for example, is irrelevant to this classification: a bank teller might deal with hundreds of thousands of dollars each month whereas a staffer in human resources never touches a dime of the bank's money, yet the bank teller is in production and the human resources staffer performs an administrative position. Similarly, it is irrelevant that Whalen's salary was relatively low or that he worked in a cubicle. What determines whether an underwriter performed production or administrative functions is the nature of her duties, not the physical conditions of her employment.

The Department of Labor has attempted to clarify the classification of jobs within the financial industry through regulations and opinion letters. In 2004, the Department of Labor promulgated new regulations discussing, among other things, employees in the financial services industry. Although these regulations were instituted after Whalen's employment with Chase ended, the Department of Labor noted that the new regulations were "[c]onsistent with existing case law." [Citation omitted.] The regulation states:

"Employees in the financial services industry generally meet the duties requirements for the administrative exemption if their duties include work such as collecting and analyzing information regarding the customer's income, assets, investments or debts; determining which financial products best meet the customer's needs and financial circumstances; advising the customer regarding the advantages and disadvantages of different financial products; and marketing, servicing or promoting the employer's financial products. However, an employee whose primary duty is selling financial products does not qualify for the administrative exemption." [Citation omitted.]

. . .

We thus turn to the job of underwriter at Chase to assess whether Whalen performed day-to-day sales activities or more substantial advisory duties. As an underwriter, Whalen's primary duty was to sell loan products under the detailed directions of the Credit Guide. There is no indication that underwriters were expected to advise customers as to what loan products best met their needs and abilities. Underwriters were given a loan application and followed procedures specified in the Credit Guide in order to produce a yes or no decision. Their work is not related either to setting "management policies" nor to "general business operations" such as human relations or advertising . . . but rather concerns the "production" of loans—the fundamental service provided by the bank.

Chase itself provided several indications that they understood underwriters to be engaged in production work. Chase employees referred to the work performed by underwriters as "production work." Within Chase, departments were at least informally categorized as "operations" or "production," with underwriters encompassed by the production label. Underwriters were evaluated not by whether loans they approved were paid back, but by measuring each underwriter's productivity in terms of "average of total actions per day" and by assessing whether the underwriters' decisions met the Chase credit guide standards.

Underwriters were occasionally paid incentives to increase production, based on factors such as the number of decisions underwriters made. While being able to quantify a worker's productivity in literal numbers of items produced is not a requirement of being engaged in production work, it illustrates the concerns that motive the FLSA. . . .

We conclude that the job of underwriter as it was performed at Chase falls under the category of production rather than of administrative work. Underwriters at Chase performed work that was primarily functional rather than conceptual. They were not at the heart of the company's business operations. They had no involvement in determining the future strategy or direction of the business, nor did they perform any other function that in any way related to the business's overall efficiency or mode of operation. It is undisputed that the underwriters played no role in the establishment of Chase's credit policy. Rather, they were trained only to apply the credit policy as they found it, as it was articulated to them through the detailed Credit Guide.

. . .

Accordingly, we hold that Whalen did not perform work directly related to management policies or general business operations. Because an administrative employee must *both* perform work directly

(Continued)

related to management policies or general business operations *and* customarily and regularly exercise discretion and independent judgment, we thus hold that Whalen was not employed in a bona fide administrative capacity. . . .

The judgment of the district court in favor of the appellee is REVERSED.

Child Labor

Another important issue the FLSA addresses is that of child labor. Generally, the FLSA restricts the number of hours a minor can work. A minor is considered a child under age 18. The FLSA provides different rules for children under age 14, children that are ages 14 and 15, and children that are ages 16 and 17. Children under 14 are generally prohibited from being employed, with some exceptions (*e.g.*, working for parents, delivering newspapers, etc.). Children that are 14 and 15 can be employed, but the number of hours are restricted during school days and the types of work are restricted (*e.g.*, no dangerous jobs such as mining). Sixteen and seventeen year-olds are not restricted on hours, but still cannot work in certain hazardous jobs. Remember that states also have regulations on child labor (and other employment issues) that may be even more restrictive than federal law. If so, the employer should comply with whichever rules are more strict.

Workers' Compensation

If an employee is injured while on the job, the workers' compensation system will provide payments to the employee. Workers' compensation is administered under state, not federal, law. Before the workers' compensation program was created, all an injured employee could do was to sue the employer under tort law. Of course, this typically would take a long time and there was still uncertainty as to whether the employee would win. Now, in return for receiving workers' compensation, employees cannot sue their employers for injuries on the job unless the employer intentionally created the hazardous working condition or acted with reckless disregard for the safety of employees. An important issue that

often arises in workers' compensation controversies is whether the employee was injured in the "scope of employment." Courts have interpreted "scope of employment" quite broadly, however, in favor of employees.

Workplace Safety

Ideally, the workers' compensation system would be rarely used because of safe work environments. Some employers, however, may be inclined to pay less attention to employee safety than they should. Consequently, the **Occupational Safety and Health Act** (OSHA) was passed to regulate workplace safety and impose fines and penalties on employers who violate safety rules. OSHA created an agency in the Department of Labor called the Occupational Safety and Health Administration to enforce the safety laws and regulations. Generally, an employer is required to comply with a set of nationwide safety standards, keep records regarding employee injuries, report workplace accidents to the Administration within a certain amount of time, and disclose to workers where hazardous areas exist or when a particular job assignment could be hazardous.

Olivier Le Queinec/Shutterstock.com

Health Insurance and Medical Information

When an employee is terminated from employment, typically a significant issue the employee must address is health insurance coverage. Although all employers are not required to provide health insurance to employees, an employer that does provide health insurance to employees must comply with the **Consolidated Omnibus Budget Reconciliation Act** (COBRA) once an employee is terminated. COBRA requires the employer to continue to provide health insurance coverage to the former employee for up to 18 months. This does not mean that the employer has to *pay* for the insurance during that time, however.

Employers with 50 or more employees must provide health insurance benefits to employees in accordance with the provisions contained in the **Patient Protection and Affordable Care Act** (also sometimes called "ObamaCare").

An employer is also required to keep medical information about an employee confidential. This is required by the **Health Insurance Portability and Accountability Act** (HIPAA). An employer may learn much about an employee's health condition because of medical claims, etc., filed through the employer's health insurance plan. HIPAA provides fines and penalties for disclosing this confidential medical information.

Family and Medical Leave

An employee may need to take time off work for an extended period of time for a family and/or medical reason. Historically, some employers would reduce the pay of an employee or in some other manner place the employee at a disadvantage when the employee would return (*e.g.*, reinstating them at a lower level job, or not giving them a promotion that they would have received if they had not taken leave). For example, a common reason for an extended leave from work is the birth of a child. The **Family and Medical Leave Act** (FMLA) protects employees from being treated unfairly for taking time off work for a reason covered by the Act. Basically, an employee is entitled to twelve weeks of unpaid leave during any twelve-month period in order to address family medical issues. Of course, key definitions in this law are "family" and "medical." A family member is typically the person's spouse, child, or parent. The medical condition must be a "serious health condition" to

What Do You Think?

Why would the federal government require only employers with 50 or more employees to comply with FMLA?

the employee or family member. The FMLA only applies to employers with 50 or more employees and to full-time employees who have been on the job more than one year. As with other laws and regulations we have discussed, however, state laws may fill in the gaps in federal law (*e.g.*, enact laws similar to the FMLA that apply to employers with fewer than 50 employees).

Unemployment Compensation

To help employees who may lose their jobs, Congress has provided a program to assist the unemployed worker for a limited period of time. This program is funded pursuant to the **Federal Unemployment Tax Act** (FUTA). Under the program, states administer unemployment compensation to employees who suddenly lose their jobs through no fault of their own. Eligibility requirements and specific procedures are governed by state law, which vary from state to state. Employers fund the program by remitting a certain amount per employee based upon the employee's wages. Many *states* also impose an unemployment tax on employers.

Social Security

If you have ever been an employee, you are likely familiar—at least to some extent— with the **Federal Insurance Contribution Act** (FICA). FICA has two components: social security and Medicare. An employer must withhold a percentage of your wages and remit the amounts to the Social Security Administration, which keeps track of how much social security payments you may be eligible for upon retirement, permanent disability, and other certain events. Of course, there is much political debate as to the solvency of the social security system and how to go about fixing the problem. An employer must also withhold Medicare taxes from an employee's wages. These funds, of course, go primarily to the elderly, among others, to assist with medical costs.

Retirement Plans

The Department of Labor regulates a business's handling of its retirement plans for employees. The federal law applicable to retirement plans is the **Employee Retirement Income Security Act** (ERISA). This law requires employers that have adopted retirement plans for their employees to disclose pertinent information to the employees and to comply with certain vesting schedules so that the employee knows when he or she is vested in the employer's contributions to the plan. There are many different types of retirement plans (*e.g.*, defined contributions, defined benefit, pension, 401(k), employee stock ownership plans (ESOPs), etc.), but a detailed explanation of each is beyond the scope of our discussion here.

Employee Privacy

To what extent can an employer monitor an employee's emails? Require an employee to take a drug test? Polygraph test? These issues pertain to employee privacy. As a general rule, an employer may monitor an employee's e-mails and other communications on employer-owned devices. Some employers actually have written policies informing employees that the employer will be monitoring electronic communications. Of course, many employers require an employee to consent to these things at the time the employee is hired. Whether an employer can require an employee (or potential employee) to take a drug test as a condition of employment generally depends on state law, which, of course, varies by state. Similarly, an employer's

right to subject an employee to a polygraph test (*i.e.*, lie detector test) is governed by state law. Some states allow polygraph tests if the reason is to investigate a potential theft within the company. Federal law (*i.e.*, the Employee Polygraph Protection Act), however, does prevent employers from administering a polygraph test as a condition of employment.

Labor Law

Occasionally, employees of a company or of a certain industry will be so upset regarding their compensation or working conditions that they band together and refuse to work. In other words, they go **on strike**. Of course, the more workers that do this the more harm the employer may suffer, thus increasing the workers' bargaining power.

In the early years of the United States courts prohibited strikes by employees, reasoning that such action was illegal and a restraint on trade. Further-

John Kershner/Shutterstock.com

more, employers would often require new employees to sign contracts (*i.e.*, "yellow-dog" contracts) promising not to join a union. Congress finally addressed the issue shortly after the Great Depression.

Congress passed the **Norris-LaGuardia Act** in 1932 to stop courts from enforcing yellow-dog contracts and from stopping employee strikes, picketing, etc. Next, Congress passed the **National Labor Relations Act** (also called the Wagner Act or NLRA) in 1935, which gave workers the right to form unions, elect representatives and engage in **collective bargaining** with management on behalf of members of the union. The NLRA created the

National Labor Relations Board (NLRB), which administers the NLRA. One of the NLRB's functions is to investigate charges of unfair labor practices. When management and the union cannot come to an agreement on terms, union workers may go on strike or management may **lockout** the employees and prevent them from coming to work. After a short time following the enactment of the NLRA, unions obtained significant power. Some union organizations engaged in criminal activities and misused union power and union funds. Consequently, Congress passed the **Labor-Management Relations Act** (LMRA) in 1947 to curb these union abuses and establish rules for unfair labor practices by both unions and employers. For example, employers cannot prohibit employees from participating in union activities. Consider the following case decided by the United States Court of Appeals for the District of Columbia Circuit (Illustrative Court Case 31.2).

ILLUSTRATIVE COURT CASE 31.2

Bally's Park Place, Inc. v. National Labor Relations Board

Court of Appeals for the District of Columbia Circuit

646 F.3d 929 (2011)

OPINION

Garland, *Circuit Judge*: Bally's Park Place, Inc. petitions for review of a decision and order of the National Labor Relations Board (NLRB). The Board found that the company committed unfair labor practices in violation of . . . the National Labor Relations Act . . . when it discharged employee Jose Justiniano because of his support for the United Auto Workers. For the reasons set forth below, we deny Bally's' petition and grant the Board's cross-application for enforcement of its order.

I.

Bally's operates a casino in Atlantic City, New Jersey. The company hired Justiniano as a table dealer in 2000, and through 2006 it repeatedly praised him as a good employee. . . . In November of that year, the United Auto Workers (UAW) began a campaign to organize casino dealers in the Atlantic City area, including those working at Bally's. Justiniano attended numerous meetings held by the union, became a supporter, and signed an authorization card. He spoke to other Bally's employees on a daily basis about the need for a union – in the employees' lounge, in the cafeteria, and as they were coming to and going from work. He also appeared in a promotional video that the union prepared and mailed to casino workers in and around Atlantic City.

In January 2007, at a time when no customers were present at his table, Justiniano spoke to another employee about the union's organizing efforts. It is undisputed that Bally's allowed dealers to have social conversations in such circumstances. Nonetheless, Justiniano's supervisor told the two that they could not talk about the union while on the casino floor.

On March 19, 2007, Justiniano got into a dispute with a manager over break time. When the supervisor threatened to discipline him, Justiniano responded that such threats were the reason the employees needed a union. The manager then began yelling at him, saying that he was not allowed to talk about "union" on the casino floor and that he could be "fired for talking about unions." [Citation omitted.] A short while later, Justiniano was instructed to report to another supervisor, who told him that he was "not allowed to talk about the Union on the casino floor whatsoever." And on March 22, Justiniano was escorted to speak to the shift manager, who asked him about the previous incident. The shift manager told Justiniano that he should not talk about the union on the casino floor and issued him a written warning for acting "in an unprofessional manner."

(Continued)

. . .

On March 31, Justiniano was scheduled to work at the casino from 12:00 noon to 8:00 p.m. The night before his shift, the mother of his 13-year-old daughter called and asked him to take care of the girl beginning at 12:30 p.m. the next day. Justiniano's daughter suffered from severe asthma that required treatment every four hours. He had previously taken leave to care for her, without incident, pursuant to the Family and Medical Leave Act (FMLA). . . . Justiniano called Bally's at 6:00 a.m. on the morning of March 31 and left a message that he would be taking FMLA leave that day; he called back at 9:00 a.m. to confirm that Bally's had received the message.

Later that morning, the UAW held a rally outside the Trump Plaza casino as part of its effort to organize Atlantic City casino dealers. The rally was scheduled to last from 10:30 a.m. until about 12:15 p.m. Justiniano attended the rally and waved a "Union Yes" sign. On his way to work, one of Bally's' managers saw Justiniano holding the sign. Upon arriving at the casino, the manager informed Bally's' vice president of table games, Michael May, that he had just seen Justiniano at the rally. . . .

When Justiniano returned to work, he signed a form requesting paid family leave for his entire shift on March 31. On April 9, May took Justiniano to meet with Bally's' director of operations, Richard Tartaglio. Tartaglio informed Justiniano that he had been seen at the UAW rally on the morning of March 31, and he asked Justiniano when he left the rally. Justiniano acknowledged that he was at the rally until it ended at about 12:20 p.m., and said that he had then gone home to care for his daughter. Based on the information Justininao provided, Tartaglio and May concluded that Justiniano had been at the rally for 20 minutes after the start of his scheduled shift and that he had therefore spent 20 minutes of FMLA leave time attending the rally. On April 12, Bally's terminated Justiniano for "violation of Work Rule Number 3 in the employee handbook stating that employees will be honest and forthcoming in all communication." [Citation omitted.]

Following Justiniano's termination, the UAW filed unfair labor practice charges against Bally's. Based on those charges, the NLRB's General Counsel issued a complaint alleging that the company had violated . . . the NLRA, which . . . make[s] it an unfair labor practice for an employer "to interfere with, restrain, or coerce employees in the exercise of" their rights to form, join, or assist labor organizations . . . and "by discrimination in regard to . . . tenure of employment . . . to encourage or discourage membership in any labor organization." [Citation omitted.] . . .

The Administrative Law Judge (ALJ) found that Bally's violated [the NLRA] by telling Justiniano—once in January and three times in March, 2007—that he could not discuss union issues on the casino floor even though employees were permitted to discuss other nonwork-related matters there. . . .

Bally's now petitions for review of that determination.

II.

. . .Bally's does not challenge the Board's conclusion that the General Counsel established a prima facie case of discriminatory motive. And for good reason. As Bally's well knew, the union was attempting to organize its employees and Justiniano was an outspoken union supporter. Its managers had unlawfully instructed him on three recent occasions not to discuss the union with other employees on the casino floor. Indeed, one manager threatened that he could be "fired for talking about unions," and he was given a written warning. A supervisor had also unlawfully solicited his grievances with the implied promise to remedy them if he refrained from supporting the union. Justiniano's discharge came less than three weeks after the firing threat, even closer in time to the unlawful solicitation, and within days of a manager observing him at a pro-union rally. As the board rightly found, this "evidence of a discriminatory motive is strong." [Citation omitted.] . . .

Where, as here, the General Counsel makes a strong showing of discriminatory motivation, the employer's rebuttal burden is substantial. . . . Bally's argues that it met that burden by demonstrating that it maintained a "zero-tolerance" policy with respect to the misuse of family leave time. As the Board noted, however, Bally's had no written zero-tolerance policy, and there is no evidence that it ever announced such policy to its employees.

. . .

As the Board reasonably concluded, "at most, this evidence establishes that [Bally's] had a practice of terminating employees who fraudulently requested or extended FMLA leave, i.e., telling [Bally's] that they required leave to fulfill family responsibilities or out of medical necessity and then using the leave for a completely different purpose." . . . By contrast, "Justiniano did not intentionally and fraudulently request FMLA leave for a purpose not covered by the FMLA." [Citation omitted.]

Bally's offers only two examples of employees who, like Justiniano, used some but not all of their FMLA leave time for its intended purpose. One requested leave to care for her ailing father, but then failed to return to work for a month after her father died. The other requested leave to attend to his wife who, he claimed, required constant care. After an investigation, however, Bally's discovered that he was operating a bed-and-breakfast with his wife. These employees are also reasonably distinguishable from Justiniano, who misused only a tiny fraction of the time they did. . . .

III.

For the foregoing reasons we deny the petition for review and grant the Board's cross-application for enforcement.

What Do You Think?

In the Bally's case just presented, was Justiniano acting ethically to go to the pro-union rally on a day that he requested FMLA time to take care of his daughter?

QUESTIONS FOR REVIEW

1. Explain briefly each of the following acts passed by Congress:

   a. FLSA

   b. OSHA

   c. COBRA

   d. HIPAA

   e. FMLA

   f. FUTA

   g. FICA

   h. ERISA

2. If an employee is injured on the job, what are the employee's options?

3. Discuss generally whether an employer can monitor an employee's emails, voice messages, and other communications.

4. Explain briefly each of the following acts passed by Congress:

   a. Norris-LaGuardia Act

   b. National Labor Relations Act

   c. Labor-Management Relations Act

5. Summarize the *Davis v. J.P. Morgan* case.

6. Summarize the *Bally's Park Place v. NLRB* case.

INTERNET ACTIVITIES

1. Visit the United States Department of Labor website at www.dol.gov.

   a. Click on the "Topics" tab. Click on the "Work Hours" link. Click on the "Breaks & Meal Periods" link. Summarize the rules regarding whether an employer must compensate employees for breaks and meal periods.

   b. Go back to the home page. Click on the "Topics" tab. Click on the "Wages" link. Click on the "Tips" link. Summarize the discussion on tips.

2. Conduct a search for the website of your state agency that administers workers' compensation.

   a. What is the agency's name?

   b. What is the agency's website?

   c. Summarize how an injured employee makes a workers' compensation claim in your state.

3. Conduct an internet search and provide a synopsis of the requirements placed on employers under the Patient Protection and Affordable Care Act.

Part XI

Employment Discrimination

Employment Discrimination Based on Race, Color, National Origin, Gender, and Religion

For what reasons can an employer fire an employee? What if you wear bright orange shoes to work one day and your boss doesn't like orange? What if you have a visible tattoo on your neck and the employer has a policy against visible tattoos? What if you refuse to work on a religious holiday because you want to go to worship services? What if you make disparaging remarks to a member of the opposite sex? Assume you own a moving company and you need to hire another employee. Can your job advertisement say, "Strong *men* wanted who can lift up to 75 lbs."? Assume instead that you own a women's swimsuit store. Can your job advertisement say, "Only *women* need apply"? Can you discriminate based upon eyesight? Weight? Height? The answers to these questions depend upon whether you are discriminating against classifications of people that the law protects.

As a general rule, an employer can fire an employee for any reason at any time and an employee can quit for any reason at any time (*i.e.*, **employment at will**). Important exceptions exist, of course. One exception is if the employer and employee are parties to a contract that specifically limits the reasons for which an employee could be fired. This includes union contracts with employers. Another very important exception is that an employer cannot terminate an employee

or refuse to hire a person for reasons prohibited by law. The most important federal legislation governing employment discrimination is **Title VII of the Civil Rights Act of 1964**.

Title VII of the Civil Rights Act of 1964

Title VII of the Act basically states that an employer cannot discriminate on the basis of race, color, national origin, religion, or gender. These categories are referred to as **protected classes**.

The Act created the **Equal Employment Opportunity Commission** (EEOC). The role of the EEOC is to investigate claims by employees of discrimination by their employers. In fact, the employee must typically first file a claim with the EEOC, and then the EEOC will evaluate the claim to decide whether to file suit against the employer on behalf of the affected employee(s). The employee(s) can still file suit against the employer if the EEOC decides not to pursue the claim.

What Constitutes Discrimination?

Establishing a universal definition of "discrimination" that would apply in every situation is difficult. Nevertheless, the courts have established certain tests to which a particular situation can be evaluated. Basically, discrimination is either intentional or unintentional. Intentional discrimination exists if there is **disparate treatment** of an employee or potential employee and the employee is in a protected class. Suppose you are an employer and are hiring eight people. Sixty women apply and 10 men apply. You hire seven men and one woman. Is this discrimination? Does the rate of hiring have to correspond to the pool of applicants? Not necessarily, but it could be an important factor that a woman who does not get hired could assert.

In short, disparate treatment means that if the employee (or job applicant) can show a prima facie case of intentional discrimination (*i.e.*, sufficient evidence that shows on its face that the employer may have discriminated) then the burden shifts to the employer to show why the action was *not* discriminatory. If the employer argues that the particular action taken regarding an employee was justified for business reasons (*e.g.*, not qualified for the job, or the employee has past poor performance), then the employee's claim may be rejected by the courts (see discussion later in this chapter regarding an employer's potential defenses to discrimination claims).

Regarding *unintentional* discrimination, if an employee can show that particular actions of the employer have a **disparate impact** on the employee or class of employees, then the employer may be liable for discrimination. Disparate impact basically means that notwithstanding the lack of the employer's intentional discrimination, unfair results occurred. For example, suppose an employer requires that all applicants take a test to ensure that the applicant has the requisite knowledge required for the job. Suppose further that only applicants from one particular race pass the test even though applicants from several races actually took the test. Is this discrimination based on race? See the *Ricci* case later in this chapter (Illustrative Court Case 32.2) for the United States Supreme Court's analysis of this issue.

Discrimination Based on Gender

Many court cases are filed each year against employers on the basis of gender discrimination. Gender, of course, is a protected class. Sexual harassment is also a form of discrimination. The courts have identified two types of sexual harassment: (1) *quid pro quo* harassment; and (2) hostile work environment harassment. *Quid pro quo* (*i.e.*, "this for that") harassment is the more serious type of harassment. Basically, to prevail on a *quid pro quo* harassment claim the plaintiff must show unwelcome sexual harassment that the employer knew about and failed to remedy. In addition, the employee must show that tangible aspects of the employee's employment (*e.g.*, compensation, terms, conditions, or privileges of employment) were negatively affected.

aerogondo2/Shutterstock.com

Consider the following court case from the United States Court of Appeals for the Fourth Circuit (Illustrative Court Case 32.1).

Hostile work environment harassment is not quite as direct as *quid pro quo* sexual harassment. Nevertheless, as discussed in the *Okoli* case (Illustrative Court Case 32.1), a claim for hostile work environment harassment can be made if the employee is the target of unwelcome conduct and such conduct is sufficiently "severe" or "pervasive" to constitute abusive conduct.

Employers should establish sexual harassment policies and procedures to handle claims by employees. Moreover, an employer should make

Okoli v. City of Baltimore

Court of Appeals for the Fourth Circuit

648 F.3d 216 (2011)

OPINION BY: GREGORY

OPINION

GREGORY, Circuit Judge:

Appellant challenges the grant of summary judgment for her employer when her boss forcibly kissed her, fondled her leg, propositioned her, asked sexually explicit questions, described sexual activities he wished to perform, and then, after she spurned the advances and filed a harassment complaint, fired her. Because those allegations are sufficient to make out claims of hostile work environment, quid pro quo harassment, and retaliation, we vacate and remand.

I.

. . .

John P. Stewart is the director of Baltimore's Commission on Aging and Retirement ("CARE") and serves in the Mayor's cabinet. On June 21, 2004, Stewart hired Okoli, an African-American woman, to serve as his executive assistant. The parties agree that for the first few months, Stewart and Okoli worked well together.

Beginning in September 2004, things changed for the worse: Namely, Stewart began propositioning Okoli to have sex with him in a Jacuzzi as part of his sexual fantasy. He first did so on September 13, 2004, during a visit to a CARE facility. During a September 24, 2004 work meeting, Stewart then asked Okoli whether she was wearing any underwear, what color it was, and whether she would come to work the next day without underwear. Next, on October 4, 2004, Stewart told Okoli about a sexual experience he had with an African-American woman and her daughter. Okoli reacted with shock and disgust, which Stewart noticed. Another time, Stewart again mentioned this sexual experience with a mother and daughter. Okoli reiterated that the daughter would despise and regret having such a lewd sexual encounter with her mother. Stewart laughed it off and returned to work, as Okoli suggests he often did.

Stewart continued to proposition Okoli about his Jacuzzi fantasy, and on November 10, 2004, asked her to sit on his lap and to join him in a Jacuzzi in Las Vegas. Whenever Stewart traveled, he continued to request Okoli to join him in his Jacuzzi, and became angry when she rejected his advances. Furthermore, Stewart touched Okoli's legs under the conference table "two or three times" during their morning meetings. Whenever this occurred, Okoli would move away from Stewart and tell him "don't do that." In November 2004, Okoli met with a manager about transferring to another department, and in January, Stewart gave her an "informal" performance review with areas of suggested improvement.

On January 10, 2005, Stewart asked Okoli to come back in a conference room, then forcibly grabbed and kissed her. Okoli pushed him away and ran out the door. She was so distraught that she went home and remained there for the day. When she returned to work the next day, Okoli stressed to Stewart that she still wanted to have only a professional relationship. While he initially said "O.K.," Stewart repeated his Jacuzzi fantasy again that same day.

Okoli then began reaching out for help in various ways, to no avail: On January 26, 2005, Okoli emailed Alvin Gillard, the Executive Director of the Baltimore Community Relations Commission,

(Continued)

asking to speak with him about "a complaint." Gillard never responded. On March 23, 2005, Okoli emailed Gillard with a "high" importance flag, stating her desire to "file a harassment complaint against my supervisor, Mr. John P. Stewart." Gillard suggested she speak with an intake specialist during work hours. Okoli also emailed Michael Enright, the First Deputy Mayor, as well as Clarence Bishop, the Mayor's Chief of Staff, with a "high" importance request to meet with the Mayor as soon as possible.

Enright promptly forwarded that complaint on to Stewart through Enright's special assistant. . . . Later that afternoon, Stewart fired Okoli.

. . .

On September 26, 2006, Okoli initiated a pro se action against Stewart, Enright, O'Comartun, the Mayor, CARE, and the City Council of Baltimore (hereinafter, collectively known as "the City"). She asserted claims under Title VII, 42 U.S.C. §§ 1983, 1985, 2000e, common law, and Article 4 § 3-1 of the Baltimore City Code.

On November 16, 2006, the City filed a notice of removal to federal court, where Okoli amended her complaint. Both parties moved for summary judgment and the district court granted the City's motion. The court analyzed the same three issues which arise in this appeal, hostile work environment, quid pro quo harassment, and retaliation: First, regarding hostile work environment, the court stressed that there were "[j]ust three or four incidents [of physical contact] over a five month period," and no physical threat to Okoli. The court also reasoned that Stewart ceased his conduct on his own and "according to [Okoli's] own positive assessment of her job performance, it is clear that she does not believe that Stewart's conduct interfered with her work performance." The court emphasized that Okoli over-read certain inferences and innocuous gifts, and cited cases where similar or "more egregious" conduct did not constitute a hostile work environment. [Citations omitted.]

Second, regarding quid pro quo, the district court found that there was a legitimate basis to fire Okoli due to "performance issues," namely her attitude, errors, and absence. The court found these to be valid grounds for terminating an at-will employee and concluded that her other allegations of adverse actions were not actionable.

. . .

II.

. . .

A.

First, Okoli alleges she was subject to a hostile work environment. "To demonstrate sexual harassment and/or a racially hostile work environment, a plaintiff must show that there is '(1) unwelcome conduct; (2) that is based on the plaintiff's sex [and/or race]; (3) which is sufficiently severe or pervasive to alter the plaintiff's conditions of employment and to create an abusive work environment; and (4) which is imputable to the employer.'" [Citations omitted.]

The third factor is dispositive here: whether Stewart's treatment was severe or pervasive enough. The City contends it was not, characterizes Stewart's conduct as sporadic and infrequent, depicts Stewart as promptly stopping this conduct once Okoli objected, and questions whether some of Stewart's comments and gifts were sexual at all.

We conclude that Okoli presents a strong claim for hostile work environment. Here, we look to the totality of the circumstances, including the "'frequency of the discriminatory conduct; its severity; whether it is physically threatening or humiliating, or a mere offensive utterance; and whether it unreasonably interferes with an employee's work performance.'" [Citations omitted.] Okoli . . .

(Continued)

suffered upwards of twelve (12) incidents in just four months: (1) disparaging jokes about gays and lesbians; (2) comments about Okoli and Jacuzzi fantasy; (3) comments about Okoli and group sex fantasy; (4) questions about Okoli's underwear; (5) comments about sexual relations with another African-American woman; (6) additional inquiries about Okoli sitting on lap and Jacuzzi fantasy; (7-10) three incidents of fondling her leg under a table; (11) forcible kissing; (12) more propositions to join in a Jacuzzi fantasy. These events took place from September 8 through January 11. Functionally, these incidents span fondling, kissing, propositioning, describing sexual activities, and asking intimate questions. Some of the incidents may have been severe enough to be actionable in and of themselves.

. . .

Finally, the district court's reasoning was flawed in two other ways. First, the court over-emphasized the role of Stewart's gifts in light of the extensive remarks and touching here. Some of those gifts, such as a holiday card, flag, or tea set, may seem innocuous when viewed alone or out of context. But our legal analysis "requires careful consideration of the social context in which particular behavior occurs and is experienced by its target." [Citation omitted.] Here, Okoli alleges Stewart was engaging in an escalating pattern of sexual advances. Gifts could certainly have been a part of his effort to coerce Okoli into having sex. A gift which may seem harmless in the abstract can have sexual connotations when delivered with a suggestive comment (this flag is "[a] sign of bigger and better things to come,") or symbol (*i.e.*, a phallic or sexual allusion).

Second, the district court reasoned that Stewart's advances could not have interfered with Okoli's work since she had a high opinion of her performance. But this conflates aspects of Stewart's hostile work environment and retaliation claims. Okoli can argue that Stewart negatively impacted her work, while still defending her performance against the City's attempt to show a legitimate basis for firing her. Indeed "[t]he fact that a plaintiff continued to work under difficult conditions is to her credit, not the harasser's." [Citation omitted.] Overall, Okoli presents a strong claim for hostile work environment, when "objective[ly viewing the] severity of harassment . . . from the perspective of a reasonable person in the plaintiff's position." [Citation omitted.]

B.

Second, Okoli claims she experienced quid pro quo discrimination. This requires an employee prove five elements:

1. The employee belongs to a protected group.

2. The employee was subject to unwelcome sexual harassment.

3. The harassment complained of was based upon sex.

4. The employee's reaction to the harassment affected tangible aspects of the employee's compensation, terms, conditions, or privileges of employment. The acceptance or rejection of the harassment must be an express or implied condition to the receipt of a job benefit or cause of a tangible [*17] job detriment to create liability. Further, as in typical disparate treatment cases, the employee must prove that she was deprived of a job benefit which she was otherwise qualified to receive because of the employer's use of a prohibited criterion in making the employment decision.

5. The employer, as defined by Title VII, 42 U.S.C. § 2000e(b), knew or should have known of the harassment and took no effective remedial action.

[Citation omitted.] With the fourth element, "[a] tangible employment action constitutes a significant change in employment status, such as hiring, firing, failing to promote, reassignment with significantly different responsibilities, or a decision causing a significant change in benefits." [Citations omitted.]

(Continued)

If the plaintiff makes a prima facie showing, the burden shifts to the employer to articulate a legitimate, non-retaliatory reason for the adverse action. [Citations omitted.] Then, if the employer satisfies its burden, the burden returns to the plaintiff to establish that the employer's proffered reason is a pretext for discrimination. [Citation omitted.]

In this case, the inquiry turns on the fourth factor: whether Okoli's reaction to Stewart's advances affected "tangible aspects" of her employment. The parties focus mostly on whether Stewart's decision to conduct an informal performance feedback—as opposed to a formal, periodic performance review—was "tangible" enough. Performance reviews are clearly related to employment and promotion. But the record contains no details about what reviews are standard or required by office policy. The more "tangible" employment action taken by Stewart was Okoli's allegation that Stewart fired her for rejecting his advances and complaining about his conduct.

. . .

In this case, there is some evidence that Okoli occasionally had scheduling conflicts and made typographical errors. But it appears deeply suspicious that Stewart fired Okoli only hours after she culminated her rejection of him by complaining to the Mayor. . . .

III.

For these reasons, the grant of summary judgment is vacated and the case is remanded for further proceedings.

attempts to remedy the situation once the employer is aware of alleged sexual harassment.

What Do You Think?

At what point do comments rise to the level of sexual harassment? When does a hostile work environment exist? How much should the law tolerate before holding the employer responsible for the actions of employees that are sexually harassing other employees?

Discrimination Based on Race, Color, National Origin

The legal doctrines of discrimination because of disparate treatment or disparate impact also apply to the protected classes of race, color, and national origin. Of course, ethnic minorities have been discriminated against for decades. But what if the alleged discrimination based on race is "reverse discrimination" (e.g., discriminating

against white males)? Consider the United States Supreme Court case that follows (Illustrative Court Case 32.2).

What Do You Think?

Are exams a fair way to determine promotions? What if only members of a particular race or gender pass the exam even though that was not the employer's intention?

Federal law also prohibits discrimination based on race in the formation and enforcement of contracts. This provides another legal avenue for employees who can show that they were discriminated against in a manner relating to an employment contract.

One method of remedying past racial and gender discrimination is **affirmative action** programs. Affirmative action is the concept that people in protected classes ought to be strongly considered

Ricci v. DeStefano

Supreme Court of the United States

129 S. Ct. 2658 (2009)

[**Note:** For convenience of the reader, the following language is from the Syllabus of the case as provided by the U.S. Supreme Court Reporter of Decisions.]

New Haven, Conn. (City), uses objective examinations to identify those firefighters best qualified for promotion. When the results of such an exam to fill vacant lieutenant and captain positions showed that white candidates had outperformed minority candidates, a rancorous public debate ensued. Confronted with arguments both for and against certifying the test results—and threats of a lawsuit either way—the City threw out the results based on the statistical racial disparity. Petitioners, white and Hispanic firefighters who passed the exams but were denied a chance at promotions by the City's refusal to certify the test results, sued the City and respondent officials, alleging that discarding the test results discriminated against them based on their race in violation of, *inter alia*, Title VII of the Civil Rights Act of 1964. The defendants responded that had they certified the test results, they could have faced Title VII liability for adopting a practice having a disparate impact on minority firefighters. The District Court granted summary judgment for the defendants, and the Second Circuit affirmed.

Held: The City's action in discarding the tests violated Title VII.

(a) Title VII prohibits intentional acts of employment discrimination based on race, color, religion, sex, and national origin, . . . (disparate treatment), as well as policies or practices that are not intended to discriminate but in fact have a disproportionately adverse effect on minorities, . . . (disparate impact). Once a plaintiff has established a prima facie case of disparate impact, the employer may defend by demonstrating that its policy or practice is "job related for the position in question and consistent with business necessity." [Citation omitted.] If the employer meets that burden, the plaintiff may still succeed by showing that the employer refuses to adopt an available alternative practice that has less disparate impact and serves the employer's legitimate needs.

(b) Under Title VII, before an employer can engage in intentional discrimination for the asserted purpose of avoiding or remedying an unintentional, disparate impact, the employer must have a strong basis in evidence to believe it will be subject to disparate-impact liability if it fails to take the race-conscious, discriminatory action. The Court's analysis begins with the premise that the City's actions would violate Title VII's disparate-treatment prohibition absent some valid defense. All the evidence demonstrates that the City rejected the test results because the higher scoring candidates were white. Without some other justification, this express, race-based decisionmaking is prohibited. The question, therefore, is whether the purpose to avoid disparate-impact liability excuses what otherwise would be prohibited disparate-treatment discrimination. The Court has considered cases similar to the present litigation, but in the context of the Fourteenth Amendment's Equal Protection Clause. . . . In those cases, the Court held that certain government actions to remedy past racial discrimination—actions that are themselves based on race—are constitutional only where there is a "strong basis in evidence" that the remedial actions were necessary. [Citations omitted.] In announcing the strong-basis-in-evidence standard, the [Court previously] recognized the tension between eliminating segregation and discrimination on the one hand and doing away with all governmentally imposed discrimination based on race on the other. [Citation omitted.] It reasoned that "[e]videntiary support for the conclusion that remedial action is warranted becomes crucial when the remedial program is challenged in court by nonminority employees." [Citation omitted.] The same

(Continued)

interests are at work in the interplay between Title VII's disparate-treatment and disparate-impact provisions. Applying the strong-basis-in-evidence standard to Title VII gives effect to both provisions, allowing violations of one in the name of compliance with the other only in certain, narrow circumstances. It also allows the disparate-impact prohibition to work in a manner that is consistent with other Title VII provisions, including the prohibition on adjusting employment-related test scores based on race. . . . Thus, the Court adopts the strong-basis-in-evidence standard as a matter of statutory construction in order to resolve any conflict between Title VII's disparate-treatment and disparate-impact provisions.

(c) The City's race-based rejection of the test results cannot satisfy the strong-basis-in-evidence standard.

(i) The racial adverse impact in this litigation was significant, and petitioners do not dispute that the City was faced with a prima facie case of disparate-impact liability. The problem for respondents is that such a prima facie case—essentially, a threshold showing of a significant statistical disparity . . . and nothing more—is far from a strong basis in evidence that the City would have been liable under Title VII had it certified the test results. That is because the City could be liable for disparate-impact discrimination only if the exams at issue were not job related and consistent with business necessity, or if there existed an equally valid, less discriminatory alternative that served the City's needs but that the City refused to adopt. Based on the record the parties developed through discovery, there is no substantial basis in evidence that the test was deficient in either respect.

(ii) The City's assertions that the exams at issue were not job related and consistent with business necessity are blatantly contradicted by the record, which demonstrates the detailed steps taken to develop and administer the tests and the painstaking analyses of the questions asked to assure their relevance to the captain and lieutenant positions. The testimony also shows that complaints that certain examination questions were contradictory or did not specifically apply to firefighting practices in the City were fully addressed, and that the City turned a blind eye to evidence supporting the exams' validity.

(iii) Respondents also lack a strong basis in evidence showing an equally valid, less discriminatory testing alternative that the City, by certifying the test results, would necessarily have refused to adopt. Respondents' three arguments to the contrary all fail. First, respondents refer to testimony that a different composite-score calculation would have allowed the City to consider black candidates for then-open positions, but they have produced no evidence to show that the candidate weighting actually used was indeed arbitrary, or that the different weighting would be an equally valid way to determine whether candidates are qualified for promotions. Second, respondents argue that the City could have adopted a different interpretation of its charter provision limiting promotions to the highest scoring applicants, and that the interpretation would have produced less discriminatory results; but respondents' approach would have violated Title VII's prohibition of race-based adjustment of test results. Third, testimony asserting that the use of an assessment center to evaluate candidates' behavior in typical job tasks would have had less adverse impact than written exams does not aid respondents, as it is contradicted by other statements in the record indicating that the City could not have used assessment centers for the exams at issue. Especially when it is noted that the strong-basis-in-evidence standard applies to this case, respondents cannot create a genuine issue of fact based on a few stray (and contradictory) statements in the record.

(iv) Fear of litigation alone cannot justify the City's reliance on race to the detriment of individuals who passed the examinations and qualified for promotions. Discarding the test results was impermissible under Title VII, and summary judgment is appropriate for petitioners on their disparate-treatment claim. If, after it certifies the test results, the City faces a disparate-impact suit, then in light of today's holding the City can avoid disparate-impact liability based on the strong basis in evidence that, had it not certified the results, it would have been subject to disparate-treatment liability.

based upon their protected class status. Recent court decisions have held that affirmative action programs are acceptable if there is no "quota" in place. Nevertheless, race or gender, can be taken into consideration as one factor among many factors (*e.g.*, or in other words, a 'positive' factor, but not the 'only' factor).

Discrimination Based on Religion

The Civil Rights Act of 1964 also prohibits employment discrimination based on religion. Can you fire an employee for his or her refusal to work on a religious holiday? What if an employee demands time off to pray on particular days or at particular times of each day?

DPiX Center/Shutterstock.com

Of course, these issues can be sensitive too. As a fundamental rule, an employer must "reasonably accommodate" an employee's religious practices unless the employee's religious practices would constitute an "undue hardship" on the employer. In other words, an employer should be flexible and perhaps a little creative to accommodate an employee's sincerely held religious beliefs. If not, the employer should be able to demonstrate reasons why such accommodation would be an undue hardship.

Equal Pay Act

To address gender discrimination related to compensation, Congress passed the **Equal Pay Act** in 1963. Basically, the Equal Pay Act requires employers to compensate both men and women in a similar manner for similar working conditions, skill, effort and responsibility. Of course, the law allows difference in pay if the difference is not based on gender. For example, differences in pay are allowed if based on shift differential, seniority, merit systems, production, etc.

An Employer's Defenses to Discrimination Claims

Employers have a few defenses to employment discrimination claims. For example, what if a filmmaker is producing a documentary based on early Native American life and the lead role is for a Native American? Clearly, the filmmaker can limit the potential applicants for the acting job to Native Americans. An employer's defenses include (1) business necessity, (2) bona fide occupational qualifications, and (3) seniority systems.

Business Necessity

An employer can defend against a claim of disparate impact discrimination (*i.e.*, unintentional discrimination) by arguing that the action taken was a business necessity. Suppose the employer states that as part of the requirement for a job, an applicant must have a bachelor's degree. Suppose then that it turns out that 45 of the 50 applicants are of one particular race. An employer must be able to show that a bachelor's degree is legitimately necessary for the job in question. If the employer can do this, then the "business necessity" defense may prevail.

Bona Fide Occupational Qualification

In some situations, an employer, for example, may only want to hire females. Although this appears discriminatory on its face, perhaps the employer's business is a lingerie store, or a women's-only fitness club. Thus, the law recognizes that it may be inappropriate for a male to be hired in a women's lingerie store. Nevertheless, the employer must be able to show that being female is reasonably necessary to meet the job requirements. This **bona fide occupational qualification** (BFOQ) defense is only available for situations involving gender or religion, but not race, color, or national origin.

Seniority Systems

Promotions based on seniority have survived court scrutiny if there is no intention to discriminate. Consequently, it is generally acceptable for a promotion system to advance employees who have been with the employer the longest.

QUESTIONS FOR REVIEW

1. What is the role of the Equal Employment Opportunity Commission?

2. Explain generally what Title VII of the Civil Rights Act of 1964 provides.

3. What is the difference between disparate treatment discrimination and disparate impact discrimination?

4. What is the basic difference between *quid pro quo* sexual harassment and hostile work environment sexual harassment?

5. May an employer set a "quota" of the number of minority employees that should be hired? Why or why not?

6. When may an employer not reasonably accommodate an employee's religious practices?

7. What defenses does an employer have to claims of discrimination? What is a BFOQ?

8. Summarize the *Okoli v. City of Baltimove* case.

9. Summarize the *Ricci v. DeStefano* case.

INTERNET ACTIVITIES

1. Visit the EEOC website at www.eeoc.gov. Click on the "About EEOC" tab, then the "Newsroom" link.

   a. Find a recent release relating to a religious discrimination claim. Who was the employer? Summarize the complaint.

   b. Find a recent release relating to a sex discrimination or sexual harassment claim. Who was the employer? Summarize the complaint.

2. Visit the EEOC website at www.eeoc.gov. Click on the "Employees & Applicants" tab. Then click on the link regarding "How to File" a charge of discrimination. Summarize the process how someone files a charge of discrimination with the EEOC.

Chapter 33

Employment Discrimination Based on Age and Disability

In addition to discrimination based on race, color, national origin, gender, and religion (discussed in Chapter 32), federal law prohibits discrimination based on age and disability.

Age Discrimination

To combat employers discriminating based on age, Congress passed the **Age Discrimination in Employment Act** (ADEA). Consider the section of the ADEA that follows (Illustrative Federal Statute 33.1).

The law only applies to age discrimination against individuals who are 40 years-old or older. Also, the Act applies only to employers that have at least 20 employees. Remember, state laws may

ilkercelik/Shutterstock.com

supplement federal law to fill in the gaps (*e.g.*, age discrimination laws applicable to smaller employers).

ILLUSTRATIVE FEDERAL STATUTE 33.1

29 U.S.C. § 623

§ 623. Prohibition of age discrimination

(a) Employer practices. It shall be unlawful for an employer—

1. to fail or refuse to hire or to discharge any individual or otherwise discriminate against any individual with respect to his compensation, terms, conditions, or privileges of employment, because of such individual's age;

2. to limit, segregate, or classify his employees in any way which would deprive or tend to deprive any individual of employment opportunities or otherwise adversely affect his status as an employee, because of such individual's age; or

3. to reduce the wage rate of any employee in order to comply with this Act.

. . .

Cortez v. Wal-Mart Stores, Inc.

Court of Appealas for the Tenth Circuit

460 F.3d 1268 (2006)

OPINION

MURPHY, Circuit Judge.

Plaintiff Robert Cortez sued defendant Sam's Club for discrimination in violation of the Age Discrimination in Employment Act (ADEA), on account of the company's failure to promote him to the position of general manager. During the trial, the district court twice denied Sam's Club's motions for judgment as a matter of law . . ., and the case went to the jury. The jury found that Sam's Club had violated the ADEA and awarded damages to Cortez. . . . [W]e affirm.

BACKGROUND

Cortez worked for Sam's Club from April 28, 1986, to April 29, 2003. On the day he resigned, he was 48 years old and had been an assistant manager of several Sam's Club stores in Texas and New Mexico. The highest level that he reached in the company was the position of co-general manager of a store in Puerto Rico, where he worked from 1996 to 1998. When Cortez returned to the United States from his Puerto Rico assignment, he let it be known generally throughout the company that he wished to be promoted to general manager. He specifically asked Carlos Doubleday, the director of operations for Sam's Club stores in El Paso and Albuquerque, if any general manager positions were available in his region. Doubleday told him there were not. Accordingly, Cortez accepted a demotion and took a position as assistant manager of a store in El Paso.

From 1998 until his resignation in 2003, Cortez continued to press for promotions that never materialized. During that same time period, however, at least three other Sam's Club assistant managers were promoted to general manager positions in Texas and New Mexico. Two of those promoted were in their early 30's and the other was in his late 20's. Cortez told several executives in the company that he was concerned that he was being passed over because of his age. However, only one, Stephanie Sallinger, the personnel manager, ever followed up with him. When she did, she was under the apparently mistaken impression that a promotion for Cortez was imminent.

On October 30, 2003, Cortez filed a complaint against Sam's Club under the ADEA alleging that despite his qualifications Sam's Club consistently failed to promote him because of his age. He also alleged that he had filed a charge of discrimination with the Equal Employment Opportunity Commission (EEOC) on or about June 11, 2003, and had received a right-to-sue letter on or about August 4, 2003, within 90 days of filing his district court complaint. In its answer, Sam's Club denied that it had discriminated against Cortez . . .

The case was tried [by] a jury in February 2005. At trial, Cortez argued that although he was qualified for the position of general manager, Sam's Club consistently denied him promotional opportunities in favor of younger employees, many of whom he had helped to train. With respect to his qualifications, Cortez argued that his long years of assistant managerial experience taught him the requisite skills to be a general manager. He also argued that he had already demonstrated his ability to be a general manager in his position as co-general manager of the store in Puerto Rico. In addition, he adduced evidence of his laudable role in opening a new store in Albuquerque in record time for the company.

. . .

Sam's Club argued that Cortez was not promoted not because of his age, but because of the active performance "coaching" in his file, in accordance with its "Coaching for Improvement" policy.

According to the *Club Manual*, "Coaching for Improvement occurs when an Associate's behavior (job performance or misconduct) fails to meet the Company's expectations." The manual goes on to explain that coaching for job performance is appropriate when an associate's behavior "does not meet the reasonable expectations/standards set for all Associates in the same or similar position." Misconduct is defined as "behavior other than job performance, which falls below stated expectations, or violates Company policy, does or may interfere with safe, orderly, or efficient operations or which creates a hostile or offensive environment for Associates, Customers, and/or Vendors." The Coaching for Improvement section of the *Club Manual* also has a subheading entitled "File Retention/Active Period." That section provides that "Coaching for Improvement documentation must be maintained in the Associate's personnel file for 12 months under an 'active' status. Twelve months after the last Coaching for Improvement session, if the behavior does not reoccur, the Coaching for Improvement documentation becomes 'inactive'."

. . .

At the close of evidence, the jury was instructed that in order to find for Cortez on the age discrimination claim, it would have to find that Cortez proved the following elements by a preponderance of the evidence: (1) that he was at least 40 years of age at the time he was denied a promotion; (2) that he applied for or sought an available promotion, and was qualified for that position; (3) that, despite his qualifications, he was not promoted to the position; and (4) that his age was a motivating factor or determining factor in Sam's Club's decision not to promote him. . . .

DISCUSSION

. . .

II. Legal Framework

The ADEA makes it unlawful for an employer to "discriminate against any individual with respect to his compensation, terms, conditions, or privileges of employment, because of such individual's age." [Citation omitted.] In disparate treatment cases such as this, where the plaintiff alleges that he was singled out for discrimination, "liability depends on whether the protected trait (under the ADEA, age) actually motivated the employer's decision. That is, the plaintiff's age must have actually played a role in the employer's decisionmaking process and had a determinative influence on the outcome." [Citation omitted.] . . .

We have traditionally distinguished between employment decisions based on objective criteria, which are generally immune to employer manipulation, and those based on subjective criteria, "which are particularly easy for an employer to invent in an effort to sabotage a plaintiff's prima facie case and mask discrimination." [Citation omitted.]. . . .

III. The No-Coaching Qualification

It is undisputed that Cortez received a written coaching on April 2, 2001, and Cortez admitted that Sam's Club has a policy with respect to promotions whereby employees are not eligible for a promotion within one year of receiving a written coaching. The question, therefore, is whether this no-coaching qualification is a truly objective criterion, such that Cortez's failure to establish it defeated his prima facie case. Sam's Club maintains that its no-coaching qualification is an objective measure that forms part of its promotion criteria. . . .

(Continued)

Certainly, as Sam's Club argues, the question of whether an employee has an active coaching in his file can be objectively answered. The problem, however, is that the coaching itself can be premised on almost limitless subjective bases, and in that regard it is only facially objective. . . .

IV. Sufficiency of the Evidence

Within this legal framework, we must now decide whether the evidence supported the jury's finding of discrimination, keeping in mind that "it is not the function of the appeals court to reverse merely if it believes the evidence might have supported a different verdict." [Citation omitted.] Unless Sam's Club can show that there is no evidentiary basis to support the verdict, we will not disturb the jury's determination, "even where there is substantial contradictory evidence that could have supported an opposite verdict." Sam's Club has not made such a showing.

At trial, Cortez presented evidence that he had more than ten years of assistant managerial experience at Sam's Club and that he had earned accolades for his leadership in opening a new store in Albuquerque during the same time period that he was seeking a promotion. He was also the co-general manager of a Sam's Club store in Puerto Rico for three years where he shared responsibility with the general manager for the entire store's operations. He also testified that he lost out on promotions even as he was receiving above-average performance ratings. Sam's Club challenged Cortez's qualifications. It adduced evidence that Cortez had received declining performance evaluations and written coachings during the relevant time period and that certain of Cortez's managers had not recommended him for promotion. Viewed in the light most favorable to Cortez, however, we conclude that the evidence could have convinced a rational jury that Cortez was objectively qualified to be a general manager. This evidence, combined with the relatively young age of the individuals who received the challenged promotions was sufficient to establish a prima facie case of discrimination.

. . .

The judgment of the district court is AFFIRMED.

Consider the *Cortez v. Wal-Mart Stores, Inc.* court case from the United States Court of Appeals for the Tenth Circuit (Illustrative Court Case 33.1).

What Do You Think?

Why would Congress choose the age of 40 as the time when an employee should be protected from age discrimination?

As a general rule, if an employee believes they have been discriminated against, the process is similar to the procedures for claims under Title VII (discussed in Chapter 32). In short, the plaintiff must show a prima facie case that adverse action occurred based upon the plaintiff's age. If the employee meets this burden, then the burden shifts to the employer to show that the reason for the adverse action against the employee was not on account of age. If the employer meets this burden, then the burden shifts back to the employee to show notwithstanding the employer's stated reasons for the adverse action, age discrimination nevertheless occurred.

Disability Discrimination

To yet again fight discrimination by employers, Congress passed the **Americans with Disabilities Act (ADA)**. Of course, one issue that is often debated is what constitutes a **disability**. The term as it is intended to mean in the ADA is very broad in scope. A disability is basically any "mental or physical impairment that substantially limits one or more major life activities." Examples of disabilities include, but are not limited to, muscular dystrophy, heart disease, cancer, cerebral palsy, diabetes, AIDS, and even morbid obesity and alcoholism. If the disability can be corrected (*e.g.*, poor eyesight), then the condition is not considered a disability.

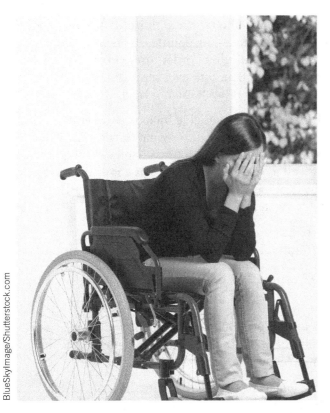
Employees and employers obviously should communicate clearly when dealing with disabilities and related leaves of absence that may be a result of a disability.

As a broad, general rule, an employer must "reasonably accommodate" an employee with a disability unless the accommodation would constitute an "undue hardship" on the employer.

Of course, in addition to not discriminating against employees, businesses also must not discriminate against customers with disabilities. This means, as a general rule, that the business must be wheelchair accessible, no artificial barriers are in place, the restrooms must be useable and accessible to people with disabilities, etc. Consider the Ninth Circuit Court of Appeals case that follows (Illustrative Court Case 33.2).

Employer Defenses

With regard to age and disability discrimination claims, employers have the defenses of business necessity, bona fide occupation qualification, seniority systems, that were discussed in Chapter 32. With regard to discrimination issues, an employer should be able to document through an employee's file over time that any adverse action taken against an employee was not based upon age, disability, or the other "protected classes"

ILLUSTRATIVE COURT CASE 33.2

Antoninetti v. Chipotle Mexican Grill, Inc.

United States Court of Appeals for the Ninth Circuit

643 F.3d 1165 (2010)

FRIEDMAN, Circuit Judge:

This case presents several issues involving the application of the Americans with Disabilities Act ("Disabilities Act" or "Act") to a wheelchair-bound customer of the well-known Mexican fast-food restaurants operated by Chipotle Mexican Grill, Inc. ("Chipotle"). The question on the merits is whether the actions Chipotle took to accommodate the customer's disability satisfied the requirements of the Act and its implementing guidelines. We hold that they did not and accordingly that Chipotle violated the Act. . . .

I.

A. The case arises out of visits by the appellant, Maurizio Antoninetti, to two Chipotle restaurants in California, one in San Diego and one in Encinitas. Antoninetti is a paraplegic who uses a wheelchair for mobility. He visited the San Diego restaurant six times, four times as a customer and twice to gather evidence for this litigation. He visited the Encinitas restaurant twice, once as a customer and once in connection with discovery proceedings in this case.

(Continued)

The physical arrangements of the two restaurants were, insofar as the issues in this case are involved, substantially the same. Customers walk along a line that is next to a long counter containing the different foods that are available and on which the customers' individual orders are prepared. The customers' walking line is separated from this "food preparation counter" by a separator wall. This wall rises 45 inches above the floor; the food preparation counter is 34-35 inches high.

As customers proceed through the line, they see the different foods available by looking over the wall, and they tell the food service employees behind the food preparation counter what they want. There are many kinds of foods available—such as salsa, guacamole, cheese, and lettuce—and each ingredient is described on written menus in the restaurant as well as on large menu boards above the food preparation counter. The employees then assemble the customer's order—customizing the burrito, taco, or other Mexican food selected—while the customer watches.

At the end of the food preparation counter is a 4 foot-long counter containing the cash register and a 2-3 foot-long empty space. This counter, called the "transaction station," is 34 inches high, and is where the customer pays for and receives the order. The wall ends where this counter begins. Beyond the transaction station is a dining room with fixed seating, which customers may use after receiving their order.

The parties stipulated that the average eye level of persons in wheelchairs is 43 to 51 inches above the restaurant floor; and that, at a distance of 12 inches from the wall, a person at any height within that average range cannot see the food preparation counter or the food on display there.

According to Chipotle, it "strives to offer a unique experience consisting of the architecture, décor, and music of its restaurants, the aroma of the food, the appearance of a customer's entrée, friendly staff, a tradition of excellent customer service, [the] ability to customize one's entrée, and . . . the taste of the food." It describes this as the "Chipotle experience."

Prior to this litigation, Chipotle had an unwritten policy of accommodating customers in wheelchairs who wanted to see the available food ingredients or watch the preparation of their food. When customers in wheelchairs so indicated, employees were required to show them samples of the available foods in serving spoons, held in tongs or in plastic portion cups, or to assemble the food either at the "transaction station" or at a table in the restaurant's seating area.

In February 2007, because of this litigation, Chipotle adopted its written "Customers With Disabilities Policy" (the "written policy"). This policy provides that "the restaurant staff will offer . . . [a] customer with a disability (for example, a visual or mobility impairment) a suitable accommodation based on the individual circumstances, and will be responsive to the customer's requests. . . .

II

Title III of the Disabilities Act requires that "public accommodations' built for first occupancy after January 26, 1993, be "readily accessible to and usable by individuals with disabilities." [Citation omitted.] To satisfy this standard, "[n]ew construction and alterations . . . [must] comply with the standards for accessible design" promulgated by the Attorney General of the United States. [Citation omitted.] The Attorney General has issued detailed, primarily architectural, standards—known as the Guidelines—that govern the applicability of the Acct to a variety of public accommodations. Failure to comply with the Guidelines constitutes prohibited "discrimination for the purposes of the Disabilities Act. [Citation omitted.] The parties do not dispute that the two Chipotle restaurants are places of public accommodation, built after January 26, 1993, and therefore must comply with the Guidelines. Not surprisingly, the parties disagree about which Guideline governs this case.

A. Antoninetti argues that Guideline §4.33.3 applies to Chipotle's food preparation counters. That Guideline provides, in pertinent part:

"Placement of Wheelchair Locations. Wheelchair areas shall be an integral part of any fixed seating plan and shall be provided so as to provide people with physical disabilities a choice of admission prices and lines of sight comparable to those for members of the general public. They shall adjoin an accessible route that also serves as a means of egress in case of emergency. At least one companion fixed seat shall be provided next to each wheelchair seating area. When the seating capacity exceeds 300, wheelchair spaces shall be provided in more than one location. Readily removable seats may be installed in wheelchair spaces when the spaces are not required to accommodate wheelchair users."

. . .

B. Chipotle argues, and the district court held, that Guideline §7.2 provides the governing standard here. That Guideline, titled "Sales and Service Counters, Teller Windows, Information Counters," . . . provides:

"At ticketing counters, teller stations in a bank, registration counters in hotels and motels, box office ticket counters, and other counters that may not have a cash register but at which goods or services are sold or distributed, either:

(i) a portion of the main counter which is a minimum of 36 [inches] . . . in length shall be provided with a maximum height of 36 [inches] . . . or

(ii) an auxiliary counter with a maximum height of 36 [inches] . . . in close proximity to the main counter shall be provided; . . ."

We agree with the district court that this provision applies. The food service areas of the two restaurants are "counters" and the preparation of the customers' food orders is the sale and distribution of "goods or services." The "goods are the food itself, and the "services" are the preparation of the meal the customer orders.

C. The next question is whether the two restaurants comply with that Guideline, which includes the requirement that "a portion of the main counter" have "a maximum height" of 36 inches. Chipotle contends that this requirement is satisfied because the food preparation counter adjoins the transact-t5ion station, which is 34 inches high, and therefore that either a "portion of the main counter" or an "auxiliary counter' is below the 36 inch maximum height. The district court properly rejected this argument.

. . .

IV

Under the Disabilities Act, "the court . . . in its discretion, may allow the prevailing party . . . a reasonable attorney's fee, including litigation expenses, and costs." [Citation omitted.]

. . .

Antoninetti sought attorney's fees of $546,151.33. Because of his limited success, the court "FOUND that the plaintiff is entitled to one-quarter of the attorneys' fees that he has requested," and awarded him $136,537.83.

The results of this litigation are now quite different than they were when the district court made that award. Under our decision today, Antoninetti has prevailed on the two major issues that he lost before the district court. We have held that Chipotle's treatment of him in the two restaurants violated the Disabilities act, and that the district court must provide injunctive relief.

In light of this changed outcome, the district court should reexamine and reconsider its attorney's fee award. We express no view on what would be a reasonable fee in light of the changed circumstances. That determination is one that initially is for the informed discretion of the district court.

(*Continued*)

V.

. . .

CONCLUSION

The judgment of the district court is affirmed insofar as it ruled that Chipotle's unwritten earlier policy violated the Disabilities Act. The portions of the judgment determining that Chipotle's written policy did not violate the Act and that Antoninetti was not entitled to an injunction are reversed, and the case is remanded to the district court to enter a judgment that Chipotle violated the Disabilities Act and to issue appropriate injunctive relief. The portions of the judgment that awarded an attorney's fee of $136,537.83 and awarded damages of $5,000 under the California Act are vacated and the case is remanded for the district court to reconsider those issues.

discussed in Chapter 32. Rather, any adverse action should be based on qualifications, job performance evaluations, seniority, etc.

QUESTIONS FOR REVIEW

1. What is the ADEA?

2. At what age does the ADEA protect an employee from age discrimination?

3. What is the ADA?

4. Explain what a "disability" is for purposes of the ADA.

5. Summarize the *Cortez v. Wal-Mart* case.

6. Summarize the *Antoninetti v. Chipotle Mexican Grill* case.

INTERNET ACTIVITIES

1. Visit the EEOC website at www.eeoc.gov. Click on the "About EEOC" tab, then the "Newsroom" link. Find a recent release relating to an age discrimination claim. Who was the employer? Summarize the complaint.

2. Visit the EEOC website at www.eeoc.gov. Click on the "About EEOC" tab, then the "Newsroom" link. Find a recent release relating to a disability discrimination claim. Who was the employer? Summarize the complaint.

Part XII

Rights of Creditors, Secured Transactions, and Bankruptcy Law

Chapter 34

Rights of Creditors

What rights does a creditor have if a debtor fails or refuses to pay a legitimate debt? This chapter and Chapter 35 discuss this issue. A discussion of bankruptcy is reserved for Chapter 36.

Credit in General

The ability to borrow money often can facilitate a person's or business's objectives. For example, perhaps you have borrowed some money in order to pay for tuition and books or some other related expenses concerning your education. A business may wish to expand or acquire another business and may borrow some money in order to accomplish that objective.

The lender is called the **creditor**. The borrower, of course, is called the **debtor**. A creditor lends the money generally either on a secured basis or unsecured basis. A debt is **secured** if the creditor can repossess specific assets of the debtor if the debtor fails to pay. A debt is **unsecured** if the creditor only has a general claim against the debtor, but has no ability to repossess a specific asset.

Various processes are in place for a creditor to obtain a secured interest in debtor property. Chapter 35 covers secured transactions in more detail, but we will discuss the basic rights of creditors here.

Liens

Suppose you are a roofer and install shingles on homes. When a home is constructed, the homeowner typically does not pay every contractor separately. Rather, the homeowner typically will pay the general contractor and the general contractor will pay the subcontractors. Since, as a roofer, you would likely be a subcontractor, what can you do if you do not get paid for your roofing services by the general contractor? Can you try to recover payment from the homeowner? What if the homeowner has already paid the general contractor?

One common approach to protect service providers that fix or make improvements to property is for the service provider to place a **lien** on the property. By placing a lien on the property, this indicates that the **lienholder** claims that they still have been unpaid for certain work. Thus, if the property owner wants to sell the property, the property owner will have to pay the lienholder to get the lien **released**. The lien provides security for the service provider. Liens of the type just discussed (*i.e.*, liens placed on real property by a service provider who made the improvements) are called **mechanic's liens**. Note that this term can be misleading because the lien is placed on real property and is not limited to "mechanics" as that term is most commonly used. Mechanic's liens are usually filed with a government agency at the state or local level, and the fact that a property is subject to a mechanic's lien is public information. Consider the following case relating to mechanics' liens (Illustrative Court Case 34.1).

Other types of liens include artisan's liens and judicial liens. An **artisan's lien** typically arises in situations involving property other than real property (*i.e.*, personal property). Suppose, for example, that you take your bicycle to be fixed at a bicycle repair shop. You leave your bicycle there for a few hours and come back to pick it up. The bicycle shop indicates that the repair charge is $50. What if you do not pay the $50 bill? Can the bicycle repair shop refuse to return your bike? As a general rule, the common law gives an artisan's lien to the bicycle shop and the bicycle shop can retain your bike until you pay the bill. Sometimes the terms "mechanic's lien" and "artisan's lien" get used interchangeably, however, A **judicial lien** can be placed on property of a person who loses a court case. At the request of the creditor, the judge can place a lien on the debtor's property so as to protect the court's monetary award to the creditor. Moreover, the judge can ultimately order the sheriff to seize the debtor's property that is subject to the judicial lien in order to satisfy the creditor's claims.

Mortgages and Deeds of Trust

A creditor who loans money to someone in order to purchase or build on real property will likely require the borrower to sign a **mortgage** document. The lender/creditor is sometimes

ILLUSTRATIVE COURT CASE 34.1

Thigpen v. Father & Sons Home Improvement II, Inc.

United States Bankruptcy Court for the Northern District of Illinois, Eastern Division

2014 Bankr. LEXIS 1127 (2014)

OPINION

The debtors, Phillip and Paula Thigpen, brought this adversary proceeding seeking to "strip off" a mechanic's lien filed against their home by Father & Sons Home Improvement II, Inc. They allege that their mortgage lender has a higher priority lien and that there is no collateral value to support Father & Sons' mechanic's lien. Father & Sons filed a motion for summary judgment, arguing that its mechanic's lien has first priority to the extent of the value of the improvements it made to the debtors' property. It therefore contends that its lien is supported by collateral value and cannot be "stripped off" in a chapter 13 [bankruptcy] plan. Father & Sons is correct. Its motion for summary judgment will be granted.

Background and Undisputed Facts

Father & Sons built a second floor addition on the debtors' home in 2009 for a cost of approximately $184,000. It properly perfected its mechanic's lien. U.S. Bank Home Mortgage holds a mortgage lien that was filed before the mechanic's lien. U.S. Bank is owed approximately $235,000. The debtors contend that their home is now worth only $126,000. They argue that U.S. Bank's lien has higher priority than Father & Sons' lien because it was filed first. The debtors therefore seek to "strip off" the Father & Sons' mechanic's lien – meaning treat it as wholly unsecured – because there is no collateral value to support its lower priority lien.

Father & Sons moved for summary judgment, arguing that it has a first priority lien under the Illinois Mechanic's Lien Act ("Act") to the extent of the value of the improvements it made to the debtors' home. It therefore contends there is collateral value to support its lien, so it cannot be "stripped off" and paid as an unsecured claim.

The debtors do not contest the validity of Father & Sons' mechanic's lien; they contest its priority. They argue that the Act does not give a mechanic's lien claimant a first priority lien, but instead grants only the right to receive payment in the event of a sale. There will be no sale in this chapter 13 case, so the debtors contend that the Acct does not give Father & Sons priority over U.S. Bank.

. . .

Priority Under the Illinois Mechanic's Lien Act

The Act determines the priority of the liens against the debtors' property in this case. Section 16 of the Act provides that a lien created by the Act must be satisfied before any other lien, filed before or after the mechanic's lien, has been satisfied. . . . It further provides that, when the proceeds of sale are insufficient to pay all lien holders, previous lien holders have priority over mechanic's lien holders only to the extent of the value of the property before the improvements were made, while mechanic's lien holders have priority for the value they added to the property. . . .

The debtors . . . assert that the general rule of first-in-time, first-in-right applies to give U.S. Bank the first priority lien on the property, leaving Father & Sons with no collateral value to support its mechanic's lien.

. . .

Father & Sons has a first priority lien under the Act to the extent of the value of the improvements it made to the debtors' home. While the parties dispute the actual value of the home, there is no doubt that Father & Sons added significant value to the home by adding an entire second floor. It holds a first priority lien to the extent of the value of this addition, which provides collateral value for its lien. Its lien, therefore, cannot be stripped off in the debtors' chapter 13 plan. Instead, under [Illinois law], the debtors must pay Father & Sons the allowed amount of the secured claim, which is the value added to the home by Father & Sons . . . .

The court need not determine in this adversary proceeding the value of the collateral supporting Father & Son's first priority lien. The debtors sought in their complaint only to strip off the lien as wholly unsecured. Based on the undisputed facts and Illinois law, there is collateral value supporting Father & Sons' lien so it cannot be stripped off. Father & Sons is therefore entitled to summary judgment.

Conclusion

Father & Sons' motion for summary judgment is granted. It has a first priority lien on the debtors' property to the extent of the value it added to the home. The debtors may not "strip off" this first-priority lien and treat it as an unsecured claim.

called the **mortgagee** and the borrower/debtor is the **mortgagor**. A mortgage basically gives the creditor a lien on the borrower's property that the borrower obtains with the loan proceeds. Creditors will also document their mortgage interest in the property by filing the mortgage with the local county recorder's office. If a debtor fails to pay the mortgage, the creditor can **foreclose** on the property typically through the courts. A debtor usually has a **right of redemption** before the property is sold at a foreclosure sale, but in order to successfully assert this right of redemption, the debtor has to satisfy the original debt, pay applicable interest, and certain other fees the creditor may have incurred in the foreclosure process. Ultimately, if the creditor's attempt to foreclose is successful, the creditor becomes the owner of the property.

A borrowing arrangement somewhat similar to a mortgage is a **deed of trust** (or sometimes called a **trust deed**). Some states use the deed of trust method of granting the creditor a security interest in the property rather than through the mortgage process. In a deed of trust arrangement, the lender is the **beneficiary** of a trust that is created when the money is borrowed. The borrower is the **trustor**, and a **trustee** becomes involved if the creditor is not paid and the creditor wishes to initiate the foreclosure process. Some advantages and disadvantages accompany the deed of trust arrangement as compared to a mortgage, but such detailed explanation is beyond the scope of our

Terrance Emerson/Shutterstock.com

discussion here.

Suretyship and Guaranty

In situations where a creditor determines that the borrower may not quite qualify financially for a loan, the creditor may ask the borrower to find someone else (*i.e.*, a third party) who can "co-sign" for the loan. Technically, two different arrangements can be made with respect to the co-signer. The first arrangement is a **suretyship**. This is an arrangement where the creditor enters into a direct contract with the third party wherein the third party is also *primarily* liable for the debt along with the debtor. Thus, the creditor could attempt to collect the debt directly from the third party (called the **surety**). The second arrangement could be a **guaranty** contract between the creditor and the third party (called the **guarantor**). In this situation, the third party is *secondarily* liable for the debt, and the creditor must first try to collect the debt from the borrower. If the borrower cannot pay, only then does the creditor attempt to collect from the guarantor.

Garnishment

If a creditor wins a judgment against a debtor and the debtor still does not pay, the creditor can seek a **garnishment**. A garnishment is when a judge orders a third party to withhold funds from the debtor and remit those funds to the creditor. The most common form of garnishment is on a debtor's wages. The debtor's employer is ordered to withhold a certain percentage of the debtor's paycheck and remit it to the court or wherever the court orders the employer to send the funds. The garnishment process is governed by state law and thus may vary from state-to-state. The amount that is garnished from the debtor's paycheck is limited by state and federal law and may vary depending on the debtor's personal circumstances. Certain income that the debtor receives may be exempt from being garnished. Consider the following case from the Supreme Court of Vermont relating to garnishments (Illustrative Court Case 34.2).

Cote v. Cote

Supreme Court of Vermont

2011 VT 92 (2011)

OPINION BY: BURGESS

Alan Cote appeals from . . . the Family Court's garnishment order directing the Social Security Administration to withhold defendant's Social Security disability benefits in the amount of $1569 per month to offset alimony arrearages. Husband receives $1569 in Social Security disability and $2721 in veterans' disability benefits each month. He contends the garnishment order violates . . . a provision of the Federal Consumer Credit Protection Act, which imposes a cap on the percentage of aggregate disposable earnings that any court, state or federal, may garnish. While the trial court garnished only husband's Social Security disability benefits and not his veterans' disability benefits, the court did include the latter in its calculation of aggregate disposable earnings. This broad calculation of disposable earning increased the percentage of husband's Social Security payments subject to garnishment. Husband contends that, as defined and excluded from such a calculation by federal law, his particular veterans' disability benefits are not to be counted as earnings because they are not paid for a service related disability and are not received in lieu of retirement payments to which he would otherwise be entitled as earnings. We agree, and so reverse and remand.

In 2000, Carol and Alan Cote divorced. The court's final divorce order directed husband to pay spousal support to wife in the amount of $2000 per month. Husband did not pay the full amount of his support obligation, instead he made partial payments each month while contributing to wife's living expenses by paying some of her rent and mortgage payments, purchasing a vehicle for her, and making payments to a daughter. Husband ceased partial payments in 2008.

Wife filed a motion to enforce the support order. Husband submitted an itemization of his income and expenses indicating income consisting of veterans' disability pay and Social Security disability pay. Husband moved to modify the spousal maintenance award, and requested relief from judgment. The court denied husband's motions and entered an order granting judgment to wife for husband's arrearages in the amount of $95,385.33, together with post-judgment interest at 12% per annum. Despite the court's order, husband made no payments to wife and shortly thereafter ceased making her mortgage payments.

After receiving a foreclosure letter from her mortgagee in 2009, wife filed an emergency motion to enforce the spousal support award asking the court to garnish the entirety of husband's Social Security disability benefits to satisfy the judgment. Husband objected. Citing [federal law], husband argued that wife was entitled to garnish only a fraction of his monthly Social Security disability check. This law limits garnishment to 55% of husband's aggregate disposable income. [Citation omitted]. Husband claimed that [federal law] excluded his veterans' disability benefits from "aggregate disposable earnings" subject to garnishment. Thus, asserted husband, the court could garnish a maximum of $862.95, which is 55% of his Social Security disability income, but not 55% of his total monthly benefits, which include both his Social Security benefits and veterans' disability benefits payments.

In August 2009, the family court granted wife's motion to garnish, noting that "federal statutes authorize garnishment of husband's Social Security disability payments for payment of alimony arrearages." Not persuaded by husband's argument, however, the family court entered a garnishment order requiring the Social Security Administration to withhold 100% of husband's Social Security disability benefits in the amount of $1569 and to forward the payments to wife. In its order the court noted that "the sum of $1569.00 is less than 55% of defendant's aggregate disposable earnings

(Continued)

of $4290.00/mo. The defendant is supporting a spouse." Absent from the court's garnishment order was any mention of husband's veterans' benefits, but these were evidently included in the court's calculation to arrive at its figure for aggregate disposable earnings of $4290 per month. His monthly Social Security benefits are $1569, and his veterans' disability benefits are $2721, which added together total $4290.

On appeal, husband again argues that the garnishment order violates the limits on the total amount of an individual's earnings that may be garnished . . . because the court impermissibly included his veterans' disability benefits as aggregate disposable earnings. Husband notes that federal law restricts garnishment of veterans' disability benefits to only those benefits paid as "remuneration for employment." [Citation omitted.] Husband posits that because his veterans' disability payments are (1) compensation for a non-service-connected disability, and (2) are not received as a substitute for a pension or other post-work benefit based on prior employment, these benefits are not "remuneration for employment" as defined by federal law.

Accordingly, husband maintains, since his veterans' disability benefits are not "remuneration for employment," they cannot be considered "disposable earnings" and should have been excluded from the trial court's aggregate disposable earnings calculation. . . . Husband contends that the family court's inclusion of the veterans' disability benefits incorrectly inflated his disposable income available for garnishment. As a consequence, rather than limiting its garnishment to 55% of husband's aggregate disposable income as represented by his Social Security benefits, the family court garnished 55% of all of those earnings in violation of [federal law].

Husband's argument "presents a pure issue of law which we review de novo." [Citation omitted.] Applying this standard, we hold that federal law precludes the inclusion of non-service-connected veterans' disability benefits not received in lieu of retired or retainer pay in calculating aggregate disposable earnings available for garnishment. The family court's garnishment order was therefore erroneous.

Vermont law . . . does not preclude the trial court's order, but garnishment is limited by federal statute. [Citation omitted.] Congress has established an expansive regulatory scheme dictating how garnishments to enforce a support order must be processed and what moneys may be so diverted. One part of that scheme . . . limits the percentage of an individual's income subject to garnishment. In particular, [federal law] limits the amount of an individual's "aggregate disposable earnings" subject to garnishment to 55%, if the individual being garnished is supporting a spouse and the garnishment is in connection with enforcement of a spousal support order with respect to a period prior to the last earning period. Both parties agree that the court was authorized to garnish husband's Social Security disability benefits and, by extension, count those benefits in the calculation of aggregate disposable earnings under federal garnishment law. [Citation omitted.]

The parties' dispute centers on whether husband's veterans' disability benefits can also be counted as part of his aggregate disposable earnings. According to husband, his veterans' benefits are non-service connected disability pay given as compensation for "injuries and/or diseases that were made worse by his active military service." In addition, husband asserts he did not meet armed forces eligibility requirements for military pension benefits included in "earnings' for purposes of garnishment. [Citation omitted.] Nor did husband waive any such pension pay in order to receive the disability compensation in lieu of earnings. Wife does not dispute these characterizations.

To determine if husband's benefits fall into "aggregate disposable earnings" we look to the applicable federal statutes. For purposes of [federal law], "earnings" are in relevant part defined as "compensation paid or payable for personal services, whether denominated as wages, salary, commission, bonus, or otherwise." [Citation omitted.] "Disposable earnings" are broadly defined as "earnings" less amounts like payroll and withholding taxes that are "required by law to be withheld." [Citation omitted.]

Military pensions and other veterans' benefits are included in "earnings." As part of the Child Support Enforcement Act of 1975 (CSEA), which amended the Social Security act to enforce "support obligations owed by absent parents to their children," . . ., Congress authorized garnishment of moneys "due from, or payable by, the United States . . . to any individual, including members of the Armed Forces," for the purposes of enforcing an individual's "legal obligation . . . to provide . . . alimony." [Citation omitted.] The United States Code . . . lists specific forms of moneys due from or payable by the United States that are subject to garnishment process, including service-connected disability benefits paid by the Veterans Administration to a former serviceman, but only to the extent the veteran waives military pension pay to receive the disability payments instead. [Citation omitted.] All such benefits are considered to be "remuneration for employment." [Citation omitted.]

As observed by husband, however. [Federal law] clarifies that all other veterans' benefits are not "remuneration for employment" and thus not garnishable. . . .

. . .

Husband's veterans' disability benefits are not remuneration for employment and may not be included in calculating the portion of his aggregate disposable earnings available for garnishment under [federal law]. The family court may include husband's Social Security disability benefits and any other eligible income. The court may not direct the Social Security Administration to withhold more than 55% of his aggregate disposable earnings for garnishment.

Reversed and remanded for proceedings consistent with this opinion.

QUESTIONS FOR REVIEW

1. Discuss the meaning of the following terms:

    a. debtor

    b. creditor

    c. lien

    d. lienholder

    e. mechanic's lien

    f. artisan's lien

    g. judicial lien

2. Discuss the meaning of the following terms:

    a. mortgage

    b. mortgagor

    c. mortgagee

    d. foreclosure

    e. deed of trust

    f. surety

    g. guaranty

    h. garnishment

3. Summarize the *Thigpen v. Father & Sons Home Improvement* case.

4. Summarize the *Cote v. Cote* case.

INTERNET ACTIVITIES

1. Summarize how to file a mechanic's lien in your state.

2. Summarize the foreclosure process in your state.

Chapter 35

Secured Transactions

n Chapter 34 we discussed the basic rights of creditors. In this chapter we further our discussion regarding debtor/creditor relationships. In particular, we address how creditors can strengthen their positions on claims against the debtor and the debtor's property. As with many other areas of law, understanding the applicable terminology is a necessary first step. Then we will discuss in a bit more detail how creditors can better **secure** themselves if and when a debtor defaults.

Terminology

Article 9 of the Uniform Commercial Code (UCC) contains provisions that states can adopt to govern the area of **secured transactions**. A secured transaction is one in which the creditor obtains an interest in specific property of the debtor. In other words, the creditor (or **secured party**) has a **security interest** in the debtor's property. The secured party is often called a **secured creditor**. A creditor that has no interest in specific property of the debtor is called an **unsecured creditor**. The debtor's property in which the secured party has a security interest is called the **collateral**. Typically, the secured party obtains a security interest in the collateral by having the debtor sign a **security agreement**. A security interest is said to **attach** when the security agreement is signed and the creditor has an interest in the collateral.

An example is in order here. Suppose you borrow $10,000 from some friends. Further suppose that your friends says that they will only agree to the deal if, in the case you fail to pay them back, they can come and get your grand piano to go toward satisfying the portion of the debt you have not repaid. You agree to this arrangement. Consequently, you, the *debtor*, enter into a *security agreement* with your friends that gives them—now the *secured parties*—a *security interest* in the

ESLINE/Shutterstock.com

collateral. Of course, your friends' security interest in the grand piano *attached* when the security agreement was signed. Now, they have a greater interest (or "priority") in your piano than would any *unsecured creditor.*

Perfecting a Security Interest

What if the debtor has given a security interest in the same collateral to two or more creditors? State law provides a relatively straightforward way for one creditor to have priority over another. A creditor who has a **perfected** security interest in the collateral of the debtor will prevail against a creditor—even a secured creditor—that does not have a perfected security interest. Typically, a creditor perfects a security interest by filing a UCC **financing statement** with the applicable state agency (*e.g.*, Secretary of State's office). The financing statement acts as a notice to the world that the creditor has a claim against the collateral of the debtor. Thus, any subsequent creditor should check the government agency's database for any existing security interests filed against the debtor and the debtor's collateral. Consider the following case from the Court of Civil Appeals of Oklahoma (Illustrative Court Case 35.1).

Ultimately, once the debtor satisfies the debt to the creditor, the creditor files a **termination statement** with the state agency.

In some situations a creditor may have a security interest in inventory of the debtor. Of course, inventory levels will fluctuate as inventory is sold and purchased. A creditor can include in the security agreement a **floating lien** provision. This basically means that it is possible for the creditor to have a perfected security interest in new inventory that is acquired after the creditor filed the financing statement. An important concept to remember here, however, is that if *in the ordinary course of business* a customer purchases an item from the debtor's inventory, the customer obtains the goods free from the security interest of the creditor.

The UCC provides that, in some instances, a security interest automatically is perfected without the filing of a financing statement. One example of this situation is a **purchase money security interest** (PMSI). Although state laws vary, as a basic rule, a PMSI arises when a seller extends credit to a buyer of

---

ILLUSTRATIVE COURT CASE 35.1

Farm Credit Services of America, Inc. v. Wilson

Court of Civil Appeals of Oklahoma

247 P.3d 1199 (2010)

OPINION BY: BELL

In this action for foreclosure of security interest and an order of delivery, Plaintiff/Appellant, Farm Credit Services of America, Inc., a Nebraska Corporation (Farm Credit), seeks review of the trial court's order granting summary judgment to Defendants/Appellees, Daniel M. Wilson and Nancy L. Wilson. For the reasons set forth below, we reverse and remand for further proceedings.

On or about March 26, 2005, Dustin R. Sherwood and Jennifer J. Sherwood purchased a 2005 John Deere 1690 Planter in Missouri, and financed the purchase through Farm Credit. The Sherwoods signed a promissory note and loan agreement, and granted Farm Credit a purchase money security interest in the Planter. Farm Credit filed its security interest with the Missouri Secretary of State on April 4, 2005. On March 2, 2007, the Sherwoods sold the Planter to Defendants for $14,000.00 plus the value of Defendants' trade-in planter. Defendants did not search the Missouri UCC records before they purchased the Planter. Defendants brought the Planter to Oklahoma.

Farm Credit learned about the sale, and, on March 13, 2008, filed a UCC-1 financing statement on the Planter in Oklahoma. On April 7, 2008, Farm Credit filed the instant action against the defendants, seeking foreclosure on its security interest and [recovery] of the Planter. Defendants denied the allegations of Farm Credit and asserted several affirmative defenses.

Defendants subsequently filed a motion for summary judgment, asserting they had no knowledge of Farm Credit's security interest when they purchased the Planter from the Sherwoods. Defendants also argued that, because Farm Credit had not perfected its security interest in Oklahoma within one year of the sale, Farm Credit no longer possessed any valid claim to the Planter under [Oklahoma statutory law]. Farm Credit's response argued that it did not know of, or consent to, the sale of the Planter to Defendants, and that Defendants had constructive notice of its filed security interest in Missouri at the time of purchase. Farm Credit consequently asserted superiority of its purchase money security interest over any claim of Defendants.

The trial court concluded that Farm Credit's security interest in the Planter expired . . . when it failed to file its financing statement in Oklahoma within one year of the sale, and held Defendants were entitled to judgment as a matter of law. Farm Credit now appeals. . . .

"Summary judgment is proper [only] when there is no dispute as to any material fact and the moving party is entitled to judgment as a matter of law." [Citation omitted]. . . .

"To perfect a security interest in collateral, a creditor . . . must file a financing statement which complies with the requirements of [Oklahoma statutory law]." [Citation omitted.] "The purpose of the filing system is 'to give notice to creditors and other interested parties that a security interest exists in property of the debtor.'" [Citation omitted.] A properly filed and perfected security interest constitutes constructive notice of its existence to the world. [Citation omitted.]

Furthermore, "a security interest continues in collateral notwithstanding its sale 'unless the secured party authorized the disposition free of the security interest.'" [Citation omitted.] Consequently, the failure to perfect a security interest affects only the priority of the claim, not its validity: "An unperfected security interest is a security interest without priority over conflicting security interest rather than one without validity. [Citation omitted.]

In the present case, Farm Credit properly perfected its security interest in the Planter at the time the Sherwoods purchased it. Defendants were charged with constructive notice of Farm Credit's pre-existing and superior security interest at the time they purchased the Planter from the Sherwoods. The failure of Farm Credit to refile its security interest in Oklahoma within one year of the Sherwoods' sale to the Defendants . . . affected only the priority Farm Credit may have enjoyed over other security interests, and *did not completely extinguish* Farm Credit's claim. [Citation omitted.]

Because Defendants were charged with constructive notice of Farm Credit's outstanding and superior security interest at the time they purchased the Planter from the Sherwoods, they acquired the Planter subject to Farm Credit's security interest. Farm Credit's claim is superior to Defendants, and the trial court erred in holding otherwise. Accordingly, the order of the trial court is reversed and the case is remanded for further proceedings.

REVERSED AND REMANDED

Woven Treasures, Inc., v. Hudson Capital, L.L.C.

Supreme Court of Alabama

46 So.3d 905 (2009)

OPINION BY: SMITH

Woven Treasures, Inc., and Mina Esfahani appeal the trial court's summary judgment in favor of Hudson Capital, L.L.C. We affirm.

Facts and Procedural History

The action arises from the liquidation of the inventory of a retail store known as Old Mobile Furniture by defendant Hudson Capital. Woven Treasures, a seller of oriental rugs, and Esfahani, the owner of Woven Treasures (hereinafter referred to collectively as "the plaintiffs"), sued Hudson Capital . . . asserting that Hudson Capital improperly possessed and sold rugs the plaintiffs say they had consigned to the owner of Old Mobile Furniture, Richard Clarke. The plaintiffs asserted claims of conversion, trespass to property, unjust enrichment, negligence, and wantonness.

Old Mobile Furniture was the name under which a company known as TSR Imports, Inc., operated. Sometime in 2005 TSR Imports defaulted on a loan from Compass Bank that it had secured in part with the inventory of old Mobile Furniture. A representative of Compass Bank subsequently contacted Hudson Capital, a company engaged in the inventory-liquidation business, to see whether Hudson Capital was interested in purchasing the inventory of Old Mobile Furniture.

Hudson Capital, after conducting a walk-through of Old Mobile Furniture and a Uniform Commercial Code ("UCC") search regarding the merchandise at the store, decided to purchase Compass Bank's interest in TSR Imports. On August 26, 2005, TSR Imports, Compass Bank, and Hudson Capital entered into a tripartite "Agreement to Conduct a 'Going Out of Business Sale'" whereby Hudson Capital agreed to pay Compass Bank $385,000 for the right to conduct a liquidation sale of the merchandise at Old Mobile Furniture and to retain all proceeds of the sale as well as the unencumbered rights to all unsold merchandise. Pursuant to the agreement, the sale would begin on or about August 29, 2005, and continue for 10 weeks. . . .

The agreement defines the term "Merchandise" as "all of [TSR Imports'] owned retail inventory located at the Store on the Sale Commencement Date. . . ."

On August 26, 2005, Hudson Capital and TSR Imports also entered into a security agreement whereby TSR Imports granted Hudson Capital "a security interest in and to (i) all of the Merchandise located in the Store. . . . The agreement expressly authorized Hudson Capital to file a UCC financing statement describing the merchandise in order to perfect the lien granted to it by TSR Imports.

Among the merchandise Hudson Capital obtained from Old Mobile Furniture were rugs the plaintiffs had allegedly consigned to Richard Clarke individually and/or to Reproduction Galleries, a furniture store Clarke had previously owned and that was operated by an entity known as Reproduction Galleries, Inc. In January 2001, Reproduction Galleries and Woven Treasures entered into an agreement pursuant to which Reproduction Galleries would display rugs provided by Woven Treasures on a consignment basis. . . .

. . .

Approximately two years after Reproduction Galleries and Woven Treasures had executed the consignment agreement, Reproduction Galleries went out of business. Esfahani testified that Clarke told her that he would be opening a furniture store in a new location and that she replied, "[T]hat's a great idea." Esfahani further testified that Clarke specifically told her that he would move the consigned rugs to the new store, Old Mobile Furniture, and that she told him, "it's fine with me." Esfahani did not personally transfer the consigned rugs to Old Mobile furniture, but she testified that "I see [sic] my rugs at the new location" and that she regularly sent her employees to Old Mobile Furniture to inventory the consigned rugs. Esfahani further testified that she believed that displaying the rugs at Old Mobile Furniture was a continuation of the consignment agreement Woven Treasures had entered into with Reproduction Galleries.

After the consigned rugs were moved to the new location of Old Mobile Furniture, TSR Imports defaulted on its loan with Compass Bank. The bank sought to sell its interest in the inventory of Old Mobile Furniture, and several Hudson Capital employees walked through the store with Clarke when Hudson Capital was considering whether to purchase the bank's interest in TSR Imports. The chief operating officer of Hudson Capital, Fulton Stokes, testified that during the walk-through he asked Clarke whether any of the merchandise in the store was on consignment and that Clarke responded that it was not. Stokes further testified that he specifically asked Clarke whether any of the rugs in the store were on consignment and that Clarke responded that he previously had had some rugs on consignment but that "the lady" had picked up those rugs the previous evening. Hudson Capital then conducted a search of UCC records for TSR Imports and Old Mobile Furniture to ensure that the inventory was not claimed by someone else because, as Stokes testified, "when you deal with people in distress, you never know if they're telling the truth." In an affidavit, an attorney with the law firm that conducted the UCC search represented that the firm found no filings by or on behalf of Esfahani and/or Woven Treasures naming TSR Imports or Old Mobile Furniture as the debtor. Indeed, it is undisputed that the plaintiffs never filed any financing statements related to the consigned rugs.

In August 2005, Hudson Capital commenced the liquidation sale at Old Mobile Furniture. Esfahani testified that she saw an advertisement for the sale in the Mobile Press-Register and thought, "[w]hat's going on, where [are] my rugs?" Esfahani then went to Old Mobile Furniture in an attempt to speak with Clarke. Esfahani testified that, when she went to the store, she spoke with Angelo Nichols, an employee of Hudson Capital. Esfahani described her conversation with Nichols as follows:

"I went up there and I said, I want to see [Clarke]. And [Nichols] said . . . he's not here or he's no longer here or something like that. And there was some lady cleaning the floor, and I think she said, he's not here anymore. And I said, I need to . . . I think I said I want to see [Clarke], my rugs are here. And [Nichols] said something like, oh, those rugs are gone, something like that."

. . .

After the sale, Hudson Capital perfected its security interest in the merchandise of Old Mobile Furniture and the proceeds arising therefrom by filing a financing statement with the Alabama Secretary of State. The plaintiffs later requested that Hudson Capital tender a sum equal to the fair-market value of the rugs they had originally consigned to Reproduction Galleries. Hudson Capital refused.

In January 2007, the plaintiffs sued Hudson Capital alleging that Hudson Capital improperly possessed and sold consigned rugs in which they maintained an unperfected security interest. As referenced earlier, the plaintiffs asserted claims of conversion, trespass to property, unjust enrichment, negligence, and wantonness.

(*Continued*)

Hudson Capital subsequently moved for a summary judgment based upon the following arguments: (1) that the plaintiffs cannot establish that Hudson Capital took possession of the consigned rugs; (ii) that Hudson Capital properly obtained and perfected a security interest in the rugs; and (iii) that Hudson Capital obtained title to the rugs as a good-faith purchaser for value. . . .

Discussion

A threshold issue in this case is whether the plaintiffs produced substantial evidence indicating that the consigned rugs were among the merchandise possessed and sold by Hudson Capital. The plaintiffs produced scant documentary evidence indicating that the consigned rugs were ever among the merchandise at Old Mobile Furniture, but they have produced deposition testimony in which several individuals stated that they saw oriental rugs at the store during the liquidation sale or several weeks before the sale. Specifically, the plaintiffs submitted deposition testimony from Esfahani in which she stated that she went to Old Mobile Furniture several weeks or months before the sale and that the store was closed but that "[I] could see my rugs from the distance that I could see from the window or door." The plaintiffs also produced deposition testimony from Angelo Nichols, a Hudson Capital employee, in which he stated that at the time Hudson Capital inventoried the merchandise at Old Mobile Furniture, "[t]here [were] oriental rugs throughout the store." Another employee of Hudson Capital, Jo Swingle, testified that she "saw rugs on the floor" of Old Mobile Furniture, particularly a very large rug, which, as described by Swingle, resembled a rug Esfahani testified that Woven Treasures had consigned to Reproduction Galleries.

. . .

Assuming that the rugs were among the merchandise Hudson Capital possessed and sold, the issue then becomes whether Hudson Capital wrongfully converted the rugs to its possession. Although the plaintiffs present numerous arguments as to why Hudson Capital lacks rights to and title to the rugs and, therefore, why the trial court erred in entering a summary judgment in favor of Hudson Capital, these arguments consist of two primary contentions: (1) that Hudson Capital did not acquire a security interest in the rugs; and (2) that Hudson Capital did not acquire title to the rugs as a good-faith purchaser for value.

In response, Hudson Capital argues that the trial court did not err in entering a summary judgment in its favor because, it contends, its perfected security interest in the consigned rugs is senior to the plaintiffs' unperfected security interest. We agree. Stated another way, TSR Imports granted Hudson Capital a security interest in all the merchandise displayed at Old Mobile Furniture (including the consigned rugs), and Hudson Capital perfected this interest, while the plaintiffs never filed a financing statement asserting their interest in the rugs.

In analyzing whether Hudson Capital obtained a security interest in the rugs, we begin by examining TSR Imports' ability to grant a security interest in the consigned rugs. As referenced in the facts, TSR Imports displayed the rugs at the Old Mobile Furniture store on a consignment basis. Consequently, TSR Imports was a consignee as to the rugs. As a consignee of the rugs, TSR Imports obtained the rights and the title to the rugs identical to those of the plaintiffs under [Alabama statutory law]. . . .

. . .

Even apart from the fact that one of the consignment slips listed Old Mobile Furniture as a consignee, we find that a consignment between the plaintiffs and TSR Imports (d/b/a Old Mobile Furniture) arose when the plaintiffs permitted Clarke to move the rugs from Reproduction Galleries to Old Mobile Furniture and to display the rugs at that store on a consignment basis. Under Alabama law, a "consignee" is "a merchant to which goods are delivered in a consignment" . . . and there is no requirement that a consignment be in writing; . . .

. . .

The plaintiffs further argue that if Hudson Capital is found to have a security interest in the rugs, its interest is inferior to their unperfected security interest because Hudson Capital perfected its interest in the rugs after the liquidation sale had ended and some of or all the rugs had been sold. . . .

This argument is without merit because Hudson Capital's security interest in the rugs attached before the sale began and continued after the rugs had been disposed of. [Alabama law] clearly provides that "(1) a security interest . . . continues in collateral notwithstanding sale . . . or other disposition thereof . . . and (2) a security interest attaches to any identifiable proceeds of collateral." . . . [W]hen Hudson Capital perfected its security interest in the rugs it also perfected its security interest in any proceeds from the sale of the rugs, and the fact remains that the plaintiffs never filed a financing statement reflecting their security interest in the rugs.

Based on the foregoing, the plaintiffs' claims of conversion, trespass to property, unjust enrichment, negligence, and wantonness must fail because Hudson Capital has a superior security interest in the consigned rugs. Accordingly, the trial court did not err in entering a summary judgment in favor of Hudson Capital as to all the plaintiffs' claims.

Conclusion

We affirm the trial court's summary judgment in favor of Hudson Capital.

AFFIRMED.

---

consumer goods for personal, family, or household use. The seller-creditor automatically has a perfected security interest in the collateral (*i.e.*, no UCC financing statement need be filed) and the seller has a higher priority in the consumer goods in comparison to other creditors of the debtor.

Now that you have been introduced to the fundamentals of secured transactions, consider the court case from the Supreme Court of Alabama (Illustrative Court Case 35.2).

Foreclosing on a Security Interest

If a debtor fails to pay the creditor, the creditor now has the practical problem of how to go about foreclosing on the security interest and repossessing the collateral. For example, what if the collateral is a grand piano that is sitting in the debtor's family room? How should the creditor go about repossessing the grand piano? The UCC contains a provision addressing this issue. Consider the following Michigan state UCC statute as an example (Illustrative State Statute 35.1).

Notice that if the creditor attempts to take possession of the collateral without judicial process (*i.e.*, **self-help** repossession), the creditor must take the collateral without breaching the peace. Breaching the peace in this context typically includes, for example, breaking and entering and assault and battery. The same general rules apply if the creditor hires an independent third party to execute the repossession.

MCL § 440.9609

§ 440.9609. Secured party's right to take possession after default.

Section 9609. (1) After default, a secured party may do 1 or more of the following:

(a) Take possession of the collateral.

(b) Without removal, render equipment unusable and dispose of collateral on a debtor's premises. . . .

(2) A secured party may proceed under subsection (1) either pursuant to judicial process, or without judicial process if it proceeds without breach of the peace.

(3) If so agreed, and in any event after default, a secured party may require the debtor to assemble the collateral and make it available to the secured party at a place to be designated by the secured party that is reasonably convenient to both parties.

QUESTIONS FOR REVIEW

1. Discuss the meaning of the following terms:

   a. secured transaction

   b. secured party

   c. security agreement

   d. collateral

   e. attachment

2. What does it mean to "perfect" a security interest?

3. What is a "floating lien"?

4. What is a purchase money security interest? What is unique about it?

5. Explain generally the rights and obligations of a creditor that tries to repossess collateral from a debtor who is in default.

6. Summarize the *Farm Credit Services of America v. Wilson* case.

7. Summarize the *Woven Treasures v. Hudson Capital* case.

INTERNET ACTIVITIES

1. What is the name of the agency in your state where a financing statement is filed?

2. Find the United States District Court for the Eastern District of Wisconsin case *Operating Engineers Local 139 Health Benefits Fund v. HUML Contractors, Inc.*, 2012 U.S. Dist. LEXIS 25193 (February 28, 2012).

   a. What is the issue or issues in the case?

   b. What was the holding of the court?

   c. Summarize the court's analysis.

Chapter 36

Bankruptcy Law

When entrepreneurs first start a business, bankruptcy law is likely the last thing on their minds. Nevertheless, it is inevitable that some businesses—and individuals—will not be able to pay their debts. How should the law treat the debtor? The creditors? Of course, the law strives to find a fair result to provide the debtor a **fresh start**, but at the same time try to protect—at least to some extent—the contractual rights of the debtor's creditors. This chapter discusses the fundamentals of bankruptcy law and the bankruptcy process.

Bankruptcy Law and the Constitution

The drafters of the United States Constitution recognized that there was a need for uniform laws on bankruptcy, and that such laws should be made at the federal level. Hence, the Constitution contains the following provision regarding bankruptcy.

UNITED STATES CONSTITUTION

Article I, Section 8. The Congress shall have Power . . . [t]o establish . . . uniform Laws on the subject of Bankruptcies throughout the United States . . .

Congress has passed extensive laws relating to bankruptcies and placed those laws in Title 11 of the United States Code.

Fundamental Terminology and Bankruptcy Procedure

You may have heard in the news or from a friend who may have declared bankruptcy that there are different types of bankruptcy. The most common types are known as **Chapter 7**, **Chapter 11**, and **Chapter 13** bankruptcies. The fundamental differences among these types of bankruptcies will be discussed later in this chapter.

The Petition

Bankruptcy law requires that an individual filing for bankruptcy must first receive counseling relating to the effects of a bankruptcy filing. A bankruptcy then begins when a bankruptcy **petition** is filed in **U.S. Bankruptcy Court**. The bankruptcy court judge appoints a bankruptcy **trustee** to oversee the assets properly included in the debtor's bankrupt **estate**. A bankruptcy petition can either be **voluntary** (filed by the debtor) or **involuntary** (filed by the debtor's creditors). Once a petition is filed, an **automatic stay** takes effect, which prevents creditors from continuing collection actions or trying to enforce other judgments that may have already been obtained against the debtor.

The Schedules

In order for the judge and creditors to know what assets the debtor owns, the debtor must complete various **schedules** listing the debtor's assets.

Greg Kushmerek/Shutterstock.com

In addition, the debtor must disclose, among other things, the debtor's financial affairs, evidence of the debtor's monthly income, and the debtor's federal income tax returns.

Exemptions

If the creditors could make a claim against *all* of a debtor's assets, then a debtor could possibly not have a home, vehicle, or other basic personal items. Consequently, Congress has provided that some assets are **exempt** from the bankruptcy estate. Consider the following statute from the Bankruptcy Code listing, in part, items exempt from inclusion in the bankruptcy estate (Illustrative Federal Statute 36.1).

ILLUSTRATIVE FEDERAL STATUTE 36.1

11 U.S.C. § 522

§ 522. Exemptions

. . .

(b)(1) Notwithstanding section 541 of this title, an individual debtor may exempt from property of the estate the property listed in . . . paragraph (2) . . . of this subsection. . . .

(b)(2) Property listed in this paragraph is property that is specified under subsection (d). . . .

(d) The following property may be exempted under subsection (b)(2) of this section:

(1) The debtor's aggregate interest, not to exceed $25,150 in value, in real property or personal property that the debtor or a dependent of the debtor uses as a residence, . . ., or in a burial plot for the debtor or a dependent of the debtor.

(2) The debtor's interest, not to exceed $4,000 in value, in one motor vehicle.

(3) The debtor's interest, not to exceed $625 in value in any particular item or $13,400 in aggregate value, in household furnishings, household goods, wearing apparel, appliances, books, animals, crops, or musical instruments, that are held primarily for the personal, family, or household use of the debtor or a dependent of the debtor.

(4) The debtor's aggregate interest, not to exceed $1,700 in value, in jewelry held primarily for the personal, family, or household use of the debtor or a dependent of the debtor.

. . .

(6) The debtor's aggregate interest, not to exceed $2,525 in value, in any implements, professional books, or tools, of the trade of the debtor or the trade of a dependent of the debtor.

. . .

(10) The debtor's right to receive—

(a) a social security benefit, unemployment compensation, or a local public assistance benefit;

(b) a veterans' benefit;

(c) a disability, illness, or unemployment benefit;

(d) alimony, support, or separate maintenance, to the extent reasonably necessary for the support of the debtor and any dependent of the debtor;

. . .

(11) The debtor's right to receive, or property that is traceable to—

(a) an award under a crime victim's reparation law;

. . .

(d) a payment, not to exceed $25,150, on account of personal bodily injury, not including pain and suffering or compensation for actual pecuniary loss, of the debtor or an individual of whom the debtor is a dependent; or

(e) a payment in compensation of loss of future earnings of the debtor or an individual of whom the debtor is or was a dependent, to the extent reasonably necessary for the support of the debtor and any dependent of the debtor.

(12) Retirement funds to the extent that those funds are in a fund or account that is exempt from taxation under [the Internal Revenue Code].

. . .

Obviously a debtor has an incentive to try to claim exemptions for as much property as possible. Consider the following case from the United States Supreme Court (Illustrative Court Case 36.1).

ILLUSTRATIVE COURT CASE 36.1

Clark v. Rameker

Supreme Court of the United States

134 S. Ct. 2242 (2014)

[**Note:** For convenience of the reader, the following language is from the Syllabus of the case as provided by the U.S. Supreme Court Reporter of Decisions.]

When petitioners filed for Chapter 7 bankruptcy, they sought to exclude roughly $300,000 in an inherited individual retirement account (IRA) from the bankruptcy estate using the "retirement funds" exemption. See 11 U.S.C. §522(b)(3)(C). The Bankruptcy Court concluded that an inherited IRA does not share the same characteristics as a traditional IRA and disallowed the exemption. The District Court reversed, explaining that the exemption covers any account in which the funds were originally accumulated for retirement purposes. The Seventh Circuit disagreed and reversed the District Court.

Held: Funds held in inherited IRAs are not "retirement funds" within the meaning of §522(b)(3)(C).

(a) The ordinary meaning of "retirement funds" is properly understood to be sums of money set aside for the day an individual stops working. Three legal characteristics of inherited IRAs provide objective evidence that they do not contain such funds. First, the holder of an inherited IRA may never invest additional money in the account. Second, holders of inherited IRAs are required to withdraw money from the accounts, no matter how far they are from retirement. Finally, the holder of an inherited IRA may withdraw the entire balance of the account at any time—and use it for any purpose—without penalty.

(Continued)

(b) This reading is consistent with the purpose of the Bankruptcy Code's exemption provisions, which effectuate a careful balance between the creditor's interest in recovering assets and the debtor's interest in protecting essential needs. Allowing debtors to protect funds in traditional and Roth IRAs ensures that debtors will be able to meet their basic needs during their retirement years. By contrast, nothing about an inherited IRA's legal characteristics prevent or discourage an individual from using the entire balance immediately after bankruptcy for purposes of current consumption. The "retirement funds' exemption should not be read in a manner that would convert the bankruptcy objective of protecting debtors' basic needs into a "free pass."

. . .

[The Seventh Circuit Court of Appeals decision is] affirmed.

ILLUSTRATIVE COURT CASE 36.2

In re Longview Aluminum, L.L.C.

Court of Appeals for the Seventh Circuit

2011 U.S. App. LEXIS 18302 (2011)

OPINION BY: BAUER

Longview Aluminum, L.L.C. ("Longview") filed for Chapter 11 bankruptcy and its trustee brought an adversary action to set aside and recover payments made less than one year before the bankruptcy filing to Dominic Forte, one of Longview's members. The bankruptcy court found that Forte qualified as an "insider" of Longview and that the trustee could void and recover the transfers. The district court affirmed the bankruptcy court. For the following reasons, we affirm.

I. BACKGROUND

Longview is a limited liability company organized under the laws of Delaware. Longview was formed pursuant to the Amended and Restated Limited Liability Agreement of Longview Aluminum, L.L.C. ("Longview LLC Agreement") by five members, who made up a Board of Managers (the "Board"). The Board consisted of Michael Lynch (50% interest), Michael J. Ochalski (13% interest), John L. Kolleng (20% interest), McCall Enterprises, L.L.C. (5% interest), and Forte (12% interest).

From 2001 until June 2002, Forte requested that Longview provide him with business records or allow him to inspect all of Longview's records; Forte's requests were repeatedly denied. On July 10, 2002, Forte sued Lynch, the Board member with the highest percentage interest in Longview, alleging that Lynch had used his controlling interest to bar Forte from reviewing any of Longview's business records and to exclude Forte from participating in any management decision. . . .

On August 20, 2002, the members of the Board other than Forte executed a majority written consent, formally suspending Forte's right to access Longview's information and records until the conclusion of (1) Longview's investigation in to whether Forte's requests were made for an improper purpose; (2) an audit of Longview's account; and (3) the discovery in an unrelated case in which Longview was a party. On November 7, 2002, Forte and the defendants to that lawsuit entered into a settlement agreement under which $400,000, plus attorney's fees and costs, would be paid to Forte in exchange for Forte's agreement to leave the Board. On that same day, Longview delivered a $200,000 cashier's check to Forte as an initial payment. On January 16, 2003, Longview delivered a second check to Forte in the amount of $15,000 which represented payment for Forte's attorney's fees and costs.

On March 4, 2003, Longview filed a Chapter 11 petition for bankruptcy relief. The trustee in bankruptcy proceedings filed the instant adversary action against Forte, seeking to recover the settlement payments as preferential transfers made to an insider within one year of Longview's bankruptcy petition. Forte conceded that the $15,000 payment was a preferential transfer made within three months of Longview's bankruptcy petition and returned the funds. However, Forte denied that the $200,000 payment constituted a preferential transfer. The bankruptcy court ruled in favor of the trustee, finding that Forte was an insider as defined by . . . the Bankruptcy Code, thereby enabling the trustee to void and recover the $200,000 transfer. The district court affirmed the bankruptcy court. Forte appealed.

II. DISCUSSION

. . .

Pursuant to [bankruptcy law], a bankruptcy trustee is able to avoid certain transfers made by a debtor prior to filing for bankruptcy. Generally, all transfers within 90 days of the debtor's bankruptcy filing are considered preferential and subject to avoidance. [Citation omitted.] When the creditor is an "insider" of the debtor, however, the Bankruptcy Code enlarges the time period for avoidance to one year before the bankruptcy filing. [Citation omitted.] The Bankruptcy Code defines an insider of a corporation as a: (i) director of the debtor; (ii) officer of the debtor; (iii) person in control of the debtor; (iv) partnership in which the debtor is a general partner; (v) general partner of the debtor; or (vi) relative of a general partner, director, officer, or person in control of the debtor. [Citation omitted.] Courts regularly treat this definition as illustrative of types of insider relationships and not as an exhaustive list. [Citation omitted.]

The insider analysis is a case-by-case decision based on the totality of the circumstances, and bankruptcy courts have used a variety of factors in their determinations. One approach focuses on the similarity of the alleged insider's position to the enumerated statutory categories, while another approach focuses on the alleged insider's control of the debtor. If the alleged insider holds a position substantially similar to the position specified in the definition, a court will often find that individual to be an insider. But, based on the legislative history of the statute, our case law has also held that the term insider can also encompass anyone with a "sufficiently close relationship with the debtor that his conduct is made subject to closer scrutiny than those dealing at arm's length with the debtor." [Citation omitted.] For this second approach, courts look to the closeness of the relationship between the parties.

Forte first argues that the district court erred when it used the similarity approach to analogize a director of a corporation to a member of an LLC and expanded the term "director" in the definition to include members and managers of an LLC. We disagree.

It is well established that the definition of insider is not an exhaustive list; the definition has been expanded by bankruptcy courts to include positions analogous to those enumerated, including in the LLC context. [Citations omitted.] When the position held by the alleged insider is not enumerated in the statute, the relevant inquiry for the court is to consider whether the relationship at issue is similar to or has characteristics of any of the defined relationships.

(*Continued*)

The district court looked to both Delaware corporate and LLC law to properly analogize a director of a corporation to a member of an LLC. Under Delaware law, a corporation must "be managed by or under the direction of a board of directors. . . ." [Citation omitted.] With respect to an LLC, Delaware law states that "[u]nless otherwise provided in a limited liability company agreement, the management of a limited liability company shall be vested in its members. . . ." [Citation omitted.] The district court concluded that directors generally have the authority to manage a corporation and members generally have the authority to manage an LLC, and thus found a member analogous to a director. Forte, however, argues that because an LLC manager's powers can be specified by an LLC agreement, an LLC manager's authority can be vastly different from that of a director of a corporation, depending on the LLC agreement. This argument is unpersuasive. By default, under Delaware law, authority is vested in the members of an LLC. Furthermore, in this case Longview's own LLC agreement specifically provided its operations and affairs of [Longview] shall be vested in the Board of Managers and the Members." The district court did not err in concluding that a member of an LLC can be a statutory insider within the meaning of [bankruptcy law].

Notwithstanding the foregoing, we also recognize, as the bankruptcy court and the district court did, that "it is not simply the title 'director' or 'officer' that renders an individual an insider; rather, it is the set of legal rights that a typical corporate director or officer holds." [Citation omitted.] We thus not only look to the individual's title, but also his relationship to the company.

Here, Forte argues that because he was prevented from managing or participating in a meaningful way in some of Longview's affairs, he was in no way in control of Longview. Forte points out that as early as 2001, he was denied access to Longview's books and records, and that in August 2002, before the $200,000 transfer was made, the majority of the Board executed a formal written consent excluding him from viewing Longview's books and records. Longview responds that although the majority written consent removed Forte's unfettered access to the books and records, this was merely a temporary suspension, and, moreover, did not remove Forte from his position as a member of Longview on the Board. The district court did not find the effect of the majority written consent to be enough to remove Forte's status as an insider, and neither do we. There was never a formal vote or document executed that removed Forte's member status. Forte's surviving member status caused him to retain meaningful rights and control given to members under Longview's LLC Agreement; significantly, Forte still retained voting rights in the company. At the time of the $200,000 transfer in November, Forte still held a formal position on the Board and did not resign until after he received the transferred funds.

. . .

Finally, Forte argues that because members and managers are not contemplated within the definition in the statute, they can only be considered insiders if they fall within the non-statutory criteria, and here, there was no close relationship or less than arm's-length transaction. We acknowledge that courts consider those factors and often use the control approach, but in this situation, where the court is determining whether a member or manager of an LLC is a statutory insider, the similarity approach yields a better interpretation of the statute.

The bankruptcy and district courts applied the similarity approach, and we find that the court did not err in doing so.

III. CONCLUSION

For the foregoing reasons, we AFFIRM the judgment of the district court.

A debtor may also be tempted to transfer property in contemplation of filing a bankruptcy petition. Perhaps a debtor might think to transfer all property to relatives or friends before filing for bankruptcy, and then have them transfer the property back some time after the bankruptcy. Not surprisingly, the bankruptcy laws anticipate that some people may do this. A debtor's transfer of property within a certain time before declaring bankruptcy could be considered a **fraudulent transfer** (or **fraudulent conveyance**), and the bankruptcy trustee could reclaim such property. Also, a debtor may be tempted to pay certain creditors in full and not pay other creditors at all if the debtor is contemplating bankruptcy. The bankruptcy laws also provide rules to prevent **preferential transfers** by the debtor. Consider the case from the United States Court of Appeals for the Seventh Circuit (Illustrative Court Case 36.2).

Bankruptcy law also identifies which debts have **priority** over other debts. For example, secured creditors and tax debts will get paid before unsecured creditors. A detailed presentation of the order of priorities is beyond the scope of our discussion here, however.

Creditors Meeting and Proofs of Claim

Once the debtor has submitted schedules identifying assets, debts, income, etc., the creditors have a meeting (*i.e.*, a **creditors meeting**) to review the information submitted by the debtor. A creditor must timely submit a **proof of claim** evidencing the debt that the debtor owes the creditor. These claims then are presented to the judge as the judge ultimately approves how the assets in the debtor's bankruptcy estate will be applied to the varying creditors' claims.

Chapter 7 Bankruptcies

A Chapter 7 bankruptcy is a **liquidation bankruptcy**. The debtor's nonexempt assets are sold, the proceeds are collected, and the proceeds are paid to the creditors. Any remaining debts of the debtor are discharged unless the debts are

identified as nondischargeable under bankruptcy law (*e.g.*, the most common are alimony, child support, certain tax claims, student loans (with some exceptions), etc.).

Chapter 11 Bankruptcies

A Chapter 11 bankruptcy is a **reorganization bankruptcy**. Chapter 11 is primarily for businesses (*e.g.*, corporations, partnerships, LLCs, etc.). In these situations, the business typically desires to have the judge discharge some of the business's debt so the business can reorganize its capital structure. The business creates a reorganization plan for the judge's approval. The plan's ultimate goal, of course, is that post-bankruptcy the business can continue on as a going concern and meet its obligations.

Chapter 13 Bankruptcies

In contrast to Chapter 7 bankruptcies, a Chapter 13 bankruptcy is not a liquidation of the debtor's assets. Rather, Chapter 13 is available for individuals with regular, stable incomes that can pay back the debt if the debts were **adjusted**. Basically, the debtor sets forth a plan on how much the debtor can pay over a certain period of time (*e.g.*, three to five years). The bankruptcy judge **confirms** the plan and supervises the debtor's compliance with the plan. Debts remaining after the debtor complies with the plan are discharged (except for nondischargeable debts).

QUESTIONS FOR REVIEW

1. Bankruptcy law is contained in Title _____ of the United States Code.

2. Explain the meaning of the following terms:

   a. petition

   b. bankruptcy estate

   c. trustee

   d. automatic stay

   e. fraudulent transfer (or fraudulent conveyance)

   f. preferential transfer

   g. proof of claim

3. Explain the basic purpose of Chapter 7 bankruptcies.

4. Explain the basic purpose of Chapter 11 bankruptcies.

5. Explain the basic purpose of Chapter 13 bankruptcies.

6. Summarize the *Clark v. Rameker* case.

7. Summarize the *Longview Aluminum* case.

INTERNET ACTIVITIES

1. Visit the website www.uscourts.gov. "Services & Forms" tab. Then click on the "Bankruptcy Forms" link.

   a. What is Form B101?

   b. Click on Form B101 and download the form. What information is required on Lines 7, 9, 12, and 20?

2. Visit the website www.uscourts.gov. "Click on the "Services & Forms" tab. Then click on the "Bankruptcy Basics" link. Click on the "Chapter 13" link.

   a. According to the website, a chapter 13 bankruptcy is also called a "_____."

   b. What are advantages of Chapter 13 bankruptcy?

   c. Who is eligible to file a Chapter 13 bankruptcy?

   d. Summarize how Chapter 13 works.

Part XIII

Negotiable Instruments and Banking

Chapter 37

Negotiable Instruments and Banking

Parties to a business transaction involving the transfer of money must be confident that the payment system process will effectively carry out the transfer of funds from one party to the other. Lack of such confidence would severely hamper contractual arrangements. Consequently, to ensure relative uniformity among the states in this area, the states have adopted the Uniform Commercial Code (Article 3) relating to negotiable instruments.

What Is a Negotiable Instrument?

Basically, a **negotiable instrument** is a written promise or order to pay a fixed amount of money, with or without interest, on demand or at a definite time. The most common form of negotiable

Waxen/Shutterstock.com

instrument is a **check**, but other instruments that are considered negotiable instruments are **drafts** (a check is a form of draft), **promissory notes**, and **certificates of deposit**. Promissory notes and certificates of deposit are *promises* to pay. Checks and other drafts are *orders* to pay. In this chapter we will focus mostly on checks to illustrate the law relating to negotiable instruments.

Checks

As with most areas of the law, one must first be familiar with certain fundamental terminology in order to better understand the details.

Terminology

Suppose you write a check to pay a bill to the electric company. You are the **drawer**, the electric company is the **payee**, and your bank (or other financial institution where you have your checking account) is the **drawee**. You have a **principal-agent** relationship with your bank in that you are ordering the bank to pay to the payee a certain amount. The relationship with your financial institution is also a **contractual** relationship.

If you write a check that is payable "to the order of" a specific payee then the check is said to be an **order** instrument whereas a check that is payable to "cash" or to "bearer" is said to be a **bearer** instrument. An order instrument is safer because only the payee can properly **negotiate** the instrument. If the check is a bearer instrument then whoever possesses the check can negotiate it.

We are most familiar with personal checks, but there are other types of checks. **Cashier's checks**, for example, are checks written by a bank or other financial institution. Typically a person would purchase a cashier's check from a bank by giving the bank money for the amount of the check plus a processing fee. The payee may demand or request a cashier's check rather than a personal check to be assured that the check will clear. A **certified check** is one where a bank agrees in advance to honor a check written by the drawer and specifically sets aside funds of the drawer in anticipation of paying for the check. This, of course, gives the payee greater confidence that the check will clear.

Endorsements

A check is negotiated when the payee **endorses** the check and **presents** it for payment typically by depositing it at the payee's bank. The payee's bank then collects the funds from the drawer's bank. A payee can endorse a check in a few different ways. One way is called a **blank endorsement**, where the payee merely signs the back of the check. Once the check is endorsed with a blank endorsement, the check becomes a bearer instrument. Thus, care must be taken by the endorser that the check is not misplaced or lost once the check has been endorsed. Another method of endorsement is to write "for deposit only" above the endorser's signature. This is called a **for-deposit-only** endorsement and restricts the further transferability of the check. Yet another type of endorsement is a **special endorsement**. This is when the endorser writes above the signature to pay to the order of some other person. For example, if you write a check to your friend Shawn for $50 in return for Shawn's promise to provide cleaning services for you, Shawn could then endorse the check and transfer it to Theresa by writing "pay to the order of Theresa," and then signing "Shawn" underneath it. Theresa would then need to endorse

it also in order to either deposit it or transfer it on to someone else.

Margaret M Stewart/Shutterstock.com

Holder in Due Course

Let us continue with the example where you write a check to your friend Shawn for $50. At this point, your friend Shawn is a **holder** of the check. If Shawn endorses the check and transfers it to Theresa, Theresa is now a holder. The holder of a check typically has the same rights that the transferor had if there turns out to be a controversy relating to the check or underlying transaction. Thus, Theresa inherits the same rights that Shawn had in relation to the check. It is possible, however, that if a holder (Theresa in this case) qualifies as a **holder in due course** (HDC), the holder has even greater rights than the transferor had. A holder is an HDC if the holder took the instrument (a) in return for value, (2) in good faith, and (3) without notice that the instrument was fraudulent or altered or another party had a claim to the instrument or a defense related to the instrument.

Continuing with our example, suppose Shawn endorses the check you wrote to him. Shawn then endorses it and delivers the check to Theresa in exchange for Theresa's used textbook. Now assume that Shawn fails to provide the cleaning services to you that he agreed to. You then sue him for breach of contract and you also sue Theresa to get your $50 back. Theresa is an HDC (because she transferred the textbook for value, in good faith, and without notice of any problems regarding the check or underlying transaction). Thus, you will not prevail against Theresa, but you may very well prevail against Shawn. Theresa has an HDC defense against the breach of contract claim you have against Shawn. An HDC does not have a defense in every situation, however, but those exceptions are beyond our discussion here. Consider the following case from the Supreme Court of Maryland relating to a holder in due course (Illustrative Court Case 37.1).

ILLUSTRATIVE COURT CASE 37.1

State Security Check Cashing, Inc. v. American General Financial Services, Inc.

Supreme Court of Maryland

972 A.2d 882 (2009)

OPINION BY: Harrell

In this case we are asked to determine which party, as between the issuer of a check and the check cashing business that cashed it, is liable under [Maryland law] for the face amount of the check, when an imposter, posing successfully as another individual in securing a loan (the proceeds of which were represented by the check) from the issuer, subsequently negotiated the check at the check cashing business. We shall hold that, under the circumstances presented in this case, the issuer of the check is liable for the amount of the check.

I.

Factual and Procedural Background

On 20 June 2007, American General Financial Services, Inc., ("American General") was contacted by telephone by a man, later revealed to be an imposter posing as Ronald E. Wilder (we shall refer to this person as the "imposter", though he was not known to be so at most relevant times in this case). The imposter sought a $20,000.00 loan. Based on the information supplied by him over the telephone, American General ran a credit check on Ronald E. Wilder, finding his credit to be excellent. American General informed the imposter that it would need personal tax returns for the prior two years, and asked him what he intended to do with the proceeds of the desired loan. The imposter sent by electronic facsimile to American General the requested tax returns of Mr. Wilder and explained that he wanted the loan to renovate a property he owned. On Friday, 22 June 2007, American General's District Manager received the completed loan application and tax returns, performed a cash flow analysis, and obtained approval from senior management for an $18,000.00 loan.

On that same morning, American General informed the imposter that the loan was approved. The imposter appeared at noon at American General's Security Boulevard office in Baltimore County. He proffered an apparent Maryland driver's license bearing Mr. Wilder's personal information and the imposter's photograph. He remained in the loan office for approximately thirty minutes, meeting with the branch manager and a customer account specialist during the loan closing. After all the

(Continued)

loan documents were signed, American General issued to the imposter a loan check for $18,000.00 drawn on Wachovia Bank, N.A., and payable to Ronald E. Wilder.

Later that afternoon, the imposter presented the check to State Security Check Cashing, Inc. ("State Security"), a check cashing business. At the time the imposter appeared in State Security's office, also on Security Boulevard in Baltimore County, only one employee was on duty, Wanda Decker. Decker considered the same driver's license that the imposter presented to American General, and reviewed the American General loan documents related to the check. She also compared the check to other checks issued by American General which had been cashed previously by State Security. Deeming the amount of the check relatively "large," Decker called Joel Deutsch, State Security's compliance officer, to confirm that she had taken the proper steps in verifying the check. Deutsch directed Decker to verify the date of the check, the name of the payee on the check, the address of the licensee, the supporting loan paperwork, and whether the check matched other checks in State Security's system from the issuer. Decker confirmed the results of all of these steps, and, upon Deutsch's approval, cashed the check, on behalf of State Security, for the imposter for a fee of 3–5% of the face value of the check.

On Monday, 25 June, the next business day after the imposter negotiated the check at State Security, the real Ronald E. Wilder appeared at the offices of American General indicating that he had been notified by the U.S. Secret Service that a person applied for a loan in his name. At that time, the true Ronald E. Wilder completed an Affidavit of Forgery. As a result of the Affidavit, Thurman Toland, the Branch Manager of American General's Security Boulevard branch, called Wachovia Bank to determine whether the $18,000.00 check had been presented for payment. Learning that the check had not been presented yet, Toland placed a "stop payment" on the check.

State Security filed a civil claim in the District Court of Maryland . . . against American General for the face value of the check, plus interest, asserting that it was a holder in due course of American General's check, that it received the check in good faith, without knowledge of fraud, and that it gave value for the check. On 3 December 2007, the District Court conducted a bench trial. During the trial, the testimonies of Deutsch and Toland revealed three additional, potentially important points: (a) had State Security personnel called American General on 22 June 2007 to verify that American General issued a check to Ronald E. Wilder for $18,000.00, Toland would have confirmed that to be the case; (b) State security employed a thumb print identification system for its check-cashing business, but, at the time the imposter cashed the check, it was unclear whether it was functional; and (c) although, as part of the loan application process, American General obtained names and telephone numbers of personal references from the imposter, it did not call any of the references before delivering the check.

On 19 December 2007, the District Court held in favor of American General. . . .

The District Court concluded that . . . State Security had not exercised ordinary care in paying the imposter's check, and that its failure to exercise ordinary care contributed substantially to the loss.

State Security appealed to the Circuit Court for Baltimore County. A hearing was held on 24 July 2008, based on the record made in the District Court. On 8 August 2008, the Circuit Court . . . [affirmed] the judgment of the District Court . . . .

State Security pressed on. It filed a petition for writ of certiorari with this Court . . . seeking review of the Circuit Court's judgment. We issued the writ. [Citation omitted.]

II.

Discussion

. . .

Section 3-302 of [Maryland's] Commercial Law Article provides . . . that the definition of a "holder in due course" is as follows:

"(a) "[h]older in due course" means the holder of an instrument if:

(1) The instrument when issued or negotiated to the holder does not bear such apparent evidence of forgery or alteration or is not otherwise so irregular or incomplete as to call into question its authenticity; and

(2) The holder took the instrument (i) for value, (ii) in good faith, (iii) without notice that the instrument is overdue or has been dishonored or that there is an uncured default with respect to payment of another instrument issued as part of the same series, (iv) without notice that the instrument contains an unauthorized signature or has been altered, (v) without notice of any claim to the instrument . . ., and (vi) without notice that any party has a defense . . . ."

. . .

The first prerequisite to being deemed a holder in due course is that the item held must be an "instrument." As used in Title 3 of the Commercial Law Article, "'instrument' means a negotiable instrument." . . .

The parties do not dispute that the check issued to the imposter by American General satisfies the definition of a negotiable instrument for purposes of Title 3 of the Commercial Law Article.

. . .

American General argues that, because of the "suspicious circumstances" under which the imposter negotiated the check with State Security, State Security failed to satisfy the Title 3 requirement of good faith. In support of this position, American General advances five points, which, the company argues, when considered together, should defeat State Security's claim: (1) State Security's failure to develop any special procedures to validate the authenticity of large checks being presented at its check cashing business, as confirmed by the testimony of Decker and Deutsch that all checks are treated the same, regardless of amount, and that when Decker called Deutsch for assistance, Deutsch merely re-traced the steps Decker already had taken; (2) State Security "should have known that no competent businessman uses a check-cashing facility for an $18,000 check unless a stop payment order is likely"; (3) Wilder had not been a customer of State Security previously and was not a member of State Security's business; (4) State Security's failure to use its thumbprint identification system, even though the system may not have been functioning at the time of the transaction was critical because "[h]ad State Security told the impostor that it would not complete the transaction without his thumbprint, he likely would not have proceeded and looked instead for a more careless victim"; and (5) the imposter presented the check to State Security on a Friday afternoon, "just hours before most banks and businesses closed for the weekend."

State Security retorts that, under the circumstances of this case, its actions were sufficient to satisfy the good faith statutory requirement. State Security argues:

"It cannot be seriously argued that State Security did not act in good faith. There was no evidence that it had any idea that the person presenting the check was not Ronald E. Wilder. To the contrary, all the evidence points to State Security having made all commercially reasonable efforts to verify that the person presenting the check was the person who was intended to have the check. By matching the signatures on the loan documents with the signature of the person who presented the check, and by verifying that against the driver's license, State Security did all that could be expected of it."

(Continued)

The definition of "good faith," for the purposes of Title 3 of the Commercial Law Article, is . . . "'Good faith' means honesty in fact and the observance of reasonable commercial standards of fair dealing."

. . .

We conclude here that State Security is entitled to enforce the check because it has met its burden of proving that it took the check in good faith.

. . .

American General's position that State Security did not take the check in good faith seems anomalous when State Security relied on the same document for personal identification, as well as the loan documents that American General generated in issuing the check to the imposter, when cashing the check. Because the check was issued by American General as the proceeds of a loan, a transaction verified by State Security, adoption of American General's position would require us to hold State Security, a check cashing business, to a higher commercial standard than American General, simply because the financial institution was duped into issuing the check to an imposter.

American General's desire that we hold the check cashing company here to a higher standard shall not carry the day. . . .

. . .

[W]e resolve that State Security was a holder in due course of the check cashed by the imposter.

Regarding our imposter in the present case, the District Court ruled . . . that State Security did not exercise ordinary care in paying the check presented by him, and that the failure to exercise such care contributed substantially to the loss.

. . .

The District Court's ruling in favor of American General erred in two respects: a) the ruling is not in accord with the statutory definition of "ordinary care," in light of the uncontradicted testimony of Deutsch, State Security's compliance officer, and b) the ruling erred by shifting the default burden of loss in an imposter case to the subsequent holder, State Security, rather than the party who was in the best position to detect the fraud, the drawer, American General.

JUDGMENT OF THE CIRCUIT COURT FOR BALTIMORE COUNTY REVERSED; CASE REMANDED TO THAT COURT WITH DIRECTIONS TO REVERSE THE JUDGMENT OF THE DISTRICT COURT AND REMAND THE CASE TO THE DISTRICT COURT WITH DIRECTIONS TO ENTER JUDGMENT IN FAVOR OF [STATE SECURITY]; COSTS TO BE PAID BY [AMERICAN GENERAL].

Unique Issues Related to Honoring Checks

Sometimes unique situations arise with regard to checks. This section discusses post-dated checks, stale checks, stop-payment orders, forged and altered checks, overdrafts, and inconsistencies.

Undated and Post-Dated Checks

An undated check is still negotiable. A post-dated check is still negotiable and a bank can pay the check even before the date indicated on the check. According to the UCC, a drawer must notify the bank in a separate writing regarding the post-dated check to give the bank notice of the check. If the drawer does this, then the bank is liable for any loss suffered by the drawer if the bank pays the check prematurely.

Stale Checks

If the payee does not present the check for payment within a six month period, the check is said to be **stale**. This means the drawer's bank has no obligation to pay the amount on the check.

Stop-Payment Orders

A drawer may contact the drawer's bank and request that the bank not pay a check that the drawer has written. This is called a **stop-payment order**. If the drawer makes the request orally, the bank is bound by the request for 14 calendar days. If the request is in writing, the bank is bound for six months. If the bank pays the check even though there is a stop-payment order on the check, the bank cannot take the money out of the drawer's account.

Forged and Altered Checks

Typically the drawer's bank is obligated to make sure that the signature on the check is, indeed, the drawer's signature. If the drawer's signature is forged and the drawer's bank pays the check anyway, then the drawer's bank can sue the forger. If a check is altered, the general rule is that the drawer or any bank that may suffer a loss because of the altered check can sue the person who altered the check. Otherwise, the bank that was in the best position to first discover that the check was altered will likely suffer the loss.

Overdrafts

If a drawer writes a check for more money than the drawer has in his or her bank account, this is called an **overdraft**. Depending upon bank policy and/or the contractual arrangement between the bank and the customer, the bank may still pay the check notwithstanding the overdraft (*i.e.*, **overdraft protection**). Often, the bank may charge a fee for paying the check. Alternatively, the drawer's bank can reject payment on the check due to **insufficient funds**. Typically, the drawer pays fees as a result of writing a check without sufficient funds in his or her account.

Inconsistencies

Suppose the numerical amount on the check differs from the written-out portion of the check. For example, $100.00 is written in the box on the right side of the check, but the written portion says, "Ten and 00/100 dollars." Is the check negotiable for $10.00 or $100.00? The UCC indicates that words outweigh the numerical figures. Thus, the check is payable for $10.00. Moreover, handwritten terms prevail over printed terms.

Other Related Banking Issues

Technology has impacted banking tremendously in recent years. Thus, banking laws and payment processing systems have had to adapt. We discuss a few related banking issues here.

The Federal Reserve System

The Federal Reserve System was created by Congress in 1913 to help facilitate the banking system in the United States. The Federal Reserve consists of 12 banks located in varying regions across the country. These Federal Reserve banks also have branches in other cities. For example, the San Francisco Federal Reserve bank has branches in Los Angeles, Portland, Salt Lake City, and Seattle.

Although there are many functions of the Federal Reserve, one function is to facilitate payments from one bank to another. For example, if you write a check to your friend, your friend will likely deposit the check in a bank (*i.e.*, the **depository bank**). The depository bank ultimately seeks payment from your bank, but rather than send the check to your bank, the depository bank may get paid by an **intermediary** (or **collecting**) **bank**, which will then collect the amount of the check from your bank. The Federal Reserve banks often act as intermediary banks to facilitate the processing of checks.

Debit Cards and Electronic Banking

The use of **debit cards** has increased significantly in recent years. Debit cards are basically substitutes for checks. When a debit card is swiped at a **point of sale** terminal, the money to pay for the transaction is electronically transferred from the customer's account to the seller's. Obviously, this process is much faster than the check depositing and collecting process.

Most all banks and financial institutions now allow online banking where customers can monitor balances, make balance transfers, and pay bills. Of course, banking laws have evolved to address the increased electronic nature of banking. Electronic banking also is common now for automatic deposits for employee payroll purposes. **Automatic teller machines** (ATMs) also serve as forms of electronic banking. Customers can withdraw cash, make deposits, transfer funds from one account to another, etc.

Diego Cervo/Shutterstock.com

What Do You Think?

Due to the prevalence of online banking and the ease of using debit cards, should the use of checks be discontinued?

Dodd-Frank Wall Street Reform and Consumer Protection Act

One of the most significant Congressional acts to overhaul the United States financial system occurred in 2010. This act, the **Dodd-Frank Wall Street Reform and Consumer Protection Act**, was in response to the actual and perceived abuses of financial institutions and investment firms relating to the financial crisis that began in 2007. The Act is extraordinarily detailed and provides a host of regulatory reforms. For example, the Act creates new agencies such as the Financial Stability Oversight Council and streamlines other agencies. The Act also requires these agencies to regularly report to Congress. New lending regulations are also part of the Act as an attempt to limit financial institutions from making "bad" loans and then immediately selling those loans, oftentimes to Freddie Mac and Fannie Mae.

The Act also permanently increased the ceiling on insured amounts at **FDIC** (Federal Deposit Insurance Corporation) insured banks. Accounts at FDIC insured banks are insured up to $250,000. Thus, if the bank fails, the account holder will be paid by the FDIC up to $250,000. Further details of the Dodd-Frank Act are beyond the scope of our discussion here.

QUESTIONS FOR REVIEW

1. What is a negotiable instrument?

2. Name two instruments that are "promises" to pay, and two instruments that are "orders" to pay.

3. Explain the meaning of the following terms:

    a. drawer

    b. payee

    c. drawee

    d. order instrument

    e. bearer instrument

    f. blank endorsement

    g. special endorsement

    h. holder

    i. holder in due course

4. Explain the general rules that apply to these unique issues regarding checks:

    a. undated check

    b. post-dated check

    c. check with inconsistent numbers and word description

    d. stale checks

    e. forged checks

    f. altered checks

    g. stop-payments

    h. insufficient funds

5. Discuss generally the purpose of the Federal Reserve System.

6. Discuss generally the purpose of the Dodd-Frank Act.

7. What is the role of the FDIC?

8. Summarize the *State Security v. American General* case.

INTERNET ACTIVITIES

1. Visit the website of the Federal Reserve at www.federalreserve.gov.

    a. Click on the "About the Fed" tab. Who is the current Chair of the Board?

    b. Click on the "News & Events" tab. Click on the "Press Releases" link. Summarize a recent press release.

2. Visit the website of the Federal Deposit Insurance Corporation at www.fdic.gov.

    a. Click on the "Consumer Protection" tab. Click on the "Consumer Assistance & Information" link. Click on "Consumer Protection Topics". Click on "Credit Reports". Provide a brief summary of the consumer protections available.

    b. Click on the "Industry Analysis" tab. Click on the "Failed Banks" link. Click on "Failed Bank" list. When was the last bank to fail in your state? What was the bank's name? If your state is not listed, use the state of Georgia.

Part XIV

Administrative, Consumer, Environmental, and Antitrust Law

Chapter 38

Administrative Law

As discussed in Chapter 2, government consists of numerous departments and agencies. A federal administrative agency is created by Congress through **enabling legislation**. Nearly all businesses must interact with one or more goverment agencies. For example, all businesses must comply with income tax rules, regulations and filing requirements established by the IRS. Businesses that serve or manufacture food must comply with national and/or local health regulations imposed by government agencies. Airlines must deal with the FAA, manufacturers with OSHA, and pharmaceutical companies with the FDA, etc.

Questions often arise as to how much power an agency has, and how arbitrary its rules and regulations can be to make operating a business more difficult. Agencies have broad authority to interpret statutes and to enforce its own rules and regulations. Nevertheless, such rulemaking and enforcement actions must be within the scope of authority granted to the agency by Congress (or in the case of a state agency, by the state legislature). Of course,

agencies must abide by certain rules of fairness and must establish procedures for aggrieved parties to follow when dealing with the agency. These rules are contained primarily in the Administrative Procedure Act.

Administrative Procedure Act

Although the **Administrative Procedure Act** (APA) gives agencies wide latitude in establishing procedures, rules, and regulations within the respective agency's area of expertise, the agency actions cannot be unconstitutional, **arbitrary** or **capricious**. In other words, there must be a rational reason behind the agency's action. Consider the United States Supreme Court case (Illustrative Court Case 38.1) that explains the law applicable to an agency's use of its discretionary authority. More specifically, the case addresses the situation where the Federal Communications Commission sought to regulate television stations that broadcasted a live event where celebrities used expletives.

ILLUSTRATIVE COURT CASE 38.1

Federal Communications Commission v. Fox Television Stations, Inc.

Supreme Court of the United States

129 S. Ct. 1800 (2009)

[**Note:** For convenience of the reader, the following language is from the Syllabus of the case as provided by the U.S. Supreme Court Reporter of Decisions.]

(Continued)

Federal law bans the broadcasting of "any . . . indecent . . . language," [citation omitted], which includes references to sexual or excretory activity or organs . . . . [Citation omitted.] Having first defined the prohibited speech in 1975, the Federal Communications Commission (FCC) took a cautious, but gradually expanding, approach to enforcing the statutory prohibition. In 2004, the FCC's *Golden Globes Order* declared for the first time that an expletive (nonliteral) use of the F-Word or the S-Word could be actionably indecent, even when the word is used only once.

This case concerns isolated utterances of the F- and S-Words during two live broadcasts aired by Fox Television Stations, Inc. In its order upholding the indecency findings, the FCC . . . stated that the *Golden Globes Order* eliminated any doubt that fleeting expletives could be actionable; declared that under the new policy, a lack of repetition weighs against a finding of indecency, but is not a safe harbor; and held that both broadcasts met the new test because one involved a literal description of excrement and both invoked the F-Word. The order did not impose sanctions for either broadcast. The Second Circuit set aside the agency action, declining to address the constitutionality of the FCC's action but finding the FCC's reasoning inadequate under the Administrative Procedure Act (APA).

Held: The judgment is reversed, and the case is remanded.

1. The FCC's orders are neither "arbitrary" nor "capricious" within the meaning of the APA.

(a) Under the APA standard, an agency must "examine the relevant data and articulate a satisfactory explanation for its action." [Citation omitted.] In overturning the FCC's judgment, the Second Circuit relied in part on its precedent interpreting the APA and [a prior Supreme Court case] to require a more substantial explanation for agency action that changes prior policy. There is, however, no basis in the Act or this Court's opinions for a requirement that all agency change be subjected to more searching review. Although an agency must ordinarily display awareness that it *is* changing position . . . and may sometimes need to account for prior factfinding or certain reliance interests created by a prior policy, it need not demonstrate to a court's satisfaction that the reasons for the new policy are *better* than the reasons for the old one. It suffices that the new policy is permissible under the statute, that there are good reasons for it, and that the agency *believes* it to be better, which the conscious change adequately indicates.

(b) Under these standards, the FCC's new policy and its order finding the broadcasts at issue actionably indecent were neither arbitrary nor capricious. First, the FCC forthrightly acknowledged that its recent actions have broken new ground, taking account of inconsistent prior FCC and staff actions, and explicitly disavowing them as no longer good law. The agency's reasons for expanding its enforcement activity, moreover, were entirely rational. Even when used as an expletive, the F-Word's power to insult and offend derives from its sexual meaning. And the decision to look at the patent offensiveness of even isolated uses of sexual and excretory words fits with [a] context-based approach. Because the FCC's prior safe-harbor-for-single-words approach would likely lead to more widespread use, and in light of technological advances reducing the costs of bleeping offending words, it was rational for the agency to step away from its old regime. The FCC's decision not to impose sanctions precludes any argument that it is arbitrarily punishing parties without notice of their actions' potential consequences.

(c) None of the Second Circuit's grounds for finding the FCC's action arbitrary and capricious is valid. First, the FCC did not need empirical evidence proving that fleeting expletives constitute harmful "first blows" to children; it suffices to know that children mimic behavior they observe. Second, the court of appeals' finding that fidelity to the FCC's "first blow" theory would require a categorical ban on *all* broadcasts of expletives is not responsive to the actual policy under review since the FCC has always evaluated the patent offensiveness of words and statements in relation to the context in which they were broadcast. The FCC's decision to retain some discretion in less egregious cases does not invalidate its regulation of the broadcasts under review. Third, the FCC's prediction that a *per se* exemption for fleeting expletives would lead to their increased use merits deference and makes entire sense.

(d) Fox's additional arguments are not tenable grounds for affirmance. Fox misconstrues the agency's orders when it argues that that the new policy is a presumption of indecency for certain words. . . . And Fox's argument that the FCC's repeated appeal to "context" is a smokescreen for a standardless regime of unbridled discretion ignores the fact that [this Court has] endorsed a context-based approach.

2. Absent a lower court opinion on the matter, this Court declines to address the FCC orders' constitutionality.

Notice how the Supreme Court allows an agency (the FCC in this case) to change its enforcement policy as long as there is a rational reason to do so.

designer491/Shutterstock.com

Once an individual or business complies with the administrative procedure in whatever dispute the person has with the agency, the person usually has the ability to appeal an adverse decision to the courts. In fact, in many situations a court will not hear a case unless the person has **exhausted the administrative remedies** available to the person.

Freedom of Information Act

So as to provide government transparency, Congress enacted the **Freedom of Information Act (FOIA)**. This requires government agencies to make publicly available the rules, regulations, and decisions that it makes. Moreover, most agency hearings and meetings must be open to the public.

Someone desiring information from the government may make a FOIA request. Of course, there are some limitations on what information a person can obtain through a FOIA request. Examples include information that may compromise national security, criminal investigations, and information about another individual.

Privacy Act of 1974

As a general rule, the Privacy Act of 1974 prohibits government agencies from sharing information about you to other government agencies without first obtaining your consent. Not surprisingly, there are exceptions to this rule too (*e.g.*, national security issues, criminal investigations, etc.).

QUESTIONS FOR REVIEW

1. An agency's decision cannot be arbitrary or capricious. What does this mean?

2. Generally, do agencies have broad or narrow latitude in making rules and regulations?

3. What does FOIA stand for? What is the purpose of the FOIA?

4. Before a court hears a case between a person and a governmental agency, the person usually must first exhaust his or her administrative remedies. What does this mean?

5. Summarize the *FCC v. Fox Television* case.

INTERNET ACTIVITIES

1. Visit the Freedom of Information Act website at www.foia.gov. Click on the "Learn about FOIA" tab. Summarize how to make a FOIA request and where to make a FOIA request.

2. Locate the United States Supreme Court case *Motor Vehicle Manufacturers Association v. State Farm Automobile Insurance*, 463 U.S. 29 (1983).

   a. What is the issue or issues in the case?

   b. What was the Court's holding?

   c. Summarize the Court's analysis, including the analysis of the meaning of "arbitrary and capricious."

Chapter 39

Consumer Protection

What role should the government have in protecting consumers from dangerous or faulty products? Should the government be able to force a recall of the products? Or at least warn the public? The United States government does undertake consumer protection in many different areas of commerce. Consumer protection laws cover a broad array of products and services, many of which we will discuss in this chapter.

Advertising and Sales Practices

Have you ever wondered whether the late-night commercial promoting a magic product that you can wear that builds your ab muscles while you're sitting on the couch watching TV eating chocolate cake was deceptive advertising? The government realizes the possibility of deceptive and unfair trade practices and has assigned the **Federal Trade Commission** (FTC) as the primary federal agency to be responsible for consumer protection. Since the FTC is such a large organization, a special sub-agency—the **Bureau of Consumer Protection**—was created to deal with consumer protection matters involving unfair, deceptive or fraudulent practices by businesses.

Deceptive Advertising

One major function of the FTC is to address issues related to deceptive advertising. Basically, a business is engaged in deceptive advertising if the business makes an **expressly false statement** regarding the product's quality, ingredients, or effectiveness. If the FTC determines that a business has engaged in deceptive advertising, the FTC can issue **cease-and-desist** letters basically requiring the business to stop the advertising. Additionally, the FTC can order the business to engage in **corrective advertising** to address the problem. The FTC can also order the business to **disgorge** the profits it made as a result of the deceptive advertising. Consider the United States Court of Appeals for the Second Circuit case that follows (Illustrative Court Case 39.1).

In addition to deceptive advertising, companies may be tempted to engage in a tactic called **bait and switch**. This basically means that a business advertises something at a very low price (*e.g.*, the "bait"), but when the customer arrives at the business the salesperson pressures the customer to purchase something else (*e.g.*, the "switch"). The FTC investigates this type of "unfair" advertising also.

Labeling and Packaging

Much of what we buy must meet strict labeling and packaging requirements set forth in various acts passed by Congress, including the **Fair Packaging and Labeling Act** (FPLA). This Act is intended to prevent deceptive advertising on the product itself (as opposed to just on television, radio, or in newspapers). Of course, the labeling and packaging requirements vary depending upon the product being sold and what ingredients and/or parts

Federal Trade Commission v. Bronson Partners

Court of Appeals for the Second Circuit

2011 U.S. App. LEXIS 17203

OPINION

Gerard E. Lynch, Circuit Judge:

In 2003 and 2004, Bronson Partners, LLC, Martin Howard, H&H Marketing, and Sandra Howard (collectively, "Bronson") advertised and sold two purportedly miraculous weight loss products. According to advertisements, Bronson's Chinese Diet Tea "SHEDS POUND AFTER POUND OF FAT — FAST!" Among other claims, Bronson's advertisements also proclaimed that the Chinese Diet Tea "[e]liminates an amazing 91% of absorbed sugars," "[p]revents 83% of fat absorption," and "[d]oubles your metabolic rate to burn calories fast." Over the same time period, Bronson advertised its Bio-Slim Patch as a way to achieve "LASTING weight loss." The advertisements promised that by "carry[ing] on with your normal lifestyle" and wearing the Bio-Slim Patch, "[r]epulsive, excess ugly fatty tissue will disappear at a spectacular rate." Bronson now admits that it engaged in deceptive advertising of both products in violation of the Federal Trade Commission Act. . . . Bronson nevertheless appeals from a January 5, 2010 judgment of the United States District Court for the District of Connecticut . . . that entered a permanent injunction against Bronson and ordered it to pay $1,942,325 in monetary equitable relief plus statutory interest. Bronson contests the judgment on the grounds that: (1) the statute on which the district court's jurisdiction was based . . . does not permit a court to order monetary relief; and (2) even if monetary relief may be awarded, the district court calculated its award incorrectly by awarding legal rather than equitable relief. We hold that [the Act] empowers a court to award ancillary equitable remedies, including disgorgement of wrongfully obtained funds, and that the district court's monetary award was appropriately calculated. Accordingly we AFFIRM the judgment of the district court.

. . .

Section 19 [of the Act] authorizes the district court to hear suits to enforce the Commission's cease-and-desist orders and, where appropriate, to award "such relief as the court finds necessary to redress injury to consumers," which may include "the refund of money or return of property." [Citation omitted.] Because . . . the Commission may bring suit only where the defendant has been the subject of a prior order entered in the wake of a lengthy administrative process, that provision has the disadvantages of creating substantial opportunities for delay as well as allowing merchants who knowingly engage in fraud at least one free shot at violating the Act. In contrast, Section 13 requires only that the Commission establish that the defendant's conduct on a particular occasion violated the general prohibitions of the statute. In sum, . . . the FTC Act permits courts to award not only injunctive relief but also ancillary relief, including monetary relief.

. . .

B. Calculating Equitable Monetary Relief

To guide the district court on remand, [this court has] adopted a two-step burden-shifting framework for calculating monetary relief under Section 13(b). "This framework requires the FTC to first show that its calculations reasonably approximated the amount of the defendant's unjust gains, after which the burden shifts to the defendants to show that those figures were inaccurate." [Citation omitted.] After the burden shifts, the risk of uncertainty "fall[s] on the wrongdoer whose illegal conduct created the uncertainty."

. . .

In sum, . . . [t]he district court properly assessed Bronson's unjust gains as $1,942,325, the amount Bronson received in revenues from sales of the Chinese Diet Tea and the Bio-Slim Patch after check refunds.

CONCLUSION

For the foregoing reasons, we AFFIRM the district court's judgment in full.

---

are included with the product. For example, toys typically will indicate that the toy is appropriate for children over a certain age and if the product could be a choking hazard to small children. Serving sizes must be on food labels, etc. Other similar legislation passed by Congress includes:

- The Nutrition Labeling and Education Act
- The Food, Drug, and Cosmetic Act
- Poison Prevention Packaging Act
- Wool Products Labeling Act
- Flammable Fabrics Act
- Hazardous Substance Act
- Cigarette Labeling Act
- Fur Products Labeling Act

Monkey Business Images/Shutterstock.com

Door-to-Door Sales, Telemarketing, and Mail Order Sales

Salespeople who go door-to-door attempting to make sales are also governed by the FTC. In short, the salespeople must inform customers that the door-to-door sale can be cancelled within three days (the "cooling off period"). Of course, the federal government also regulates solicitation by telemarketers. The national "Do Not Call" list is a good example. Regulations applicable to mail order sales require companies to ship the product within the time frame advertised. In some cases, consumers may also have rights to cancel the mail order, particularly if a product arrives unsolicited by the consumer.

Credit and Financial Protection

During the last several years, Congress has tightened considerably the regulation of the financial industry. This, of course, is in response to the downturn in the economy that began toward the end of 2007. This downturn was significantly impacted by banks and other financial institutions creating and trading questionable financial instruments that were backed by unstable loans to consumers who were over-extended financially. In 2010, Congress created the **Consumer Financial Protection Bureau** (CFPB) to protect consumers by enforcing federal consumer financial laws and regulations. This includes rule-making, taking consumer complaints, monitoring financial markets for new financial products that may pose a risk, and restrict unfair, deceptive, or abusive acts or practices in the financial markets. The CFPB does not regulate the securities markets, however, which is regulated by the Securities and Exchange Commission (SEC).

Regulation of credit transactions has been in effect for decades. The primary legislation impacting credit transactions is the **Consumer Credit Protection Act**. This Act is voluminous and actually addresses a variety of topics and encompasses smaller acts by Congress that have been incorporated into the CCPA.

Fair Debt Collection Practices Act

The **Fair Debt Collection Practices Act** restricts debt collectors from certain practices in attempting to collect debts. This includes, for example, harassing the debtor by, among other things, calling at inconvenient times, contacting the debtor's employer for certain purposes,

continuing to contact the debtor after the debtor has retained an attorney, etc. Moreover, a debt collection agency must give the debtor at least 30 days from the initial contact to dispute the debt that is asserted to be owed by the creditor. It is important to understand that this Act defines "debt collector" very broadly, so care is in order if you are engaged in business and trying to collect a debt. Consider the following case from the United States Supreme Court addressing issues related to the FDCPA (Illustrative Court Case 39.2).

ILLUSTRATIVE COURT CASE 39.2

Jerman v. Carlisle

Supreme Court of the United States

130 S. Ct. 1605 (2010)

[**Note:** For convenience of the reader, the following language is from the Syllabus of the case as provided by the U.S. Supreme Court Reporter of Decisions.]

The Fair Debt Collection Practices Act (FDCPA) . . . imposes civil liability on "debt collector[s]" for certain prohibited debt collection practices. A debt collector who "fails to comply with any [FDCPA] provision . . . with respect to any person is liable to such person" for "actual damage[s]," costs, "a reasonable attorney's fee as determined by the court," and statutory "additional damages." [Citation omitted.] In addition, violations of the FDCPA are deemed unfair or deceptive acts or practices under the Federal Trade Commission Act (FTC Act) . . . , which is enforced by the Federal Trade Commission (FTC). A debt collector who acts with "actual knowledge or knowledge fairly implied on the basis of objective circumstances that such act is [prohibited under the FDCPA]" is subject to civil penalties enforced by the FTC. [Citation omitted.] A debt collector is not liable in any action brought under the FDCPA, however, if it "shows by a preponderance of evidence that the violation was not intentional and resulted from a bona fide error notwithstanding the maintenance of procedures reasonably adapted to avoid any such error." [Citation omitted.]

Respondents, a law firm and one of its attorneys (collectively Carlisle), filed a lawsuit in Ohio state court on behalf of a mortgage company to foreclose a mortgage on real property owned by petitioner Jerman. The complaint included a notice that the mortgage debt would be assumed valid unless Jerman disputed it in writing. Jerman's lawyer sent a letter disputing the debt, and, when the mortgage company acknowledged that the debt had in fact been paid, Carlisle withdrew the suit. Jerman then filed this action, contending that by sending the notice requiring her to dispute the debt in writing, Carlisle had violated . . . the FDCPA, which governs the contents of notices to debtors. The District Court, acknowledging a division of authority on the question, held that Carlisle had violated [the Act] but ultimately granted Carlisle summary judgment under [the Act's] "bona fide error" defense. The Sixth Circuit affirmed, holding that the defense . . . is not limited to clerical or factual errors, but extends to mistakes of law.

Held: The bona fide error defense . . . does not apply to a violation resulting from a debt collector's mistaken interpretation of the legal requirements of the FDCPA.

(a) A violation resulting from a debt collector's misinterpretation of the legal requirements of the FDCPA cannot be "not intentional" under [the Act]. It is a common maxim that "ignorance of the law will not excuse any person, either civilly or criminally." [Citation omitted.] When Congress has intended to provide a mistake-of-law defense to civil liability, it has often done so more explicitly than here. In particular, the administrative-penalty provisions of the FTC Act, which are expressly incorporated into the FDCPA, apply only when a debt collector acts with "actual knowledge or knowledge fairly implied on the basis of objective circumstances" that the FDCPA prohibited its action. [Citation omitted.] [I]t is fair to infer that Congress permitted injured consumers to recover damages for "intentional" conduct, including violations resulting from a mistaken interpretation of the FDCPA, while reserving the more onerous administrative penalties for debt collectors whose intentional actions reflected knowledge that the conduct was prohibited. Congress also did not confine FDCPA liability to "willful" violations, a term more often understood in the civil context to exclude mistakes of law. [Citation omitted.] . . .

(c) Today's decision does not place unmanageable burdens on debt-collecting lawyers. The FDCPA contains several provisions expressly guarding against abusive lawsuits, and gives courts discretion in calculating additional damages and attorney's fees. Lawyers have recourse to the bona fide error defense . . . when a violation results from a qualifying factual error. To the extent the FDCPA imposes some constraints on a lawyer's advocacy on behalf of a client, it is not unique; lawyers have a duty, for instance, to comply with the law and standards of professional conduct. Numerous state consumer protection and debt collection statutes contain bona fide error defenses that are either silent as to, or expressly exclude, legal errors. To the extent lawyers face liability for mistaken interpretations of the FDCPA, Carlisle [has] not shown that "the result [will be] so absurd as to warrant" disregarding the weight of textual authority. [Citation omitted.] Absent such a showing, arguments that the FDCPA strikes an undesirable balance in assigning the risks of legal misinterpretation are properly addressed to Congress. [Citation omitted.]

[R]eversed and remanded.

Truth in Lending Act

Federal law requires lenders to disclose certain information to borrowers as part of the credit transaction. The **Truth in Lending Act** (TILA) specifically applies to lenders who are in the business of extending credit to consumers for personal, family, or household purposes. The TILA also provides that the Federal Reserve Board can issue regulations if necessary to further the purposes of the act. The Federal Reserve has, in fact, issued regulations, the most important of which is likely **Regulation Z**. This Regulation requires that the lender disclose to the consumer the finance charge and the annual percentage rate (APR). The finance charge portion of the disclosure basically states how much interest the consumer will pay over the life of the loan. The APR is the interest rate the consumer will pay, as a percentage, on a yearly basis throughout the term of the loan. TILA also requires the lender to notify the borrower that the borrower has three days to cancel the transaction. Failure to properly notify the borrower of this right could cause the borrower to have up to three years to cancel the transaction.

Fair Credit Reporting Act

Many lenders will base the decision whether to grant credit to an applicant on the applicant's **credit score**. This credit score is developed by credit reporting agencies based on the consumer's credit history. The **Fair Credit Reporting Act** (FCRA) requires that credit reporting agencies provide at least one copy of a consumer's credit report to the consumer upon request free of charge each year. Moreover, if a consumer is declined credit based on the credit report, the consumer has a right to view the credit report. The FCRA also provides dispute procedures, and requires the credit reporting agencies to remove information that is out-dated (*e.g.*, bankruptcies over a decade ago) or inaccurate.

Equal Credit Opportunity Act

Pursuant to the **Equal Credit Opportunity Act** (ECOA), lenders cannot discriminate against potential borrowers based on race, color, national origin, religion, gender, age or marital status.

Electronic Funds Transfer Act

Electronic commerce is, of course, more popular than ever. Moreover, many people prefer to do their banking electronically also. The **Electronic Funds Transfer Act** (EFTA) regulates transferring funds electronically between consumers, banks and other financial institutions. ATM and debit card transactions, for example, are governed by and protected by the EFTA. The Act also provides consumers the right to challenge disputed transactions and limits a consumer's liability for a lost or stolen card.

Credit Card Accountability and Disclosure Act

The **Credit Card Accountability and Disclosure Act** (CARD) requires credit card companies to disclose information such as how much total interest a consumer will pay if the consumer only makes the minimum payment each month. The CARD Act also requires credit card companies to give 45-day notice to consumers of increases in interest rates. Additionally, the Act requires the company mail the statement to the consumer at least 21 days before the credit card bill is due.

Health and Safety Protection

Given the vast number of products in the marketplace and the potential for malfunctions and design problems, the government has agencies to regulate and test some of those products. Primarily the products regulated have some connection to public health and safety.

The **Food and Drug Administration** (FDA) is an important agency involved in the regulation of food and drug safety. New drugs, medicines, and some medical procedures must generally receive approval from the FDA before the product or service can be marketed to the public. Of course, businesses involved in food and drug research and manufacturing pay very close attention to FDA regulations and rulings.

The **Department of Transportation** (DOT) also is heavily involved in the protection of public health and safety. The DOT is composed of several agencies, including the high-profile Federal Aviation Administration and National Highway Traffic Safety Administration (NHTSA). These agencies regulate air and highway travel, respectively, including airplane and vehicle manufacturing specifications and safety features. The NHTSA, for example, conducts crash tests on new vehicles and provides safety ratings (*e.g.*, 5-star, 4-star, etc.) to help the public be more informed on the safety of vehicles. Other government agencies regulate the railroad and maritime industries.

Regarding most products other than food, drugs, and vehicles, the regulating agency is the **Consumer Product Safety Commission** (CPSC). The CPSC was created to administer the Consumer Product Safety Act. The purpose of the Act is set forth in Illustrative Federal Statute 39.1.

The CPSC fields consumer complaints, issues recalls, and otherwise provides the public information regarding the safety of products. The Commission's website provides the latest updates on recalls, hazards, and links to regulations governing certain products. The CPSC may issue these regulations and standards under authority from Congress. Consider Illustrative Federal Statute 39.2.

Remember also that in addition to the federal consumer protection laws, most states also have a consumer protection agency and regulations that businesses must comply with.

15 U.S.C. § 2051

§ 2051. Congressional findings and declaration of purpose

(a) The Congress finds that –

(1) an unacceptable number of consumer products which present unreasonable risks of injury are distributed in commerce;

(2) complexities of consumer products and the diverse nature and abilities of consumers using them frequently result in an inability of users to anticipate risks and to safeguard themselves adequately;

(3) the public should be protected against unreasonable risks of injury associated with consumer products;

(4) control by State and local governments of unreasonable risks of injury associated with consumer products is inadequate and may be burdensome to manufacturers;

(5) existing Federal authority to protect consumers from exposure to consumer products presenting unreasonable risks of injury is inadequate; and

(6) regulation of consumer products the distribution or use of which affects interstate or foreign commerce is necessary to carry out this Act.

(b) The purposes of this Act are—

(1) to protect the public against unreasonable risks of injury associated with consumer products;

(2) to assist consumers in evaluating the comparative safety of consumer products;

(3) to develop uniform safety standards for consumer products and to minimize conflicting State and local regulations; and

(4) to promote research and investigation into the causes and prevention of product-related deaths, illnesses, and injuries.

15 U.S.C. §2056

§ 2056. Consumer product safety standards

(a) Types of requirements. The Commission may promulgate consumer product safety standards in accordance with the provisions [of the Act]. A consumer product safety standard shall consist of one or more of any of the following types of requirements:

(1) Requirements expressed in terms of performance requirements.

(2) Requirements that a consumer product be marked with or accompanied by clear and adequate warnings or instructions, or requirements respecting the form of warnings or instructions.

Any requirement of such a standard shall be reasonably necessary to prevent or reduce an unreasonable risk of injury associated with such product.

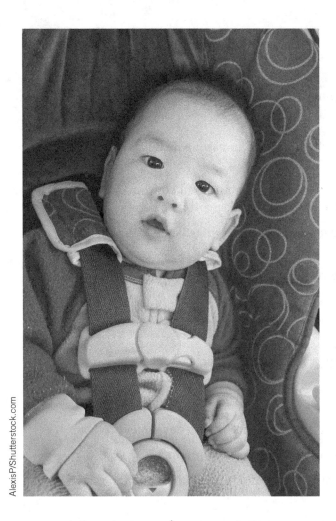

4. Explain the "bait-and-switch" tactic.

5. With regard to door-to-door sales, what is the "cooling off" period?

6. In 2010, Congress created the Consumer Financial Protection Bureau. What is the purpose of the CFPB?

7. Discuss briefly some protections provided to debtors by the Fair Debt Collection Practices Act.

8. What is Regulation Z?

9. Explain briefly the CARD Act.

10. Discuss some of the purposes of the Consumer Product Safety Act as set forth by Congress.

11. Summarize the *FTC v. Bronson Partners* case.

12. Summarize the *Jerman v. Carlisle* case.

INTERNET ACTIVITIES

1. Visit the Federal Trade Commission website at www.ftc.gov. Click on the "Enforcement" tab. Click on the "Cases and Proceedings" Link.

   a. Select a case or proceeding. What company was it against? Summarize the FTC's enforcement action against the company.

   b. Select a different case or proceeding. What company was it against? Summarize the FTC's enforcement action against the company.

2. Find the website of your state's consumer protection agency.

   a. What is the official name of your state's consumer protection agency? (Note: Some states' consumer protection agency is within the Attorney General's office while other states have a stand-alone consumer protection agency.)

   b. Summarize an recent action taken by your state's consumer protection agency.

What Do You Think?

Should government be in the business of regulating the safety of all products sold to consumers? If not, how should the government determine which products to regulate? Car seats? Skateboards? Pencils? Textbooks? Dolls? As a taxpayer, are you willing to pay for all of this regulation?

QUESTIONS FOR REVIEW

1. What is the primary role of the Federal Trade Commission?

2. What is deceptive advertising?

3. What can the FTC require a business to do if the business is engaged in deceptive advertising?

Chapter 40

Environmental Law

The United States government largely ignored business activities creating environmental hazards until the 1970s. At that point, Congress enacted laws significantly restricting air pollution, water pollution, hazardous wastes, ocean dumping, etc. As part of this major attempt to regulate pollution and other environmental hazards, Congress created the Environmental Protection Agency.

Environmental Protection Agency

The mission of the **Environmental Protection Agency** (EPA) is to protect human health and the environment. Thus, Congress has charged the EPA with the primary responsibility of enforcing environmental laws passed by Congress and issuing regulations of its own. Additionally, the EPA encourages compliance with these laws and regulations and can assess fines for violations. Congress also gives some business tax credits and other incentives to encourage compliance with environmental regulations. The EPA engages in research in an attempt to identify potential risks and hazards to the environment. What if the EPA fails to act in regulating what many consider to be an environmental hazard? Consider the United States Supreme Court case that follows (Illustrative Court Case 40.1).

ILLUSTRATIVE COURT CASE 40.1

Massachusetts v. Environmental Protection Agency

Supreme Court of the United States

127 S. Ct. 1438 (2007)

[**Note:** For convenience of the reader, the following language is from the Syllabus of the case as provided by the U.S. Supreme Court Reporter of Decisions.]

Based on respected scientific opinion that a well-documented rise in global temperatures and attendant climatological and environmental changes have resulted from a significant increase in the atmospheric concentration of "greenhouse gases," a group of private organizations petitioned the Environmental Protection Agency (EPA) to begin regulating the emissions of four such gases, including carbon dioxide, under . . . the Clean Air Act, which requires that EPA "shall by regulation prescribe . . . standards applicable to the emission of any air pollutant from any class . . . of new motor vehicles . . . which in [the EPA Administrator's] judgment cause[s], or contribute[s] to,

---

(Continued)

air pollution . . . reasonably . . . anticipated to endanger public health or welfare," [Citation omitted.] The Act defines "air pollutant" to include "any air pollution agent . . . , including any physical, chemical . . . substance . . . emitted into . . . the ambient air." [Citation omitted.] EPA ultimately denied the petition, reasoning that (1) the Act does not authorize it to issue mandatory regulations to address global climate change, and (2) even if it had the authority to set greenhouse gas emission standards, it would have been unwise to do so at that time because a causal link between greenhouse gases and the increase in global surface air temperatures was not unequivocally established. The Agency further characterized any EPA regulation of motor-vehicle emissions as a piecemeal approach to climate change that would conflict with the President's comprehensive approach involving additional support for technological innovation, the creation of nonregulatory programs to encourage voluntary private-sector reductions in greenhouse gas emissions, and further research on climate change, and might hamper the President's ability to persuade key developing nations to reduce emissions.

Petitioners, now joined by . . . Massachusetts and other state and local governments, sought review in the D. C. Circuit. Although each of the three judges on the panel wrote separately, two of them agreed that the EPA Administrator properly exercised his discretion in denying the rulemaking petition. One judge concluded that the Administrator's exercise of "judgment" as to whether a pollutant could "reasonably be anticipated to endanger public health or welfare," . . . could be based on scientific uncertainty as well as other factors, including the concern that unilateral U. S. regulation of motor-vehicle emissions could weaken efforts to reduce other countries' greenhouse gas emissions. The second judge opined that petitioners had failed to demonstrate the particularized injury to them that is necessary to establish standing . . . , but accepted the contrary view as the law of the case and joined the judgment on the merits as the closest to that which he preferred. The court therefore denied review.

Held:

1. Petitioners have standing to challenge EPA's denial of their rulemaking petition.

(a) [T]he proper construction of a congressional statute is an eminently suitable question for federal-court resolution, and Congress has authorized precisely this type of challenge to EPA action. Contrary to EPA's argument, standing doctrine presents no insuperable jurisdictional obstacle here. To demonstrate standing, a litigant must show that it has suffered a concrete and particularized injury that is either actual or imminent, that the injury is fairly traceable to the defendant, and that a favorable decision will likely redress that injury. [Citation omitted.] However, a litigant to whom Congress has "accorded a procedural right to protect his concrete interests," [citation omitted]—here, the right to challenge agency action unlawfully withheld . . . —"can assert that right without meeting all the normal standards for redressability and immediacy," [citation omitted.] Only one petitioner needs to have standing to authorize review. [Citation omitted.] Massachusetts has a special position and interest here. It is a sovereign State and not . . . a private individual, and it actually owns a great deal of the territory alleged to be affected. The sovereign prerogatives to force reductions in greenhouse gas emissions, to negotiate emissions treaties with developing countries, and (in some circumstances) to exercise the police power to reduce motor-vehicle emissions are now lodged in the Federal Government. Because Congress has ordered EPA to protect Massachusetts (among others) by prescribing applicable standards . . . , and has given Massachusetts a concomitant procedural right to challenge the rejection of its rulemaking petition as arbitrary and capricious . . . , petitioners' submissions as they pertain to Massachusetts have satisfied the most demanding standards of the adversarial process. EPA's steadfast refusal to regulate greenhouse gas emissions presents a risk of harm to Massachusetts that is both "actual" and "imminent," [citation omitted], and there is a "substantial likelihood that the judicial relief requested" will prompt EPA to take steps to reduce that risk. [Citation omitted].

(b) The harms associated with climate change are serious and well recognized. The Government's own objective assessment of the relevant science and a strong consensus among qualified experts indicate that global warming threatens, [among other things], a precipitate rise in sea levels, severe and irreversible changes to natural ecosystems, a significant reduction in winter snowpack with direct and important economic consequences, and increases in the spread of disease and the ferocity of weather events. That these changes are widely shared does not minimize Massachusetts' interest in the outcome of this litigation. [Citation omitted.] According to petitioners' uncontested affidavits, global sea levels rose between 10 and 20 centimeters over the 20th century as a result of global warming and have already begun to swallow Massachusetts' coastal land. Remediation costs alone, moreover, could reach hundreds of millions of dollars.

. . .

(d) While regulating motor-vehicle emissions may not by itself reverse global warming, it does not follow that the Court lacks jurisdiction to decide whether EPA has a duty to take steps to slow or reduce it. [Citation omitted.] Because of the enormous potential consequences, the fact that a remedy's effectiveness might be delayed during the (relatively short) time it takes for a new motor-vehicle fleet to replace an older one is essentially irrelevant. Nor is it dispositive that developing countries are poised to substantially increase greenhouse gas emissions: A reduction in domestic emissions would slow the pace of global emissions increases, no matter what happens elsewhere. The Court attaches considerable significance to EPA's espoused belief that global climate change must be addressed.

. . .

3. Because greenhouse gases fit well within the Act's capacious definition of "air pollutant," EPA has statutory authority to regulate emission of such gases from new motor vehicles. That definition—which includes "any air pollution agent . . . , including any physical, chemical, . . . substance . . . emitted into . . . the ambient air . . . ," —embraces all airborne compounds of whatever stripe. Moreover, carbon dioxide and other greenhouse gases are undoubtedly "physical [and] chemical . . . substance[s]." EPA's reliance on post-enactment congressional actions and deliberations it views as tantamount to a command to refrain from regulating greenhouse gas emissions is unavailing. Even if post-enactment legislative history could shed light on the meaning of an otherwise-unambiguous statute, EPA identifies nothing suggesting that Congress meant to curtail EPA's power to treat greenhouse gases as air pollutants. The Court has no difficulty reconciling Congress' various efforts to promote interagency collaboration and research to better understand climate change with the Agency's pre-existing mandate to regulate "any air pollutant" that may endanger the public welfare. [Citation omitted.] Also unpersuasive is EPA's argument that its regulation of motor-vehicle carbon dioxide emissions would require it to tighten mileage standards, a job (according to EPA) that Congress has assigned to the Department of Transportation. The fact that DOT's mandate to promote energy efficiency by setting mileage standards may overlap with EPA's environmental responsibilities in no way licenses EPA to shirk its duty to protect the public "health" and "welfare." [Citation omitted.]

. . .

[The Circuit Court's opinion is] reversed and remanded.

Air Pollution

The EPA enforces the **Clean Air Act** (CAA), which primarily sets nationwide limits on air pollutants. The EPA also works in concert with state and local agencies to reduce air pollution. The Act regulates various pollutants, including lead, carbon monoxide, sulfur dioxide, to name a few. The EPA has developed standards that apply nationally. These standards, called the **National Ambient Air Quality Standards**, primarily focus on protecting human health.

Joseph Sohm/Shutterstock.com

course, in addition to regulating pollutants emitted by factories, manufacturing plants, and other stationary sources of air pollution, the EPA regulates emissions from mobile sources of air pollution. These mobile sources of air pollution, such as motor vehicles, also must meet fuel economy standards set by the EPA.

What Do You Think?

How would you rate the air quality where you live?

The Clean Air Act requires that businesses that emit pollutants into the air use **maximum available control technology** (or sometimes called "best" available control technology) to minimize pollution. Thus, businesses must assess whether the machinery and equipment being used are minimizing pollutants as much as possible. If not, the business must make changes (over a certain period of time) to improve its pollution reduction equipment. Of

Water Pollution

In addition to combating air pollution, Congress has passed the **Clean Water Act** (CWA) to combat water pollution. Consider Congress's policy objectives as set forth in the Clear Water Act (Illustrative Federal Statute 40.1).

ILLUSTRATIVE FEDERAL STATUTE 40.1

33 U.S.C. §1251

§1251. Congressional declaration of goals and policy

(a) Restoration and maintenance of chemical, physical and biological integrity of Nation's waters; national goals for achievement of objective. The objective of this Act is to restore and maintain the chemical, physical, and biological integrity of the Nation's waters. In order to achieve this objective it is hereby declared that, consistent with the provisions of this Act –

(1) it is the national goal that the discharge of pollutants into the navigable waters be eliminated by 1985;

(2) it is the national goal that wherever attainable, an interim goal of water quality which provides for the protection and propagation of fish, shellfish, and wildlife and provides for recreation in and on the water be achieved by July 1, 1983;

(3) it is the national policy that the discharge of toxic pollutants in toxic amounts be prohibited;

(4) it is the national policy that Federal financial assistance by provided to construct publicly owned waste treatment works;

(5) it is the national policy that areawide waste treatment management planning processes be developed and implemented to assure adequate control of sources of pollutants in each State;

(6) it is the national policy that a major research and demonstration effort be made to develop technology necessary to eliminate the discharge of pollutants into the navigable waters, waters of the contiguous zone, and the oceans; . . .

Most industrial and government facilities that may discharge pollutants into navigable waters or surface waters must first obtain a permit to do so. Individuals can also be fined for violating regulations under the CWA.

Similar to the Clean Air Act, the CWA requires businesses that may engage in discharging pollutants into the water to use the best available control technology to minimize pollutants. Federal laws and regulations also govern drinking water (Safe Drinking Water Act), oil pollution (Oil Pollution Act), ocean dumping (the Marine Protection, Research, and Sanctuaries Act), and wetlands preservation.

What Do You Think?

Do U.S. lakes, rivers, streams, and other waterways still contain too much pollution notwithstanding the Clean Water Act?

Hazardous Waste and Toxic Substances

Pesticides, herbicides, asbestos, nuclear waste, etc., are also subject to federal regulation through the EPA. The manufacturers of these substances usually are required to affix very descriptive labeling and warnings to the product packaging.

Additionally, the EPA has extensive regulations determining which substances are, in fact, "hazardous" and how those materials should be disposed.

Have you ever seen a junky, empty lot or parcel of land and wondered whether any hazardous materials may exist on or under the land? It is possible, of course, that businesses or individuals buried or otherwise discharged hazardous chemicals long before the federal government began strict regulation of environmental safety. Acknowledging that this may be a problem Congress enacted the **Comprehensive Environmental Response Compensation and Liability Act** (CERCLA). The intent of CERCLA is to impose liability on **principally responsible parties** (PRP) for the clean-up costs of sites identified by the EPA as a hazardous toxic waste site. Typically, PRPs are current owners of the site or prior owners of the site or operators of a business on the site during the time the hazardous materials were disposed of at the site. PRPs are jointly and severally liable for the costs (*i.e.*, each PRP individually or the PRPs collectively are liable for the costs). The EPA will typically attempt to negotiate with the PRPs a clean-up plan and who will bear the costs of the plan. If the PRPs do not cooperate, then the federal government can unilaterally create a plan and even engage in the clean-up process. In this case, the government would then sue the PRPs to recover the cost of the clean-up. The federal government maintains a fund to help cover the costs when the government engages in the clean-up. This fund is frequently called the **Superfund**.

Environmental Impact Statements

As part of the government's increasing regulation on actions impacting the environment, Congress passed the **National Environmental Policy Act** (NEPA), which requires that an **environmental impact statement** be prepared whenever a governmental project significantly impacts the environment. Since private individuals and businesses may also engage in actions that significantly impact the environment, the government may require the private individual or business to prepare an environmental impact statement as a condition to receiving a permit allowing a particular activity.

QUESTIONS FOR REVIEW

1. What is the EPA? What are its responsibilities?

2. In the *Massachusetts v. EPA* case, what was the reasoning of the Supreme Court as to why the EPA should regulate greenhouse gases?

3. The government requires businesses that may emit pollutants to use what standard of technology in order to control the level of pollution?

4. Name two federal laws other than the Clean Water Act that regulate water pollutants.

5. What is CERCLA? What is its purpose? What is the potential consequence of being named a principally responsible party?

6. What is the Superfund?

7. What is an environmental impact statement?

INTERNET ACTIVITIES

1. Visit the Environmental Protection Agency's website at www.epa.gov.

   a. Who is the current EPA administrator?

   b. Click on a news release. Summarize two recent news releases by the EPA.

2. Find the website of your *state's* environmental protection agency.

   a. What is the official name of your state's environmental protection agency?

   b. Summarize two recent news releases by your state's environmental protection agency.

Chapter 41

Antitrust Law

StudioSmart/Shutterstock.com

The United States economy is founded on the idea that business competition is a good thing. As a result of competition, customers often benefit from lower prices and higher quality products and services. Nevertheless, should the federal government allow several companies in one industry to meet together and agree to fix prices higher than would otherwise be the case? As a result of some tendency for businesses to engage in anti-competitive activities, the federal government has instituted some laws regulating businesses and the competitive marketplace.

In the late 1800s and early 1900s some businesses like Standard Oil (owned by John D. Rockefeller), organized their enterprises by conveying their stock in various corporations they owned into a trust arrangement that was governed by trustees. This business structure provided significant advantages for the businesses and ultimately allowed the conglomerate (*e.g.*, the Standard Oil Trust) to dominate and eliminate competition in the marketplace.

The federal government ultimately determined that such domination in the marketplace was unhealthy for the economy and for fair competition. Consequently, Congress passed "antitrust" legislation. The foremost among the antitrust laws is called the **Sherman Antitrust Act**.

The Sherman Antitrust Act

The primary purpose of the Sherman Antitrust Act is to prohibit unfair **restraints on trade**. The Act provides that some activities are, by their very nature, restraints on trade and are prohibited (*i.e.*, the **per se** test). Other activities, although perhaps not as egregious as *per se* violations, may also be viewed as too anticompetitive and not considered fair or reasonable business practices (*i.e.*, the **rule-of-reason** test). Factors involved in determining whether the rule-of-reason test has been violated are (1) the purpose of the restraint, (2) the scope of the restraint, (3) the effect on competitors, and (4) the intent of the activity. Activities that may be violations of certain provisions of the Sherman Act are often broken down into two

341

broad categories: *horizontal* restraints on trade and *vertical* restraints on trade. Monopolization can also violate the Sherman Act.

Horizontal Restraints

Examples of horizontal restraints on trade include "horizontal price fixing," "horizontal division of markets," and "horizontal boycotting." **Horizontal price fixing** typically occurs when two or more competitors get together and decide on what price to charge for a particular product or service. The price agreed on is likely higher than what the price would be otherwise. Such a practice, of course, ultimately harms consumers and is against the law. A **horizontal division of markets** exists, for example, when companies in the same industry divide up the market along geographic lines or product lines. Suppose Company A and Company B, both sports products manufacturers, agree that only Company A can sell to customers in Texas and Oklahoma, and only Company B can sell to customers in Arkansas and Louisiana. Alternatively, the companies may agree that only Company A can sell baseball bats in Texas, Oklahoma, Louisiana, and Arkansas, and only Company B can sell football helmets in those four states. Either of these arrangements would be a *per se* violation of the Sherman Act. A **horizontal** boycott arrangement is also generally a *per se* violation of the Sherman Act. This exists, for example, if two or more competitors agree to *not* purchase goods or services from a particular business. This action, of course, harms the boycotted business and serves to frustrate fair competition.

Vertical Restraints

Vertical restraints on trade typically involve agreements between or among manufacturers and distributors rather than direct competitors. Like businesses engaged in horizontal restraints on trade activities, businesses participating in vertical restraints on trade are prohibited from price fixing, vertical division of markets, and vertical boycotting. Of course, manufacturers can *suggest* the price at which their products should be sold. But if the manufacturer forces the distributor to sell at a specific price, then the manufacturer may have violated the Sherman Act by vertically fixing prices. Vertical anti-competitive practices are usually judged by the rule-of-reason standard rather than the *per se* standard.

Consider the United States Supreme Court case that follows involving the National Football League, the Sherman Antitrust Act and the rule-of-reason (Illustrative Court Case 41.1).

ILLUSTRATIVE COURT CASE 41.1

American Needle, Inc. v. National Football League

Supreme Court of the United States

130 5.Ct. 2201 (2010)

[**Note:** For convenience of the reader, the following language is from the Syllabus of the case as provided by the U.S. Supreme Court Reporter of Decisions.]

[The] National Football League (NFL) is an unincorporated association of 32 separately owned professional football teams. . . . The teams, each of which owns its own name, colors, logo, trademarks, and related intellectual property, formed . . . National Football League Properties (NFLP) to develop, license, and market that property. At first, NFLP granted nonexclusive licenses to [American Needle] and other vendors to manufacture and sell team labeled apparel. In December 2000, however, the teams authorized NFLP to grant exclusive licenses. NFLP granted an exclusive license to . . . Reebok International Ltd. to produce and sell trademarked headwear for all 32 teams. When [American Needle's] license was not renewed, it filed this action alleging that the agreements between [the NFL and its teams] violated the Sherman Act, . . . which makes "[e]very contract, combination . . . or, conspiracy, in restraint of trade" illegal. [The NFL and its teams] answered that they were incapable of conspiring within [the Sherman Act's] meaning because the NFL and its teams are, in antitrust law jargon, a single entity with respect to the conduct challenged. The District Court granted [the NFL and its teams] summary judgment, and the Seventh Circuit affirmed.

Held: The alleged conduct related to licensing of intellectual property constitutes concerted action that is not categorically beyond [the Sherman Act's] coverage.

(a) The meaning of "contract, combination . . . , or, conspiracy" in . . . the Sherman Act is informed by the Act's "basic distinction between concerted and independent action." [Citation omitted.] [The Sherman Act] "treat[s] concerted behavior more strictly than unilateral behavior," . . . because, unlike independent action, "[c]oncerted activity inherently is fraught with anticompetitive risk" insofar as it "deprives the market place of independent centers of decision making that competition assumes and demands," [citation omitted]. And because concerted action is discrete and distinct, a limit on such activity leaves untouched a vast amount of business conduct. That creates less risk of deterring a firm's necessary conduct and leaves courts to examine only discrete agreements. An arrangement must therefore embody concerted action in order to be a "contract, combination . . . or, conspiracy" under [the Sherman Act].

(b) In determining whether there is concerted action under [the Sherman Act], the Court has eschewed formalistic distinctions, such as whether the alleged conspirators are legally distinct entities, in favor of a functional consideration of how they actually operate. The Court has repeatedly found instances in which members of a legally single entity violated [the Sherman Act] when the entity was controlled by a group of competitors and served, in essence, as a vehicle for ongoing concerted activity. [Citation omitted.] Conversely, the Court has found that although the entities may be "separate" for purposes of incorporation or formal title, if they are controlled by a single center of decision making and they control a single aggregation of economic power, an agreement between them does not constitute a "contract, combination . . . or, conspiracy." [Citation omitted.]

(c) The relevant inquiry is therefore one of substance, not form, which does not turn on whether the alleged parties to contract, combination, or conspiracy are part of a legally single entity or seem like one firm or multiple firms in any metaphysical sense. The inquiry is whether the agreement in question joins together "separate economic actors pursuing separate economic interests," [citation omitted], such that it "deprives the marketplace of independent centers of decision making," [citation omitted], and therefore of diversity of entrepreneurial interests and thus of actual or potential competition. If it does, then there is concerted action covered by [the Sherman Act], and the court must decide whether the restraint of trade is unreasonable and therefore illegal.

(d) The NFL teams do not possess either the unitary decision making quality or the single aggregation of economic power characteristic of independent action. Each of them is a substantial, independently owned, independently managed business, whose "general corporate actions are guided or determined" by "separate corporate consciousnesses," and whose "objectives are" not "common." [Citation omitted.] They compete with one another, not only on the playing field, but to attract fans, for gate receipts, and for contracts with managerial and playing personnel. [Citation omitted.] Directly relevant here, the teams are potentially competing suppliers in the market for intellectual property. When teams license such property, they are not pursuing the "common interests of the whole" league, but, instead, the interests of each "corporation itself." [Citation omitted.] It is not dispositive, as [the NFL and its teams] argue, that, by forming NFLP, they have formed a single entity, akin to a merger, and market their NFL brands through a single outlet. Although the NFL [and its teams] may be similar in some sense to a single enterprise, they are not similar in the relevant functional sense. While teams have common interests such as promoting the NFL brand, they are still separate, profit maximizing entities, and their interests in licensing team trademarks are not necessarily aligned. Nor does it

(Continued)

matter that the teams may find the alleged cooperation necessary to compete against other forms of entertainment. Although decisions made by NFLP are not as easily classified as concerted activity, the NFLP's decisions about licensing the teams' separately owned intellectual property are concerted activity and thus covered by [the Sherman Act] for the same reason that decisions made directly by the 32 teams are covered by [the Sherman Act]. In making the relevant licensing decisions, NFLP is "an instrumentality" of the teams. [Citation omitted.]

(e) Football teams that need to cooperate are not trapped by antitrust law. The fact that the NFL teams share an interest in making the entire league successful and profitable, and that they must cooperate to produce games, provides a perfectly sensible justification for making a host of collective decisions. Because some of these restraints on competition are necessary to produce the NFL's product, the Rule of Reason generally should apply, and teams' cooperation is likely to be permissible. And depending upon the activity in question, the Rule of Reason can at times be applied without detailed analysis. But the activity at issue in this case is still concerted activity covered for [Sherman Act] purposes.

Vladimir Mucibabic/Shutterstock.com

Monopolization

The Sherman Antitrust Act also prohibits monopolization. This extends to *attempts* to monopolize and *conspiracy* to monopolize. Of course, a business that grows so large that it can shut out competition also has the ability to fix prices for the goods and services it offers. Attempts to monopolize may also be evidenced by **predatory pricing** (*e.g.*, setting prices artificially low in an attempt to drive competitors out of business). The federal government—primarily through the Federal Trade Commission and Department of Justice—scrutinizes proposed mergers and analyzes the possible anti-competitive and monopolistic results that may occur.

What Do You Think?

Is Microsoft Corporation a monopoly?

Clayton Act

By passing the **Clayton Act**, Congress has extended laws prohibiting anticompetitive activities to include "exclusive dealing contracts" and "tying" arrangements.

Exclusive Dealing Contracts

Occasionally, a buyer of goods will sign an agreement with a supplier of goods that the buyer will only buy from the supplier. These **exclusive dealing contracts**, of course, preclude other sellers from potentially selling their goods to the buyer. While the courts historically have not looked favorably upon such arrangements, the courts now will look at the specific agreement and determine the overall anticompetitive impact of the agreement on the particular market of goods involved and the economic harm that other businesses may suffer.

Tying Arrangements

A business that makes more than one related product may try to sell both products in tandem. For example, Company R may say to Company J, "I will sell you these shoes, but only if you buy these socks also." Consider the following United States Supreme Court case (Illustrative Court Case 41.2) relating to tying arrangements.

Courts will look at tying arrangements under the rule-of-reason test rather than the *per se* test.

Thus, many factors will come into play to determine the legality of such anticompetitive arrangements.

Price Discrimination

The Clayton Act, as amended by the Robinson-Patman Act, prohibits **price discrimination**. If a business sells identical products to two different buyers at two different prices, then this could be price discrimination. If the products are not identical (*e.g.*, lower quality, smaller, larger, etc.), then price discrimination does not occur. Also, in order

---

ILLUSTRATIVE COURT CASE 41.2

Illinois Tool Works v. Independent Ink

Supreme Court of the United States

547 U.S. 28 (2006)

[**Note:** For convenience of the reader, the following language is from the Syllabus of the case as provided by the U.S. Supreme Court Reporter of Decisions.]

[Illinois Tool Works Inc. and its subsidiary Trident, Inc., collectively "ITW"] manufacture and market printing systems that include a patented printhead and ink container and unpatented ink, which they sell to original equipment manufacturers who agree that they will purchase ink exclusively from [ITW] and that neither they nor their customers will refill the patented containers with ink of any kind. [Independent Ink] developed ink with the same chemical composition as [ITW's] ink. [Independent Ink] filed suit seeking a judgment of . . . invalidity of [ITW's] patents on the ground that [ITW is] engaged in illegal "tying" and monopolization in violation of . . . the Sherman Act. Granting [ITW] summary judgment, the District Court rejected [Independent Ink's] argument that [ITW] necessarily ha[s] market power as a matter of law by virtue of the patent on [its] printhead system, thereby rendering the tying arrangements *per se* violations of the antitrust laws. After carefully reviewing this Court's tying-arrangements decisions, the Federal Circuit reversed . . . concluding that it had to follow this Court's precedents until overruled by this Court.

Held: Because a patent does not necessarily confer market power upon the patentee, in all cases involving a tying arrangement, the plaintiff must prove that the defendant has market power in the tying product.

(a) Over the years, this Court's strong disapproval of tying arrangements has substantially diminished, as the Court has moved from relying on assumptions to requiring a showing of market power in the tying product. The assumption in earlier decisions that such "arrangements serve hardly any purpose beyond the suppression of competition," [citation omitted], was rejected in *United States Steel Corp.* v. *Fortner Enterprises, Inc.,* [citation omitted], and again in *Jefferson Parish Hospital Dist. No. 2* v. *Hyde,* [citation omitted], both of which involved unpatented tying products. Nothing in *Jefferson Parish* suggested a rebuttable presumption of market power applicable to tying arrangements involving a patent on the tying good.

. . .

(Continued)

c. At the same time that this Court's antitrust jurisprudence continued to rely on the assumption that tying arrangements generally serve no legitimate business purpose, Congress began chipping away at that assumption. . . . After considering the congressional judgment reflected in the amendment, this Court concludes that tying arrangements involving patented products should be evaluated under the standards of cases like *Fortner II* and *Jefferson Parish* rather than the *per se* rule. . . . Any conclusion that an arrangement is unlawful must be supported by proof of power in the relevant market rather than by a mere presumption thereof.

d. [Independent Ink's] alternatives to retention of the *per se* rule—that the Court endorse a rebuttable presumption that patentees possess market power when they condition the purchase of the patented product on an agreement to buy unpatented goods exclusively from the patentee, or differentiate between tying arrangements involving requirements ties and other types of tying arrangements—are rejected.

e. Because [Independent Ink] reasonably relied on this Court's prior opinions in moving for summary judgment without offering evidence of the relevant market or proving [ITW's] power within that market, [Independent Ink] should be given a fair opportunity to develop and introduce evidence on that issue, as well as other relevant issues, when the case returns to the District Court.

to violate the Act, the products must *actually* be sold for different prices rather than just *offered* to be sold for different prices. A seller may have a defense if the seller can show that the prices are different because of market forces (*e.g.*, location of the buyer) or higher or lower costs incurred to sell to one buyer compared to another.

QUESTIONS FOR REVIEW

1. Why are laws prohibiting monopolies and other unfair restraints on trade called "antitrust" laws?

2. Under the Sherman Antitrust Act, what is the difference between the *per se* test and the rule-of-reason test?

3. Name at least two horizontal and two vertical restraints on trade. Discuss each restraint.

4. Which department[s] of the federal government enforce antitrust laws?

5. What is an exclusive dealing contract?

6. What is a tying arrangement?

7. Explain price discrimination.

8. Summarize the *American Needle v. National Football League* case.

9. Summarize the *Illinois Tool Works v. Independent Ink* case.

INTERNET ACTIVITIES

1. Visit the Federal Trade Commission website at www.ftc.gov. Click on the "About the FTC" tab. Then click on the "Bureaus & Offices" link. Then click on the "Bureau of Competition" link.

   a. Summarize the purpose of the FTC's Bureau of Competition.

   b. Summarize two recent news releases from the Bureau of Competition.

2. Visit the Department of Justice website at www.justice.gov. Click on the "Our Agency" tab. Click on the "Alphabetical Listing" link. Click on the "Antitrust Division" link. Then click on the "Website" link.

   a. Who is the Assistant Attorney General for the Antitrust Division?

   b. Summarize two recent antitrust division news releases.

Part XV

Insurance, Wills, and Trusts

Chapter 42

Insurance

One of the many decisions a businessperson must make is how to best manage risk. Thus, the question often arises as to whether a business should obtain insurance, and if so, how much insurance. Of course, in addition to business insurance, individuals typically enter into some insurance contracts that are not necessarily business related (*e.g.*, health insurance, dental insurance, personal automobile insurance, homeowners insurance, etc.). In this chapter we will discuss common insurance terminology, different types of insurance, and common provisions in insurance contracts.

Common Insurance Terminology

Fundamentally, insurance exists to protect against uncertain or unknown events that may occur. **Insurance** is a contractual arrangement between the **insured** and the insurance company (also called the **insurer** or **underwriter**) wherein the insurer promises to pay the insured person or business a certain amount if a certain specified event or events occur (*e.g.*, loss of life, property damage, health problems, etc.). In return for the promise to pay if a certain event occurs, the insurance company receives **premiums** from the insured. If an event occurs that is covered by the insurance policy, the insured makes a **claim** to the insurer. Sometimes the insured and insurer will modify the policy. Rather than rescind the initial policy and create a new one, the insurer will often issue

a **rider** or **endorsement**, which will be considered part of the policy.

Ivelin Radkov/Shutterstock.com

Insurable Interest

State laws govern insurance contracts. In order for someone to purchase an insurance policy, the person seeking the insurance must have an **insurable interest** in the person or property that the person is trying to insure. In general, an insurable interest exists if a person obtaining life insurance on another person has a family or other close relationship to the person or a pecuniary interest in that person's continuing to be alive (*e.g.*, business partner, key employee, etc.). A similar concept applies to property that a person wants to insure (*e.g.*, the prospective insured must be exposed to a possible financial loss if the property is damaged or destroyed). A prospective insured's failure to have an insurable interest would be akin to gambling on the likelihood that a certain event will occur, and state law will prevent a policy from being issued. Consider the following case from the United States Court of Appeals for the Eighth Circuit regarding the issue of insurable interest (Illustrative Court Case 42.1).

ILLUSTRATIVE COURT CASE 42.1

Country Life Insurance Company v. Marks

Court of Appeals for the Eighth Circuit

592 F.3d 896 (2010)

OPINION BY: BYE

This is a dispute over the death benefits on an insurance policy issued by Country Life Insurance Company (Country Life) to Johno and Debbie Marks insuring the life of Connie B. Romig. Country Life filed this declaratory judgment action seeking, in part, a determination the policy was void on the grouds the Markses had no insurable interest in Romig's life. The district court granted Country Life's motion for summary judgment concluding the Markses did not have an insurable interest as a matter of law. We reverse and remand for further proceedings.

I.

. . .

Connie Romig was a close friend of Johno Marks's parents and was present at most all of his family gatherings while he was growing up. Johno knew her from the time he was a baby until her death and had always referred to her as "Aunt Connie" in his dealing with her. In fact, Johno did not learn as to Romig not being his biological aunt until early in his adult life.

The Markses have been married for over thirteen years and have three children—Vincent, Angelina and Adrianna. Vincent suffers from a medical condition called Charcot-Marie-Tooth (CMT), a nerve disorder which causes muscle atrophy and weakness. As a consequence, the Markses incurred extra medical and travel expenses because of Vincent's condition resulting from trips to medical specialists. After the birth of their children, the couple's relationship with Romig became even closer than previously, and they would see her with considerable frequency. The Markses saw Romig on an almost daily basis during the last nine years of her life.

Romig helped support the Marks family in a variety of ways. She provided the couple with cash to assist in the expenses they incurred while traveling with their son, Vincent. She did most of the family's grocery shopping, not only donating her time and travel to the effort, but also paying for the groceries. She also frequently paid the family's rent, which was $1,000.00 per month, as well as the family's utility bills. In addition, Romig gave Johno and Debbie extra money on a regular basis, telling them she would always do what she could to help and take care of them. Romig also helped Johno in his automobile business, picking up and dropping him off at car auctions. Romig did all this for free, never asking for or receiving any compensation for all she did to assist the family financially.

Romig's husband passed away in 2005 without any life insurance. As a result of that incident, she obtained life insurance naming the Markses as beneficiaries so that when she passed away the Marks's children would be taken care of, especially Vincent because of his medical issues.

In February 2006, Romig and the Markses visited an insurance agent for Auto-Owners Insurance to obtain life insurance. She submitted to a medical examination at the request of Auto-Owners, which took place in the Marks's home. A follow-up visit took place in Romig's home where neither Johno or Debbie were present.

Because of delays in obtaining the Auto-Owners policy, the insurance agent suggested Romig visit an agent for Country Life. She was advised Country Life could provide a policy providing twice the death benefit as the Auto-Owners policy for about the same premium, so she sought a policy from Country Life while waiting for approval on the Auto-Owners policy. Romig submitted to a medical examination at the request of Country Life. On April 25, 2006, Country Life issued the Markses a life insurance policy on Romig's life, naming the couple as both owners and beneficiaries of the policy, and the Markses thereafter paid the premiums as they became due under the terms of the policy.

Romig was healthy, strong, and insurable when the two life insurance policies were issued, but did become ill and was eventually hospitalized in October 2006. She passed away on November 29, 2006. Country Life and Auto-Owners denied the Marks's claims for death benefits on the grounds the couple had no insurable interest in Romig's life and refunded the premiums the couple had paid. Both insurance companies filed this declaratory judgment action. The district court granted summary judgment in favor of the insurers and this appeal followed, with Auto-Owners settling its claim while the appeal was still pending. The claim involving the Country Life insurance policy remains the central focus of this litigation.

II.

. . .

The Markses were the beneficiaries and owners of the life insurance policy issued by Country Life. This dual beneficiary/owner role is distinct from a situation where an insured owns a policy, pays the premiums, and has the right to name whomever the insured desires as a beneficiary. Because the Markses were both beneficiaries and owners of the Country Life policy, they had to prove they had an insurable interest in the life of the insured, otherwise the policy would be unenforceable. [Citation omitted.] To establish an insurable interest under Missouri law, a party is required to show a benefit or advantage from the continuance of the life of the insured. [Citation omitted.] An insurable interest can be based upon three different types of relationships—a pecuniary relationship, a blood relationship, or a relationship based upon affinity (*i.e.*, marriage). [Citation omitted].

The Markses did not have a blood or marriage relationship with Romig, so the existence of an insurable interest turned instead upon whether there was a pecuniary relationship between them. To establish an insurable interest based upon a pecuniary relationship, "there must be a reasonable probability that [the beneficiary] will gain by the [insured's] remaining alive or lose by [her] death." [Citation omitted.] "Stated another way, any reasonable expectation of pecuniary benefit or advantage from the continued life of another creates an insurable interest in such life." [Citation omitted.] Whether a party has an insurable interest due to a pecuniary interest is a question of fact when the parties dispute (as they do here) the basis for the pecuniary interest. [Citation omitted.]

The Markses contend the disputed facts regarding their relationship with Romig, when viewed in the light most favorable to them, show they had a reasonable expectation of a pecuniary benefit or advantage from Romig remaining alive, making summary judgment inappropriate. We agree.

As an initial matter, we disagree with Country Life's contention Missouri law categorically limits a pecuniary interest in another's life to situations involving: 1) a business enterprise's pecuniary interest in the life of its manager; 2) an insured and beneficiary's common interest in a business association; 3) a business partner's pecuniary interest in the life of a partner; 4) a business owner's pecuniary interest in the life of a customer; or 5) a creditor's pecuniary interest in the life of a debtor. Missouri, like other states which follow the common law rule, indulges "great liberality" in determining whether an insurable interest exists by virtue of a pecuniary relationship. [Citation omitted.] Although the sort of benefactor-type relationship between Romig and the Markses has not been the subject of a prior Missouri case, other jurisdictions which follow the same common law rules as Missouri have recognized an insurable interest under analogous facts. Thus, if the relationship between them satisfies the general test for creating an insurable interest (*i.e.*, any reasonable expectation of pecuniary benefit or advantage from the continued life of another), we conclude Missouri courts would recognize it.

. . .

When viewed in the light most favorable to the Markses, the financial support and other services provided by "Aunt Connie" to the Markses over the course of the last nine years of her life is very similar to the gifts and support provided [in persuasive court cases from other states]. In each of these benefactor-type relationships, the courts recognized an insurable interest based on a pecuniary relationship. We therefore conclude there is an issue of material fact as to whether the pecuniary relationship between Romig and the Markses was sufficient to create an insurable interest, making summary judgment inappropriate.

III.

We reverse and remand for further proceedings.

Types of Insurance

Given that risks present themselves in almost all areas of business and personal life, insurance companies have developed a large number of insurance products. We mention a few here.

- **Life insurance.** There are a variety of different types of life insurance. Term life insurance is a policy that lasts only for a particular term (*e.g.*, five years, year-to-year, etc.). The premiums will typically increase after the end of the term. Whole life insurance is a form of insurance where the insured can actually "own" the policy and eventually have "paid up" the policy so that premiums are no longer required to be paid. Moreover, the premiums typically remain constant until such time that the policy is paid up. Other forms of life insurance also exist that are beyond the scope of this discussion.

- **Health insurance.** This type of insurance, of course, covers medical costs due to illness, accident, disease, etc. Although technically distinct from health insurance, *dental* insurance is often grouped with health insurance.

- **Automobile insurance.** State law typically requires automobile owners to be insured. This insurance usually covers damage to the automobile, injuries to occupants of the vehicle, injuries to others the insured driver may have caused, and property damage that the insured may have caused.

- **Homeowners insurance.** This typically covers damage caused to the home and attached buildings such as a garage. The policy usually also covers damage to or loss of personal property (*e.g.*, theft) within the home up to a certain dollar amount. Fire insurance is often included

in homeowners' policies, but can also be a separate policy. The policy may also cover the insured for torts committed by the insured.

- **Professional liability (or "malpractice") insurance**. Professionals on occasion may make mistakes or omissions that cause damage to a client, patient, or other person. Doctors, dentists, lawyers, accountants, engineers, and other professionals face potential lawsuits for malpractice. Some states require individuals in certain professions to carry malpractice insurance, or at least disclose the fact that they do not have any malpractice insurance coverage.

- **Business interruption insurance**. In the event business is interrupted by some stated incident (*e.g.*, fire, certain weather events, etc.), the policy pays for costs incurred to get the business back to normal operations.

- **Workers' compensation**. This is insurance that pays workers who are injured on the job. Typically, an employee that receives workers' compensation cannot then also sue the employer for the employee's injuries.

- **Disability insurance**. This is designed primarily to cover an insured's lost wages in the event the insured is disabled and becomes unable to work.

What Do You Think?

Should government be able to mandate that you carry automobile insurance? Health insurance? Why or why not?

Other insurance policies can be issued in areas in addition to those mentioned here. For example, a professional pianist might insure his fingers, and a professional singer may insure her voice. In short, a person can insure anything that an insurance company is willing to insure (and is not in violation of state law) in exchange for premium payments.

Common Provisions in Insurance Policies

Most insurance policies require that the insured pay an initial part of the cost before the insurer pays. This initial payment by the insured is called a **deductible**. Under the deductible clause in the policy, an insured may be required to pay, for example, the first $100 or $500 on a claim for property damage before the insurer will pay the insurer's part of the damages. The insurer's agreement to pay for the property damages or property loss suffered by the insured is often called **indemnification**. In other words, the insurer compensates (or "indemnifies") the insured for the loss or damage incurred by the insured. Sometimes this is called an insurer's **duty to indemnify**.

Another common provision in an insurance contract is the **incontestability clause**. The purpose of this clause is to prevent insurers from contesting several years later statements made by the insured on the application for insurance. On occasion, for example, an applicant may misstate answers to questions on the application about their medical history. Notwithstanding this misrepresentation by the insured, the insurer must cover the insured due to the incontestability clause if a certain number of years has expired (usually two years, but can vary) since the policy was issued.

In addition to a duty to indemnify, an insurer has a **duty to defend** the insured. Thus, if the insured is being sued for a reason that may be covered under the insured's policy with the insurer, the insurer must provide a lawyer for the insured to defend the case. Sometimes this can be contentious because many insurance policies have **exclusions** built in. A common provision would be that an insurer excludes itself from liability arising from any "intentional and criminal" act that the insured

Farmers Automobile Insurance Association v. Neumann

Appellate Court of Illinois, Third District

28 N.E.3d 830 (2015)

OPINION

Defendant insured, John E. Neumann, appealed from a circuit court order granting the motion of the plaintiff insurer, Farmers Automobile Insurance Association (Farmers), for summary judgment and denying Neumann's cross-motion for summary judgment, and finding that Farmers owed no duty to defend Neumann in one of two civil lawsuits that had been filed against Neumann. We reverse the grant of summary judgment in favor of Farmers and grant Neumann's motion for summary judgment.

FACTS

The defendant in this declaratory judgment action, John E. Neumann, was involved in a traffic incident on August 27, 2011, with the other defendant in this action, Christopher Bitner, wherein Neumann allegedly hit Bitner with his automobile while Bitner was directing traffic as a City of Pekin police officer. As a result of the accident, two civil lawsuits were filed naming Neumann as a defendant. The first was a complaint filed by Bitner, alleging intentional assault and intentional battery by Neumann. Neumann tendered the Bitner complaint to his insurer, the plaintiff in this action, Farmers. Farmers rejected the defense of the Bitner complaint on the basis that the automobile liability policy issued to Neumann did not cover any claims for intentional conduct.

After rejecting the defense of the Bitner action, Farmers filed the instant action for a declaratory judgment that it owed no duty to defend Neumann against the Bitner complaint. Neumann answered the declaratory judgment complaint, asserting affirmative defenses and attaching his affidavit. Neumann's affidavit asserted that he did not intend to strike nor intend to cause bodily harm to Bitner. Farmers moved to strike both the affidavit and the affirmative defenses, arguing that the affirmative defenses were not proper affirmative defenses and the affidavit was an improper attempt to assert "true but unpleaded facts." The circuit court granted both motions. Farmers filed a motion for summary judgment, arguing that it did not owe Neumann a defense to the Bitner complaint.

Thereafter, a second civil action involving the same incident on August 27, 2011, was filed against Neumann, this one by CCMSI Insurance Company, as subrogee of the City of Pekin. That action alleged that Neumann was negligent and sought to recover the amounts of worker's compensation that CCMSI would have to pay to Bitner as a result of the accident. Neumann filed a motion to consolidate the Bitner and CCMSI actions, which was granted. The consolidation order states that all filings shall reference and be filed in the first case number (the Bitner action). Farmers acknowledged, under a reservation of rights, its duty to defend Neumann against the CCMSI complaint.

Then, in this case, Neumann filed a cross-motion for summary judgment, asserting that, because the actions were consolidated, Farmers should defend both actions. The circuit court granted Farmers' motion for summary judgment and denied Neumann's motion, and Neumann appealed.

ANALYSIS

. . .

An insurer's duty to defend its insured is broader than its duty to indemnify. [Citation omitted.] In determining whether an insurer has a duty to defend its insured, a court must look to the allegations

(Continued)

in the underlying complaint and the relevant portions of the insurance policy. [Citation omitted.] The court must focus on the allegations of the complaint, liberally construed in favor of the insured. [Citation omitted.] If the allegations of the underlying complaint fall within, or potentially within, the policy coverage, then the insurer has a duty to defend. [Citation omitted.]

Neumann contends that the consolidation of the two lawsuits was equivalent to a single lawsuit with several causes of action, and since Farmers already acknowledged its duty to defend on one claim, it had to defend both claims. . . .

Although the complaints had different named plaintiffs, they both arose from a single incident, involving injury to a single person. Considering that the purpose of consolidation is to expedite the resolution of lawsuits, conserve time, and avoid duplicating efforts and unnecessary expenses, we find that the lawsuits were consolidated into one action. [Citation omitted.] Since Farmers had a duty to defend against the CCMSI action, it also had a duty to defend the consolidated Bitner action. . . .

CONCLUSION

For the foregoing reasons, we reverse the judgment of the circuit court of Tazewell County granting summary judgment in favor of Farmers and remand and order that the circuit court enter summary judgment in favor of Neumann, finding that Farmers owes a duty to defend the Bitner action.

Reversed and remanded.

engages in. Consider the case from the Appellate Court of Illinois (Illustrative Court Case 42.2).

As a final point, if an insurance company pays a claim to an insured, but someone else was at fault, the insurance company may invoke its **right of subrogation** and sue the other person or the other person's insurance company in order to recoup the money the insurer paid to the insured. In other words, the insurer "steps-into-the-shoes" of the insured and sues the wrongdoer.

QUESTIONS FOR REVIEW

1. Discuss the meanings of the following terms
   a. insurance
   b. insurer
   c. insured
   d. underwriter
   e. premium
   f. deductible
   g. insured interest
   h. claim
   i. rider/endorsement

2. What is an incontestability clause?

3. What does the term "indemnification" mean?

4. What does "subrogation" mean?

5. Discuss five different types of insurance.

6. Summarize the *Country Life Insurance v. Marks* case.

7. Summarize the *Farmers v. Neumann* case.

INTERNET ACTIVITIES

1. Find the website of the agency or department in your state that regulates insurance.
   a. What is the agency's official name?
   b. Who is the head of the agency?
   c. Summarize a recent news release from the agency.

2. Summarize the features of two different types of life insurance other than pure whole life insurance and pure term insurance. (Hint: Examples are universal life insurance and variable life insurance.)

Chapter 43

Wills and Trusts

Although the laws governing wills and trusts may not necessarily be directly related to business activity, such laws are important for business owners to understand so that the personal wealth is managed and disposed of in the manner which they prefer. Although the topic of estate planning is quite vast, we will focus on the fundamentals of wills and trusts in this chapter.

Wills

A **will** is a legal document that controls the disposition of a person's property upon the person's death. The person making the will is called the **testator**. State law controls what is necessary for the testator to create a valid will.

Requirements for a Valid Will

A testator must have the requisite **capacity** to make a will (*i.e.*, understands the importance and legal significance of what they are doing). Additionally, the will must usually be in writing, signed, and witnessed. Consider the California statute that follows (Illustrative State Statute 43.1) regarding the requirements for creating a valid will.

In very unique situations, a state may allow an *oral* will to be valid. Oral wills are often called **nuncupative** wills. These wills are also sometimes called "deathbed" wills. A person can also make a will in their own handwriting—called a **holographic** will. When a person dies, and the person has a will, the person is said to have died **testate** and the will is submitted for **probate**.

ILLUSTRATIVE STATE STATUTE 43.1

Cal. Prob. Code § 6100, § 6110

§ 6100. Persons who may make will

(a) An individual 18 or more years of age who is of sound mind may make a will.

. . .

§ 6110. Witnessed will

(a) Except as provided in this part, a will shall be in writing and satisfy the requirements of this section.

(b) The will shall be signed by one of the following:

(1) By the testator.

(2) In the testator's name by some other person in the testator's presence and by the testator's direction. . . .

(Continued)

(c)(1) Except as provided in paragraph (2), the will shall be witnessed by being signed, during the testator's lifetime, by at least two persons each of whom (A) being present at the time, witnessed either the signing of the will or the testator's acknowledgment of the signature or of the will and (B) understand that the instrument they sign is the testator's will.

(2) If a will was not executed in compliance with paragraph (1), the will shall be treated as if it was executed in compliance with that paragraph if the proponent of the will establishes by clear and convincing evidence that, at the time the testator signed the will, the testator intended the will to constitute the testator's will.

The probate process is where a judge reviews the will and hears any potential arguments from concerned individuals that the will may not be valid. The judge will also appoint a **personal representative** (or "personal administrator") of the estate of the deceased person (*i.e.*, the **"decedent"**). The will typically identifies who the testator wants as the personal representative. The personal representative is also sometimes called the **executor** of the estate. Consider the Supreme Court of Georgia court case that follows (Illustrative Court Case 43.1) regarding whether a will was validly created.

ILLUSTRATIVE COURT CASE 43.1

Swain v. Lee

Supreme Court of Georgia

700 S.E.2d 541 (2010)

OPINION BY: MELTON

On July 23, 2007, Lydia Swain, the Goddaughter of decedent Elouise Harley Collins, filed a petition to probate certain documents that she alleged constituted Collins' Will. On August 3, 2007, Bobby Eugene Lee, Collins' cousin and temporary Administrator of her estate, filed a caveat to probate on the grounds that the documents presented by Swain did not create a valid Will as a matter of law. On that same day, Betty Scott, Alvenia Turner, and Marie McIntosh, who claimed to be additional cousins of the deceased, filed a caveat to probate, challenging the Will on essentially the same grounds as those set out by Lee. The probate court found that the documents presented by Swain lacked the requisites of a Will or a codicil under Georgia law, and found that Collins died intestate. Swain appealed the ruling to the Superior Court of Glynn County, and Lee filed a motion for judgment on the pleadings in the superior court. The superior court granted Lee's motion for judgment on the pleadings, prompting Swain to appeal. As explained more fully below, because the record reveals that Swain presented a potentially viable claim that the documents she presented for probate could be read together to create a valid will, the trial court erred in granting Lee's motion for judgment on the pleadings. Accordingly, we reverse.

. . .

Here, the record that was before the superior court reveals that Collins had written an unwitnessed letter dated June 10, 1999, in which she stated, among other things, that Swain was to have "everything that's in my name." On April 12, 2005, Collins filled in a blank on a form "Last Will and Testament" naming Swain as the executrix of her estate. Although Collins signed this form before three witnesses, the remaining pages on this will form were left blank, with no disposition of any property being referenced on the form.

In her petition to probate, Swain specifically contended: "Attached to the last Will and Testament of [Collins] dated April 12, 2005, is a memorandum of instruction written by Collins dated June 10, 1999, which is to accompany and be an exhibit to the Last Will and Testament" (emphasis supplied). Furthermore, Swain specifically argued to the probate court that Collins kept both the 1999 letter and the 2005 will form together in one envelope, and that Collins took both of these documents from this envelope and presented them to the witnesses who signed the 2005 will form at the time that they signed it.

Although Collins' unwitnessed 1999 letter and the partially executed 2005 will form, by themselves, could not create valid wills . . . (will must be attested and subscribed in presence of two witnesses) and . . . (will must convey an interest accruing at death), and the 2005 document does not expressly refer to the 1999 letter such that it could revive or republish the 1999 letter as a valid will [citation omitted], this does not end our inquiry. Indeed, "[t]o determine whether an instrument is a will, the test is the intention of the maker to be gathered from *the whole instrument, read in light of the surrounding circumstances.*" [Citation omitted.] In this regard, a will need not be written on one continuous sheet of paper, [nor need the separate papers that constitute a will] necessarily be tied and fastened together. . . . [Citation omitted.] Indeed, "there is no known rule as to any precise manner in which [the will] papers shall be bound or attached together, or requiring a will to be written all on one sheet." [Citation omitted.]

. . .

Here, when the relevant documents, and the manner in which Swain claims that they were presented, are considered together, a valid will could have been created. Specifically, Swain contended in her petition to probate that Collins presented the 1999 letter and the 2005 will form as one, integrated will for the attesting witnesses to sign. In this connection, the documents could be read together to show Collins' intent to bequeath to Swain everything that was in her name and to appoint Swain as the executrix of her estate. Under such circumstances, an issue of fact has been created as to the potential validity of the will, and a judgment on the pleadings was inappropriate. [Citation omitted.] Accordingly, we must reverse the superior court's ruling.

Persons challenging the will's validity may assert, in addition to the possible argument that the will was not validly created, that the testator signed the will under duress or that the testator was subject to undue influence. Once the judge orders that the will is valid and appoints the personal representative, the judge also oversees the administration and distribution of the estate's property.

Some legal terminology is important to mention here regarding those persons who receive property from the decedent's estate. If the will makes a gift of *real property* to someone, the gift is said to be a **devise** and the recipient is called a **devisee**. If the gift by will is of personal property, the gift is said to be a **bequest** or **legacy** and the recipient is called a **legatee**. As a practical matter, however, people often call recipients of gifts by will either **beneficiaries** or **heirs** of the decedent's estate.

A person's will does not control property that may otherwise be held in a valid **living trust** (discussed later in this chapter) or property that is the subject of a **will substitute**. Suppose Sam owns a joint checking account with his brother John.

If Sam dies, all the money in the checking account will be John's even if Sam's will says otherwise. Another example would be a life insurance policy. Suppose Sam purchases a life insurance policy and names John as the beneficiary of the policy. Upon Sam's death, John will receive the proceeds from the policy even if Sam's will provides that someone else should receive Sam's property.

Amending or Revoking a Will

A testator can amend or revoke a will at any time while the testator is alive and has the requisite mental capacity. To amend a will, the testator creates a **codicil**, which basically is a statement attached to the will that sets forth the provisions of the will that the testator desires to amend and sets forth the language of the amendment(s). A testator can **revoke** a will by stating so in the subsequent creation of a new will. In some situations, a will may be revoked by physically destroying it (*e.g.*, burning it, tearing it up, etc.), if such act clearly manifests the intent of the testator to revoke it.

Dying without a Will

If a person dies without a will, the person is said to have died **intestate**. In these situations, state law will control who receives the decedent's property. Of course, this will typically be the decedent's spouse and/or children. If the decedent has no spouse or children, then the decedent's property will likely go to the decedent's parents and/or siblings. Ultimately, state law may provide that the property could go to aunts, uncles, cousins, etc., if no immediate family members can be found. These laws are called **intestacy** laws. In rare cases where no relatives can be found pursuant to the state's intestacy laws, the decedent's property will **escheat** to the state.

Trusts

A trust is a legal vehicle in which a person can place property and give instructions on how that property is to be managed and disposed of. A trust can be legally controlling while a person is alive

(compare this to a will, which is only effective when the testator dies). If a person makes a trust while that person is alive, the trust is said to be an ***inter vivos*** or **living** trust. If a will requires that the personal representative of an estate create a trust upon the decedent's death in order to manage the property on behalf of someone else, the trust is called a **testamentary** trust.

The person creating a trust is called the **grantor** or **settlor** or **trustor** of the trust. The property transferred to the trust (whether *inter vivos* or testamentary) is called the **corpus** or **principal** of the trust. The person in charge of managing the property and accounting for income and expenses is called the **trustee**. A trust is either **revocable** or **irrevocable** by the grantor, depending on what the trust document says. Of course, a grantor should be fully aware of the advantages and disadvantages of deciding to make a trust irrevocable (*e.g.*, gift tax, estate tax, qualifying for government assistance programs like Medicaid, loss of control over the property, etc.).

We have mentioned that a trust may be revocable or irrevocable, *inter vivos* or testamentary. Several other types of trusts exist also, such as a **charitable trust** (*e.g.*, a charity is a beneficiary), a **spendthrift trust** (*e.g.*, where the trust property is managed to prevent a beneficiary from being careless with the property), and a **constructive trust** (*e.g.*, a trust is *implied* for fairness purposes). Consider the following case from the Supreme Court of Utah (Illustrative Court Case 43.2) that illustrates the concept of a constructive trust.

Rawlings v. Rawlings

Supreme Court of Utah

240 P.3d 754 (2010)

OPINION BY: DURRANT

INTRODUCTION

We granted certiorari in this case to determine whether the court of appeals erred in reversing the district court's imposition of a constructive trust. The parties in this case are siblings who dispute the ownership of farm land transferred by their father [Arnold]. The oldest sibling, Donald, received the land as the grantee under a warranty deed. He contends that his father transferred the land to him in exchange for payments he made on some of his father's debts. The family's four other siblings and their spouses (collectively, the "siblings") contend that their father deeded the land to Donald in an attempt to create a family trust. During the time period surrounding this transfer, their father had been diagnosed with cancer and owning the land made him ineligible for welfare assistance. The siblings contend that their father placed the property in their older brother's name so that he could act as trustee over the land and hold it for the benefit of the family. The siblings also contend that, in the decades since the transfer, the land was treated as a family farm and that they have contributed to its care, maintenance, and profitability.

The district court credited the testimony of the siblings and found that the oldest brother had been unjustly enriched by accepting the siblings' years of contributions to the success of the farm. Accordingly, the court exercised its equitable power to award a constructive trust in favor of the siblings. The court of appeals reversed. Concluding that certain of the district court's findings of fact were inconsistent with its award of a constructive trust, the court of appeals held as a matter of law that the siblings could not prevail on any theory of constructive trust. We exercised our jurisdiction . . . and granted the siblings' petition for certiorari. We reverse the judgment of the court of appeals.

. . .

ANALYSIS

The siblings contend that the trial court was correct in imposing a constructive trust, either as a means of giving effect to an oral express trust, or as a means of remedying unjust enrichment. Thus, they argue that the court of appeals erred in two ways. First, they argue that the court of appeals misinterpreted the trial court's findings of fact and that these findings actually demonstrate Arnold's intent to create a trust to benefit the family. Second, they argue that the trial court was correct in finding that Donald had been unjustly enriched and that the court of appeals erred in holding otherwise. As such, they claim that the trial court had discretion to award a constructive trust under either theory.

In addressing the siblings' claims, we keep a number of important principles in mind. First, we affirm our prior statement that "the forms and varieties of these trusts . . . are practically without limit." [Citation omitted.] We also note that, in cases involving transfers of land, imposing a constructive trust will often "alter a deed or other writing which is regular in form and is presumed to convey a clear and unambiguous title." [Citation omitted.] We have recognized that altering deeds in this way may make it difficult for a landowner to "rest in the security of his title to the property, however solemn might be the instrument on which it was founded." [Citation omitted.] To mitigate this effect, we require that the evidence offered to overcome a deed must be "clear and convincing."

(Continued)

Even given this elevated burden of proof, we agree with the siblings with regard to their claim for unjust enrichment. . . .

I. CONSTRUCTIVE TRUSTS ARE A REMEDY THAT MAY BE IMPOSED WHERE A PARTY HAS BEEN UNJUSTLY ENRICHED OR WHERE NECESSARY TO GIVE EFFECT TO AN ORAL EXPRESS TRUST

The siblings argue that a constructive trust may be imposed under either of two distinct causes of action. One is a cause of action to establish an oral express trust. The other is a claim for unjust enrichment. Oral express trusts have "certain fundamental characteristics" in common with traditional trusts because, like traditional trusts, they are the manifestation of a settlor's intent with regard to property. The main such characteristic is the imposition of obligations on a trustee "to act for the benefit of [beneficiaries] as to matters within the scope of the [trust]." [Citation omitted.] Like trusts created by a valid writing, constructive trusts imposed to give effect to oral express trusts are adequately characterized as "a fiduciary relationship with respect to property, arising as a result of a manifestation of an intention to create it and subjecting the person in whom the title is vested to equitable duties to deal with it for the benefit of others." [Citation omitted.]

Where a transfer of land was made with the intent to create such a trust, the trust will generally fail unless evidenced by a writing that complies with the Statute of Frauds. Because oral express trusts do not meet these requirements, they will only be given effect in "certain circumstances." [Citation omitted.] "In these instances, the constructive trusts are deemed to arise by operation of law and [are] not within the statute of frauds." [Citation omitted.]

We have recognized that constructive trusts may be imposed in the circumstances set forth in Section 45 of . . . the Restatement of Trusts. This section applies when the transferor of land intends for the transfer to benefit someone other than the transferor or the transferee:

"(1) Where the owner of an interest in land transfers it inter vivos to another in trust for a third person, but no memorandum properly evidencing the intention to create a trust is signed, as required by the Statute of Frauds, and the transferee refuses to perform the trust, the transferee holds the interest upon a constructive trust for the third person, if, but only if,

(a) the transferee by fraud, duress or undue influence prevented the transferor from creating an enforceable interest in the third person, or

(b) the transferee at the time of the transfer was in a confidential relation to the transferor, or

(c) the transfer was made by the transferor in anticipation of death."

In short, the imposition of a constructive trust under this section of the Restatement of Trusts requires proof that the transferor of land intended to create a trust and that one of the three identified circumstances existed at the time of the transfer. And where proving this intent will be contrary to an otherwise valid deed, the evidence of the trust must be clear and convincing.

. . .

II. THE COURT OF APPEALS ERRED IN BASING ITS CONCLUSION SOLELY ON WHETHER ARNOLD INTENDED TO CREATE AN ORAL EXPRESS TRUST

. . .

III. THE COURT OF APPEALS ERRED IN HOLDING THAT DONALD WAS NOT UNJUSTLY ENRICHED BY THE CONTRIBUTIONS HIS SIBLINGS MADE TO THE FARM PROPERTY OVER SEVERAL DECADES

The court of appeals held that because Donald was the transferee under a deed, his acceptance of his siblings' contributions to the land could not be unjust. In so holding, the court of appeals erred. The standard for determining whether a person has been unjustly enriched requires a court to determine whether the defendant accepted and retained benefits conferred by the plaintiff under such circumstances as to make it inequitable for the defendant to retain those benefits without compensating the plaintiff.

The court of appeals' conclusion does not adequately take into consideration the circumstances under which Donald accepted many of the benefits conferred by his siblings. As found by the trial court, the reason the siblings continued to work on the trust property after Arnold's death was that Donald led them to believe it was their "Mother's farm." . . .

We hold that these findings were sufficient to support the trial court's imposition of a constructive trust.

. . .

CONCLUSION

We hold that the trial court acted within the bounds of its discretion in imposing a constructive trust in favor of the siblings. Unjust enrichment is a cause of action separate from an attempt to prove the existence of an oral express trust. Thus, even if the siblings have failed to prove the existence of an oral express trust in this case, something we assume without deciding, they were still free to pursue their claim of unjust enrichment as an independent cause of action. The trial court explicitly found that Donald had been unjustly enriched, and numerous of its factual findings support that judgment. Given the broad discretion that must necessarily be afforded trial courts when they apply the law of unjust enrichment to the facts of a given case, we disagree with the court of appeals' conclusion that imposition of a constructive trust was not an available or appropriate remedy in this case. The judgment of the court of appeals is therefore reversed.

Other Estate Planning Documents

Estate planning often consists of more than just creating a will or trust. Many estate planning lawyers will recommend that a person have a **living will** (also called an "advance health care directive"). A living will is basically instructions to health care providers as to the person's wishes if the person were to be incapacitated for a long period of time or in a vegetative state. Another common estate planning document is a **durable healthcare power of attorney**, which allows another person to make health care decisions in the event a person is incapacitated. Other types of powers of attorney may be created to allow another person to handle issues other than health care (*e.g.*, financial matters).

QUESTIONS FOR REVIEW

1. What are the necessary elements to create a valid will?

2. Explain what the following terms mean:
    a. testator
    b. devise
    c. devisee
    d. legacy
    e. legatee
    f. executor
    g. nuncupative
    h. holographic

    i. testate

    j. intestate

    k. escheat

3. What is probate?

4. Explain what the following terms mean:

    a. settlor

    b. grantor

    c. trustee

    d. inter vivos

    e. testamentary

    f. corpus

5. What is the purpose of a constructive trust? (Hint: refer to the *Rawlings v. Rawlings* case if necessary.)

6. Summarize the *Swain v. Lee* case.

INTERNET ACTIVITIES

1. Conduct a search for the Last Will and Testament of Elvis Presley.

    a. Who did Elvis appoint as the Executor of his estate?

    b. Who was the alternate Executor of his estate?

    c. Who were the witnesses to the signing of the will?

2. Conduct a search for the Last Will and Testament of Marilyn Monroe.

    a. To whom did she specifically bequeath $10,000?

    b. Who received the residuary balance of her estate?

    c. Who did Marilyn Monroe appoint as the Executor of her estate?

    d. Who was the alternate Executor of her estate?

    e. Who were the witnesses to the signing of the will?

Part XVI

International Law

Chapter 44

International Law

Advances in technology have facilitated international transactions like never before. Of course, disputes can arise between citizens of different countries as well as between governments. No universal or world government, however, makes binding laws on every country. Typically, countries voluntarily submit to be parties to international agreements in an attempt to facilitate trade and commerce as well as to further social objectives. This chapter provides a broad overview of the international legal environment of business.

Sources of International Law

Treaties and Multinational Agreements

As discussed in Chapter 2, one of the powers granted to the president by the Constitution is to enter into treaties with foreign countries. A **treaty** is basically a written agreement between two or more countries relating to particular issues such as crime, trade, patents, trademarks, taxation, etc. The U.S. Senate must approve such treaties by a two-thirds vote. The United States has entered into a wide variety of treaties (sometimes called **conventions**). You may have heard of the Geneva Convention (relating to war and the treatment of prisoners, civilians, wounded fighters, etc.) Another example is the Convention on Cybercrime, which attempts to establish consistent enforcement of computer crimes as well as provide for international cooperation regarding investigation of suspected computer crimes.

Other international agreements are more business related. For example, the United States, Canada, and Mexico have entered into agreements that provide for increased cooperation among the countries on cross-border transactions such as the elimination of tariffs on goods. Yet another business-related international agreement is the **Convention of International Sale of Goods** (CISG). The agreement facilitates business transactions in providing predictability with respect to how a sales transaction and possible disputes will be treated by the member countries.

International Court of Justice

The United Nations (addressed later in this chapter) created **The International Court of Justice** (ICJ) to serve as the judicial branch of the United Nations. The ICJ hears disputes between nations and provides some advisory decisions with regard to some international issues. ICJ decisions are typically only binding on a country if the country agrees to be bound by the decision. For example, consider the United States Supreme Court case that follows (Illustrative Court Case 44.1) and its discussion of the impact of an ICJ decision.

Medellín v. Texas

Supreme Court of the United States

552 U.S. 491 (2008)

[*Note:* For convenience of the reader, the following language is from the Syllabus of the case as provided by the U.S. Supreme Court Reporter of Decisions.]

In the *Case Concerning Avena and Other Mexican Nationals* (*Mex. v. U.S.*), 2004 I.C.J. 12 (*Avena*), the International Court of Justice (ICJ) held that the United States had violated Article 36(1)(b) of the Vienna Convention on Consular Relations (Vienna Convention or Convention) by failing to inform 51 named Mexican nationals, including petitioner Medellín, of their Vienna Convention rights. The ICJ found that those named individuals were entitled to review and reconsideration of their U.S. state-court convictions and sentences regardless of their failure to comply with generally applicable state rules governing challenges to criminal convictions. In *Sanchez-Llamas v. Oregon* . . . this Court held, contrary to the ICJ's determination, that the Convention did not preclude the application of state default rules. The President then issued a memorandum (President's Memorandum or Memorandum) stating that the United States would "discharge its international obligations" under *Avena* "by having State courts give effect to the decision."

Relying on *Avena* and the President's Memorandum, Medellín filed a second Texas state-court habeas application challenging his state capital murder conviction and death sentence on the ground that he had not been informed of his Vienna Convention rights. The Texas Court of Criminal Appeals dismissed Medellín's application as an abuse of the writ, concluding that neither *Avena* nor the President's Memorandum was binding federal law that could displace the State's limitations on filing successive habeas applications.

Held: Neither *Avena* nor the President's Memorandum constitutes directly enforceable federal law that pre-empts state [court procedures and rulings].

1. The *Avena* judgment is not directly enforceable as domestic law in state court.

(a) While a treaty may constitute an international commitment, it is not binding domestic law unless Congress has enacted statutes implementing it or the treaty itself conveys an intention that it be "self-executing" and is ratified on that basis. . . . The *Avena* judgment creates an international law obligation on the part of the United States, but it is not automatically binding domestic law because none of the relevant treaty sources . . . creates binding federal law in the absence of implementing legislation, and no such legislation has been enacted.

. . .

The ICJ Statute, by limiting disputes to those involving nations, not individuals, and by specifying that ICJ decisions have no binding force except between those nations, provides further evidence that the *Avena* judgment does not automatically constitute federal law enforceable in U.S. courts. Medellín, an individual, cannot be considered a party to the *Avena* decision.

. . .

(d) The Court's holding does not call into question the ordinary enforcement of foreign judgments. An agreement to abide by the result of an international adjudication can be a treaty obligation like any other, so long as the agreement is consistent with the Constitution. In addition, Congress is up to the task of implementing non-self-executing treaties, even those involving complex commercial disputes. Medellín contends that domestic courts generally give effect to foreign judgments, but the

(*Continued*)

judgment Medellín asks us to enforce is hardly typical: It would enjoin the operation of state law and force the State to take action to "review and reconside[r]" his case. . . .

2. The President's Memorandum does not independently require the States to provide review and reconsideration of the claims of the 51 Mexican nationals named in *Avena* without regard to state procedural default rules.

(a) The President seeks to vindicate plainly compelling interests in ensuring the reciprocal observance of the Vienna Convention, protecting relations with foreign governments, and demonstrating commitment to the role of international law. But those interests do not allow the Court to set aside first principles. The President's authority to act, as with the exercise of any governmental power, "must stem either from an act of Congress or from the Constitution itself." [Citation omitted.]

. . .

The President's Memorandum—a directive issued to state courts that would compel those courts to reopen final criminal judgments and set aside neutrally applicable state laws—is not supported by a "particularly longstanding practice." The Executive's limited authority to settle international claims disputes pursuant to an executive agreement cannot stretch so far.

What Do You Think?

Should the United States be bound by decisions made by the International Court of Justice?

The Principle of Comity

Suppose you win a court case in the United States, but before you can collect damages that a jury awarded you, the defendant moves out of the country. Now you likely face even greater difficulty in collecting the awarded damages. Under the **principle of comity**, foreign courts may enforce judgments of the courts of other countries. Of course, judgments of foreign courts are not binding on courts in other countries, but to maintain good relations with other countries, courts will often, as a courtesy, enforce foreign judgments when requested to do so. Thus, if the foreign country to which the defendant moved applies the principle of comity and adopts and enforces the United States court's judgment, you may still be able to collect from the defendant.

International Organizations

Several international bodies exist to promote cooperation among member countries. We will briefly discuss a couple here.

United Nations

In 1945, countries interested in promoting international peace, cooperation, and the development of international law, economic security, human rights, etc., formed the **United Nations** (UN). Each member country has a representative at the UN. The UN is based in New York City. The UN General Assembly, Security Council and other bodies within the UN often meet to discuss world affairs and how to best address international problems and conflicts. Often, the UN will "sanction" countries whose leaders are viewed to be acting contrary to international law and/or violating human rights. The UN occasionally imposes economic sanctions on these countries in an attempt to cause the leaders of the country to change policies or take certain actions (*e.g.*, cease producing nuclear weapons, violating human rights, etc.). The UN has several agencies including the **World Health Organization** (WHO), the **United Nations Children's Fund** (UNICEF), and the **International Monetary Fund** (IMF).

© VLuma, 2013. Under license from Shutterstock, Inc.

World Trade Organization

The **World Trade Organization** (WTO) was created in 1995 to assist countries in removing trade barriers and in negotiating with other countries with respect to business transactions. The WTO also assists with resolving trade disputes between countries and developing policies that promote consistency and predictability among trading countries.

Doing Business Internationally

"Choice of Law" Contract Provision

Many contracts entered into by parties from different countries will provide a "choice of law" provision. In such a provision, the parties will agree in advance as to which country's laws would be applicable in a dispute. Failure to include a choice of law provision could cause uncertainty and considerable cost and frustration if a dispute arises from the international transaction.

Letters of Credit

As you might expect, a seller may be very reluctant to sell to a buyer from another country on credit. What if the buyer never pays? The seller may demand more assurance of payment. Consequently, banks often act as intermediaries to facilitate international transactions. In short, a bank (*i.e.*, the

"issuing" bank) agrees to issue a **letter of credit** on behalf of the buyer promising to pay the seller. The seller's bank may act as a "confirming" bank, which would receive the payment from the issuing bank. Thus, the seller obtains more assurance that the bill will be paid, and the risk of nonpayment by the buyer is transferred to the banks. Of course, the banks will charge a fee to facilitate this transaction and take on the risk of nonpayment. Obviously, the buyer must have a sufficient relationship with an issuing bank to pursue the letter of credit.

Foreign Corrupt Practices Act

In some countries, providing a "pay-off" to a government official in order to facilitate needed approval from a government agency may be commonplace. This practice, however, is not allowed in the United States, nor are U.S. citizens or businesses allowed to bribe foreign government officials. Consider the excerpt from the **Foreign Corrupt Practices Act** that follows (Illustrative Federal Statute 44.1).

© Kurt De Bruyn, 2013. Under license from Shutterstock, Inc.

Quotas and Tariffs

Countries may impose a **quota** limiting the amount of goods that can be imported into the country. Additionally, countries often have **tariffs** (*i.e.*, taxes or fees) on goods when imported into the country. Of course, a common purpose of quotas and tariffs is to protect the domestic producers of similar goods and to raise revenue for the government. Some countries, including the United States, have **antidumping** laws. These laws impose an extra

15 U.S.C. § 78dd-2

§ 78dd-2. Prohibited foreign trade practices by domestic concerns

(a) Prohibition. It shall be unlawful for any domestic concern . . . or for any officer, director, employee, or agent of such domestic concern or any stockholder thereof acting on behalf of such domestic concern, to make use of the mails or any means or instrumentality of interstate commerce corruptly in furtherance of an offer, payment, promise to pay, or authorization of the payment of any money, or offer, gift, promise to give, or authorization of the giving of anything of value to—

(1) any foreign official for purposes of –

(A) (i) influencing any act or decision of such foreign official in his official capacity, (ii) inducing such foreign official to do or omit to do any act in violation of the lawful duty of such official, or (iii) securing any improper advantage; or

(B) inducing such foreign official to use his influence with a foreign government or instrumentality thereof to affect or influence any act or decision of such government or instrumentality,

in order to assist such domestic concern in obtaining or retaining business for or with, or directing business to, any person. . . .

tariff or tax on the importation of goods that are then sold for less than fair value, which is viewed as an attempt to undercut competition and create a larger market share for the company that manfactures the "dumped" goods.

Taxation

Engaging in international business transactions brings along international tax issues as well. To what extent could your business be taxed in a foreign country and in the United States on the same transaction? Is there any remedy for this possible double-taxation? Of course, the United States tax laws are quite complex, as are other nations' tax laws. Tax treaties may also impact the tax

consequences of parties involved in international transactions.

QUESTIONS FOR REVIEW

1. What is a treaty?

2. Explain briefly the purposes of NAFTA and the CISG.

3. Are decisions of the International Court of Justice binding upon the United States? If not, how does the United States view decisions of the International Court of Justice?

4. What is the principle of comity?

5. Name at least two agencies of the United Nations other than UNICEF.

6. Explain how a letter of credit facilitates international transactions.

7. Briefly explain the Foreign Corrupt Practices Act.

8. Summarize the *Medellin v. Texas* case.

What Do You Think?

Should U.S. corporations pay income taxes on the profits of foreign subsidiaries even if the profits have not yet been repatriated to the United States?

INTERNET ACTIVITIES

1. Visit the website of the Office of the United States Trade Representative at www.ustr.gov. Click on the "Trade Agreements" tab. Click on the "Free Trade Agreements" link.

   a. With how many countries does the United States have a free trade agreement in force?

   b. Click on the "Jordan" link. When was the agreement implemented?

2. Visit the website of the International Court of Justice at www.icj-cij.org.

   a. Click on the "Cases" tab and then on the "Judgments" link. Select one of the latest judgments. Which countries were involved?

   b. Click on the "Press Room" link. Select a recent press release and summarize its contents.

Appendix

The Constitution of the United States

We the People of the United States, in Order to form a more perfect Union, establish Justice, insure domestic Tranquility, provide for the common defence, promote the general Welfare, and secure the Blessings of Liberty to ourselves and our Posterity, do ordain and establish this Constitution for the United States of America.

Article I

Section 1

All legislative Powers herein granted shall be vested in a Congress of the United States, which shall consist of a Senate and House of Representatives.

Section 2

The House of Representatives shall be composed of Members chosen every second Year by the People of the several States, and the Electors in each State shall have the Qualifications requisite for Electors of the most numerous Branch of the State Legislature.

No Person shall be a Representative who shall not have attained to the Age of twenty five Years, and been seven Years a Citizen of the United States, and who shall not, when elected, be an Inhabitant of that State in which he shall be chosen.

Representatives and direct Taxes shall be apportioned among the several States which may be included within this Union, according to their respective Numbers, which shall be determined by adding to the whole Number of free Persons, including those bound to Service for a Term of Years, and excluding Indians not taxed,

three fifths of all other Persons. The actual Enumeration shall be made within three Years after the first Meeting of the Congress of the United States, and within every subsequent Term of ten Years, in such Manner as they shall by Law direct. The Number of Representatives shall not exceed one for every thirty Thousand, but each State shall have at Least one Representative; and until such enumeration shall be made, the State of New Hampshire shall be entitled to chuse choose three, Massachusetts eight, Rhode-Island and Providence Plantations one, Connecticut five, New-York six, New Jersey four, Pennsylvania eight, Delaware one, Maryland six, Virginia ten, North Carolina five, South Carolina five, and Georgia three.

When vacancies happen in the Representation from any State, the Executive Authority thereof shall issue Writs of Election to fill such Vacancies.

The House of Representatives shall chuse their Speaker and other Officers; and shall have the sole Power of Impeachment.

Section 3

The Senate of the United States shall be composed of two Senators from each State, chosen by the Legislature thereof for six Years; and each Senator shall have one Vote.

Immediately after they shall be assembled in Consequence of the first Election, they shall be divided as equally as may be into three Classes. The Seats of the Senators of the first Class shall be vacated at the Expiration of the second Year, of the second Class at the Expiration of the fourth Year, and of the third Class at the Expiration of the sixth Year, so that one third may be chosen every second Year; and if Vacancies happen by Resignation, or otherwise, during the Recess of the Legislature of any State, the Executive thereof may make temporary Appointments until the next Meeting of the Legislature, which shall then fill such Vacancies.

No Person shall be a Senator who shall not have attained to the Age of thirty Years, and been nine Years a Citizen of the United States, and who shall not, when elected, be an Inhabitant of that State for which he shall be chosen.

The Vice President of the United States shall be President of the Senate, but shall have no Vote, unless they be equally divided.

The Senate shall chuse their other Officers, and also a President pro tempore, in the Absence of the Vice President, or when he shall exercise the Office of President of the United States.

The Senate shall have the sole Power to try all Impeachments. When sitting for that Purpose, they shall be on Oath or Affirmation. When the President of the United States is tried, the Chief Justice shall preside: And no Person shall be convicted without the Concurrence of two thirds of the Members present.

Judgment in Cases of Impeachment shall not extend further than to removal from Office, and disqualification to hold and enjoy any Office of honor, Trust or Profit under the United States: but the Party convicted shall nevertheless be liable and subject to Indictment, Trial, Judgment and Punishment, according to Law.

Section 4

The Times, Places and Manner of holding Elections for Senators and Representatives, shall be prescribed in each State by the Legislature thereof; but the Congress may at any time by Law make or alter such Regulations, except as to the Places of chusing Senators.

The Congress shall assemble at least once in every Year, and such Meeting shall be on the first Monday in December, unless they shall by Law appoint a different Day.

Section 5

Each House shall be the Judge of the Elections, Returns and Qualifications of its own Members, and a Majority of each shall constitute a Quorum to do Business; but a smaller Number may adjourn from day to day, and may be authorized to compel the Attendance of absent Members, in such Manner, and under such Penalties as each House may provide.

Each House may determine the Rules of its Proceedings, punish its Members for disorderly Behaviour, and, with the Concurrence of two thirds, expel a Member.

Each House shall keep a Journal of its Proceedings, and from time to time publish the same, excepting such Parts as may in their Judgment require Secrecy; and the Yeas and Nays of the Members of either House on any question shall, at the Desire of one fifth of those Present, be entered on the Journal.

Neither House, during the Session of Congress, shall, without the Consent of the other, adjourn for more than three days, nor to any other Place than that in which the two Houses shall be sitting.

Section 6

The Senators and Representatives shall receive a Compensation for their Services, to be ascertained by Law, and paid out of the Treasury of the United States. They shall in all Cases, except Treason, Felony and Breach of the Peace, be privileged from Arrest during their Attendance at the Session of their respective Houses, and in going to and returning from the same; and for any Speech or Debate in either House, they shall not be questioned in any other Place.

No Senator or Representative shall, during the Time for which he was elected, be appointed to any civil Office under the Authority of the United States, which shall have been created, or the Emoluments whereof shall have been increased during such time; and no Person holding any Office under the United States, shall be a Member of either House during his Continuance in Office.

Section 7

All Bills for raising Revenue shall originate in the House of Representatives; but the Senate may propose or concur with Amendments as on other Bills.

Every Bill which shall have passed the House of Representatives and the Senate, shall, before it become a Law, be presented to the President of the United States: If he approve he shall sign it, but if not he shall return it, with his Objections to that House in which it shall have originated, who shall enter the Objections at large on their Journal, and proceed to reconsider it. If after such Reconsideration two thirds of that House shall agree to pass the Bill, it shall be sent, together with the Objections, to the other House, by which it shall likewise be reconsidered, and if approved by two thirds of that House, it shall become a Law. But in all such Cases the Votes of both Houses shall be determined by yeas and Nays, and the Names of the Persons voting for and against the Bill shall be entered on the Journal of each House respectively. If any Bill shall not be returned by the President within ten Days (Sundays excepted) after it shall have been presented to him, the Same shall be a Law, in like Manner as if he had signed it, unless the Congress by their Adjournment prevent its Return, in which Case it shall not be a Law.

Every Order, Resolution, or Vote to which the Concurrence of the Senate and House of Representatives may be necessary (except on a question of Adjournment) shall be presented to the President of the United States; and before the Same shall take Effect, shall be approved by him, or being disapproved by him, shall be repassed by two thirds of the Senate and House of Representatives, according to the Rules and Limitations prescribed in the Case of a Bill.

Section 8

The Congress shall have Power To lay and collect Taxes, Duties, Imposts and Excises, to pay the Debts and provide for the common Defence and general Welfare of the United States; but all Duties, Imposts and Excises shall be uniform throughout the United States;

To borrow Money on the credit of the United States;

To regulate Commerce with foreign Nations, and among the several States, and with the Indian Tribes;

To establish an uniform Rule of Naturalization, and uniform Laws on the subject of Bankruptcies throughout the United States;

To coin Money, regulate the Value thereof, and of foreign Coin, and fix the Standard of Weights and Measures;

To provide for the Punishment of counterfeiting the Securities and current Coin of the United States;

To establish Post Offices and post Roads;

To promote the Progress of Science and useful Arts, by securing for limited Times to Authors and Inventors the exclusive Right to their respective Writings and Discoveries;

To constitute Tribunals inferior to the supreme Court;

To define and punish Piracies and Felonies committed on the high Seas, and Offences against the Law of Nations;

To declare War, grant Letters of Marque and Reprisal, and make Rules concerning Captures on Land and Water;

To raise and support Armies, but no Appropriation of Money to that Use shall be for a longer Term than two Years;

To provide and maintain a Navy;

To make Rules for the Government and Regulation of the land and naval Forces;

To provide for calling forth the Militia to execute the Laws of the Union, suppress Insurrections and repel Invasions;

To provide for organizing, arming, and disciplining, the Militia, and for governing such Part of them as may be employed in the Service of the United States, reserving to the States respectively, the Appointment of the Officers, and the Authority of training the Militia according to the discipline prescribed by Congress;

To exercise exclusive Legislation in all Cases whatsoever, over such District (not exceeding ten Miles square) as may, by Cession of particular States, and the Acceptance of Congress, become the Seat of the Government of the United States, and to exercise like Authority over all Places purchased by the Consent of the Legislature of the State in which the Same shall be, for the Erection of Forts, Magazines, Arsenals, dock-Yards, and other needful Buildings;—And

To make all Laws which shall be necessary and proper for carrying into Execution the foregoing Powers, and all other Powers vested by this Constitution in the Government of the United States, or in any Department or Officer thereof.

Section 9

The Migration or Importation of such Persons as any of the States now existing shall think proper to admit, shall not be prohibited by the Congress prior to the Year one thousand eight hundred and eight, but a Tax or duty may be imposed on such Importation, not exceeding ten dollars for each Person.

The Privilege of the Writ of Habeas Corpus shall not be suspended, unless when in Cases of Rebellion or Invasion the public Safety may require it.

No Bill of Attainder or ex post facto Law shall be passed.

No Capitation, or other direct, Tax shall be laid, unless in Proportion to the Census or enumeration herein before directed to be taken.

No Tax or Duty shall be laid on Articles exported from any State.

No Preference shall be given by any Regulation of Commerce or Revenue to the Ports of one State over those of another; nor shall Vessels bound to, or from, one State, be obliged to enter, clear, or pay Duties in another.

No Money shall be drawn from the Treasury, but in Consequence of Appropriations made by Law; and a regular Statement and Account of the Receipts and Expenditures of all public Money shall be published from time to time.

No Title of Nobility shall be granted by the United States: And no Person holding any Office of Profit or Trust under them, shall, without the Consent of the Congress, accept of any present, Emolument, Office, or Title, of any kind whatever, from any King, Prince, or foreign State.

Section 10

No State shall enter into any Treaty, Alliance, or Confederation; grant Letters of Marque and Reprisal; coin Money; emit Bills of Credit; make any Thing but gold and silver Coin a Tender in Payment of Debts; pass any Bill of Attainder, ex post facto Law, or Law impairing the Obligation of Contracts, or grant any Title of Nobility.

No State shall, without the Consent of the Congress, lay any Imposts or Duties on Imports or Exports, except what may be absolutely necessary for executing it's inspection Laws: and the net Produce of all Duties and Imposts, laid by any State on Imports or Exports, shall be for the Use of the Treasury of the United States; and all such Laws shall be subject to the Revision and Controul of the Congress.

No State shall, without the Consent of Congress, lay any Duty of Tonnage, keep Troops, or Ships of War in time of Peace, enter into any Agreement or Compact with another State, or with a foreign Power, or engage in War, unless actually invaded, or in such imminent Danger as will not admit of delay.

Article II
Section 1

The executive Power shall be vested in a President of the United States of America. He shall hold his Office during the Term of four Years, and, together with the Vice President, chosen for the same Term, be elected, as follows:

Each State shall appoint, in such Manner as the Legislature thereof may direct, a Number of Electors, equal to the whole Number of Senators and Representatives to which the State may be entitled in the Congress: but no Senator or Representative, or Person holding an Office of Trust or Profit under the United States, shall be appointed an Elector.

The Electors shall meet in their respective States, and vote by Ballot for two Persons, of whom one at least shall not be an Inhabitant of the same State with themselves. And they shall make a List of all the Persons voted for, and of the Number of Votes for each; which List they shall sign and certify, and transmit sealed to the Seat of the Government of the United States, directed to the President of the Senate. The President of the Senate shall, in the Presence of the Senate and House of Representatives, open all the Certificates, and the Votes shall then be counted. The Person having the greatest Number of Votes shall be the President, if such Number be a Majority of the whole Number of Electors appointed; and if there be more than one who have such Majority, and have an equal Number of Votes, then the House of Representatives shall immediately chuse by Ballot one of them for President; and if no Person have a Majority, then from the five highest on the List the said House shall in like Manner chuse the President. But in chusing the President, the Votes shall be taken by States, the Representation from each State having one Vote; A quorum for this purpose shall consist of a Member or Members from two thirds of the States, and a Majority of all the States shall be necessary to a Choice. In every Case, after the Choice of the President, the Person having the greatest Number of Votes of the Electors shall be the Vice President. But if there should remain two or more who have equal Votes, the Senate shall chuse from them by Ballot the Vice President.

The Congress may determine the Time of chusing the Electors, and the Day on which they shall give their Votes; which Day shall be the same throughout the United States.

No Person except a natural born Citizen, or a Citizen of the United States, at the time of the Adoption of this Constitution, shall be eligible to the Office of President; neither shall any Person be eligible to that Office who shall not have attained to the Age of thirty five Years, and been fourteen Years a Resident within the United States.

In Case of the Removal of the President from Office, or of his Death, Resignation, or Inability to discharge the Powers and Duties of the said Office, the Same shall devolve on the Vice President, and the Congress may by Law provide for the Case of Removal, Death, Resignation or Inability, both of the President and Vice President, declaring what Officer shall then act as President, and such Officer shall act accordingly, until the Disability be removed, or a President shall be elected.

The President shall, at stated Times, receive for his Services, a Compensation, which shall neither be increased nor diminished during the Period for which he shall have been elected, and he shall not receive within that Period any other Emolument from the United States, or any of them.

Before he enter on the Execution of his Office, he shall take the following Oath or Affirmation:— "I do solemnly swear (or affirm) that I will faithfully execute the Office of President of the United States, and will to the best of my Ability, preserve, protect and defend the Constitution of the United States."

Section 2

The President shall be Commander in Chief of the Army and Navy of the United States, and of the Militia of the several States, when called into the actual Service of the United States; he may require the Opinion, in writing, of the principal Officer in each of the executive Departments, upon any Subject relating to the Duties of their respective Offices, and he shall have Power to grant Reprieves and Pardons for Offences against the United States, except in Cases of Impeachment.

He shall have Power, by and with the Advice and Consent of the Senate, to make Treaties, provided two thirds of the Senators present concur; and he shall nominate, and by and with the Advice and Consent of the Senate, shall appoint Ambassadors, other public Ministers and Consuls, Judges of the supreme Court, and all other Officers of the United States, whose Appointments are not herein otherwise provided for, and which shall be established by Law: but the Congress may by Law vest the Appointment of such inferior Officers, as they think proper, in the President alone, in the Courts of Law, or in the Heads of Departments.

The President shall have Power to fill up all Vacancies that may happen during the Recess of the Senate, by granting Commissions which shall expire at the End of their next Session.

Section 3

He shall from time to time give to the Congress Information of the State of the Union, and recommend to their Consideration such Measures as he shall judge necessary and expedient; he may, on extraordinary Occasions, convene both Houses, or either of them, and in Case of Disagreement between them, with Respect to the Time of Adjournment, he may adjourn them to such Time as he shall think proper; he shall receive Ambassadors and other public Ministers; he shall take Care that the Laws be faithfully executed, and shall Commission all the Officers of the United States.

Section 4

The President, Vice President and all civil Officers of the United States, shall be removed from Office on Impeachment for, and Conviction of, Treason, Bribery, or other high Crimes and Misdemeanors.

Article III
Section 1

The judicial Power of the United States shall be vested in one supreme Court, and in such inferior Courts as the Congress may from time to time ordain and establish. The Judges, both of the supreme and inferior Courts, shall hold their Offices during good Behaviour, and shall, at stated Times, receive for their Services a Compensation, which shall not be diminished during their Continuance in Office.

Section 2

The judicial Power shall extend to all Cases, in Law and Equity, arising under this Constitution, the Laws of the United States, and Treaties made, or which shall be made, under their Authority;—to all Cases affecting Ambassadors, other public Ministers and Consuls;—to all Cases of admiralty and maritime Jurisdiction;—to Controversies to which the United States shall be a Party;—to Controversies between two or more States;—between a State and Citizens of another State,—between Citizens of different States,—between Citizens of the same State claiming Lands under Grants of different States, and between a State, or the Citizens thereof, and foreign States, Citizens or Subjects.

In all Cases affecting Ambassadors, other public Ministers and Consuls, and those in which a State shall be Party, the supreme Court shall have original Jurisdiction. In all the other Cases before mentioned, the supreme Court shall have appellate Jurisdiction, both as to Law and Fact, with such Exceptions, and under such Regulations as the Congress shall make.

The Trial of all Crimes, except in Cases of Impeachment, shall be by Jury; and such Trial shall be held in the State where the said Crimes shall have been committed; but when not committed within any State, the Trial shall be at such Place or Places as the Congress may by Law have directed.

Section 3

Treason against the United States, shall consist only in levying War against them, or in adhering to their Enemies, giving them Aid and Comfort. No Person shall be convicted of Treason unless on the Testimony of two Witnesses to the same overt Act, or on Confession in open Court.

The Congress shall have Power to declare the Punishment of Treason, but no Attainder of Treason shall work Corruption of Blood, or Forfeiture except during the Life of the Person attainted.

Article IV
Section 1

Full Faith and Credit shall be given in each State to the public Acts, Records, and judicial Proceedings of every other State. And the Congress may by general Laws prescribe the Manner in which such

Acts, Records and Proceedings shall be proved, and the Effect thereof.

Section 2

The Citizens of each State shall be entitled to all Privileges and Immunities of Citizens in the several States.

A Person charged in any State with Treason, Felony, or other Crime, who shall flee from Justice, and be found in another State, shall on Demand of the executive Authority of the State from which he fled, be delivered up, to be removed to the State having Jurisdiction of the Crime.

No Person held to Service or Labour in one State, under the Laws thereof, escaping into another, shall, in Consequence of any Law or Regulation therein, be discharged from such Service or Labour, but shall be delivered up on Claim of the Party to whom such Service or Labour may be due.

Section 3

New States may be admitted by the Congress into this Union; but no new State shall be formed or erected within the Jurisdiction of any other State; nor any State be formed by the Junction of two or more States, or Parts of States, without the Consent of the Legislatures of the States concerned as well as of the Congress.

The Congress shall have Power to dispose of and make all needful Rules and Regulations respecting the Territory or other Property belonging to the United States; and nothing in this Constitution shall be so construed as to Prejudice any Claims of the United States, or of any particular State.

Section 4

The United States shall guarantee to every State in this Union a Republican Form of Government, and shall protect each of them against Invasion; and on Application of the Legislature, or of the Executive (when the Legislature cannot be convened), against domestic Violence.

Article V

The Congress, whenever two thirds of both Houses shall deem it necessary, shall propose Amendments to this Constitution, or, on the Application of the Legislatures of two thirds of the several States, shall call a Convention for proposing Amendments, which, in either Case, shall be valid to all Intents and Purposes, as Part of this Constitution, when ratified by the Legislatures of three fourths of the several States, or by Conventions in three fourths thereof, as the one or the other Mode of Ratification may be proposed by the Congress; Provided that no Amendment which may be made prior to the Year One thousand eight hundred and eight shall in any Manner affect the first and fourth Clauses in the Ninth Section of the first Article; and that no State, without its Consent, shall be deprived of its equal Suffrage in the Senate.

Article VI

All Debts contracted and Engagements entered into, before the Adoption of this Constitution, shall be as valid against the United States under this Constitution, as under the Confederation.

This Constitution, and the Laws of the United States which shall be made in Pursuance thereof; and all Treaties made, or which shall be made, under the Authority of the United States, shall be the supreme Law of the Land; and the Judges in every State shall be bound thereby, any Thing in the Constitution or Laws of any State to the Contrary notwithstanding.

The Senators and Representatives before mentioned, and the Members of the several State Legislatures, and all executive and judicial Officers, both of the United States and of the several States, shall be bound by Oath or Affirmation, to support this Constitution; but no religious Test shall ever be required as a Qualification to any Office or public Trust under the United States.

Article VII

The Ratification of the Conventions of nine States, shall be sufficient for the Establishment of this Constitution between the States so ratifying the Same.

The Word, "the," being interlined between the seventh and eighth Lines of the first Page, the Word "Thirty" being partly written on an Erazure in the fifteenth Line of the first Page, The Words "is tried" being interlined between the thirty second and thirty third Lines of the first Page and the Word "the" being interlined between the forty third and forty fourth Lines of the second Page.

Attest William Jackson Secretary done in Convention by the Unanimous Consent of the States present the Seventeenth Day of September in the Year of our Lord one thousand seven hundred and Eighty seven and of the Independance of the United States of America the Twelfth In witness whereof We have hereunto subscribed our Names,

G°. Washington	Presidt and deputy from Virginia
Delaware	Geo: Read, Gunning Bedford jun, John Dickinson, Richard Bassett, Jaco: Broom
Maryland	James McHenry, Dan of St. Thos. Jenifer, Danl. Carroll
Virginia	John Blair, James Madison Jr.
North Carolina	Wm. Blount, Richd. Dobbs Spaight, Hu Williamson
South Carolina	J. Rutledge, Charles Cotesworth Pinckney, Charles Pinckney, Pierce Butler
Georgia	William Few, Abr Baldwin
New Hampshire	John Langdon, Nicholas Gilman
Massachusetts	Nathaniel Gorham, Rufus King
Connecticut	Wm. Saml. Johnson, Roger Sherman
New York	Alexander Hamilton
New Jersey	Wil: Livingston, David Brearley, Wm. Paterson, Jona: Dayton
Pennsylvania	B. Franklin, Thomas Mifflin, Robt. Morris, Geo. Clymer, Thos. FitzSimons, Jared Ingersoll, James Wilson, Gouv Morris

Amendments to the Constitution of the United States of America

Amendment I

Congress shall make no law respecting an establishment of religion, or prohibiting the free exercise thereof; or abridging the freedom of speech, or of the press; or the right of the people peaceably to assemble, and to petition the Government for a redress of grievances.

Amendment II

A well regulated Militia, being necessary to the security of a free State, the right of the people to keep and bear Arms, shall not be infringed.

Amendment III

No Soldier shall, in time of peace be quartered in any house, without the consent of the Owner, nor in time of war, but in a manner to be prescribed by law.

Amendment IV

The right of the people to be secure in their persons, houses, papers, and effects, against unreasonable searches and seizures, shall not be violated, and no Warrants shall issue, but upon probable cause, supported by Oath or affirmation, and particularly describing the place to be searched, and the persons or things to be seized.

Amendment V

No person shall be held to answer for a capital, or otherwise infamous crime, unless on a presentment or indictment of a Grand Jury, except in cases arising in the land or naval forces, or in the Militia, when in actual service in time of War or public danger; nor shall any person be subject for the same offence to be twice put in jeopardy of life or limb; nor shall be compelled in any criminal case to be a witness against himself, nor be deprived of life, liberty, or property, without due process of law; nor shall private property be taken for public use, without just compensation.

Amendment VI

In all criminal prosecutions, the accused shall enjoy the right to a speedy and public trial, by an impartial jury of the State and district wherein the crime shall have been committed, which district shall have been previously ascertained by law, and to be informed of the nature and cause of the accusation; to be confronted with the witnesses against him; to have compulsory process for obtaining witnesses in his favor, and to have the Assistance of Counsel for his defence.

Amendment VII

In Suits at common law, where the value in controversy shall exceed twenty dollars, the right of trial by jury shall be preserved, and no fact tried by a jury, shall be otherwise re-examined in any Court of the United States, than according to the rules of the common law.

Amendment VIII

Excessive bail shall not be required, nor excessive fines imposed, nor cruel and unusual punishments inflicted.

Amendment IX

The enumeration in the Constitution, of certain rights, shall not be construed to deny or disparage others retained by the people.

Amendment X

The powers not delegated to the United States by the Constitution, nor prohibited by it to the States, are reserved to the States respectively, or to the people.

Amendment XI

The Judicial power of the United States shall not be construed to extend to any suit in law or equity, commenced or prosecuted against one of the United States by Citizens of another State, or by Citizens or Subjects of any Foreign State.

Amendment XII

The Electors shall meet in their respective states and vote by ballot for President and Vice-President, one of whom, at least, shall not be an inhabitant of the same state with themselves; they shall name in their ballots the person voted for as President, and in distinct ballots the person voted for as Vice-President, and they shall make distinct lists of all persons voted for as President, and of all persons voted for as Vice-President, and of the number of votes for each, which lists they shall sign and certify, and transmit sealed to the seat of the government of the United States, directed to the President of the Senate;—The President of the Senate shall, in the presence of the Senate and House of Representatives, open all the certificates and the votes shall then be counted;— The person having the greatest Number of votes for President, shall be the President, if such number be a majority of the whole number of Electors appointed; and if no person have such majority, then from the persons having the highest numbers not exceeding three on the list of those voted for as President, the House of Representatives shall choose immediately, by ballot, the President. But in choosing the President, the votes shall be taken by states, the representation from each state having one vote; a quorum for this purpose shall consist of a member or members from two-thirds of the states, and a majority of all the states shall be necessary to a choice. And if the House of Representatives shall not choose a President whenever the right of choice shall devolve upon them, before the fourth day of March next following, then the Vice-President shall act as President, as in the case of the death or other constitutional disability of the President— The person having the greatest number of votes as Vice-President, shall be the Vice-President, if such number be a majority of the whole number of Electors appointed, and if no person have a majority, then from the two highest numbers on the list, the Senate shall choose the Vice-President; a quorum for the purpose shall consist of two-thirds of the whole number of Senators, and a majority of the whole number shall be necessary to a choice. But no person constitutionally ineligible to the office of President shall be eligible to that of Vice-President of the United States.

Amendment XIII

Section 1. Neither slavery nor involuntary servitude, except as a punishment for crime whereof the party shall have been duly convicted, shall exist within the United States, or any place subject to their jurisdiction.

Section 2. Congress shall have power to enforce this article by appropriate legislation.

Amendment XIV

Section 1. All persons born or naturalized in the United States and subject to the jurisdiction thereof, are citizens of the United States and of the State wherein they reside. No State shall make or enforce any law which shall abridge the privileges or immunities of citizens of the United States; nor shall any State deprive any person of life, liberty, or property, without due process of law; nor deny to any person within its jurisdiction the equal protection of the laws.

Section 2. Representatives shall be apportioned among the several States according to their respective numbers, counting the whole number of persons in each State, excluding Indians not taxed. But when the right to vote at any election for the choice of electors for President and Vice President of the United States, Representatives in Congress, the Executive and Judicial officers of a State, or the members of the Legislature thereof, is denied to any of the male inhabitants of such State, being twenty-one years of age, and citizens of the United States, or in any way abridged, except for participation in rebellion, or other crime, the basis of representation therein shall be reduced in the proportion which the number of such male citizens shall bear to the whole number of male citizens twenty-one years of age in such State.

Section 3. No person shall be a Senator or Representative in Congress, or elector of President and Vice President, or hold any office, civil or military, under the United States, or under any State, who, having previously taken an oath, as a member of Congress, or as an officer of the United States, or as a member of any State legislature, or as an executive or judicial officer of any State, to support the Constitution of the United States, shall have engaged in insurrection or rebellion against the same, or given aid or comfort to the enemies thereof. But Congress may by a vote of two-thirds of each House, remove such disability.

Section 4. The validity of the public debt of the United States, authorized by law, including debts incurred for payment of pensions and bounties for services in suppressing insurrection or rebellion, shall not be questioned. But neither the United States nor any State shall assume or pay any debt or obligation incurred in aid of insurrection or rebellion against the United States, or any claim for the loss or emancipation of any slave; but all such debts, obligations and claims shall be held illegal and void.

Section 5. The Congress shall have power to enforce, by appropriate legislation, the provisions of this article.

Amendment XV

Section 1. The right of citizens of the United States to vote shall not be denied or abridged by the United States or by any State on account of race, color, or previous condition of servitude.

Section 2. The Congress shall have power to enforce this article by appropriate legislation.

Amendment XVI

The Congress shall have power to lay and collect taxes on incomes, from whatever source derived, without apportionment among the several States, and without regard to any census or enumeration.

Amendment XVII

The Senate of the United States shall be composed of two Senators from each State, elected by the people thereof, for six years; and each Senator shall have one vote. The electors in each State shall have the qualifications requisite for electors of the most numerous branch of the State legislatures.

When vacancies happen in the representation of any State in the Senate, the executive authority of such State shall issue writs of election to fill such vacancies: Provided, That the legislature of any State may empower the executive thereof to make temporary appointments until the people fill the vacancies by election as the legislature may direct.

This amendment shall not be so construed as to affect the election or term of any Senator chosen before it becomes valid as part of the Constitution.

Amendment XVIII

Section 1. After one year from the ratification of this article the manufacture, sale, or transportation of intoxicating liquors within, the importation thereof into, or the exportation thereof from the United States and all territory subject to the jurisdiction thereof for beverage purposes is hereby prohibited.

Section 2. The Congress and the several States shall have concurrent power to enforce this article by appropriate legislation.

Section 3. This article shall be inoperative unless it shall have been ratified as an amendment to the Constitution by the legislatures of the several States, as provided in the Constitution, within seven years from the date of the submission hereof to the States by the Congress.

Amendment XIX

The right of citizens of the United States to vote shall not be denied or abridged by the United States or by any State on account of sex. Congress shall have power to enforce this article by appropriate legislation.

Amendment XX

Section 1. The terms of the President and Vice President shall end at noon on the 20th day of January, and the terms of Senators and Representatives at noon on the 3d day of January, of the years in which such terms would have ended if this article had not been ratified; and the terms of their successors shall then begin.

Section 2. The Congress shall assemble at least once in every year, and such meeting shall begin at noon on the 3d day of January, unless they shall by law appoint a different day.

Section 3. If, at the time fixed for the beginning of the term of the President, the President elect shall have died, the Vice President elect shall become President. If a President shall not have been chosen before the time fixed for the beginning of his term, or if the President elect shall have failed to qualify, then the Vice President elect shall act as President until a President shall have qualified; and the Congress may by law provide for the case wherein neither a President elect nor a Vice President elect shall have qualified, declaring who shall then act as President, or the manner in which one who is to act shall be selected, and such person shall act accordingly until a President or Vice President shall have qualified.

Section 4. The Congress may by law provide for the case of the death of any of the persons from whom the House of Representatives may choose a President whenever the right of choice shall have devolved upon them, and for the case of the death of any of the persons from whom the Senate may choose a Vice President whenever the right of choice shall have devolved upon them.

Section 5. Sections 1 and 2 shall take effect on the 15th day of October following the ratification of this article.

Section 6. This article shall be inoperative unless it shall have been ratified as an amendment to the Constitution by the legislatures of three-fourths of the several States within seven years from the date of its submission.

Amendment XXI

Section 1. The eighteenth article of amendment to the Constitution of the United States is hereby repealed.

Section 2. The transportation or importation into any State, Territory, or possession of the United States for delivery or use therein of intoxicating liquors, in violation of the laws thereof, is hereby prohibited.

Section 3. This article shall be inoperative unless it shall have been ratified as an amendment to the Constitution by conventions in the several States, as provided in the Constitution, within seven years from the date of the submission hereof to the States by the Congress.

Amendment XXII

Section 1. No person shall be elected to the office of the President more than twice, and no person who has held the office of President, or acted as President, for more than two years of a term to which some other person was elected President shall be elected to the office of the President more than once. But this Article shall not apply to any person holding the office of President, when this Article was proposed by the Congress, and shall not prevent any person who may be holding the office of President, or acting as President, during the term within which this Article becomes operative from holding the office of President or acting as President during the remainder of such term.

Section 2. This article shall be inoperative unless it shall have been ratified as an amendment to the Constitution by the legislatures of three-fourths of the several States within seven years from the date of its submission to the States by the Congress.

Amendment XXIII

Section 1. The District constituting the seat of Government of the United States shall appoint in such manner as the Congress may direct: A number of electors of President and Vice President equal to the whole number of Senators and Representatives in Congress to which the District would be entitled if it were a State, but in no event more than the least populous State; they shall be in addition to those appointed by the States, but they shall be considered, for the purposes of the election of President and Vice President, to be electors appointed by a State; and they shall meet in the District and perform such duties as provided by the twelfth article of amendment.

Section 2. The Congress shall have power to enforce this article by appropriate legislation.

Amendment XXIV

Section 1. The right of citizens of the United States to vote in any primary or other election for President or Vice President, for electors for President or Vice President, or for Senator or Representative in Congress, shall not be denied or abridged by the United States or any State by reason of failure to pay any poll tax or other tax.

Section 2. The Congress shall have power to enforce this article by appropriate legislation.

Amendment XXV

Section 1. In case of the removal of the President from office or of his death or resignation, the Vice President shall become President.

Section 2. Whenever there is a vacancy in the office of the Vice President, the President shall nominate a Vice President who shall take office upon confirmation by a majority vote of both Houses of Congress.

Section 3. Whenever the President transmits to the President pro tempore of the Senate and the Speaker of the House of Representatives has written declaration that he is unable to discharge the powers and duties of his office, and until he transmits to them a written declaration to the contrary, such powers and duties shall be discharged by the Vice President as Acting President.

Section 4. Whenever the Vice President and a majority of either the principal officers of the executive departments or of such other body as Congress may by law provide, transmit to the President pro tempore of the Senate and the Speaker of the House of Representatives their written declaration that the President is unable to discharge the powers and duties of his office, the Vice President shall immediately assume the powers and duties of the office as Acting President.

Thereafter, when the President transmits to the President pro tempore of the Senate and the Speaker of the House of Representatives has written declaration that no inability exists, he shall resume the powers and duties of his office unless the Vice President and a majority of either the principal officers of the executive department or of such other body as Congress may by law provide, transmit within four days to the President pro tempore of the Senate and the Speaker of the House of Representatives their written declaration that the President is unable to discharge the powers and duties of his office. Thereupon Congress shall decide the issue, assembling within forty-eight hours for that purpose if not in session. If the Congress, within twenty-one days after receipt of the latter written declaration, or, if Congress is not in session, within twenty-one days after Congress is required to assemble, determines by two-thirds vote of both Houses that the President is unable to discharge the powers and duties of his office, the Vice President shall continue to discharge the same as Acting President; otherwise, the President shall resume the powers and duties of his office.

Amendment XXVI

Section 1. The right of citizens of the United States, who are eighteen years of age or older, to vote shall not be denied or abridged by the United States or by any State on account of age.

Section 2. The Congress shall have power to enforce this article by appropriate legislation.

Amendment XXVII

No law varying the compensation for the services of the Senators and Representatives shall take effect, until an election of Representatives shall have intervened.

Index